The Complete Guide to Running a Business

JOHN R. KLUG is a successful businessman and a management consultant. His Denver-based firm, Continental Communications Group, Inc., specializes in publishing management. Its many publications include *Profit Improvement, Business Perspectives, Executive Business Review,* and *Audit Survival.*

As a management consultant he counted among his clients the top management of such firms as General Motors, Holiday Inns, Victoria Station, and Great Western United.

In addition to his business experience, Mr. Klug's credentials also include a stint as a member of the faculty of the Harvard Graduate School of Business Administration, an MBA from that same school, and a Fulbright Scholarship to study business practices while at the University of Madrid.

The Complete Guide to Running a Business

BY JOHN R. KLUG

BOARDRM® BOOKS

500 Fifth Avenue
New York, NY 10110

Fifty Dollars

Acknowledgements

Few endeavors of any merit are ever done alone, and this one is no exception.

First, I would like to thank Professor W. Earl Sasser of the Harvard Business School for his encouragement over the years and for his critique of much of the material.

Second, I would like to thank Debbie Willoughby and William C. Banks for their excellent editorial assistance and advice.

Also, I would like to thank Professor Thomas Brightwell from the University of Denver, Frederick Goldstein, Esq., of the Boston law firm of Csaplar & Bok, Paul A. Prange, CPA, Denver, and Alan Talesnick, Esq., of Parcel, Talesnick, Meyer & Schwartz of Denver for their excellent critique of the tax and legal aspects of the book.

Finally, and most importantly, I would like to acknowledge the support and assistance of my wife Carol, who endured many sacrifices as the book came together.

REVISED EDITION

Library of Congress Cataloging in Publication Data

Klug, John R., 1945-
    The complete guide to running a business.

    Rev. ed. of: The basic book of business answers. 1981.
    Includes index.
    1. Business—Handbooks, manuals, etc.
I. Title.
HF5356.K68   1982   658   82-1333
ISBN 0-932648-24-X   AACR2

Printed in the United States of America

TABLE
OF
CONTENTS

PART I. How to Organize Your Business

PART II. How to Operate Your Business

PART III. How to Sell (or Buy) a Business

PART IV. Retirement, Life Insurance, and Estate Planning

CHAPTER ONE

Organizational Options

Huge, multinational corporations, such as General Motors and Exxon, have tens of thousands of shareholders and these companies must, for practical reasons, operate in corporate form. But smaller businesses have more options in selecting a business structure. The first and perhaps most vital step for any astute businessman is choosing the business form that best suits the needs of his individual circumstances.

You can always start right off modeling your company after Exxon by electing the standard corporate form. But if your firm is not quite that big yet, you might find that you can realize some handsome tax savings by electing the special Subchapter S corporation status. The Sub S enjoys most of the advantages of incorporation and yet avoids most of the drawbacks. Of course, you may want to stick with a proprietorship or partnership structure. In each case there are advantages and disadvantages in areas of management, owner's personal liability, the continuity of the firm, transferability of ownership, and costs to organize.

However, for most smaller businesses the choice of legal organizational form hinges on three major tax considerations:

1. Tax rate of profits.

2. Tax treatment of ordinary income/losses; capital gains/losses; dividends.

3. Fringe benefits that are tax free or receive tax preferred treatment.

In addition to these tax considerations, there are other important considerations, such as:

- Does the owner wish to reinvest profits in the business or take them out of the business for personal use?

- Does the owner have profits or losses from other activities that he would like to offset against those of the business?

- Does the business initially expect to show losses?

The importance of these questions will be seen further on. But let's examine first the three dominant tax considerations listed above.

Tax Rates

Sole proprietorship and partnership income is combined with the owner/partner's other taxable income and is taxed as follows:

- Income tax. The owner pays tax on the combined total of business and personal income at the individual progressive rate of from 11% (12% in 1982 only) to 50% maximum.

- Capital gains tax. The owner deducts 60% of his long-term capital gain and pays tax on the other 40% at ordinary income rates. Therefore, the maximum effective federal long-term capital gains tax is 20% for sales occurring after June 9, 1981.

- Estate tax. Paid in full by the estate if the business appreciates in value over the owner's lifetime. At the time of death the estate may have to pay capital gains as well.

Corporations are entities in and of themselves and as such are separate and distinct from the owners of the corporation. They are taxed as follows:

- A corporation pays 15% tax (16% for tax years beginning in 1982 only) on the first $25,000 of income; 18% (19% in 1982) on the next $25,00; 30% on the third $25,000; 40% on the fourth $25,000 and 46% on income over $100,000.

- Long-term capital gain may be treated as ordinary income or the corporation may pay an alternative capital gain tax of 28%.

- If a corporation accumulates more than $250,000 (other than a "personal service" corporation which is limited to $150,000) and it cannot be shown that the excess amount is needed to run the company, a penalty tax of up to 38½% will be assessed against current earnings. In this way IRS urges corporations to pay the current income out as taxable dividends to the owners. (Note that a large company such as General Motors has, at any one time, many millions of dollars accumulated on hand, but these funds are needed in GM's day-to-day operations. Therefore, what constitutes an excess corporate accumulation depends on the particular circumstances of the company.)

- The corporation's shareholders pay personal income tax on dividends received from the corporation. This constitutes, in effect, a "double tax" on the corporation's income.

- When ownership of a corporation is transferred upon the death of an owner, an estate tax is levied on the full fair market value of the ownership interest.

Subchapter S corporations are taxed only once like a partnership and yet the owner may enjoy many of the tax free benefits and other advantages of a corporation. These benefits will be explained further on.

Tax Treatment of Income/Losses; Capital Gains/Losses; Dividends

Different business structures merit different treatment of certain kinds of gains and losses. You must select and weigh the kind of treatment that best suits your needs.

Income, capital gains, and dividends

Treatment of special income items such as tax exempt interest and dividends: Owners of a corporation, unlike partners or proprietors, must pay tax on some corporate income that would normally be tax free or tax favored if the individual or partner received the income rather than the corporation. If, for example, the corporation wishes to distribute income from tax exempt municipal bond interest or lower taxed net long-term capital gain, this income loses its tax favored status and is fully taxable as ordinary income to the shareholder. On the other hand, a corporation is entitled to exclude from its income 85% of any dividends received from another domestic corporation, whereas an individual (proprietor-partner) must pay full tax on such dividend income, less an exclusion ($200 in 1981 and $100 thereafter). So the corporation has the advantage on dividend income and the proprietorship has the advantage when it comes to tax free or tax favored income.

Although in some cases a corporation may be at a disadvantage in distributing otherwise tax favored income, a corporation, if qualified, may elect Subchapter S status for a year in which there is anticipation of large capital gain. As a "Sub S," the corporation will pay no double tax on the income distributed for that year. Note, however, that this gambit will not work when the total capital gain is more than $25,000 and the gain exceeds 50% of the corporation's income.

Getting money out: If your goal is to get money out of the company immediately, the Subchapter S or proprietorship forms often are best because you avoid the corporate double tax on income. Remember, a corporation pays tax on its income and then, when the income is distributed as dividends, the stockholder pays another tax at personal income tax rates. However, in the Sub S and noncorporate forms, company income is usually taxed only once—at the personal level.

But don't shy away from the ordinary corporate form for a small business out of fear of the double tax. There are ways to reduce it or to get around it entirely. If profits don't get too high, the double tax can be greatly reduced by one or more of the following methods:

- The corporation can pay reasonable interest on loans from the shareholder-owner.

- The corporation can employ family members.

- The shareholder-owner may take as large a salary as is reasonable.

- The corporation can accumulate earnings up to a reasonable extent, with the accumulation being taxed at capital gain rates on sale or liquidation.

3

These techniques will be explained in detail in subsequent sections.

Reinvesting: If your goal is to reinvest for expansion of your business, the standard corporate form will often be better because the income can be divided into two groups. Part of the income (up to $100,000 per year) can be accumulated for the expansion and taxed at the corporate rate of 15-40% and the other part can be taken out as salary by the owner. This division of income is not possible in the noncorporate forms. In the proprietorship and partnership forms, all the business income is taxed to the owners at their personal tax rates before it may be reinvested for expansion. Quite often the result is that this business income ends up being taxed on considerably higher rates than the 15-40% corporate tax rate on the first $100,000 of corporate income.

Personal holding company (PHC): Finally, be warned that there is such a thing as personal holding company status if 60% or more of income is from passive income, such as interest, rent, or a personal service contract. There is a penalty tax of 50% if your corporation is declared a personal holding company. See page 21 for more details.

Losses

Capital loss. Treatment of losses can be just as important as treatment of gains. For the corporation, long-term capital loss may not be used to offset current income. It may only be used to offset capital gains from three years back to five years forward. An individual, however, may deduct 50% of his long-term capital loss (up to $3,000 in 1978 and beyond) from his current ordinary income. If his capital loss results in more than the deductible amount, he may carry the extra loss over to the next year and so on until the loss is used up.

Operating loss. A proprietor may use a net operating loss to offset current income that he may have from other sources. A corporation may only use a net operating loss to offset income in previous or future years. Therefore, if you are considering starting a new business and you anticipate that you will have start-up losses, you would be better off choosing a noncorporate or Subchapter S status.

Tax-Free or Tax-Favored Fringe Benefits

Fringe benefits in effect increase an employee's after-tax compensation by absorbing some important living costs. However, many fringe benefits are only available to corporate employees and not to proprietors or partners. The key factor here is *employment.* An incorporated business *hires* the person or persons who founded and run it. But a proprietor or partner is technically *not* an employee of his own business.

If you are considering incorporation, these benefits could be a major factor in your decision, although certainly you will want to take other factors (such as employment taxes and increased paperwork) into account, as well.

The Subchapter S corporation offers most of the fringe benefits of a corporation without losing certain tax advantages of a proprietorship. The following are some of the more important fringe benefits that can be made available to employees of a corporation:

> • Medical reimbursement plan. This plan allows employees and
> their dependents to be reimbursed directly by the corporation for
> their medical expenses. However, the rules have been significant-
> ly tightened and the plan cannot discriminate in favor of a certain

group of employees—for instance, stockholders or officers of the company.

• Employee death benefits. Upon the death of an employee, a corporation may pay the family or the estate of the decedent up to $5,000. In most cases, this amount is tax-free to the family, unless the deceased employee had the right to receive the payment while living. Proprietors and partners themselves do not qualify for this benefit, although they can certainly make such payments on behalf of their employees.

• Group health insurance. Under this plan the corporation buys insurance to cover the medical expenses of employees and their dependents. The corporation deducts the cost of the premium, but the employee does not include the value of the benefits or premium payments in his gross income. Such medical insurance is not a business expense for proprietors and partners. They may only deduct the premium as an itemized personal medical expense subject to certain limitations. However, premiums paid on behalf of employees are ordinarily deductible.

• Profit sharing and pension plans. A corporation may contribute up to 15% of the aggregate total salary of employee-participants to a profit sharing plan. (There is, however, an assumed maximum contribution allowable.) This contribution is deductible to the corporation and it is invested where it compounds and appre- of the fund, generally, at a lower tax cost. In the case of a combined profit sharing and pension plan, the corporation may contribute up to 25% of the salary provided the maximum dollar limitation is not exceeded. The plan need not include all the company's employees, but it cannot discriminate in favor of shareholders. Under the "Keogh" or "HR-10" plan, proprietors and partners may only contribute the law of 15% of earned income or $15,000 (whichever is less) to a "defined contribution" profit sharing or pension plan. (For more detail on retirement plans see Part 4.)

The pension and profit sharing plans for a Subchapter S corporation combine the features of a corporate plan and the Keogh plan. Generally, the rules are similar to those of a regular corporation.

However, there is an exception in the case of a stockholder-employee who owns more than 5% of stock. His contribution is taxable to the extent that it exceeds the lesser of 15% of his salary or $15,000.

• Group term life insurance. A corporation may purchase term life insurance for a representative group of employees and deduct the cost of the premium. The amount of insurance may be larger for corporate officers and other key employees. The "representative group" may, for example, be limited to all salaried employees, to the exclusion of hourly wage employees. The insurance is tax free to the employees and stockholder-employees up to $50,000 of coverage. Insurance over $50,000 is taxable to the employee based on projected premium payments. Special rules apply where less than ten employees are covered.

• Deferred compensation plans. Subject to certain rules, a corporate officer can arrange to defer part of his salary until after retirement. He then pays tax on the deferred part when he is presumably in a lower tax bracket. Proprietors and partners are taxed as income is received—therefore they may make no such tax deferral arrangements.

• Entertainment and travel expense. Personal entertainment and travel expense is not deductible, but business entertainment and travel expense is deductible. Unfortunately, it is sometimes difficult to tell the one from the other. It becomes even more dif-

Figure 1

LEGAL ORGANIZATIONAL FORMS

	Personal Liability	Continuity	Transferability of Ownership
Proprietorship	Unlimited	Business dissolved at death of sole proprietor	Freely transferable
Limited Partnership	General partners—unlimited. Limited partners—limited to amount of investment	General partners—withdrawal or death may dissolve partnership. Limited partners—withdrawal or death does not affect	All general partners must usually consent to transfer. Limited partners—generally free right of transfer in compliance with securities laws
General Partnership	Unlimited	May be dissolved at withdrawal or death of general partner	All general partners must usually consent to transfer
Corporation	Limited to amount of investment	Continuity unaffected by death or withdrawal of shareholder, in compliance with securities laws	Any proportion of ownership freely transferable by selling shares, in compliance with securities laws
Business Trust	Trustee—unlimited Beneficiaries—limited	Continuity unaffected by withdrawal or death of either trustee or beneficiary	Interest of beneficiary transferable by sale of trust certificates or shares in compliance with securites laws

ficult to tell them apart when the personal owner of the business, the proprietor, claims the deduction. But a corporation is a separate entity, distinct from the owner. Therefore, it is often easier to identify travel and entertainment on a corporate expense account.

Major Nontax Considerations

In addition to the major tax considerations discussed above, there are several non-tax factors to weigh before deciding how to organize your business. The major ones are:

Personal liability

- The liability of a corporate stockholder is limited to his stock

---

LEGAL ORGANIZATIONAL FORMS (continued)

Management	Cost and Requirements to Organize	Tax Treatment of Profits & Losses	Tax Rates
Proprietor manages with minimum formal regulation	No filing fees and minimal formal registration required	For tax purposes, business and its owner considered as single taxable entity	Same as owner's personal income tax rate
General partners— usually ruled by majority vote. Limited partners— no voice in management	Must comply with statutes. Written articles of partnership generally required. Costs more than general partnership to set up	Profits and losses usually flow (for tax purposes) directly to limited and general partners in proportion to their ownership of the partnership	Same as partner's personal income tax rate
Usually ruled by majority vote	No filing fees and minimal formal registration. Written articles advisable but not required	Profits and losses flow directly to partners in proportion to ownership	Same as partner's personal income tax rate
In control of a board of directors elected by shareholders	Significant costs to set up. Statutory requirements vary by state of incorporation and where business conducted	Profits and losses do not (except for sub-chapter S corporations) flow directly to shareholders. Profits taxed at corporate level and may then be passed to shareholders as taxable dividends. Losses in one period may be offset against taxable corporate income of other periods	Profits taxed 15% at corporate level on first $25,000; 18% on next $25,000; 30% on third $25,000; 40% on 4th $25,000 and 46% on income over $100,000
In control of a board of trustees, who do not have to be elected periodically	Written declaration of trust must be filed	Divided proportionally among holders of trust certificates	Same as owner's personal income tax rate

---

interest, unless, of course, he uses the corporation for a fraudulent activity or personally endorses a corporate obligation.

- General partners have unlimited liability, but a limited partner, who has no voice in management, is liable to the extent of his investment in the partnership.

Capital resources

- A corporation can sell different classes of stock and debentures and thus can raise capital with comparative ease.

- A partnership can raise capital by bringing in additional partners. Also, each partner has a personal borrowing capacity.

- A proprietor's ability to raise capital is limited by his personal resources and his credit.

Relative difficulty of formation

- Generally, a corporation is the most expensive and difficult structure to form. Also, the corporation is subject to franchise taxes and state regulations.

- A partnership is easier to form than a corporation but generally requires some legal documentation.

- A proprietorship is the least expensive and easiest business structure to form.

Transferring ownership

- Relatively speaking, corporate stock is more easily transferable and marketable than is an interest in a proprietorship or partnership.

- The number of people interested in buying into a partnership is generally limited, and a partner can often only sell his interest to a copartner. If he sells his interest to an outsider, he must usually get the other partner's approval.

- A proprietorship is usually the least marketable business form.

Management

- Authority within a corporation is usually carefully structured and easily recognizable to everyone.

- A partnership often has the least recognizable hierarchy and this can sometimes lead to confusion for employees and outsiders.

- A proprietorship has clear lines of authority and decision making power since the owner is the proprietor.

How long will it last?

- Corporations usually have indefinite life. Their existence does not depend on the continued participation of certain individuals.

- Partnerships and proprietorships can be dissolved through transfer of ownership or upon the insolvency, death, or insanity of any owner.

CHAPTER TWO

Subchapter S Corporations

The name "Subchapter S" comes from the part of the 1958 IRS Code that specifically authorizes a qualified corporation to elect to be taxed as a partnership. A Sub S corporation is permitted virtually all the benefits of incorporation but it doesn't have the major disadvantage—double taxation. Subchapter S corporations are also referred to sometimes as pseudocorporations, tax option corporations, or small business corporations.

In an ordinary corporation, profits are first taxed at the corporate level and then any dividends paid out to shareholders are again taxed as income at the personal level. With a Sub S corporation you pay tax only once (and probably at a lower rate than the corporation would pay). For example, if you own 51% of a Sub S corporation that made $10,000 this year, you would pay tax only once—on $5,100 of income on your personal tax return. If you had personal losses from other sources to offset this income, you might wind up paying little or no tax at all.

Without having to worry about the corporate double tax a Sub S can enjoy special tax advantages of a partnership, including splitting income with family members who are in lower tax brackets and shifting income to a lower tax year. A Sub S corporation is also allowed most of the advantages of incorporation referred to in the previous chapter: protection from personal liability; permanence and continuity; ease of transferring business interest; business paid health and group life insurance; tax-free reimbursement of medical expenses. There is one hitch though—you must qualify to make the Sub S election.

Checklist to qualify for "Sub S" election
Number of shareholders: must be 25 or less.
Shareholders' status: must be individuals (or estates). No corporations, partnerships or nonresident aliens. In limited cases, trusts may be shareholders.
Class of stock: only one class of stock allowed.

Passive income: no more than 20% of gross receipts from "passive" sources (i.e., royalties, rents, dividends, interest, annuities, etc.). However, this restriction may be waived during the first two years of operation if passive income is less than $3,000.

Affiliation: a "Sub S" corporation cannot be a member of an affiliated group of corporations.

How to make a valid "Sub S" election

If you qualify for "Sub S" (and most small and medium-sized businesses do), all you do is file Form 2553 with the IRS notifying them that you wish to be taxed as a "Sub S" corporation. Note, however, according to the Revenue Act of 1978:

• All shareholders must consent to the election in writing and the election must be made within 75 days of the time the new corporation begins business, acquires assets, or has stockholders, whichever happens first..

• For an already established corporation, the election must be made 75 days after or up to one year before the beginning of the applicable tax year.

• Once you make the election, it is valid until you cease to be qualified or revoke the election with the IRS.

All sound a bit complicated? Actually it's not and every businessman should give serious thought to becoming a "Sub S" corporation. Remember, you get all the benefits of incorporation—without the major disadvantage of double taxation. The profits from the business are taxed only one time and then they are taxed only at your personal tax rate.

Details on How a Sub S Is Taxed

As previously stated, for federal taxation purposes, income from a Sub S enjoys certain tax benefits. Generally, all of the capital gain, taxable income, or net operating losses pass through to the shareholders without tax to the Sub S itself. Instead, the shareholders must report their pro rata share of the Sub S income on their personal tax return and pay tax on any income or capital gain. Similarly, if there is a corporate operating loss, the shareholders deduct their share of the loss from other personal income they may have. But there is one exception to this tax treatment in the area of capital gains.

If the corporation has not been a Sub S since its inception or for the preceding three years, and if the capital gains exceed the corporation's other income, then the tax-free pass-through of capital gain is limited to $25,000. Capital gain in excess of $25,000 is taxed first to the Sub S and then to the shareholders.

The following offer more specifics on Sub S taxation:

• Income splitting. The income of a Sub S is distributed to anyone who is a shareholder on the last day of the company's tax year. The shareholder is not required to have held stock earlier in the year. This means that on the last day of a big profit year you may give stock to your children and shift the income from your higher tax bracket to their lower bracket.

• Two and one-half month rule. Sub S shareholders usually pay tax on cash dividends the year they receive them, but there is a special rule that states that if a cash dividend is paid within two and one-half months of the end of the corporation's tax year, the dividend is considered to have been paid during that year. For example, if both you and your corporation are on a calendar year tax basis and the corporation pays a cash dividend during the first two and one-half months of 1982, the dividend will be treated as if it had been paid in 1981. In other words, it may be credited back as income to your 1981 tax return.

• Switching income to a lower tax year. If your personal tax year differs from that of your Sub S corporation, you may be able to shift your income to a lower tax year. You may pay tax on the corporation's profit either as it is paid out to you as a dividend or on the last day of the company's tax year. Therefore, if you are on a calendar tax year and the fiscal year of your Sub S ends February 28, you may take a taxable dividend in December or you may delay taking the income until the following year, whichever course offers less tax.

• Sub S as long as you need it. You may terminate your Sub S status at any time as described below. This means you may take advantage of the tax benefits of the Sub S for as long as it suits your needs. You have an option with this structure, but once you terminate the election, you may not elect again for five years.

• Tax on undistributed income. Since a Sub S does not usually pay corporate tax, the shareholders must pay their pro rata share of Sub S income, even if the income is retained in the corporation and not paid out to the shareholders at the end of the company's fiscal year. In later years this income may be distributed without further tax. For example, suppose you are the sole shareholder in a Sub S that makes $25,000 profit this year and you take out $10,000 as dividends, leaving $15,000 in the company. You must pay personal income tax on the full $25,000. However, at any time in the future you may take the $15,000 out without further tax, as long as the corporation is still a Sub S and certain conditions are met.

Tax Saving Opportunities

In many business situations, the formation of a Subchapter S corporation will save taxes. But you can also take advantage of lesser-known strategies to increase your Sub S tax savings even further. Here are some on the special opportunities available through judicious planning and execution of your Sub S election.

Mid-year incorporation and Sub S election. Proprietors or partners may make a substantial one-time saving by incorporating in the middle of the year and immediately electing Sub S status. This is made possible by the progressive tax rate for individuals. The idea is to split up your proprietorship and Sub S incomes so you can file tax returns for two short periods, each of which falls into a lower tax bracket. However, you must be sure that the date you select for the end of your new Sub S fiscal year occurs in the year following Sub S election (i.e., if you elect Sub S in 1981, you must be sure that your new corporate fiscal year ends in calendar 1982).

Here's how it works: If your proprietorship normally earns $40,000 a year on which you might pay $10,000 in tax, you can save money by electing Sub S at mid-year. For example, on June 30, you've earned $20,000 and now you incorporate and elect Sub S status with a corporate fiscal year ending March 31. At the end of the year you file a personal tax return and pay the tax on the $20,000 your proprietorship earned in the six months of that year, about $3,000 tax. On March 31, you pay tax on nine months of operation as a Sub S in which you earned $30,000. You pay $6,000 tax on your nine months' earnings as a Sub S and begin a normal twelve month corporate tax year on April 1. Instead of paying about $13,000 tax for the fifteen month period's earnings, you pay only $9,000 for the combined six month and nine month periods. Admittedly, this requires some fiscal finesse, but this technique resulted in a tidy one-time-only saving of $4,000 in our example. That's well worth a trip to your accountant or tax lawyer for further details. Incidentally, your adviser will probably suggest that you pay a portion of the Sub S earnings to yourself as salary. This can reduce the tax savings potential somewhat, but still the gambit is well worth investigating.

Avoidance of unreasonable accumulation tax penalty. An ordinary corporation is permitted to accumulate up to $250,000 ($150,000 maximum for personal service corporation) of past earnings, but if it accumulates more than that and cannot show that the excess is needed for the operation of the business, the corporation must pay an "unreasonable accumulation" penalty tax of from 27½% to 38½% in addition to the regular corporate income tax. But a Sub S corporation is not subject to normal corporate taxation so it is not affected by the unreasonable accumulation penalty tax. Therefore, timely Sub S election and deft use of the dividend credit back rule can help an ordinary corporation to avoid paying this penalty tax.

Sub S election before disposition of major corporate asset. If the impending sale of a corporate asset promises to yield a substantial gain, it is likely that you do not want the gain to be taxed first to the corporation and then again to you as an individual. Instead, you can avoid the corporate double tax by electing Sub S status before the sale. Of course, take care that the $25,000 capital gain pass-through limitation does not affect the matter.

Return to regular incorporation. If you have already elected Sub S status, remember that you can switch back to the regular corporate form without any tax cost at any time. One reason to do this would be to have the first $100,000 of corporate income taxed at 15-40% rather than at your personal rate, which could be higher. But after the return to regular incorporation, you may not elect Sub S for five years.

Sub S election before corporate liquidation. You may elect Sub S status before you liquidate your corporation to avoid the regular double tax on the sale of corporate assets. And naturally, if you incur losses during liquidation, Sub S election allows you to take a deduction as an individual.

Multiple Sub S's. If you own two corporations, Sub S election for both allows you to offset the gains of one against the losses of the other. This is not allowed in the case of a regular corporation.

Combine Sub S operating losses with personal income to save taxes. If you elect Sub S for your corporation, you may deduct the corporate loss from your other personal income. If you retain regular corporate status, you may only carry an operating loss back three years to offset prior corporate income and obtain a corporate tax refund. Any excess loss after carryback can then be carried forward to offset future corporate income.

As you can see, you may not deduct the losses from a regular corporation from your personal income. You may, however, elect Sub S for a year in which you anticipate losses and then return to regular incorporation the following year, if you wish. Note that personal loss deduction from your Sub S may not exceed the amount you paid for your stock (its basis) plus any corporation debt due you.

Problems to Avoid with a Sub S

Naturally, Subchapter S incorporation is not totally trouble-free. Without an awareness of potential stumbling blocks, you could inadvertantly violate some IRS regulations governing this type of business structure. Watch out for the following problem areas.

Loss carryover. A corporation with a net operating loss carryover from years preceding its Sub S election may not use the loss carryover while it maintains a Sub S status. The carryover may be resurrected and put to use if the Sub S reverts to a regular corporation within the original fifteen-year carryover period. While the corporation remains Sub S, the carryover is put into a state of suspense.

Maintain Sub S qualification. You must maintain your Sub S qualifications after election if you wish to retain your Sub S status. Remember that you may have no more than 25 shareholders who are individuals, estates, or certain trusts (no corporation, or nonresident aliens) and your corporation must be domestic and normally cannot be a member of an affiliated group. Only one class of stock is allowed and at least 80 percent of income must be bona fide, earned (not passive) income.

Salaries. A Sub S must pay reasonable salaries to its working shareholders before income is divided among all shareholders.

Deductibility of operating losses. Operating losses incurred by a Sub S are passed through directly to the shareholders who then deduct them from their personal incomes. Again, deduction of losses is limited to an amount equal to the basis of the shareholder's stock and any corporate debt owed to him. Excess loss above this amount is wasted.

Sub S reversion. If your Sub S corporation reverts back to an ordinary corporation, be certain to distribute the retained income on which the shareholders have already paid tax. If you do not distribute it when you terminate your Sub S election, it will become a taxable dividend when the ordinary corporation later distributes it to the shareholders. Of course, the two and one-half month rule allows Sub S dividends to be distributed within two and one-half months of the end of the Sub S year.

CHAPTER THREE

Special
Issues

How to Incorporate Tax Free

A canny business person will search out ways to save or avoid taxes in every conceivable situation. For example, if you follow certain rules, you can incorporate your proprietorship or partnership tax free. However, the following two conditions must be met:

> 1. Transfer of assets from the proprietorship or partnership must be made only in exchange for stock or long term obligations of the corporation.

> 2. The person or persons who transferred property to the corporation must own at least 80% of the corporation's stock immediately after the exchange.

If the exchange satisfies the above two conditions and doesn't involve any of the following conditions, the incorporation is tax free. If, on the other hand, any one of the following three conditions is involved, there will be at least a partial tax as the result of incorporation.

> 1. Liabilities in excess of assets. If you transfer $30,000 in assets and $35,000 in liabilities to a corporation, you have a taxable gain of $5,000. The rule is that transferred liability in excess of the adjusted basis of the transferred property is considered taxable gain. Here the term "liabilities" also includes property that is subject to liability, but does not include trade accounts payable.

> 2. Personal service. Personal service is not deemed property in this kind of tax free transfer. If personal service is exchanged for

stock, a taxable income is created to the extent of the value of the personal service. In other words, if a person trades his skill and experience for 40% of the stock in a corporation, he must pay tax on the fair market value of the stock he receives.

3. Bad debt reserve. If a proprietor transfers his accounts receivable as property in exchange for corporate stock, he may have to treat any funds in a bad debt reserve account (for which he has taken annual deductions) as taxable income.

If you are caught in this kind of situation, there are a few things you can try to reduce the tax liability. You can elect Sub S for your corporation to avoid corporate tax so that the corporation's bad debt deduction for the new receivables passes directly to you. Or you can transfer your good receivables to the corporation and hold onto the dubious accounts. Finally, you may sell your receivables to a third party at a discount. In this last case you would want the amount of the discount to be less than the tax (that would be due) on the transfer of the reserve account to the new corporation. As long as the discount is less than the tax, you will be ahead.

Section 1244 Stock

The term "1244 stock" comes from the Internal Revenue Code. According to Section 1244 of the Code, which deals with so-called small business stock, up to $50,000 ($100,000 if a joint return) per year of deductions against ordinary income can be taken for loss on the common stock of a small business corporation. This rule applies whether the loss is incurred by selling the stock or its becoming worthless while you hold it. However, several strict rules must be followed in order to qualify as 1244 stock.

- Only common stock (voting or nonvoting) of a domestic corporation may be designated as 1244 stock.

- The amount of 1244 stock issued cannot exceed $1,000,000.

- The stock must be issued for money or property (not stock, securities, or services).

- The corporation must be an "operating" company and have derived over 50% of its revenue for the last five taxable years (or during its entire existence, if less than five years) from other than passive sources (royalties, rents, dividends, etc.).

Points to consider

Because of the special tax benefits, you may be better off purchasing 1244 stock rather than making a loan to a new company. If the business goes bad, you won't be caught in the troublesome area of trying to qualify the bad debt as a business loss (ordinary deduction) as opposed to a nonbusiness loss (short-term capital deduction).

If you own 1244 stock that is worthless, the law does not require you to sell the shares to establish the loss; rather, you should document the worthlessness of the shares and file an attachment to your tax return.

Consider qualifying the new venture as a "Subchapter S" corporation as well as under Section 1244. That way, you will get personal deductions from operating losses (Sub S) as well as an ordinary deduction if the whole firm goes bad (1244).

If the investment risk works out and you make a profit from your Section 1244 stock, it can qualify for the more favorable capital gains rates if you hold it for more than one year.

Finally, the IRS challenges expenses to investigate a new business, unless you subsequently go into the business. To be safe, consider incorporating before any money is spent—that way, you should definitely get an ordinary loss deduction if things don't pan out.

"Thin" Incorporation

"Thin incorporation" refers to the capital structure of a new corporation. Quite often, business people will transfer part of their assets to a new corporation, partly in exchange for stock (equity investment) and partly in the form of a loan (debt investment).

The tactic employed here is that the corporation can deduct the interest it pays on the loan and, as the debt is repaid, capital is returned tax free. In addition to avoiding the double tax by paying interest instead of dividends to the shareholder, thin incorporation also allows profits to be accumulated to repay debts without risking penalty tax for unreasonable accumulation. But there can be problems with this form of incorporation.

Incorporation is tax free only if the proprietor or partner receives stock and securities in exchange for his transferred assets. For this reason, the corporation's debt instrument must qualify as a security. To avoid having the IRS regard the interest payments as disguised dividends, be sure that proper notes are drawn up to reflect evidences of debt.

The IRS and the tax courts get very suspicious if they don't see a true debtor-creditor relationship. The following will help to convince them of your good intentions:*

- Establish the debt in your accounts, show it on the financial statements, and record it in the minutes.

- See that the ratio of debt to equity in the corporation does not exceed 3 to 1.

- Be sure there is a written unconditional promise to pay a reasonable, fixed rate of interest at proper intervals and that the payment of interest does not depend on corporate earnings.

- Try to establish some evidence that outside creditors would have seriously considered making the same loan you did.

- The debt holder should have the right to sue and to enforce payment and the debt itself should not be subordinate to other creditors.

- The amount of debt should be reasonable; and it should be clear to the Internal Revenue Service that if interest and payments are made on schedule, the debt can be paid off in the normal operation of the business.

However, before you leap into thin incorporation, consider the potential disadvantages. The debt may affect the corporation's credit rating, and it commits the corporation to regular payments of interest and principal that could strangle cash flow at the wrong time.

*New Section 385 regulations take effect for instruments issued after 12.31.81, which can affect these suggestions. See your tax adviser.

Your Salary—How to Be Sure It's "Reasonable"

There are three basic ways to take money out of an incorporated business: (1) salary, (2) dividends, and (3) tax-free benefits, such as a group-term life insurance plan. Clearly, the best route is tax-free benefits, but the law strictly limits the amount and type of benefits you can receive. Between salary and dividends, there is a decided advantage to salary. Even though both salary and dividends are treated as ordinary income to the individual, only salary payments are deductible to the corporation. As a result, salary emerges as the most practical and tax-wise way to get money out of most businesses. The trouble is—the IRS knows this, too, and often attacks salaries as "unreasonable" and requires a portion to be treated as dividends. Here are the facts you need to know to avoid trouble.

How to determine the "optimum" salary

Corporate earnings are federally taxed at 15% on the first $25,000 of income, 18% on the next $25,000, 30% on the next $25,000, 40% on the next $25,000 and at 46% on all income above $100,000.

From an individual's standpoint, however, taxes don't reach these levels until 1982 taxable incomes are about $7,600, $11,900, $29,900, $45,800 and $60,000, respectively. The optimum salary purely from a short-term tax standpoint for an owner-shareholder of a business would involve an interplay of corporate and individual tax rates.

Taking the larger view, however, even though retention of a certain amount of money at the corporate level results in double taxation, this is oftentimes the more desirable procedure. For instance, in the case of a corporation with taxable income before salary of $150,000, payment of a $100,000 salary and contribution of $15,000 to a profit-sharing plan would result in corporate taxable income of $35,000. Corporate tax on this amount would approximate $5,500 and the income could potentially be taxed again to the shareholder upon distribution as a dividend. However, a more common result would be to retain the income in the corporation for working capital, expansion, etc. At some future date the corporation would likely be sold or liquidated, at which time the retained earnings would be distributed to the shareholder with capital gain tax resulting on the monies received. Thus, to the extent the corporate accumulation is small enough to result in taxation at rates lower than the marginal rate of the individual, and does not create an "unreasonable accumulation," this would be the desirable strategy. Of course, part of this strategy is based upon the necessity of a fairly high salary as a basis for a substantial contribution to a profit-sharing or pension plan. Also, all compensation paid must be reasonable.

How to be sure your salary is "reasonable"

Just because a particular salary is best from a tax standpoint certainly doesn't mean that it is best from all standpoints. First, you must consider the economic situation of your company. It simply may not be able to pay out all you would like as salary. The second consideration is your standard of living. You may not be able to live on a salary which works out best in terms of taxes. Finally, there is the IRS to contend with. A favorite Treasury gambit is to claim that the salary paid is excessive and that part must either be treated as a dividend (and the corporation will lose the deduction) or be repaid to the corporation. While there are no hard and fast rules, here are several factors the IRS considers when checking the reasonableness of officer-shareholder salaries:

18

• Qualifications. What is the education and experience of the individual?

• Competitors. What salaries are paid to comparable individuals in other companies in the industry?

• Scope of work. What is the size and complexity of the business and nature of the individual's work? Is the individual full- or part-time?

• Dividend history. Does the company have a history of paying dividends or do salaries vary from year to year to minimize dividends?

• Return on capital. Are the corporate shareholders receiving an adequate return on their investment? (Although the IRS considers this factor, the courts have been favoring the taxpayer if the salary is reasonable compared with prior years and the other factors described above.)

Other means of compensation

If corporate earnings are rising and salaries are going up while dividends remain constant or are even omitted, you will probably face IRS scrutiny. In this case there are a couple of alternate strategies. The first is for officer-shareholders to perform certain services on a ''for fee'' basis. So long as the services are needed by the corporation and the fee is comparable to that paid to outsiders, the amount should be allowed. A second possible strategy is to enter into an arrangement with the corporation so that you are paid a base salary plus a percentage of sales. As long as the contract was consummated at arm's length and the percentage was reasonable at the time, high compensation results will not necessarily mean a disallowance of the deduction that is being claimed.

Don't shortchange yourself in the early years

Many businessmen pay themselves low salaries in the early years because that is all the company can afford. Later, as the dollars start to roll in, they raise their salaries to compensate—only to have the increase treated as excessive by the IRS. The solution is to pay yourself a reasonable salary from the beginning and have the corporation give you a note for any amount it can't afford to pay. This way, the corporation gets the deduction in the current period and later, when you get your back pay, there should be no problem with the IRS. If you have been in business for some time and have underpaid yourself to build up corporate funds, be sure to have the corporate records show how much you were underpaid. This way, when you eventually raise your pay, you will be able to show the IRS that the increase is justified in light of your past undercompensation. Be sure to check with your tax adviser to avoid potential problems.

Repayment agreement

A good protective tactic in the area of unreasonable salary is to have a written salary agreement that stipulates that you will repay any salary that the IRS deems excessive. Put this written agreement into the corporate minutes. Then, if the IRS does declare part of your salary to be unreasonable, you may repay the excess salary (which you have already paid tax on) and treat this repayment as a personal deduction. Naturally, the corporation loses its deduction for the amount you repay, but it does, after all, get the money back. This way, even if the IRS makes you return part of your unreasonable salary, both you and your corporation are right back where you would have been had you not been paid the excessive amount. There is no penalty for trying. Later you can try again to get money out of the corporation either under different circumstances or through other means.

Fending Off the Accumulated Earnings Tax

Corporations are allowed to accumulate up to $250,000 ($150,000 if personal service corporation) of earnings, but if they exceed that amount, they must be able to justify the excess to the IRS or else face a possible penalty tax on the excess. Although the excess that brought on the penalty tax may have been built up gradually over the years, the penalty tax is computed on the corporation's annual taxable income adjusted for several factors. In general, if an earnings accumulation is deemed unreasonable by the IRS, the company must pay 27½ % on the first $100,000 of excess accumulation income and 38½ % on excess accumulation over $100,000 in addition to the regular corporate income tax. Again, these penalties are in addition to the regular tax.

However, there are several possible ways to avoid the penalty tax on accumulated earnings:

1. Elect Sub S status. If the company elects Sub S status, profits are taxed at the shareholder's personal rate, whether the earnings are distributed or not.

2. Pay the excess out in dividends. If the excess is paid out as dividends to the stockholders in an ordinary corporation, the usual double tax is paid on the earnings. But this might be preferable to paying the penalty tax. Also, the credit back rule allows dividends that are considered paid in the first two and one-half months of a new tax year to be part of the previous year's distributions.

3. Prove that the excess is needed for operation of the business. The third (and most common) safety valve is to prove that the excess is needed for the continued operation of the company. To prove this, the corporation should be able to show specific plans for the accumulated funds and evidence of intent and conduct toward accomplishing the plans. The following are some of the accepted planned uses for accumulated earnings:

• To acquire a new business. It need not be related to the corporation's business.

• Planned construction for replacement or improvement of facilities.

• Working capital for the operating cycle. (The cycle goes from cash to inventory to sales to accounts receivable and then back to cash.)

• Retirement of preferred stock or corporate debt.

• A contingency fund for uninsurable events such as lawsuits, new legislation, strikes, etc.

The above allay IRS suspicions. A few conditions wave a red flag to the IRS:

- Large cash balances or significant investments in certificates of deposit or marketable securities.

- Long-term loans to stockholders or corporate monies spent for the personal benefit of shareholders.

- Loans to unrelated corporations when shareholders have ownership interests in both companies.

- Investment in property or stock unrelated to the business of the corporation.

- High-premium life insurance policies on the lives of stock-holder-employees.

Personal holding company status

It might seem ideal to form an investment corporation and have the corporation buy stock, using the allowed 85% dividend exclusion deduction. Then, instead of paying tax on the dividends in accordance with your personal income tax rate, you could let the dividend accumulate in the corporation at a cost of only 2.25% (15% of dividend income times the 15% corporate tax rate, which only applies to the first $25,000 of taxable income). But it doesn't work this way. You don't want to have a personal holding company (PHC) that the IRS would frown upon and would tax at a rate of 70% plus the usual corporate tax rate.

A corporation is considered to be a PHC if it meets two criteria: (1) More than 50% of its outstanding stock is owned by five or fewer individuals at any time during the last half of the tax year. (2) 60% or more of its adjusted ordinary gross income is made up of passive income, such as interest, royalties, certain income from personal service contracts, dividends, annuities, some rent income, and compensation paid to the corporation by its stockholders for use of company property. If your corporation meets both criteria, the PHC penalty tax will be assessed unless the PHC income is paid out as dividends.

In regard to ownership restrictions, a stockholder is considered the owner of shares held in his name by members of his family, relatives, or other corporations and partnerships in which he has ownership interest. This attribution of ownership is common in close corporations. The trick is to avoid meeting the income criterion.

Dividends and interest are obviously passive income that will be examined for the 60% passive income test. Income from leases to shareholders is also generally considered passive income. Your tax adviser should carefully look over your sources of income to see whether or not it will put you in a PHC status.

It is advisable to play it safe in the area of PHC. Beware of falling within the five person 50% ownership restriction, and be certain that no more than 59% of the corporation's earnings is from passive sources.

Family Partnerships

A family partnership allows a proprietor to split his income with family members who are in a lower tax bracket. By paying less tax on the same income, the collective wealth of the family increases. And it should also be noted that a proprietor's estate tax may be reduced as well, because his children will already own part of the business when he dies.

Since a family partnership can save a great deal on taxes, special rules (IRS § 704) have been established to prevent abuse. The rules apply to partnerships whose members are related by blood or marriage and include husband, wife, children, parents, grandparents, grandchildren, or a trust set up for any of these persons. The more stringent family partnership rules do not apply to partnerships that include a brother, a sister, an in-law, an aunt, or an uncle.

Special rules

In addition to adhering to the laws governing a general partnership, a family partnership must follow these special rules:

> • If a child is to be a partner, his interest generally must be held under a trust or a guardianship. In many states, the guardianship of a minor trust must be reviewed annually by the court. A minor of any age may be a partner.

> • A family member may be an "inactive" partner only if capital (real estate, equipment, inventories, plant, etc.) is a material income-producing factor. On the other hand, in a service industry, the family member must regularly perform a valuable service.

> • The donor or seller of a partnership interest must take out a reasonable salary for his service before the remaining profit is divided among the family partners, if capital is a material income producing factor. A new partner may not receive a greater proportionate distributive share of profit than the old partner.

The donor or seller of the partnership interest can retain limited management control consistent with true ownership after transfer of interest. Guidelines used include:

> • The old partner may not control the assets so that he owns them and leases them to the partnership.

> • The new partner must have an unlimited right to liquidate or sell his interest with no strings attached.

> • Generally speaking, all partners are entitled to vote in management decisions.

> • The new partner must be treated publicly as a partner.

Additional details

The gift of a partnership is subject to gift tax. But you can usually get around this tax by giving a small piece of the business to a new partner each year, the value of which does not exceed the annual $10,000 federal gift tax exclusion per donee ($3,000 prior to 1982).

A spouse's share of the profits or the share belonging to a minor may be left in the partnership for the purpose of business expansion. However, actual distributions to a donee partner tend to substantiate the reality of his partnership interest. No matter how much income a child receives from the partnership, the parent may continue to claim him as a dependent (so long as all dependency exemption tests are met). If your spouse is a partner, you will not reduce your annual income because you will still file a joint return. However, it may reduce your future estate tax, and your spouse may benefit from Social Security coverage.

CHAPTER FOUR

Basic Management Overview

What Does It Take to Start (and Run) a Successful Business?*

"Know yourself, and it must follow, as the night the day, you cannot then be false to any man."

The fact is that few businesspeople know very much about the characteristics that account for success.

And even fewer can recognize these characteristics in their children and subordinates.

Entrepreneurs, by definition, are "doers." Their aggressiveness usually (and necessarily) causes conflict and disruption.

If you have people in your organization with entrepreneurial characteristics, act now to channel their talents in directions which will be healthy for your business. Act as their mentor, keep them under the business umbrella, and reap the rewards of their energy and purpose.

Take this quiz, and see if you recognize anyone you know—perhaps even yourself!

1. Was your father or a close relative in business for him/herself?

The available data show that the majority of entrepreneurs had a father or other close relative in business for themselves. The importance of a role model in entrepreneurship is well documented.

2. Have you ever worked for a small firm where you had close contact with the person who started it?

Those who work in the smaller firm environment usually get more opportunities to

*Portions of this material reprinted with permission from *Do You Have What It Takes to Start Your Own Business?* by the Entrepreneurship Institute and Jeffrey C. Susbauer.

work closely with the top management and/or founders of those firms. Thus, their "entrepreneurship experience" is more varied and useful.

3. Is your work experience in a variety of functional areas, such as marketing, finance, and production?

The more functional area experiences, the better. An entrepreneur is a jack of all trades, at least initially. The entrepreneur needs to be conversant with the total functions of the enterprise, as he cannot generally afford experts at first.

4. Have you ever had an employer reject a "better mousetrap" idea?

More companies are started for negative reasons than for positive ones, and the rejection of an idea is a common negative reason. Large corporations frequently do more to unwittingly encourage entrepreneurship by discouraging creativity than they know.

5. Do you like to do things, rather than plan things?

Most entrepreneurs like to do, not read, write, think, or plan. Entrepreneurs are people of action. If you are one of those fortunate persons who is at home both planning and acting, consider yourself a prime candidate for entrepreneurship.

6. Have you lived in three or more cities in your life?

Mobility is a key factor in the decision to start a company. This relates to flexibility, a necessity in the beginning stages of a firm. Receptivity to new ideas and situations can be enhanced by variety, and movement frequently forces this flexibility.

7. Have you ever been fired?

Most entrepreneurs rebel at working for others. If you answered no to this question, and you think you are entrepreneurial material anyway, you probably quit before you got fired.

8. If you are married, is your spouse supportive of your work?

Entrepreneurs get very much married to their firms. Their families usually suffer in the start-up years and even beyond. Can your spouse/family withstand the competition of your new spouse and family (the firm) and the time/financial demands imposed by it? If not, which is more important, the firm or your family? Before you start, talk this over very seriously at length with your spouse and family.

9. When things happen to you, is it because you made them happen, rather than waiting for chance or luck?

Successful entrepreneurs operate in the middle ground between pure chance and luck, where they, not chance or luck, influence what happens to them and their firms. If you feel you make things happen, this is called internal focus of control. If you feel other forces make things happen to you, this is called external focus of control. Entrepreneurs consistently score in the direction of being internally focused.

10. If you had to make a choice between working for a firm you did not own for twice the money or running your own firm at your present compensation, would you choose to start your own firm?

Most entrepreneurs desire the independence of owning and managing their own firms far more than the financial security of working for someone else. This does not mean that entrepreneurs don't desire financial independence, and most entrepreneurs start companies with the anticipation of making and retaining more money —eventually—than they are now making. That's not the overriding consideration, though.

11. When a problem comes up that seems unsolvable, do you usually try to figure out ways to solve it?

Entrepreneurs are usually inventive, inquisitive, and aggressive. They like challenges. Solving the "unsolvable" when everyone around you gives up makes for fortunes and also for valuable employees (which may or may not be recognized and rewarded by your present employer). Solving the unsolvable is a capability few have, and it can be useful in your own firm.

12. As a child, did you sell lemonade or have a paper route?

Developmental psychologists maintain that personality and other traits are developed quite early in life. If you had a paper route, sold lemonade, or ran your own band, that's a positive (but not conclusive) entrepreneurial sign.

13. Do you get along well in general with other people? (or) Do your subordinates respect you and work hard for you, even if they don't necessarily like you and/or your style of operating?

If you are a potentially successful entrepreneur and you don't get along well with other people, you can still be successful, but you'll certainly have a difficult time starting the next Xerox or Itel. It does help, however, if you command the respect and dedication of your employees, even if they don't necessarily like you and your manner. This is called leadership, and the ability to attract and retain people who will work hard for and with you will help build your enterprise.

Strengths and Weaknesses of a Smaller Business*

Many small businessmen (those who employ fewer than five hundred people) worry that larger competitors will drive them out of business. However, small businesses actually do have many significant advantages over large companies. Knowledge of these strengths—and weaknesses—will help you avoid costly mistakes and protect your business from encroachments by competitors.

Small company weaknesses

Financial limitations. Balancing "cash in" and "cash out" is a struggle, especially when a company is trying to expand. Instead of receiving the red carpet treatment by financiers when floating a loan, the small businessman is often made to feel like a second-class citizen. And small companies can't use credit as a selling tool as readily as companies with large financial reserves. Additionally, many small companies have trouble staying afloat while waiting for their products to win acceptance in the marketplace.

Manpower problems. Small companies cannot pay top salaries and provide the opportunities and status normally associated with a big company job. Small company management must also concentrate on the day-to-day problems of running the business and generally have little time left to think about the company and its problems objectively.

Higher direct costs. A small company cannot buy raw materials, machinery, or supplies as cheaply as a large company or obtain a large producer's economies of scale. So per unit production costs are usually higher for a small company, but overhead costs are generally somewhat lower.

Too many eggs. A large diversified company can take a licking in one sector of its business and still remain strong. This is not so for the small business with only a few product lines. A small company is vulnerable if a new product doesn't catch on, if one

*Portions of this section are condensed from Alfred Arose, "Meeting the Competition of Giants," *Harvard Business Review,* May-June 1967.

of its markets is hit by a sharp recession, or if an old product suddenly becomes obsolete.

Lack of acceptance. The public accepts a large company's products because its name is well known and usually respected. A small company must struggle to prove itself each time it offers a new product or enters a new market. Its reputation and past successes in the marketplace seldom carry weight.

Small company strengths

Personal touch. Customers will often pay a premium for personalized attention. In fact, in many industries where product and price differences are minimal, the human factor emerges as a prime competitive advantage.

Greater motivation. Top management of a small company normally consists of the owners or major stockholders. Consequently, they work harder, longer, and with more personal investment. Profits and losses have more meaning for them than salaries and bonuses have to employees of a larger company.

Greater flexibility. The small company has the prime competitive advantage of agility. A big business cannot close a plant without opposition from organized labor or even raise prices without possible intervention from Washington, but a small company can react quickly to competitive changes. A small company also has shorter lines of communication. Its product lines are narrow, its markets limited, and its factories and warehouses close. It can quickly spot trouble or opportunity and take appropriate action.

Less bureaucracy. Grasping the big picture is difficult for executives of large companies. This "management myopia" leads to redundant actions and bureaucratic inefficiencies. In a small business the whole problem can be understood readily, decisions can be made quickly, and the results can be checked easily.

Unobtrusive. Because it is not readily noticeable, the small company can try new sales tactics or introduce new products without attracting undue attention and opposition. Large companies are constantly faced with proxy battles, antitrust actions, and government regulations.

Opportunities in the giant's shadow

Too many businessmen panic in the face of competition from a large company and overcompensate by drastic price cuts, expanded services, or the introduction of unproven products. The most important rule is never compete head on with a giant—you'll invariably lose. Here is a plan of action for circumventing the competition:

> Aim at specialized segments. To maximize sales volume and production efficiency, large companies concentrate on the needs of average customers—often bypassing large market segments that desire specialized products or services. By carefully studying the unique needs of this market, the small businessman can usually find numerous opportunities that are both secure and profitable.

> Localize your business. Certain local preferences exist for almost every product and service. For example, food, beverages, clothing, and household items have regional and local variances. Large companies cannot efficiently cater to individual markets. In national promotions, the giant must appeal to as many and irritate as few people as possible. Its copy becomes bland and generalized. Stress the uniqueness of your localization by using local people, backgrounds, and motifs in your advertising.

> Personal touch. No large company can compete with the per-

sonal touch of a smaller local businessman. Don't become so absorbed in your operational problems that you fail to get out to see customers. In those cases where you are not competitive in price, extra personal service can often swing the sale your way.

In an expanding economy large companies generally concentrate on expanding markets and new product areas, bypassing lower yield market segments. Sometimes, however, the opposite is true. To maintain sales, the large company begins to enter more specialized market segments, threatening smaller businesses. Be alert to this potential threat and take action to protect yourself.

How to Formulate a Business Strategy

Formulating a corporate strategy is an imposing-sounding undertaking. On one hand you might say, "That's just for huge conglomerates—not for my relatively simple business." But you might be surprised if you knew how many large firms are floundering because they don't have a coherent or consistent strategy—or just how many little firms are rapidly getting larger because they do!

What is a corporate strategy?

Strategy—no panacea or mystery—consists of three simple but profound questions that you should regularly ask yourself:

- What business am I really in?

- What is happening in the business environment that could affect my company?

- How do I organize all the resources I have (human, financial, material, etc.) to meet the business challenge ahead? In other words, strategy means to constantly ask, "Where am I going—and how do I plan to get there?"

Why is a business strategy important?

Because if you don't know where you are going, how can you ever get there? Strategy formulation forces you to:

- Focus on the future as well as on your present problems.

- Consider risks and obstacles ahead and plan adequately to meet them.

- Define your corporate purpose.

- Set objectives to meet your goals.

Business definition

What business are you really in? This is the first mistake many businessmen make. Let's take a classic example:

Earlier this century, there was hardly an industry more powerful than the railroads. Today many are practically bankrupt. What happened? Well, the railroads were insular and isolated in their thinking. They scoffed at the idea that trucks could ever carry volumes of freight as efficiently from place to place as the railroads. And, of course, to think of carrying major cargo by air—well, that was ridiculous. Or so it seemed at the time. They defined their business as railroading and it was king! What they failed to realize until too late was that they were really in the transportation business. Rather than integrate naturally into other transportation businesses, including trucking and the airlines, which they could have done, they stuck to the rails and fought a bitter battle to try and kill other forms of freight and passenger haulage. Today, the results of the myopic and literal, rather than functional, definition of their business are all too evident.

And so it is that first you must define your business in functional, not product, terms: what do you do for your customers, not what do you sell them. McDonald's doesn't sell just hamburgers and french fries—they also sell quality, service, and convenience. That's what the customer wants. Hamburgers he can get anywhere.

Environmental trends

Once you have properly defined your corporate purpose, you must then assess how social, political, economic, and technological trends affect your business. For example:

> Social. If you are in high fashion, what does the ''back-to-nature'' movement mean to you?

> Political. What effect will such governmental actions as price controls, taxes, zoning restrictions, or import quotas have on your business?

> Economic. How is your business affected by changes in interest rates, the general economic climate, or inflation? (And what about raw materials and the energy shortage? If you are in trucking, lack of energy is obviously an ominous threat. If you are in the insulation business, it could be a splendid opportunity.)

> Technological. Is there danger of technological obsolescence in your business? What must you do to keep up? Can you afford to keep up?

What resources do you have?

In other words, once you've considered the risks and opportunities ahead for your business, what capabilities do you have to cope with them? What are your strengths and weaknesses in each of the following areas?

> Human. Do you have enough people, and can they be properly trained to shift to a slightly (or perhaps radically) different type of business?

> Financial. What money will be required and how can it be made available?

> Physical. Will new or different facilities, machinery, or raw materials be needed?

Strategic choices and internal consistency

After you have defined your business and assessed relevant environmental trends and your capabilities to cope with them, you must choose among several strategic options, such as:

- Maximize short-term or long-term profits.

- Invest in present markets or expand into new markets.

• Invest profits back in the company (growth) or commit to shareholders (dividends).

You must insure, however, that your strategy is internally consistent. For example, rapid short-term growth is not consistent with paying out most profits as dividends. In addition, analyze if the proposed strategy is acceptable in terms of:

• Risk. A subjective judgment based on (1) resources available for commitment, (2) duration of commitment, (3) proportion of total resources committed to a single venture.

• Time horizon. How long until results are evident? How long do you have?

A major problem of managers in many companies is that they are completely pre-occupied with day-to-day problems. They never have the time to appraise current performance and assess the long-term needs and prospects of their business. It is a form of ad hoc decision-making—not management. In brief, take time to manage your company.

How to Consult to Your Own Company

"He can't see the forest for the trees." How often have you heard that about a business associate who is so close to his problem that he can't be objective about a solution? How often have you had the same lack of objectivity in your business?

Management consultants make a living by solving other people's problems. However, professional consultants are expensive, and they are not always available or convenient. Therefore, why not try taking the management consultant's approach to a problem? In other words, consult to yourself.

The problem-solving approach

What is the management consulting approach to problems? Basically, it is the same four-step process used to solve any problem: (1) Define the problem; (2) Gather information; (3) Analyze data and draw conclusions; (4) Implement change. Let's see how this actually works for a typical problem.

John Jones is the president and owner of Gifts by Mail, a mail-order business whose sales come from catalog orders. Jones's mailing and customer lists are kept on computer. Although he works closely with his liaison at the computer service bureau, he is disturbed by the lack of control he has over his accounts. Programming errors have resulted in many orders that were filled erroneously, payments that were not credited properly, and inventory over- and understock. Jones has cash flow problems, disgruntled customers, and in-office disorganization. He is dangerously close to going out of business.

How does Jones get back on his feet?

1. Defining the problem.

What, exactly, is Jones's problem? And how does he go about solving it?

The first step in defining a problem is limiting the scope. Instead of tackling cash flow, personnel management, inventory error, and computer problems all at once, Jones decided that most of his difficulties stem from one common source: lack of control over his mailing lists. This, in turn, is attributable to poor service from his computer bureau.

The next step is setting objectives. To do this, Jones asked himself: "What would be the ideal reasult? What do I hope to accomplish?" He wrote his objective in measurable terms, such as "All orders will be filled within ten days."

Jones then made a list of questions to be researched.

Finally, Jones prepared a schedule. He estimated the time necessary to gather information, decide on a course of action, and implement change. He set a target date of four months ahead to begin his new system—although at this stage of the problem-solving process he had no idea what the new system would be.

2. Gathering information.

Jones located five basic sources of information, which he utilized to gather data for the study of his problem:

   • Records and files. The balance sheets, inventory records, sales records, interoffice memos, customer complaints, and business plans of Gifts by Mail gave Jones an overall view of how his company was progressing and problem areas that were developing.

   • Personnel. Jones interviewed his employees. He encouraged them to give him frank answers to questions such as, "How do you perceive this operation? Where do you think we need to become more efficient? Where are the strong spots? The weak spots?"

   • Trade associations. Jones found his mail-order trade association to be an excellent source of information on industry trends and competition. In addition, the magazines and newsletters published by the associations shed insight into how other companies in his field coped with similar problems.

   • The marketplace. Jones talked to other computer service bureaus. He surveyed his customers. He discussed the problem with executives of competing businesses.

   • The government. The reams of information published by the government every day gave Jones perspectives on statistics, trends, and industrial reports.

3. Analysis and conclusions.

After Jones had utilized every source available to him, he was ready to analyze his findings. He broke them down into two categories:

   Quantitative (objective) analysis consisted of the figures and statistics he had gathered. He used actual figures where he had them and estimated where he only had projections.

   Qualitative (subjective) analysis was succinctly described by Benjamin Franklin. He said, "When confronted with two courses of action, I jot down on a piece of paper the arguments in favor of each one—then on the opposite side I write the arguments against each one. Then by weighing the arguments, pro and con, and cancelling them out one against the other, I take the course indicated by what remains."

Jones, too, organized his information into a logical display. By this time, his analysis had shown the problem to be, "Should I stay with my current computer bureau and work with them to modify their procedures, or should I change systems entirely?"

To analyze this question qualitatively, Jones made up a matrix divided into four parts, which contained all the information he had gathered about:

- The advantages of staying with the current system.

- The disadvantages of staying with the current system.

- The advantages of switching to a new system.

- The disadvantages of switching to a new system.

4. Implementing change.

When all of the information was down in black and white, Jones, through Ben Franklin's process of elimination, found the most efficient and advantageous course of action would be to work within his existing system. It was clear to him, however, that changes would have to be made, and he was now aware of what those changes were. To implement the changes, he took the following action:

He defined and listed all the steps to bring about the change.

He set up a schedule to implement the system.

He assigned responsibility for implementation to one person.

He reviewed progress regularly.

He adjusted and modified the system wherever necessary.

How to Make Your Business Succeed Beyond One Generation—The Sears Example

Many managers are so engrossed in the day-to-day operational details of running their businesses (and surviving) that they sometimes lose sight of where their companies are going. Often studying the experiences of other successful companies can yield a rewarding sense of perspective. Here's a brief case study of one of the most consistently successful companies in the country. It is not accident, as you will see.

In the beginning...

Sears, Roebuck and Company was founded around the turn of the century with the objective of tapping a totally separate and distinct market—the farmer. Separate because his isolation made other distribution channels virtually inaccessible to him; distinct because his needs were different in many respects from his urban counterparts'.

To reach this market, new distribution channels had to be created. Merchandise had to be produced for the farmer's specific needs and made available at low prices. Finally, the merchandise and company had to have a reputation for reliability and honesty, since the farmer's geographic isolation made it impractical for him to inspect the merchandise beforehand or seek redress if swindled. To accomplish these needs, innovations were necessary in five distinct areas:

Supply. Arrangements had to be made with vendors to furnish to Sears the quantity and quality of goods needed.

Distribution. The mail order catalog had to be developed as a substitute for big city shopping.

Quality. The famous (and revolutionary at the time) guarantee of "your money back and no questions asked" was initiated.

Processing. A mail order plant had to be built to inventory huge quantities of merchandise and process large numbers of customer orders.

Organization. When Sears began, there were no buyers, accountants, artists, clerks, etc., with the necessary skills. Everything had to be developed.

While Richard Sears gave the company its name, it was Julius Rosenwald who oversaw the necessary innovations and built the initial enterprise. Rosenwald is not only the father of Sears but of the twentieth century distribution revolution. By targeting a specific market and building an organization to serve it, by the end of World War I Sears grew into a national institution with its "wish book," the only literature, outside of the Bible, found in many farm homes.

A major strategic shift

The second phase of Sears' growth began in the 1920s and was dominated by General Robert E. Wood. When Wood joined Sears, the original market was rapidly changing. The farmer was no longer isolated; he now had an automobile to take him to town where he could shop. Hence, many of the systems and innovations instituted by Rosenwald were no longer appropriate.

At the same time a vast urban market was developing that consisted of lower income groups who were rapidly acquiring both the money and the desire to buy the same goods as upper class consumers. It was Wood who perceived that the country was becoming one large homogeneous and mobile market. As a result of this analysis, Sears made the decision to make a major strategic shift and switch its emphasis to retail stores equipped to serve both the more mobile farmer and the city dweller.

Still more innovation

A whole series of innovations were necessary to implement the new thrust of the company:

Merchandise. Many items had to be redesigned—goods appropriate for the farmer had to be changed to appeal to the mass market. New suppliers had to be created and often trained by Sears.

Management. Running a retail store is different from a mail order business. For almost fifteen years Sears' greatest bottleneck was a shortage of retail store managers. Internal management development programs were begun and became the models for many other companies.

Organization. Mail order was a highly centralized operation for Sears. Running retail stores throughout the country required a complete shift to a decentralized organizational structure. Everything possible was done to encourage local autonomy.

Site selection. Major innovations were necessary to determine the optimum location for new stores. The suburban shopping center, which is thought to be a relatively recent phenomenon, is really a copy of many of the concepts developed by Sears before World War II.

32

Modern day

The automobile changed Sears' market once and seems to be affecting it again. Pollution, gas shortages, and lack of parking all affect the urban shopper today. Also, more women are entering the work force and so have less time to shop. Many customers are shifting back to catalog-ordering—although more often by phone than by mail. In short, Sears must run as fast today as it did 75 years ago.

The major conclusion we can draw from the Sears story is that people determine the destiny of any business. It took Rosenwald 25 years to build the basic enterprise—and Wood another 25 to insure its continued growth. In contrast, it took Sewell Lee Avery only a few years to wreck Sears' only major competitor, Montgomery Ward, by his premonition of a depression following World War II.

As you struggle to stay on top of your business, keep one eye on the future. Few businesses are successful beyond one generation simply because they cannot adapt to the ever-changing competitive environment.

Service Industries: A Future Trend

It may surprise you to learn that over two-thirds of our gross national product is created by services, and eight out of every ten new jobs are created in the service sector of the economy. Businesspeople come in contact with services every day. Perhaps you should take a few moments to learn a little more about this fastest-growing part of the U.S. economy.

Just what is a service?

Keep a list of every purchase where you end up empty-handed. For example, you may pay rent, an insurance premium, or a highway toll. Or you may see a doctor, go to a movie, take a trip, or have a plumber unstop a drain. In each case, you have purchased a service—you received something for your money, but it was not tangible.

Actually, there are many definitions of a service, but they all revolve around two main characteristics. One is intangibility; the other is that production and consumption of a service occur almost simultaneously. A dinner in a fine restaurant or at a hamburger stand certainly involves a tangible product, but in both cases the meal is produced and consumed over a relatively short period of time, so restaurants and fast-food chains are also generally referred to as service establishments.

What is different about a service?

There are several differences between services and goods. Here are a few:

> No ownership. It is easy to transfer possession of physical property, whether a house or a bottle of aspirin. Services, on the other hand, cannot be owned or patented. This results in a very fast product life cycle for new service innovations. When Hertz offered the Number One Club that cut red tape, note how quickly the Wizard of Avis followed.

> Interaction of buyer and seller. Since production and consumption occur almost simultaneously, the buyer and seller must come together, so the physical location of operating units can be very important.

> No inventory. Unlike a goods-producing business where one can create a backlog of inventory to meet seasonal needs or peak demand, services cannot be stored. Only the capability to pro-

33

duce can be stockpiled. A consulting firm can take on extra professionals in anticipation of an increasing workload, but until additional work actually comes in, the individual cannot produce.

Cannot be transported. Unlike manufactured goods, services cannot be transported to the consumer. As a result, a service business tends to have many units—each run as a separate business. Much of the impetus behind the franchise boom was to obtain competent, committed managers to own and run local units.

Difficult to define quality. The quality of most services (except perhaps food) is difficult for the consumer to evaluate. As a result, the reputation of the service producer for providing quality is of major importance. Of equal importance is the education and training of employees, agents, franchisees, and other people involved in the business. In effect, training is often a service firm's only lever on quality control.

Why have we become a service economy?

About two-thirds of the gross national product, nearly three-fourths of the jobs, and almost half of personal consumption dollars go for services—and the figures are steadily rising. The reasons are simple:

First, the development of many services is the result of today's increased emphasis on experiences rather than possession of physical goods. We are encouraged to do our own thing, not own our own thing.

The second reason is the need for specialization due to exploding technological changes and new informational requirements. Consultants, computer time-sharing companies, personnel agencies, leasing companies, and many other services are used by businesses because of their need to specialize where they have a definite competitive advantage and leave supporting services to be performed by others.

Implications for the businessman

The continued trend toward a service-dominated economy is inescapable, as more and more companies realize that future growth will be in services. No matter how bad the times, over half of service expenditures are relatively fixed commitments. Take a look at what you sell. Is there a related service you could offer? Services could improve your sales and profits in our increasingly service-oriented economy.

How to Select the Most Effective Organizational Structure for Your Business

What is an organizational structure and why is it so important? Consider the analogy of a football team coming to the line of scrimmage. The way resources are deployed and what sort of formation is used obviously depends on the competitive situation and what the team is trying to accomplish. It's the same way in business. Like a football team, a business organization is people who must be properly organized to be effective. No business, whether it is large or small, can prosper and grow without an appropriate organizational structure.

Types of organizational structures

Size is a major factor which influences what organizational structure is best for a particular business. As a business grows, managerial style as well as organizational shape must also change, or the company may be effectively stymied.

Entrepreneurial stage. Most small companies (those employing up to about 25 people) are characterized by lack of organizational structure. Here, the owner-manager gets involved in almost everything—selling, accounting, manufacturing, hiring/firing, buying, etc. Typically, the company has few product lines at this stage. (See Figure 1.)

Functional structure. In order for a business to grow beyond about 25 employees, the owner-manager must devote more time to higher-level problems and less to daily operations. As a result, a second echelon of middle management must be developed to take over the specialized functions, such as sales, production, and administration. The shift from the entrepreneurial stage to a functional structure is usually gradual, and the dividing line is somewhat arbitrary. However, the key to a successful transition is the owner's ability to delegate responsibility to subordinates and to work through people rather than supervising the work directly. Many business owners cannot make this shift from entrepreneur to manager and their companies often stagnate or fail completely.

The functional structure (see Figure 2) is highly adaptive and used by most medium-sized companies as well as many large ones. It works best when there are relatively few products using similar production processes and distribution channels. However, a functional structure has several serious weaknesses:

Profit responsibility. Each functional area (sales, production, etc.) tends to think only in terms of costs. Only top management has direct responsibility for profits.

Figure 1

ENTREPRENEURIAL STAGE

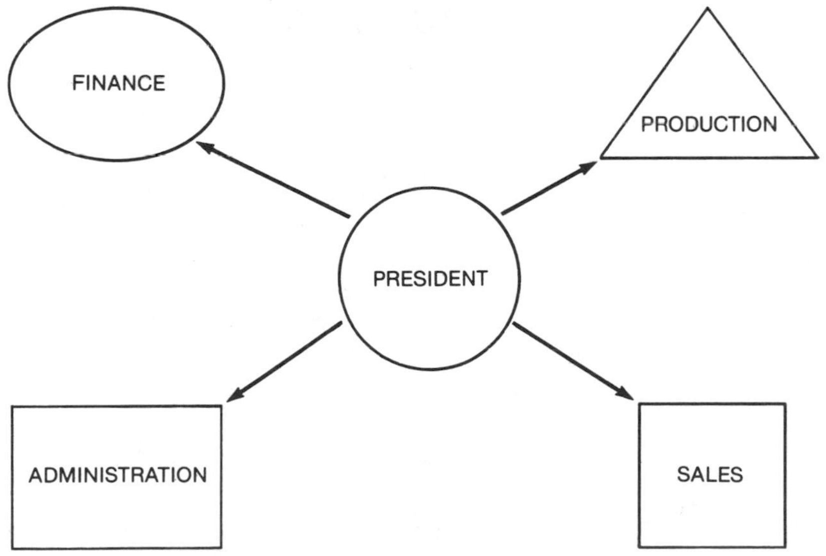

Parochialism. Each functional specialty tends to think only of its own problems. For example, it can be difficult to coordinate the insular perspectives of production and sales. Production may be concerned with even work flow and minimal disruptions while sales may promise a customer early delivery. Conflict naturally arises.

Market responsiveness. A functional structure can be unresponsive to shifting demand since no one has overall responsibility for each product. For example, the production department can be busily cranking out Product A without learning from the sales department that Product A just isn't selling. For a functional structure to work successfully, therefore, the burden is on top management to carefully monitor and coordinate each functional area.

Product structure. To overcome the weaknesses of a functional structure, many companies use a ''product-oriented'' structure in which the company is structured according to its primary products instead of its functional areas (see Figure 3).

The chief advantage of this structure is that each product manager can be given overall profit and loss responsibility for his product. As a result, decisions are decentralized and the company can be more responsive to the marketplace. The great disadvantage of this structure, however, is that it can result in expensive duplication of functional specialties. For example, instead of one production manager for the whole company, a different one may be needed for each product.

Project management or matrix structure. To overcome the expense of a product structure and still retain control of certain important products, some companies use what is known as a matrix

Figure 2

FUNCTIONAL STRUCTURE

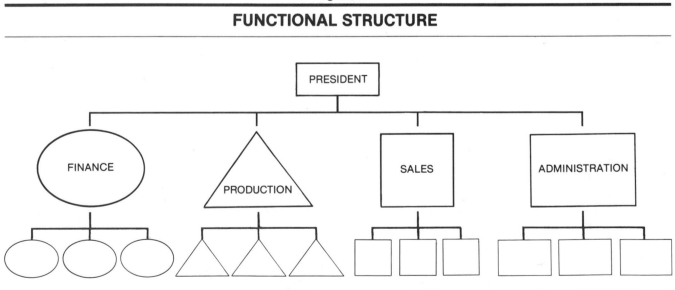

structure. With this type of organization, a manager is assigned the responsibility of coordinating a particular product with each functional area. He reports directly to top management (see Figure 4). By cutting across functional areas, however, the structure has an inherent instability, and it is best applied to products needing intensive but rather short-term attention.

How to design an organizational structure for your company

No matter how big your company is, consider its organizational structure. You don't need to draw up formal charts and distribute them to employees—many managers don't. Nevertheless, you should have a clear idea of how your company is organized. Here is a summary of the factors to consider once you are beyond the entrepreneurial stage.

Competitive situation. If the market in which you operate is stable and predictable, a functional structure is probably best. A product structure is more appropriate when the competitive situation is volatile and decisions must be made quickly at a decentralized level.

Cost. A functional structure is more efficient in terms of manpower. However, if many products are being produced, the time to coordinate all products with each functional area may obviate any real savings. In such a case, a product structure may be more appropriate.

Type of product. Products which are heavily R&D-oriented or likely to require continual updates or modifications usually fit best in a matrix or a functional structure. However, if the product is well established and primary emphasis is on sales rather than development, the more market-oriented product structure is generally best.

Figure 3

PRODUCT STRUCTURE

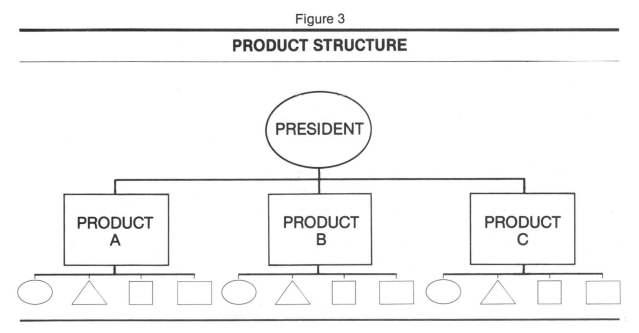

37

Figure 4

MATRIX STRUCTURE

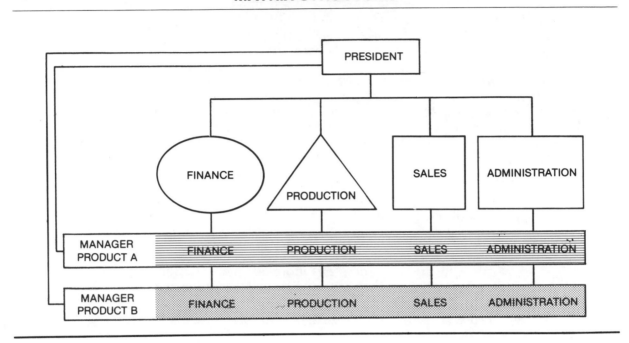

Special Problems—Conflicts That Plague Family Businesses*

Most successful small- and medium-sized companies are started and run by business executives who are essentially entrepreneurs. However, their own business success often results in intense personal and family problems that are rarely encountered by professional managers of larger companies. Psychological research reveals three general causes for these problems:

    • An entrepreneur characteristically has unresolved conflicts with his father. Because of his discomfort when under supervision, he starts his own business both to outdo his father and to escape authority.

    • An entrepreneur's business is simultaneously his "baby" and his "mistress." When anyone else tries to obtain any power, including family members, trouble results. This dominance and centralization of power is why so many organizations cannot grow beyond the entrepreneurial stage and often decline or fail when the founder ages or dies.

    • For the entrepreneur, the business is essentially an extension of himself and a medium for personal gratification and achievement. While he may be concerned with what happens to the business after he dies, generally that concern takes the form of thinking about what kind of monument he can leave behind rather than

*Portions of this section were condensed from: Harry Levinson, "Conflicts that Plague Family Businesses," *Harvard Business Review,* March-April 1971.

making sure that the business can continue to thrive and grow without him.

Father/offspring rivalry

The entrepreneur-founder often has difficulty dealing with his children. While consciously he would like to pass the business on to his children, unconsciously he is afraid to give up his "baby," his source of social power, and whatever else the business may mean to him. Most of all, the father unconsciously needs to assert himself and demonstrate competence. "After all, I'm the one who built this business and no one else can make it run the way I can." As a result, the father really doesn't want his children to take over the business because he's afraid that he may be displaced as the central figure. The result is predictable. The children feel increasingly frustrated by a lack of true autonomy and authority commensurate with their maturity. The father looks on the children as ungrateful, implies that they will never be able to run the business, and refuses to retire, despite repeated promises to do so. And, of course, even if the children do gain control, the scions cannot win. No matter how much they improve the business, their contribution will always be minimized. "After all, their father really built that business."

Sibling rivalry

The rivalry between children for parental approval begins early in life. In a succession situation, the problem can become especially acute if the parent shows that he favors one child over the other. The natural result is continuous family conflict.

> • Perceptions of the eldest child. Traditionally, the oldest child succeeds his father. This custom reaffirms the perception of the younger sibling (or siblings) that the oldest is indeed the favorite. Also, because the oldest is generally largest, physically strongest, and most knowledgeable merely because of age, the younger children rarely have the opportunity to match the skills, competence, and experience of the eldest. By that time, the nature of the relationship is so well established that the oldest sibling has difficulty regarding the younger ones as adequate and competent. Moreover, because the eldest is in earlier and longer contact with his parents, their control efforts fall heaviest on him. The result is that older children tend to expect more of themselves and control themselves more rigidly than younger children. Being already a harsh judge of himself, the eldest is likely to be an even harder judge of his younger siblings.

> • Perceptions of the younger child. The younger sibling attempts to compensate for the effects of the childhood relationships by carving out a niche of the business that he can nurture in order to prove his capabilities. He guards it jealously and resents any incursion into his domain. Even if the siblings own equal shares of the business and are all on the board, the younger feels subservient, and friction and distrust are likely to occur. Furthermore, if for some reason the younger replaces the oldest, and particularly if the latter becomes subordinate to him, the younger often feels guilty for having usurped the role of the senior.

Other relatives

In some families, it is expected that any relative who wants to join the business can

39

do so. The results can be devastating, especially if the jobs are sinecures. The chief executive of a family business naturally feels a heavy responsibility to preserve and enlarge the family fortunes. If he is weighed down by unproductive relatives, internecine warfare results, bringing casualties but no peace. Rational planning and decision making are frustrated, and often the only solution is to sell the business. This solution is costly because it results in loss of the business as a means of employment, betrayal of a family tradition, and dissolution of close ties that have been maintained through the business.

What can be done

    • Father-offspring rivalry. Most entrepreneur-fathers are unable to resolve this problem themselves because they find it difficult to accept outside advice. In these cases, it is generally advantageous for the children to form their own ventures. This can often be done under the corporate umbrella or outside it without deserting the father. For example, one father in retailing set up a store in different communities for each of his children. While collaborating on overall policy and buying, each child could run his own store, and the father also could continue to run his.

    • Sibling rivalry. It is important for siblings to realize that their relationship recapitulates ancient rivalries. And since there is love and hate in all relationships, theirs cannot, by definition, be pure. Nevertheless, they should confront and discuss the worries, anger, fears, and disappointments they cause each other. If this does not help, they should consider separate organizations.

    • Relatives. Few family businesses can sustain regeneration over a length of time solely through family members. Every family business must give thought to eventually bringing in outside professional management. In some cases, family members have gotten entirely out of day-to-day business operations while forming a trust to oversee their interests. This enables the family to act in concert and fosters cohesion while also preserving the family's role in the business.

CHAPTER FIVE

Aids in Decision-Making

Complex Problems Made Easy with "Decision Trees"

Every businessman has to make decisions. Whether they are routine or agonizingly complicated, decisions are what the business runs on, and anything specifically designed to help with that process is worth knowing about.

Just what is a decision tree?

A decision tree is a simple mathematical tool enabling the planner or decision-maker to:

- Consider various courses of action.

- Make comparisons to determine the best alternative.

- Modify these results by their probability of achievement.

- Assign financial results to them.

Actually drawn out on a piece of paper with a branch for each course of action and for each event that could stem from such actions, the structure does look like a tree laid on its side.

How does it work?

A decision tree is used to structure business problems and present in a formalized way the decision process that every executive is probably doing intuitively. The clearest way to explain this is through an example. In this instance, a commonplace business decision is reduced to a decision tree—in fact, two decision trees, for the further benefit of comparison.

41

Figure 1

DECISION TREE

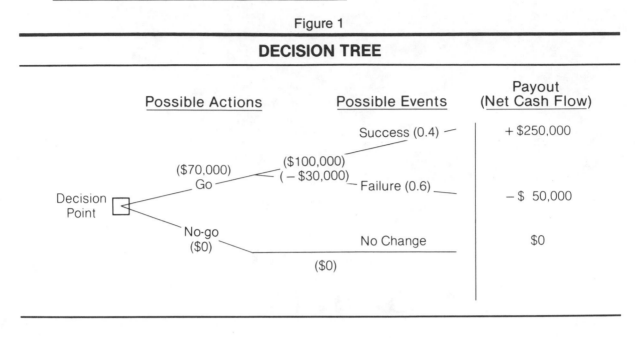

The president of Acme Tool Company has the opportunity to invest $50,000 in an exciting project. After carefully considering all the data and information, he is convinced that Acme will make a $250,000 profit if the project succeeds. However, the company is bound to lose the whole $50,000 investment if the idea fails. Furthermore, the project is more likely to fail than succeed. Being ruthlessly objective about it, he and the company's treasurer agree that the chances of succeeding are only 40%, implying that the probability of failure is 60%. Both acknowledge, however, that the loss of $50,000 is far from disastrous. They are faced with a "go/no-go" decision and quickly draw up a decision tree showing possible actions, possible events, and payout or net cash flow (Figure 1).

Figure 2

DECISION TREE

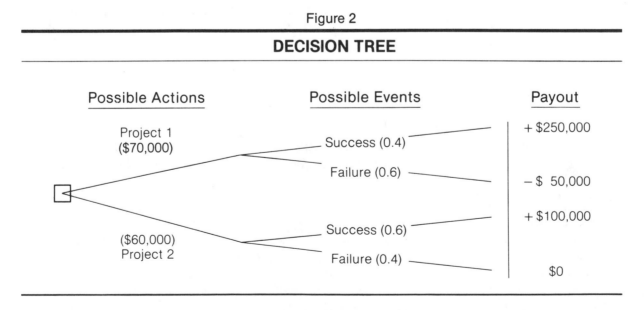

The two men then multiply out the financial consequences of the alternatives by the agreed probability that either will occur.

Working from right to left, the value of success is put at $100,000 ($250,000 × 0.4), while the loss from failure is assigned − $30,000 (− $50,000 × 0.6). Adding the two financial "results" together, a positive cash flow of $70,000 is deducted from the "go" choice against nothing from the "no-go" decision. The treasurer looks concerned, but the president explains he is doing no more than playing the odds on the upside potential against the downside risk. He rationalizes by saying that if he could make the same decision ten times, he would succeed four times for a positive cash flow of $1,000,000 (4 × $250,000) and fail six times for a loss of $300,000 (6 × $50,000)—altogether a net cash flow of $700,000 or an average of $70,000 each time.

The treasurer accepts the theory but correctly points out that, in reality, the project can only be done once, not ten times, and that a $70,000 gain will not be made. It will either be a larger profit of $250,000 or a complete loss, not a theoretical figure in between. Wouldn't it be better to pursue an alternate project, he says, where, for the same investment, they could possibly make a $100,000 profit and, in the worst possible case, at least get their $50,000 back and break even.

The president looks at the proposal. He agrees with the treasurer's figures, and they both agree that the chance of success is about 60% for the second project versus 40% for the first project. It is obviously better to go with the second. Acme cannot lose, and it stands a better chance of making $100,000.

Just to put the issue beyond doubt, they draw up another decision tree to compare the alternatives (Figure 2).

Both are amazed to discover that the first project is still the better decision. The assigned value of the first is $70,000 (as before), while the value of the second is only $60,000—($100,000 × 0.6) + ($0 × 0.4).

The conclusion goes against intuition—it is clear that the best business decision is not necessarily to prepare for the most likely event or to take the most cautious approach! Needless to say, the above example is rather simplistic, and, in practice, the problems committed to decision trees are generally diverse and complex. Nevertheless, the technique can be a useful discipline whenever the problem has more separable elements than the decision-maker can comfortably take account of in his own head.

Not a mechanical substitute

It is important to recognize that a decision tree is far from being a mechanical replacement for executive judgment and experience. Both these qualities, together with all hard facts and data available, are essential inputs to the three basic steps to drawing up the decision tree:

• Stipulate what decision alternatives are to be considered in the analysis of a problem.

• Make an assessment of the probabilities of the occurrence of each uncertain event.

• Quantify the possible financial consequences of the various alternatives under consideration.

After this has been done, the arithmetic will do the rest. Large corporations have computer programs to handle the mathematics when the problem is complex, and "the tree gets so bushy, it is positively hairy," but the input to the problem must depend on nonmechanical items.

43

Benefits of growing a decision tree

The discipline involved in tabulating alternatives, determining the financial consequences, and assessing the probabilities of various outcomes forces a careful and complete consideration of the factors to be taken into account.

The gamble of decision making is reduced. The prudent businessman acts when the odds of highest payoff are in his favor. It is the gambler who deviates from the odds.

Better decision analysis can be logically performed and if properly communicated can remove the burden of being cautious in the interest of job security rather than in the best interest of the company.

Linear Programming*

One problem facing businesspeople today is how to get maximum efficiency and profits from existing facilities. For example, a manufacturer must decide how to use his machinery to get the most output at minimum costs; a retailer is concerned with how much floor space to allocate to different products to get maximum sales and profits. Each situation involves the question of how to allocate limited resources (machines and shelf space) among competing demands (Product X or Product Y) to maximize profits.

What is linear programming?

Linear programming is a rather imposing title for a commonly used management technique that helps solve resource allocation problems. The word "programming" simply means problem solving. The term linear comes from the expectation that relationships within the problem will be linear. For example, if it takes five hours to produce one item, then to produce two is presumed to require ten hours, and so on. A simple example should illustrate the technique.

How many sofas?

A small furniture manufacturer is attempting to set his production schedule for the coming month. The market is not the limiting factor, and he can sell any quantity of his two main products—tables and sofas—that the plant can produce. His objective is to produce tables and sofas in whatever combination maximizes total contribution to profit and overhead. For a table, the contribution (sales price less direct expenses) is $40 per unit, versus $60 per unit for a sofa.

At first glance, it would seem logical to produce only sofas, since they yield the highest contribution per unit. However, the tables and sofas require different production times (see Figure 3).

The optimum production mixture

We know that our objective is to maximize total profit contribution and that each table yields $40 contribution versus $60 for a sofa. If we let "T" represent tables and "S" sofas, then the total profit contribution ("P") from any mixture of tables and sofas produced could be represented as: $P = 40T + 60S$.

Similarly, the time constraints at each of the machine centers can also be

---

*For further information on the many applications of linear programming, two excellent sources are: (1) *Introduction to Linear Programming* by R. Stansbury Stockton (Allyn and Bacon, Inc., Boston) and (2) *A primer of Linear Programming* by Kurt Meisels (New York University Press, New York).

Figure 3

PRODUCTION TIME FOR TABLES VS. SOFAS

Machine center	Capacity of center during month (hours)	Time required to produce (hours) Table	Sofa
A	1,200	2	1
B	2,000	2	3
C	1,000	1	2

represented. We know that tables require two hours and sofas require three hours at machine center B. Each month the maximum number of tables and sofas would be processed when the number of tables processed times two hours per table plus the number of sofas times three hours each totals less than or equal to 2,000 hours. If you are confused, study Figure 4, which summarizes these relationships.

By using an algebraic method known as the simplex method, the above equations can be solved. As it works out, the optimum solution is to produce 462 tables and 269 sofas. No other production mixture will yield a greater total profit.

How can linear programming help you?

Linear programming can be used to maximize profits or minimize expenses whenever there are competing demands for limited resources. We've already described how it can be applied to manufacturing and retailing. Another common use is in transportation. For example, suppose you ship your products from three different warehouses. By using linear programming, you could minimize transportation costs while, at the same time, maintaining a desired inventory level at each warehouse. This is accomplished by using linear programming to determine how much of each product to ship from each warehouse.

"Critical Path Method"—
How to Track Complicated Projects

The Critical Path Method (CPM) has been used in aerospace, construction, and research and development for some time, and now more and more businessmen are adopting it as an aid to their planning, scheduling, and cost control problems. The basic requirements are surprisingly simple—common sense and arithmetic—yet CPM

Figure 4

OPTIMUM PRODUCTION MIXTURE

This is the objective	These are the constraints	
Maximize total profit contribution (P) where: $P = 40T + 60S$	Machine center A	$2T + 1S \leq 1,200$ hours
	Machine center B	$2T + 3S \leq 2,000$ hours
	Machine center C	$1T + 2S \leq 1,000$ hours

Figure 5

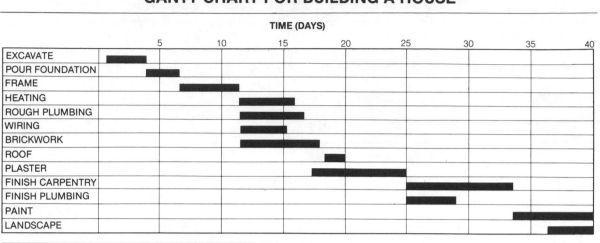

GANTT CHART FOR BUILDING A HOUSE

can produce results which, as one project manager says, "are so good I wish we could keep it a secret."

The evolution of graphical control techniques

Whether building a new addition to a plant or planning a marketing campaign, businessmen have always faced problems whenever multiple, and often interrelated, tasks have to be completed in order to finish a particular job on time and within a budget. During the early 1900's Henry T. Gantt developed the familiar bar chart or "Gantt" chart, as it is often called, which depicts a plan of action for completing tasks within a project according to a time schedule. Figure 5 shows a Gantt chart for a simple example—building a house.

Gantt charts are useful for planning and scheduling, but they have one major limitation—they can't show the interrelationship of the various tasks within the project. In other words, the bar chart does not make clear which activities must be finished before others can begin.

Figure 6

CRITICAL PATH METHOD

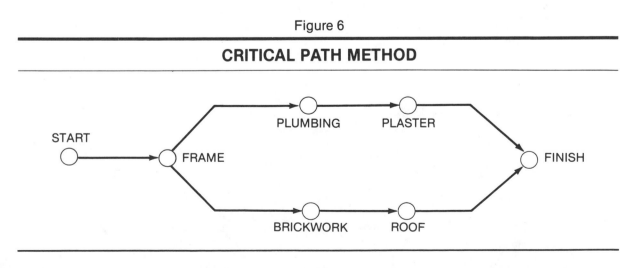

Development of the critical method

In 1957 the Du Pont company developed the critical path technique to help shorten the long time lag between completion of research and development on a new product and the construction of facilities for manufacturing the product. Basically, the technique consists of reducing a project to a graphic model called a "network plan" or "arrow diagram." Referring to the building example, let's condense it for simplicity and assume that there are only five tasks to be performed. First the house has to be framed, then plumbing and brickwork can be done simultaneously, and finally plastering and roofing can be completed. Graphically, the project could be represented as shown in Figure 6.

The flow of work is represented by arrows. Each node (circle) represents the end of one activity and the beginning of another.

Preparing a critical path chart

Planning: Determine all the major activities of a project—using the example above, framing, plumbing, etc., are each definite and separate tasks. Once this is accomplished, the interrelationship of the tasks must be established. For example, framing must be completed before plumbing and brickwork can begin; plumbing must be finished before plastering can start, etc.

Scheduling: Determine from experience the normal time necessary to complete each activity and note it within the nodes.

Control: Determine the longest path (in terms of time) through the arrow diagram. This is the critical path because each activity along this route represents a bottleneck holding up completion of the overall project.

Building a house on the critical path

Figure 7 shows a completed CPM chart for our house-building example. Note that the time to complete each activity is listed, and the interrelationship of all activities is

Figure 7

COMPLETED CPM CHART

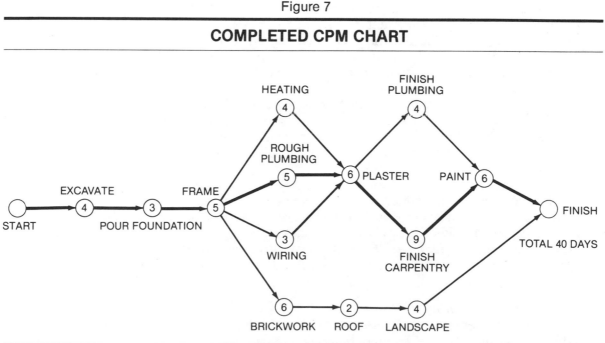

clear. The critical path is marked as the darker line and is 40 days long. Leeway or "float" on noncritical jobs (the amount of time they can be delayed without changing the critical path) can also be determined. With this stage completed, the businessman can see which jobs are critical to his finish date. For the other jobs he knows how much leeway or float time he has.

CPM as a cost-cutting tool

Once a manager knows which activities are critical to timely completion of a project, he can determine how to allocate his resources. For example, the builder above may decide that it is worth the cost to put extra men on plastering in order to finish the overall house in less time since plastering is on the critical path. Similarly, he can see that roofing and wiring are not on the critical path and may decide to reduce manpower in those areas. The ability to see the interrelationship between activities of a complex project and to make cost-saving changes is the great advantage of the critical path method.

The critical path diagram can be as simple or complex as the project it represents. In some cases computer programs are built to handle the immense amount of data that can be involved in large-scale undertakings.

Even so, the logic and method of the critical path are basically straightforward. Their main purpose is improving the planning and scheduling of interrelated tasks by drawing out information which may be too complex to be left to intuition or experience—however expert. The economic benefits follow naturally from these processes. Try using CPM on the next complicated project you tackle. The discipline of breaking the project into stages and making time estimates to complete each phase should be well worth the effort.

The Learning Curve

Practice makes perfect. A task can always be done better each time it is repeated. In industry, the theory is just as simple. A worker learns as he works, and the more he repeats a task, the more efficient he becomes with the result that direct labor per unit produced declines. This decline in cost with cumulative experience is known as the "learning curve." And far from being esoteric and "nice to know but useless," the learning curve is an underlying characteristic of organizational activity that is crucially important to the business manager.

Even before World War II, when the learning curve theory was put to use in the aircraft industry, definite studies had shown that each time the number of units produced doubled, direct man hours per unit declined about 20%. Figure 8 is a classic example that shows how the learning curve resulted in progressively lower prices for the Model T Ford.

When the same curve is plotted on ratio paper (i.e., logarithmic coordinates), it actually becomes a straight line. In more recent years, it has been found that the learning curve describes not only the increasing skill of an individual or group of production workers, but the whole complex organism of a company—some in line function, others in staff. In other words, as the cumulative output of a company's product doubles, all costs attributable to the product (direct and indirect) decrease at a fairly predictable rate.

Practical application

Pricing. Whenever long production runs are being quoted, costs (in constant dollars) should decline by a definite percentage each time cumulative volume doubles. Knowledge of this fact could give you a competitive edge when pricing a job. (Only after the British government decided to let Rolls Royce go bankrupt because the RB211 engine could not be produced at a profit was it discovered that the government's cost estimates had not considered the learning curve. According to many reports, the company would probably have at least broken even once the engine was in production.)

Strategic decisions. If you can grow faster than your competitors in a market, your

Figure 8

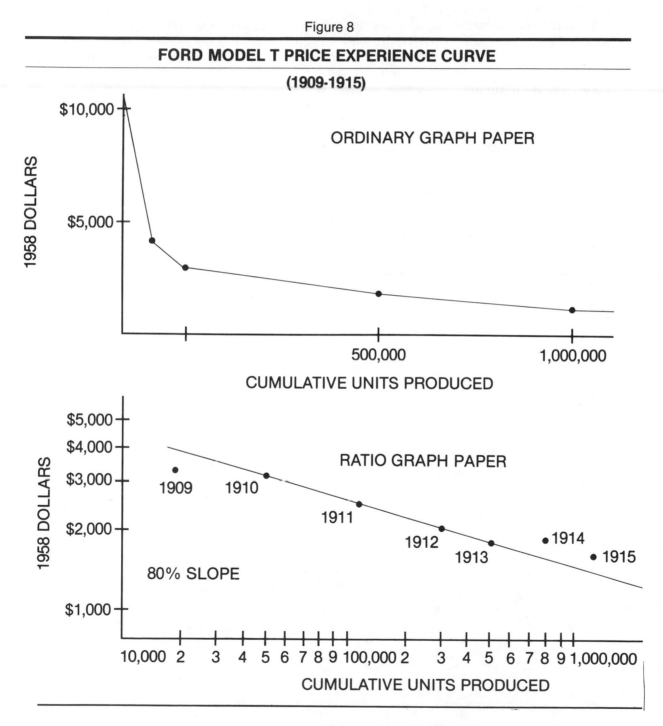

costs will be lower (according to the learning curve) because of your greater cumulative experience. By undercutting the competitors, your market share will grow further, leading to lower production costs, and so on. However, to get the initial jump on competitors, you have to price at a loss until volume catches up and your costs begin to fall. This has been the Texas Instrument strategy in the calculator market. Cut prices, build market share, cut prices again until, eventually, most of the competition is driven out.

Cost control. If you know costs should decrease by a certain amount, you can take remedial action when the reduction does not occur.

Learning is a characteristic of all living organisms. But progress and growth—and reduced costs—do not always occur without stimulation and encouragement from management. Be aware that learning curves exist for competitors as well. If you don't find ways to cut costs as your productive experience grows, you may begin to lose your position in the marketplace.

CHAPTER SIX

Financial Analysis and Control

Why Financial Analysis Is Important to Help You Protect Your Company

From time to time you should take stock of your company and plan defensively to insure that your business remains viable and strong no matter what misadventures might lie ahead.

How do you begin this process of defensive planning? First, you should define your company's "key success variables." Think about your business. What factors are crucial to its viability and success? Where do you have the most flexibility to respond to a changing business environment?

Income statement
Certain factors are keys to success in every industry. A good way to learn some of the leverage points in your particular business is by looking at your business's score sheet—its income statement. Glance down each line and ask yourself, "How critically does this item affect my business: sales, labor, materials, interest expense, overhead? Which ones most vitally affect success?" No doubt they all seem important, so let's take a closer look.

Contribution vs. fixed costs
Proper management response to any change in sales or expenses depends heavily on two factors affecting your firm's cost structure:

- Gross margin, or so-called "contribution" from your products. Defined as the net sales price less those expenses that vary directly with sales volume, i.e., "variable expenses."

- Level of fixed costs. Includes such expenses as rent, heat, administrative salaries, and depreciation, which do not vary appreciably with sales volume.

Cost structure matrix

The matrix of fixed costs vs. contribution (Figure 1) shows representative examples of each type of business. Take a look at your income statement and try to identify which description best fits your firm. For example, if the majority of your expenses are fixed at your present volume level and your per unit contribution is less than 40 % of the sales price, your firm would probably be best characterized as a high fixed cost, low contribution business.

Volume vs. cost dependent

What does all this mean for defensive planning? High fixed cost businesses, such as railroads or supermarkets, are critically volume dependent. They must keep sales up to be able to cover their fixed costs. That is why specialty clothing stores, for example, are so quick to go out of business if they ever happen to falter on an important fashion trend.

On the other hand, low contribution businesses, such as truck lines and most service companies, are critically cost dependent. In other words, since most of their revenue goes to paying variable expenses, any rise in these expenses (which cannot be passed on to the consumer) has a disastrous effect on profitability.

It should be readily apparent that if you are in a high fixed cost and low contribution business, any adverse changes in sales volume and expenses have a doubly debilitating effect. For example, consider the truckers' plight when the speed limit was cut to 55 mph. They could not travel at normal speed (hence, sales capacity was effectively cut) and, at the same time, had to pay more for fuel (costs were up)—all while not being able to pass the economic effects of these factors on to the consumer because of fixed ICC freight rates.

Capital vs. labor intensive

High fixed cost ("capital intensive") firms generally have substantial money tied up in plant and equipment while low fixed cost ("labor intensive") businesses usually have people as the critical resource. If yours is a capital intensive business, one of your main concerns should be financial management—adequate bank lines to allow for contingencies. On the other hand, a labor intensive firm's flexibility to reduce the

Figure 1

COST STRUCTURE MATRIX

| | | CONTRIBUTION | |
		High (greater than 40% of sales)	*Low* (less than 40% of sales)
FIXED COSTS	*High*	Radio or T.V. Station Airline or Railroad Specialty Clothing Store	Truck Line Supermarket Machine Shop
	Low	Executive Placement Agency Real Estate Broker Insurance Agent	Janitorial Service Guard Service Temporary Hire (Kelly Girls)

work force during a downturn is a distinct advantage—take care not to lose it during union negotiations.

Pricing structure

Inflation is the one constant we can count on. How flexible are your prices? To avoid getting trapped with older products with established and less flexible prices, perhaps you should consider an aggressive policy of introducing new products as soon as possible where you could establish prices at an attractive level.

Cash management

Most businessmen have a fairly good feel for the lifeblood of their business—cash. They know what money is expected in, and what must be paid out. But one thing they practically never do is slip the receivables by one month. That's right: extend the date when your accounts receivable come in by just 30 days. Unless you have considerable cash reserves, you will probably be frightened when you see the result. Now, obviously, this won't happen overnight, but in every economic downturn, customers take longer to pay. Here are some defensive steps you can take to counteract this problem:

- Accounts receivable management. Watch all major accounts closely and take an aggressive stance with any late payers.

- Bank lines. "Money is always available when you don't need it and rarely when you do," goes the cliche. It might be prudent to line up a standby loan now at the bank for possible use at a later time.

- Inventory control. Closely monitor your inventory. If sales are down, don't get caught with a large inventory. On the other hand, however, if raw materials are in short supply, be certain to maintain an adequate inventory to cover any supplier delays.

Many businesses take the attitude that, if receivables slip, they will extend their payables accordingly. While this may be a formula for survival, it certainly is no way to build a business. Suppliers will remember who pays on time, and as we enter a supply dominated economy, ready access to raw materials will progressively become a key ingredient to competitive success.

How to Do Your Own Internal Audit

It doesn't matter if your business is retail, wholesale, service, or manufacturing: top-notch accounting records are a must. Besides providing internal control of the business, they help furnish vital financial information for outsiders such as bankers, stockholders, and credit agencies.

Rather than have an accountant come in (at considerable expense), here is a checklist of questions to help you conduct your own internal audit. First, we'll look at controls and procedures you should have in order to prevent internal theft and fraud; then, we'll consider some additional points to be sure your financial reporting is first rate.

Internal control

Internal control of the assets of a business is of prime importance. No matter how much profit the firm makes, if it is dissipated by poor control, the firm cannot remain profitable.

1. Does one person handle the receipt of cash and also deposit the receipts in the bank?

If you answered "yes" to this question—and it is someone other than yourself—you have a weak system of internal control. There should be separation of duties. The person who receives the cash should not be the one who deposits the receipts in the bank and records collections. Because cash is the most liquid asset of a firm, it is also the most susceptible to abuse.

2. If someone other than yourself writes checks for amounts owed, does he or she also sign the checks?

Again, this indicates weak internal control. Even your most trusted and valued employee should clear disbursements with top management.

3. If you sign all of the company's checks, do you make certain that the bills that are paid by check are brought to you at the same time the checks are brought in for signature?

The bills that are paid by the check written should all be marked with the check number and the payment date in order to prevent duplicate payments.

4. Do you scrutinize bills carefully to make certain the check is to the right company for the correct amount and for goods and services which you purchased?

If you answered this question "no," you could be exposing your employees to the opportunity to steal from you.

5. Do you reconcile your bank statement monthly, or does your accountant take care of it?

Good internal audit control requires a monthly reconciliation by someone other than the person who writes your checks. The bank may send back some checks you have deposited because there were insufficient funds in the maker's account, or there may be checks on which your signature has been forged. An independent reconciliation will focus attention on any discrepancies.

6. Do you have any type of mechanical check protection?

A device such as a check imprinting machine that records the amount will make it more difficult for stolen checks to be cashed.

7. Is a separate petty cash fund maintained for small and regular disbursements?

The use of petty cash will limit the temptation to use current cash receipts to pay small bills. Vouchers, with receipts attached, should be put into the petty cash box for any payouts. Limit the amount of petty cash to an average of one to two weeks' expenditures. Replenish petty cash by writing a check for the amount necessary to bring it up to the amount set, and keep the petty cash vouchers as backup detail for the transaction.

8. Do you deposit all of each day's cash receipts in the bank intact and without delay?

Cash should not be kept on the premises, and it should be possible to trace the receipts for the day to the bank deposit for the same period. This prevents "lapping"—the use of the next day's receipts to make up for money taken.

9. Are your checks prenumbered?

Each check written—whether used or voided—should be kept in numerical sequence with cancelled checks. Any checks voided should have the signature torn off and should be kept in a safe place until the cancelled checks are returned by the bank.

Then the voided check may be placed in its proper sequence.

10. Do you use prenumbered duplicate sales checks, invoices, and receipts?

If so, the prenumbered set can be controlled, you can indicate who is responsible for which numbers, and that person will have to account for the duplicates. From this you will have a control over payments received and payments made.

11. Do you maintain a control account for your accounts receivable?

If your outstanding accounts receivable are numerous, you should have them reconciled to the control account on a monthly basis. This prevents an account from getting "lost," either accidentally or deliberately. It also makes it difficult for someone to keep the money collected from an account.

12. Do you compare current bills for utilities, supplies, and other expenses with the amounts budgeted for these items?

Any expense that is out of line with the amount budgeted for it should be investigated before payment is made. The billing may be incorrect, or the budget may need to be revised.

13. Are time records kept on hourly employees?

The Wage and Hour Division requires that accurate records be kept on all employees covered under the Wage-Hour Act. Overtime should be recorded accurately.

14. Are W-4 forms on file for all employees?

These forms are necessary so that you can determine the correct amount of federal and state income tax to withhold from the employee's periodic wage.

15. Are individual payroll records maintained that show the regular and overtime wage; the amounts withheld for Social Security, federal and state income tax, and other deductions; and the net amount paid?

There should be a cumulative record of this information for each employee for the entire year.

16. Are periodic payments made to a federal depository of taxes withheld from employees' pay?

Failure to deposit payroll tax liability may result in substantial penalties and interest on the unpaid accounts (plus potential personal liability).

17. Have you considered the use of an outside source to prepare the payroll and keep records on each individual employee?

Your accountant, the local bank, or a computer service bureau may have such a service available at a relatively nominal charge.

Financial information

Once you are satisfied that your internal controls are adequate, you should then ensure that you can obtain timely information for preparation of financial statements, budgets, and tax returns. Poor records can cause the loss of tax deductions, make budgeting difficult, and result in misleading financial statements.

18. Are your records kept on the double-entry system?

The checks and balances built into a double-entry system help to ensure that all receipts, disbursements, and purchases are accounted for.

19. Are special journals used for sales, purchases, and disbursements?

Use of separate journals permits work on financial information by more than one individual. It also permits the development of detailed information on sales by locality or by type of service and on purchases and expenses by type of item.

20. Do you receive a monthly income statement?

Income statements should be prepared for a business no less than quarterly and preferably on a monthly basis. The income statement should show income for the current period and for the year to date. It should also show how operations compare with the budget plan.

21. Are balance sheets (statements of financial position) and statements of changes in financial position prepared at least once a year?

A full set of financial statements is usually desired by your bank or a major creditor at least annually. These should be comparative statements, which will permit the development of trends and ratios. Also, consider using these statements to develop comparative ratios, or similar data, on other firms in your industry.

22. Do you analyze your financial statements to determine any trends that may be developing?

Besides the raw dollar amounts, expenses should always be expressed as a percent of sales. This will permit you to compare figures on a monthly, quarterly, or annual basis to determine shifts in expenses. Determine your current and quick ratios to estimate your debt-paying ability. Check the turnover of your inventory. And estimate the days' sales which are uncollected in your accounts receivable. These are the minimum analyses that should be done. Your accountant can assist you with other meaningful analyses.

Cash Flow

What is cash flow?

Like any profession, business has many specialized and sometimes confusing terms. It's important to use them properly, however, because often bankers, lawyers, and other professionals will judge your commercial expertise simply by how well you handle your business vocabulary and a few simple business techniques.

Cash flow is a term that many people use—but not too many understand what it means. More often it is used in reference to a "cash flow statement" which is the

Figure 2

CASH FLOW PROJECTION

	J	F	M	A	M	J	J	A	S	O	N	D
Cash In:												
1 Patients			100	200	300	400	500	750	1000	2000	2500	2500
2 Insurance					100	200	300	300	350	350	350	350
Total in	0	0	100	200	400	600	800	1050	1350	2350	2850	2850
Cash Out:												
1 Equipment	1000											
2 Nurse		500	500	500	500	500	500	500	500	500	500	500
3 Rent	200	200	200	200	200	200	200	200	200	200	200	200
Total out	1200	700	700	700	700	700	700	700	700	700	700	700
Net Cash Flow	(1200)	(700)	(600)	(500)	(300)	(100)	100	350	650	1650	2150	2150
Cumulative Balance	(1200)	(1900)	(2500)	(3000)	(3300)	(3400)	(3300)	(2950)	(2300)	(650)	1500	3650

single most important document to every businessman.

"Profits," "income," and "revenue" are all accounting terms. They may be important to Wall Street analysts and accountants, but they mean practically nothing to the average businessman. Cash is the lifeblood of any business and in most circumstances, cash does not equal income. For example, you have to meet your payroll with cash in the bank this week, although the item you have manufactured may not be sold for several weeks. And even after you sell the item (and recognize income on your books), you may not actually receive the cash payment for several more weeks. All the while you have to pay out cash. Keep this in mind—you can't spend income. You can only pay bills with cash.

Now let's see how to prepare a cash flow forecast. Let us assume that there is a new doctor in town who wishes to open a medical practice. He has approached the local banker with a cash flow projection (see Figure 2).

Let's go through this forecast point by point. First, note that the doctor plans to rent an office for $200 per month and pay $1,000 for his equipment in January. By February he will open his doors, hire a nurse for $500 per month, and begin to see patients. He expects business to be slow at first and patients won't start to pay until the next month (March). Also, some patients will probably have insurance, but because of the paperwork involved, no money will be received from insurance until May.

As you can see, the doctor estimated $1,200 Cash Out in January and nothing for Cash In for a Net Cash Flow of minus $1,200. In February it will be minus $700, which, added to the deficit from January, gives a Cumulative Balance of minus $1,900. Note that Net Cash Flow won't turn positive until July and the Cumulative Balance is negative until November.

What does this statement tell us? Well, it means that if you were the doctor, you would have to ask the banker for a line of credit of at least $3,400, which is your peak point of negative balance in June.

Now, how can we criticize this statement? If you were the banker, you would probably query several of the doctor's assumptions. For example:

- How confident is he of getting patients?

- What controls does he plan to use to make sure patients and insurance companies pay according to schedule?

- Will he need more equipment or nursing staff later?

- Most importantly, how does the doctor plan to support himself?
He has shown no figure for his own salary.

Hopefully you can now appreciate the importance of the cash flow statement. It is generally the first document that any lender wishes to see and can be the basis for you to control every aspect of your business. It can be prepared on a daily, weekly, or monthly basis. You can use it to project out as far as you feel comfortable in forecasting. Most importantly, it lets you see at any point where you are (or should be) in terms of business lifeblood—cash.

Hidden Cash:
How to Unlock the Financial
Power of Your Business

For nearly two decades after World War II, each of the elements of production (capital, energy, labor, and raw materials) was relatively cheap. In the Seventies,

Figure 3

CASH CYCLE

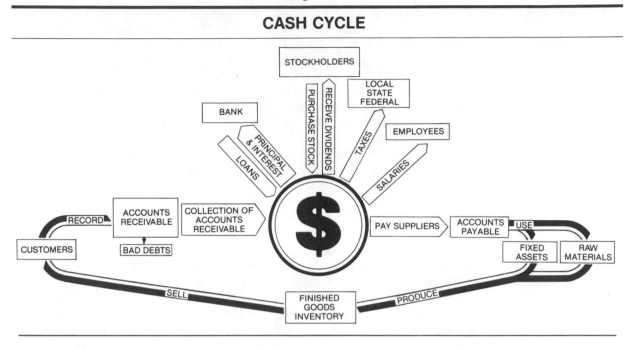

however, the situation became vastly different, and only the best managers can now cope with the prevalent shortages.

There is a way to dig deep within your own company to unlock the most critical asset of all—cash.

The cash flow cycle

At first glance, the chart at Figure 3 may seem elementary to you. It shows the flow of cash through a typical business. Yet, we've seen Fortune 500 controllers draw this same kind of diagram and plot the cash flow cycle for their companies in exactly this way.

As you can see, the cash flow cycle starts with the production or purchase of inventory (or a service, as the case may be). It takes raw materials, fixed assets, and employees to start the cycle.

After the goods or services are sold, however, cash still isn't realized. At this point, an account receivable is booked. It's only after the receivable is collected that hard cash is obtained that can be used to pay suppliers, banks, stockholders, employees, and taxes.

Where the theory and practice part company is in timing. This is why a tremendously profitable business can go bankrupt. If any point in the cash flow pipeline becomes blocked for a length of time, there simply will be no cash to clear checks, and a company with high inventory, sales, and receivables can easily go into receivership. Let's take a closer look at each point in the cycle for places where cash can be realized.

Accounts payable

The key to the management of accounts payable is to take advantage of the normal lag between the time goods are received and payment is made. But retention of suppliers' money must be kept within reasonable limits. An abuse of trade terms could damage a firm's reputation and lead to threats of "CODs only," which could worsen your cash position.

Some suppliers offer a cash discount of 2-5% on bills paid within a certain period, usually 10 days. Prompt payment is a good source of potential savings. But the savings must be balanced against the time value of the money paid out. Keep in mind that

---

Figure 4

HOW TO PINPOINT PROBLEMS AND UNLOCK CASH*

PROBLEM	RED FLAGS	POSSIBLE CAUSES
DETERIORATION OF WORKING CAPITAL	• *Current ratio (current assets ÷ current liabilities) lower than industry average* • *Acid test ratio (cash accounts receivable ÷ current liabilities) lower than industry average* • *Trade payables building; cash discounts not taken on purchases* • *Bank balance low; overdrafts and returned checks occurring regularly* • *Loan payments delinquent; suppliers threaten CODs only* • *Owner continually chasing dollars instead of running the business*	• Continuing operational losses • Unusual, nonrecurring losses (theft, fire, adverse court judgments) • Payments of excessive salaries, bonuses, dividends • Overinvestment in fixed assets from working capital • Temporary cash shortage caused by buildup of expenses for a large contract and/or slow payment of a large receivable • Lengthening of collection periods on accounts receivable • Overinvestment in slow-moving inventories
SLUGGISH SALES	• *Market position slipping* • *Sales figures stabilized; no growth apparent* • *Actual sales below those forecasted* • *Sales-to-inventory ratio (sales ÷ inventory) low compared to industry standards* • *Customer complaints frequent, merchandise returns climbing*	• Satisfaction with the status quo; obsolete or unsalable items in sale lines • Failure to develop new products and services • Location inadequacies; changing traffic patterns or deterioration of neighborhood • Inattention to or inaction within a changing market • Poorly developed marketing efforts; erratic price cuts; aggressive sales tactics substituted for coordinated marketing plan • Nonexistent market; initial failure to research • Poor employee training in areas of sales or service
DECLINING PROFITS (OR INCREASING LOSSES)	• *Net profit-to-sales ratio (net profit before taxes ÷ sales) low compared to industry statistics* • *Net-profit-to-tangible-net-worth ratio (net profit ÷ net worth) below industry standard* • *Operation expense ratios (expense ÷ gross sales) higher than industry average*	• Lack of inventory balance; erosion of profits by costs of deadweight items • Poor organization within firm; hampered cost control efforts due to lack of responsibility delegation by owner or manager • Lack of planning, improper scheduling, inadequate equipment maintenance with resultant delays or duplication of efforts • Security leaks • Improper pricing policies, not reflective of actual costs
MOUNTING DEBT	• *Firm unable to take advantage of cash discounts* • *Trade payables building* • *Ratio of current liabilities to inventory (current liabilities ÷ inventory) higher than industry average* • *Business the target of legal actions such as filing of creditors' tax liens, etc.*	• Overinvestment in fixed assets • Overpurchase of merchandise or materials • Slow sales • Increased expenses • Inadequate share of ownership capital invested • Failure to plan cash flow position

*Portions of this table are reprinted with permission from Bank of America, "Beating the Cash Crisis," *Small Business Reporter,* © 1975.

passing up "2/10 net 30" terms means you effectively pay 36% per year for use of your suppliers' money.

Some cash-conscious managers regulate payment dates to their own advantage rather than making all payments on the same date each month. To save time, checks are prepared in a batch, then stored by their release dates. This payment method can make the money owed available to the company for a few days longer. For instance, if Vendor X billed on the 10th of the month and Vendor Y on the 20th, and each offered a 3% discount on invoices paid within 10 days of receipt, then X could be paid on the 20th of the month and Y on the 30th. The alternative—paying all suppliers on the 20th, for example—would eliminate the free use of Vendor Y's money for an extra 10 days.

Fixed assets

To generate as much cash as possible without borrowing, consider selling and leasing back fixed assets such as company-owned cars, major equipment items, and real estate.

Also, lease rather than buy new equipment when cash is tight. Although it is almost always more financially advantageous to buy outright, leasing makes more sense cash-flow-wise.

Inventory

Inventory can be a big cash trap if not watched carefully. Each $100 in inventory on hand costs the company between $15 and $25 per year, taking into consideration interest, storage space expenses, facilities, handling, insurance, deterioration, and obsolescence.

Periodically review stock movement figures to weed out items that are not selling. Move these items at cost, or below, to get them off the floor. But don't go overboard. Too lean an inventory can cause stockouts requiring special runs, single item purchases, and rush orders—all expensive!

Accounts receivable

Accounts receivable represent a large part of working capital. Your job is to convert them to cash. Be sure to establish a stiff credit-granting policy followed up with a good control system for collections. Have your bookkeeper prepare a periodic "receivables aging" statement showing the percentage of accounts that are 30, 60, and 90 days past due. Consider cash discounts for prompt payment, be sure to charge for overdue accounts, and don't be afraid to vigorously pursue late payers. Remember, an uncollected account receivable is the same as having a thief in your pocket.

How to spot and unplug cash blocks

At this point you might say, "Well, I see the general idea, but how do I really dig in deeper and both identify specific problems and arrive at solutions?" A good point! What a businessperson really wants is a monitoring system so that, in effect, a red flag goes up when one area of the cash cycle is not flowing properly. Here is where your financial records and operating ratios can be so valuable. Figure 4 will help you use your records to pinpoint both the sources of problems and the corrective action you can take.

Contribution Analysis

One of the most important concepts for every businessman to understand is "contribution analysis." Its proper use is fundamental to practically all competent and knowledgeable decision making.

Definition of contribution

Contribution is defined as the selling price of a product less the variable costs associated with its production and marketing.

Variable costs

Business expenses can be broken down into variable and fixed categories (sometimes called direct and indirect expenses). By variable costs, we mean only those costs that vary directly with the number of items produced. These would include the direct costs of material, labor, shipping costs, and selling commission. For example, if you are making widgets and each one contains $1.00 of steel and costs $2.00 in direct labor to produce, it will have a variable cost per unit to manufacture of $3.00. Now let's say you pay $2.00 per unit to ship the widget and you pay 10% commission to a salesman for selling it (based on a selling price of $10.00). The net contribution attributable to manufacturing and marketing each widget would be $4.00 per unit, as shown in Figure 5.

Fixed costs

As we said before, variable expenses are those that vary according to the volume produced. Fixed expenses are those that stay practically the same over a wide range of number of units produced. These include such overhead items as heat, lights, water, rent, office staff, and manager's salary. Now, taking our simplified example, for every widget we produce and sell, we have $4.00 left over after paying all the variable expenses to "contribute" toward paying the fixed expenses (i.e., overhead) of the business and hopefully having something left over to provide a profit. That's why the term "contribution" is really an abbreviation of its full title, "contribution to fixed overhead and profit" (see Figure 6 for a schematic diagram of how the contribution from each product is applied to overhead and profit).

Why think in terms of contribution?

Every business has a certain capacity to produce within a given level of fixed overhead. Let's look at two examples. A machine shop has several different kinds of products it can produce and yet its overhead won't vary appreciably. Similarly, a consultant may be able to do several different kinds of studies and still his heat, water, lights, clerical costs, etc., will stay about the same. In both these cases the manager

---

Figure 5

WIDGET CONTRIBUTION

Selling Price		$10.00
Less Variable Costs		
Steel	1.00	
Labor	2.00	
Shipping	2.00	
Marketing (10% × $10)	1.00	
Contribution		$ 4.00

---

should always try to concentrate on the type of work that produces the highest contribution to the fixed overhead and profit.

Common sense

That is just good common sense, of course, but most businessmen think in a different way. They either attempt to maximize sales or they try to maximize profit—not contribution. Let's take two more examples, one from the realm of merchandising and the other from that of manufacturing.

Sales

Given two nearly identical items on the shelf, one at $4.00 and one at $5.00, a merchandise manager should push the $5.00 item—right? Not necessarily. It depends on their relative contribution. The $5.00 item may have cost $3.00 (contrib-

Figure 6

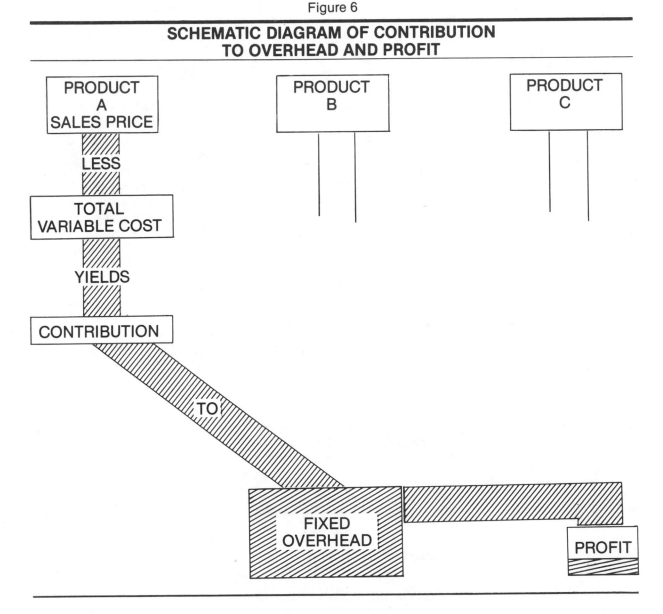

**SCHEMATIC DIAGRAM OF CONTRIBUTION
TO OVERHEAD AND PROFIT**

Figure 7

PRODUCTS A, B, AND C

Product	Sales Price Per Unit	Sales Per Year	$ Sales	Direct Costs to Manufacture & Sell
A	$100	500 units	$50,000/yr	$90/unit
B	$100	500 units	$50,000/yr	$60/unit
C	$100	500 units	$50,000/yr	$30/unit

---

ution = $2.00) while the $4.00 item cost $1.50 (contribution = $2.50). On this basis it would be better to focus attention on the $4.00 item and thereby not attempt to maximize sales dollars, but contribution.

Now before we begin to shift product lines or remove things from the shelf, let's refine our thinking one more step. It is not always possible to sell just high contribution items. What our merchandise manager should really consider is the optimum mix of merchandise to have a full product line and maximize total contribution per year. To do this, he may have to carry a few loss leaders. Also, turnover is important. Although the per unit contribution of the $5.00 item may be less, if you can sell it twice as fast, it would contribute more per year than the $4.00 item.

Profit

Other managers often try to maximize profit. But profit is an accounting term and depends on proper allocation of all the fixed costs such as depreciation, rent, water, heat, and lights. It is far easier and more accurate to maximize the contribution a given product makes to fixed overhead and profit. Consider the following minicase study. You manage a company that sells products A, B, and C.

Product A costs the most to make and sell, but you are forced to price it at only $100 because of competition. Product B provides a nice profit margin, but Product C is your real moneymaker because it is a new product and you have little competition thanks to patent protection. It will be difficult, however, to sell more than 500 units per year of Product B or C because they have very specialized and limited markets (see Figure 7).

The total overhead for this company is $45,000 per year. No matter how you allocate the overhead (by product line, dollar sales, or units produced), it works out that Product A is a big money loser. (See Figure 8.) For every unit of Product A you

Figure 8

PRODUCTS A, B, AND C: PROFIT AND LOSS

Product	Direct Costs to Manufacture & Sell	Overhead	Total Cost to Produce	Selling Price	Profit (Loss)
A	$90/unit	$30/unit	$120	$100	($20) Loss/unit
B	$60/unit	$30/unit	$ 90	$100	$10 Profit/unit
C	$30/unit	$30/unit	$ 60	$100	$40 Profit/unit

---

sell, you lose $20. You should definitely drop it before you go broke—right?

Wrong! This is a classic trap that brings large and small companies alike to their financial knees and often to bankruptcy, as it did a large and famous English aircraft manufacturer. Don't make the same mistake!

Let's restate the figures, but this time in terms of contribution. As you can see from Figure 9, Product A does contribute toward fixed overhead and profit. Obviously Products B and C contribute more per unit than Product A, but we assumed for purposes of this example that the market for Products B and C was fixed at 500 units each. On this basis you should definitely not drop Product A so long as two factors are present:

- It has a positive contribution.

- It does not utilize productive capacity that could be used to produce higher contribution products than A.

Every well-run business must attempt to maximize contribution in a slightly different way. Supermarkets and retailers try to maximize contribution per year per square foot of floor space. Salesmen and doctors maximize contribution per working hour; airlines maximize contribution per flight hour; and so on. You will find this concept vital in your decision making.

Breakeven Analysis: Key Planning and Control Tool

Breakeven analysis is one of the most important planning and control tools available to the businessperson.

"Breakeven" refers to the sales volume (either in dollars or units) at which a business neither makes a profit nor incurs a loss. In other words, it is the point where sales revenue just equals expenses. Using a simple graphic technique known as "breakeven analysis," it is possible to calculate your company's breakeven level as well as analyze a number of important management problems, such as setting prices, projecting profit and loss at different sales volume levels, and estimating the impact of major capital expenditures on profitability.

Three main factors affect the profitability of every business:

- Sales volume.

- Expenses.

- Sales price.

The problem is that each of these factors is constantly changing. For example, what

Figure 9

PRODUCTS A, B, AND C: CONTRIBUTION

Product	Selling Price	Direct Costs to Manufacture & Sell	Contribution
A	$100/unit	$90/unit	$10/unit
B	$100/unit	$60/unit	$40/unit
C	$100/unit	$30/unit	$70/unit

Figure 10

FIXED VS. VARIABLE EXPENSES

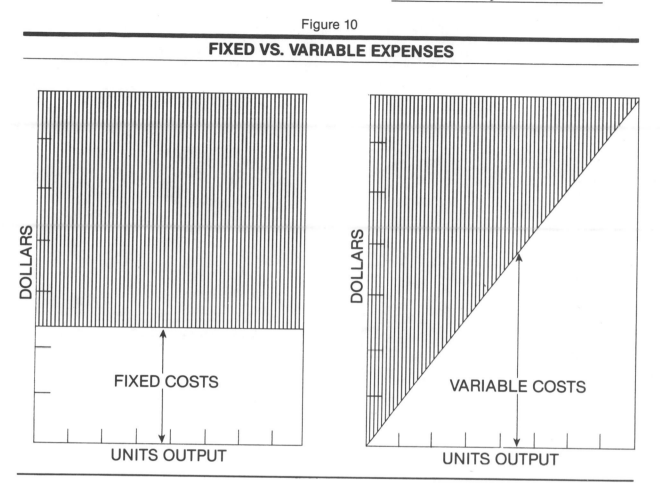

would be the profit level of your particular business if sales were off 10%, costs went up 5%, and your sales price per unit stayed the same?

Chances are you find it rather hard to give a quick answer. But businesspeople face this situation every day—costs up, volume changing, should we raise our price, what will that do to profits? It's essential that you have an analytical method to help you make quick decisions concerning the key economic components of your business.

Cost categories

The costs of every business can be separated into two broad categories. "Fixed" costs are those which do not vary appreciably with sales or production volume, depreciation, insurance, property taxes, administrative salaries, etc. In contrast, "variable expenses" vary in direct proportion to changes in sales or production volume. They include such items as direct labor and materials, sales commissions, and direct shipping expenses. There is another category of expenses known as semivariable that change with increases or decreases in sales or production, but not in direct proportion to such changes. Examples would be telephone service and advertising. For the most part, however, practically all expenses can be categorized as either fixed or variable; therefore, we will not concern ourselves with semivariable expenses at this time. Graphic examples of fixed and variable costs are shown in Figure 10. Note that the fixed costs remain constant, regardless of the production out-

Figure 11

TOTAL COSTS

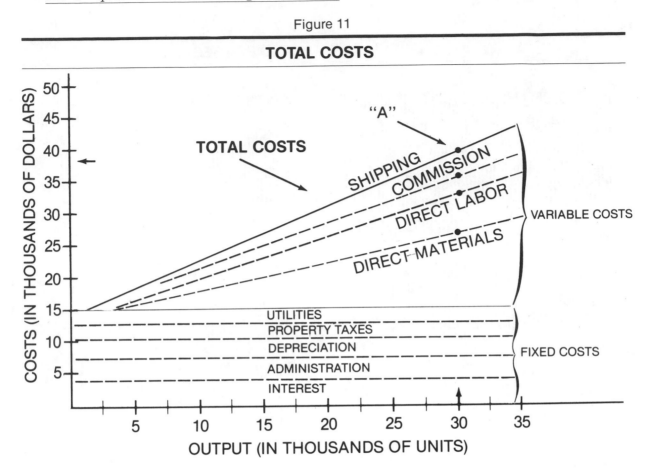

put, while the variable costs are in a directly proportional relationship to the output volume.

Total costs

Now that we can visualize the differences in fixed and variable costs, let's take a specific example and determine the total costs at any given volume level. Suppose that you are in the manufacturing business and your product sells for $1.30 each. Your direct costs per item are $0.37 for materials, $0.23 for direct labor, $0.13 for salesman's commission, and $0.07 for shipping expenses. Total variable costs, therefore, come to $0.80 per item. Now, to run your plant costs $15,000 a month, come rain or shine, for depreciation, administration, taxes, etc. Therefore, you have $15,000 of fixed costs per month. Taking the fixed and variable costs from Figure 10 and graphically adding them together, we can construct a chart (Figure 11) which gives the total costs at any output level.

To verify the figures, pick a point, such as 30,000 units of output. The fixed costs will be $15,000, and the variable costs will equal 30,000 units times $0.80 per unit = $24,000. Therefore, total costs at a volume level of 30,000 units equal $15,000 fixed costs plus $24,000 variable costs or $39,000. This can be seen as point "A" in Figure 11.

Determining the breakeven point

Let's go to the next step and determine the breakeven level for this particular business. As noted before, the sales price is $1.30 per unit. We can now superimpose a "Sales Revenue" line on the chart, as shown in Figure 12.

As can be seen in Figure 12, the breakeven point is the point where the Sales Revenue line crosses the Total Costs line. At any sales volume less than this point, the company loses money; at any greater volume, the company makes money. The exact amount of the Profit or Loss is the difference in the Sales Revenue and Total Costs at the given volume level.

Solutions to other management problems

As we mentioned earlier, breakeven analysis provides a flexible management tool to solve a number of problems involving the complex interrelationship of costs, volume, and profitability. Let's take one such problem and see how easily you might solve part of it using the techniques we have discussed.

Suppose that your manufacturing firm discussed above is considering raising prices from $1.30 to $1.50 per unit. You are concerned, however, that you analyze all relevant factors before making such a decision. How would you approach the problem in this case?

Well, part of the solution is quite easy: You should analyze the result of the price increase on your firm's cost and profit structure. Figure 12a is the same chart as Figure 12, but this time we have plotted a new Sales Revenue line (dotted line) which projects the effect of the price increase.

As you can see, the price increase caused the breakeven point to shift rather

Figure 12

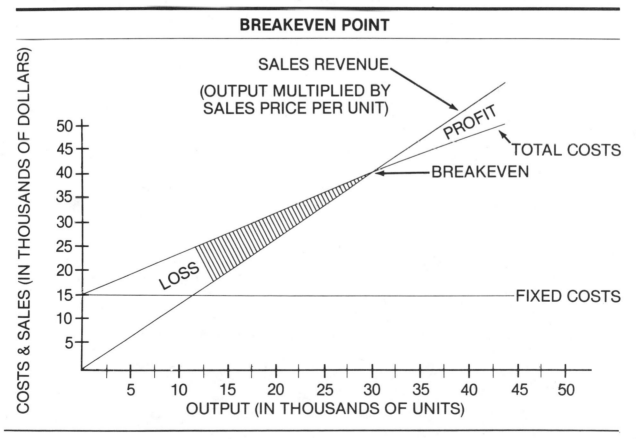

Figure 12a

REVISED BREAKEVEN POINT

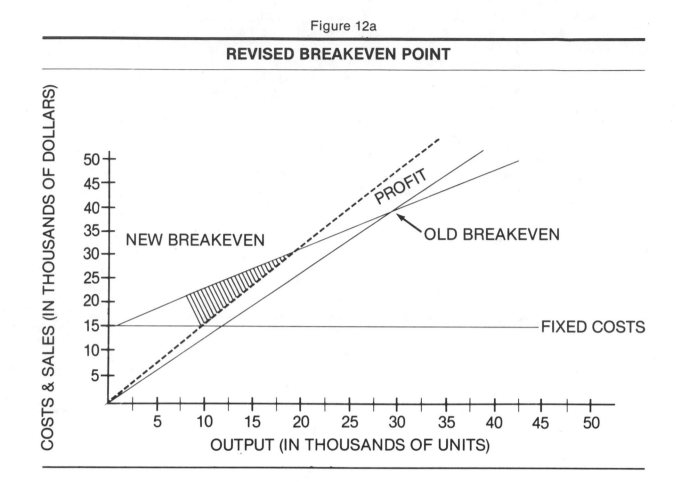

dramatically from the previous 30,000 units to only about 21,000 units (21,428 to be exact). And, of course, the profit and loss areas shift as well. This information is essential because the question now becomes, what is the "price sensitivity" of the product? Although the company will make more profit per unit at the higher price, will the market absorb as many units as before? Breakeven analysis can't answer this final question, but it does aid management by providing a picture of profits at various prices and levels of sales.

Impact of changing costs on profit
We looked only at varying prices in the above example, and projected the impact on profitability. Similarly, you could study the effect of changing fixed or variable costs on your profit structure.
Breakeven analysis provides a flexible management tool to:

> • Study information concerning volume, price, and expenses in an analytical manner.

> • Determine expense and revenue projections under alternative management and economic assumptions.

> • Control costs through the integration of breakeven analysis with budgeting techniques.

Figure 13

COMPOUNDING INTEREST

Year	Amount at beginning of year	Plus	One year's Interest on that amount	Equals	Amount at end of year
1	$100.00	+	$100.00 × 10%	=	$110.00
2	$110.00	+	$110.00 × 10%	=	$121.00
3	$121.00	+	$121.00 × 10%	=	$133.10

- Consider in a systematic manner the impact of price changes on profit.

- Project the impact of breakeven volume of major capital expenditures such as plant expansion.

Try to use the breakeven analysis method wherever possible in your decision making. If you do, you may find it will give you an insight into your business that you've never had before!

Time Value of Money

The time value of money is a straightforward concept with widespread application to business decision making. Inflation makes an understanding of the time value of money more important than ever because money used inefficiently will quickly decline in value.

The mathematics of the time value of money is simple. Any businessman prefers $100 today as opposed to $100 next year because the $100 can be invested to earn as much as 10% to 12% at high interest rates. Or it can be invested in the business as working capital or in equipment purchases. Thus, $100 today is really worth $110 next year (at a 10% interest rate). This compounding process can be carried out for future years. (See Figure 13.)

Fortunately, there are tables that speed this process by supplying an appropriate multiplier—called the "accumulation factor." The original figure is multiplied by the accumulation factor to yield the final amount accumulated. In Figure 13, the accumulation factor for compounding at 10% interest for three years is 1.331 since $100.00 × 1.331 = $133.10. These factors can be found by specifying the annual in-

Figure 14

PRESENT VALUE

X	×	1.331	=	$100.00
(Amount to be set aside)		(Accumulation factor)		(Amount to be accumulated)

Therefore: $\mathbf{X} = \$100.00 \times \frac{1}{1.331} = \$75.13$

Figure 15

ACCUMULATION FACTORS

[Value in the future of $1.00 received today]

Interest Rate

Years	5%	6%	7%	8%	9%	10%	12%	14%	15%	16%	18%	20%
1	1.050	1.060	1.070	1.080	1.090	1.100	1.120	1.140	1.150	1.160	1.180	1.200
2	1.102	1.124	1.145	1.166	1.188	1.210	1.254	1.300	1.322	1.346	1.392	1.440
3	1.158	1.191	1.225	1.260	1.295	1.331	1.405	1.482	1.521	1.561	1.643	1.728
4	1.216	1.262	1.311	1.360	1.412	1.464	1.574	1.689	1.749	1.811	1.939	2.074
5	1.276	1.338	1.493	1.469	1.539	1.611	1.762	1.925	2.011	2.100	2.288	2.488
6	1.340	1.419	1.501	1.587	1.677	1.772	1.974	2.195	2.313	2.436	2.700	2.986
7	1.407	1.504	1.606	1.714	1.828	1.949	2.211	2.502	2.660	2.826	3.185	3.583
8	1.477	1.594	1.718	1.851	1.993	2.144	2.476	2.853	3.059	3.278	3.759	4.300
9	1.551	1.689	1.838	1.999	2.172	2.358	2.773	3.252	3.518	3.803	4.435	5.160
10	1.629	1.791	1.967	2.159	2.367	2.594	3.106	3.707	4.046	4.411	5.324	6.192
11	1.710	1.896	2.105	2.332	2.580	2.853	3.479	4.226	4.652	5.117	6.176	7.430
12	1.796	2.012	2.252	2.518	2.813	3.138	3.896	4.818	5,350	5.936	7.288	8.916
13	1.886	2.133	2.410	2.720	3.066	3.452	4.363	5.492	6.153	6.886	8.599	10.699
14	1.980	2.261	2.579	2.937	3.342	3.797	4.887	6.261	7.076	7.988	10.147	12.839
15	2.079	2.397	2.759	3.172	3.642	4.177	5.474	7.138	8.137	9.266	11.974	15.407
16	2.183	2.540	2.952	3.426	3.970	4.595	6.130	8.137	9.358	10.748	14.129	18.488
17	2.292	2.693	3.159	3.700	4.328	5.054	6.866	9.276	10.761	12.468	16.672	22.186
18	2.407	2.854	3.380	3.996	4.717	5.560	7.690	10.575	12.375	14.463	19.673	26.623
19	2.527	3.026	3.617	4.316	5.142	6.116	8.613	12.056	14.232	16.777	23.214	31.948
20	2.653	3.207	3.870	4.661	5.604	6.728	9.646	13.743	16.367	19.461	27.393	38.338

terest rate and the number of years involved and then finding the appropriate accumulation factor as supplied in the tables to be found in any standard accounting or finance textbook.

If you need to know how much to set aside today at 10% interest to accumulate $100 in three years, simply reverse this compounding process. At a 10% interest rate, the $75.13 is called the "present value" of $100.00 received three years from now. It is called present value because that amount, at the present, will grow to $100.00 in three years at a 10% interest rate. As shown in Figure 14, the present value can be easily figured by multiplying the desired amount by the inverse of the accumulation factor. This new multiplier, the discount factor, can be found in the same tables that contain accumulation factors. Abbreviated discount and accumulation factor tables are shown in Figures 15 and 16.

A graphic display of the time value of money is shown in Figure 17. The center of the horizontal axis represents time zero, the increase in value from compounding is shown to the right, and the decrease in value from discounting is shown to the left. Note that both the amount of time involved and the interest rate affect the time value of money.

When to pay

Let's take a couple of common business problems and illustrate the importance of

Figure 16

DISCOUNT FACTORS

[Value today of $1.00 received in the future]

Interest Rate

	5%	6%	7%	8%	9%	10%	12%	14%	15%	16%	18%	20%
1	.952	.943	.935	.926	.917	.909	.893	.877	.870	.862	.847	.833
2	.907	.890	.873	.857	.842	.826	.797	.769	.756	.743	.718	.694
3	.864	.840	.816	.794	.772	.751	.712	.675	.658	.641	.609	.579
4	.823	.792	.763	.735	.708	.683	.636	.592	.572	.552	.516	.482
5	.784	.747	.713	.681	.650	.621	.567	.519	.497	.476	.437	.402
6	.746	.705	.666	.630	.596	.564	.507	.456	.432	.410	.370	.335
7	.711	.665	.623	.583	.547	.513	.452	.400	.376	.354	.314	.279
8	.677	.627	.582	.540	.502	.467	.404	.351	.327	.305	.266	.233
9	.645	.592	.544	.500	.460	.424	.361	.308	.284	.263	.226	.194
10	.614	.558	.508	.463	.422	.386	.322	.270	.247	.227	.191	.162
11	.585	.527	.475	.429	.388	.350	.287	.237	.215	.195	.162	.135
12	.557	.497	.444	.397	.356	.319	.257	.208	.187	.168	.137	.112
13	.530	.469	.415	.368	.326	.290	.229	.182	.163	.145	.116	.093
14	.505	.442	.388	.340	.299	.263	.205	.160	.141	.125	.099	.078
15	.481	.417	.362	.315	.275	.239	.183	.140	.123	.108	.084	.065
16	.458	.394	.339	.292	.252	.218	.163	.123	.107	.093	.071	.054
17	.436	.371	.317	.270	.231	.198	.146	.108	.093	.080	.060	.045
18	.416	.350	.296	.250	.212	.180	.130	.095	.081	.069	.051	.038
19	.396	.331	.276	.232	.194	.164	.116	.083	.070	.060	.043	.031
20	.377	.312	.258	.215	.178	.149	.104	.073	.061	.051	.037	.026

Years

Note: As you can see, the accumulation and discount factors at a given interest rate and year are the inverse of each other.

the time value of money concept. Suppose you are enlarging your plant and the contractor gives you the following payment options:

1. $10,000 when work begins,

2. $11,200 when work is completed (expected to be one year), or

3. $12,000 deferred payment plan (due in two years).

The time value of money can be used to compare these alternatives by discounting the payments in options (2) and (3) back to the time when work begins. At this point, the payments are on an equivalent basis, and we can compare their present values. Using a 10% interest rate, you eventually pay out more dollars under option (3); it has the lowest effective cost in terms of time value of money. So you should choose the third option. (See Figure 18.)

Lease or buy?

Another common decision faced by businessmen is the lease versus buy decision for facilities, office equipment, company vehicles, and so on. This decision involves differential cash flows over time, and the time factor must be analyzed.

Suppose you have the option of either purchasing office equipment with a five-year expected life or leasing the same equipment for five years. If the equipment costs

Figure 17

DISCOUNT AND ACCUMULATION FACTORS

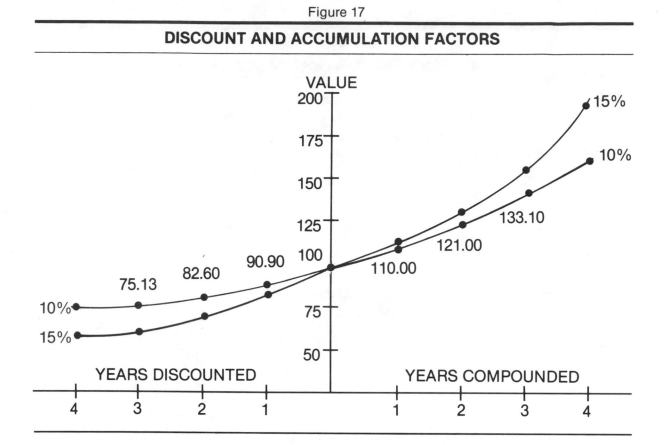

$5,000 new with an anticipated trade-in value of $500 in five years and rents for $1,100 per year, the cash flows might be graphed as shown in Figure 19.

The discounting aspect of this problem is straightforward. Because both cash outflows (purchase cost and lease fees) as well as cash inflows (investment credit, cost recovery, and salvage value) are involved, the discounted figures must be algebraically added to determine the net present value of each alternative. (See Figure 20.)

As you can see, the correct decision is to lease since that alternative has the lowest net cost in terms of the time value of money. Actually, this decision probably goes against the intuitive judgment of many businessmen who would argue that buying

Figure 18

PRESENT VALUE OF PAYMENT OPTIONS

	Present Value		1 Year	2 Years
Option 1	$10,000		$11,200	$12,000
		Discount Factor		
Option 2	$10,181	.909		
Option 3	$ 9,912	.826		

Figure 19

LEASE VERSUS BUY OPTION

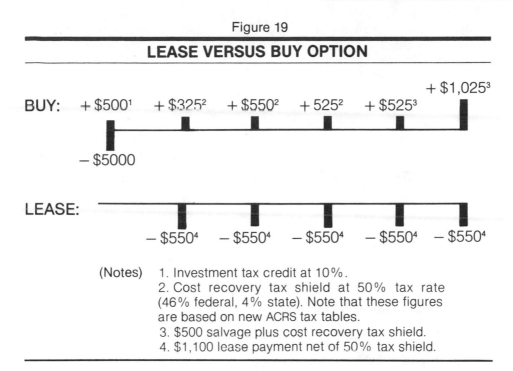

BUY: + $500[1]   + $325[2]   + $550[2]   + 525[2]   + $525[3]   + $1,025[3]

− $5000

LEASE: − $550[4]   − $550[4]   − $550[4]   − $550[4]   − $550[4]

(Notes) 1. Investment tax credit at 10%.
2. Cost recovery tax shield at 50% tax rate (46% federal, 4% state). Note that these figures are based on new ACRS tax tables.
3. $500 salvage plus cost recovery tax shield.
4. $1,100 lease payment net of 50% tax shield.

costs less money ($5,000 to purchase versus $5,500 to lease) and that the cost to purchase is reduced even further by the effects of the investment credit ($500) and salvage value ($500). With this total difference of $1,500 between lease and purchase, how could it possibly be cheaper to lease? What makes the difference is the timing of the cash flows. To buy required complete payment in year one, while the lease fees are paid out over the five-year period. When the time value of these dollars is considered, it definitely works out (as you can see from the figures) that it is cheaper to lease.

Present value problems can sometimes get complicated in detail, but the effort will definitely be worth it in times of high cost money. Remember these steps when making the time-value decisions, and you should avoid any trouble.

1. List the incoming and outgoing cash flows of each alternative.

2. Apply the appropriate tax rate to determine the after tax effect of these cash flows. Remember that lease fees and cash recovery expenses are tax deductible. The investment credit yields an effective cash inflow because it directly reduces income taxes.

3. Select an interest rate representative of your investment op-

Figure 20

NET PRESENT VALUE OF LEASE VERSUS BUY OPTION

BUY: Net Present Value = − $5,000 + 500 + 375(.909) + 550(.826)
+ 525(.751) + 525(.683) + 1025(.621) = − $2,315
LEASE: Net Present Value = − $550(.909) − 550(.826) − 550 (.751)
− 550(.683) − 550(.621)   = − $2,084

portunities. Do not set the rate too low. Even though we used an unrealistically low 10% in the previous example just for simplicity, you should certainly use a rate above current interest rates, and many companies consider the "opportunity cost" of their capital to be as high as 30%.

4. Discount the cash flows to arrive at the net present value.

5. Choose the alternative with lowest cash outflow or highest net cash inflow.

Capital Investment Analysis

Any time a business invests money (capital) today in the hopes of earning a return on this money in the future, it has made a special investment decision. It is vital that problems of this type be analyzed correctly because: (1) they often involve large amounts of money, and (2) they generally lock the business into a course of action for a period of several years. The most common types of capital investment decisions are:

- Expand plant vs. stay "as is."

- Lease equipment vs. buy.

- Buy new equipment vs. keep the old.

- Introduce new products vs. stick with the old.

Steps in analysis

In each of these cases, the following steps must be considered:

1. *Alternatives.* All capital investment decisions involve alternatives. The starting point, therefore, is to be sure that the proper alternatives are being considered. For example, perhaps the decision should not be buy new equipment versus keep the old, but rather refurbish the old versus let it wear out. Or maybe the alternatives should not be introduce new product versus scrap old product, but rather introduce the new product on a regional basis versus go national.

It is difficult to reach the right decision unless you analyze the right alternatives. Before proceeding, you should make a careful study of all the options and reduce the list to those that are relevant and most viable.

2. *Isolate relevant costs.* It is important to recognize which decisions are capital investment decisions.

- Differential costs. Since capital investment decisions involve alternatives, we are not concerned with the absolute cost of an alternative but only with the difference in cash flows between the alternatives.

- Future cash flows vs. sunk costs. Most accountants and businesspeople worry about past costs, saying, "What was our raw materials cost on that part?" or "What was our utility bill last quarter?" When analyzing a capital investment decision, however, only future cash flows are relevant. Any expenditures made in the past are considered "sunk," i.e., they can't be recouped and are therefore irrelevant to any decisions involving the future. This is a crucial (and sometimes difficult) concept to grasp. A couple of examples may clarify these concepts.

Buy new equipment vs. keep the old: This is a common problem that faces most business managers. First, consider all alternatives. For example, if the old machine is broken beyond repair, there really is no analytical problem—it must be replaced. If, however, the old machine is working satisfactorily but a new one would be faster and more efficient, then we have a genuine capital investment decision. Consider the following case: Company X has an old machine with an estimated salvage value of $2,500. To replace the old machine, which originally cost $7,000, with a new one will cost $10,000 plus $2,000 to install it. This new machine will save $1,500 a year in operating costs, it has an estimated useful life of five years, and furthermore it can be salvaged for $2,000 at the end of that time period. The company desires a minimum return of 15% on all of its investments. Should or shouldn't the company buy the new machine?

First, it is vital to know how much money will have to be invested in the new machine. Here we are concerned only with future costs. The book value of the old machine (its cost less accumulated cash recovery deductions) is irrelevant as is its original cost since both are past history. What is relevant is how much the old machine can be

Figure 21

SHOULD COMPANY X BUY NEW MACHINE

	0	1	2	3	4	5
Cash Outflows						
Cost of new machine	$10,000					
Savings from investment credit	(666)					
Installation charge	2,000					
Sale of old machine	(2,500)	(cash flows discounted at 15%)				
Net investment in new machine	$ 8,834					
Cash Inflows						
Savings @ $1,500/year						
year 1	$1,305 ◄— ($1500 × .870)					
year 2	1,134 ◄— ($1500 × .756)					
year 3	987 ◄— ($1500 × .658)					
year 4	858 ◄— ($1500 × .572)					
year 5	746 ◄— ($1500 × .497)					
Total for 5 years	$5,030					
Scrap value, end of 5 years	994 ◄— ($2000 × .497)					
Present Value of Cash Inflows	$6,024					
Net Present Value (Inflows-Outflows)	($ 2,810)					

sold for and anything else such as the investment tax credit that will reduce the net cost of the new machine. Taking all these factors into account, the net investment comes to $8,500.

The second step is to calculate the effect of savings from the new machine. In other words, what will be the return on the proposed investment? Note that when we speak of savings, it means the differential in all costs to operate the new machine versus the old. This includes labor, cash recovery, utilities, and maintenance. At first glance you might say, "We'll save $1,500 a year times five years plus the $2,000 we'll get when we scrap it—that equals $9,500. That's well above our net investment of $8,500. Let's buy it!"

But you aren't going to realize those savings until sometime in the future, and the investment of $8,500 has to be made today. It's like comparing apples and oranges. We have to take the time value of money into account (see the preceding section) and discount those savings by the 15% you would like to earn on your money. Otherwise it could be a bad investment.

As you can see, when the savings are discounted at your desired 15% rate, the present value of the inflows is only $6,024 versus the $8,500 you would have to pay out today. You would technically lose $2,476 in net present value on your investment—certainly not a 15% return! There may, of course, be nonmonetary factors that influence the decision, such as a requirement to buy new machinery to meet industry safety standards. But simply on the basis of the above economic analysis, the proposal to buy the new machine should be rejected.

Introduce new product: suppose that Company Y has spent $25,000 to develop and test market a new product. The decision of whether or not to commit an additional $25,000 to go into full production and introduce the project nationwide is now before the board of directors. The vice president of marketing tells the directors, "We've spent $25,000 to develop and test market our new product. While I'll concede that the test market results weren't as good as we had hoped, we'll never know for sure if this product is a winner until we go national. We've got $25,000 in this thing already, and we stand a good chance of making $100,000 over the next five years before the competition catches up. We must protect our investment, and I for

Figure 22

NEW PRODUCT PROPOSAL

	Time (years)					
Cash Outflows	0	1	2	3	4	5
Capital Investment	$25,000					
Increase in Working Capital	15,000					
Total Investment	$40,000					
Cash Inflows						
Present Value of				(discounted at 15%)		
Potential Profit	$66,550	$10,000	$20,000	$40,000	$20,000	$10,000
Present Value of Working Capital Released in Year 5	7,455					$15,000
Total Present Value of Inflows	$74,005					
Net Present Value (Inflows – Outflows)	$34,005					

one think it's a good place to put our money." The treasurer, however, counters, "I agree we've spent a lot of money, but that's no reason to throw good money after bad. What we've spent is gone. We have to look at this product strictly on its future merits." With that, the treasurer distributed his analysis (see Figure 22).

The treasurer continued, "I think several things should be apparent from this analysis. First, we are really considering making a capital investment of an additional $40,000, not $25,000 as was suggested, because increased working capital of $15,000 will be needed to finance accounts receivable during the five years. We'll get it back, however, at the end, and I've shown its present value of $7,455 after discounting at our standard required return of 15%. The $25,000 we've already spent is not, as I've stated, relevant to this decision of whether to go ahead or not. The $100,000 we stand to make over five years is worth $77,500 today if discounted at our desired return rate of 15%. The net present value of this investment decision (inflows minus outflows) is $34,005. What we have to decide is whether comparable investment alternatives available to us yield more or less than this one. We should also determine the probability of our realizing the $100,000 figure we have been using. While this alternative yields a high rate of return if all goes well, I think the inconclusive test marketing results cast considerable doubt on the projected figures."

After a lengthy discussion and a careful consideration of the graphic evidence presented by the treasurer, the board agreed with the treasurer's assessment of the risks and voted down the proposal.

Many decisions that were made based on gut feelings in the past can be subjected to critical, unemotional analysis with surprising results. Take a few minutes to review these techniques again. Don't worry unduly about whether you should stipulate a 10% or 20% return on your investments. It's the methodology and approach to these problems that are important.

Return on Investment Analysis

Return on investment (ROI) analysis is an invaluable tool for profit planning. You can use ROI analysis for intercompany or interindustry comparisons and for various pricing, cost, inventory, and investment decisions.

As shown below, however, you must take care that consistent definitions of sales, profit, and total investment are applied.

Sources of profit

Two factors determine how much dollar return sales of your product or service will provide on your investment: margin and turnover (see Figure 23). To ensure the consistency we mentioned above, let's define our terms:

> • Sales—Net (after returns and allowances) rather than gross sales.

> • Profit—Net operating income before tax. Any items of non-operating income, such as income from leased property or interest, are excluded.

> • Total investment—All fixed and current assets normally used in the business to produce the net operating profit.

Basic formula

Now, let's get to the interesting part! Figure 24 shows the basic formula for return on investment (ROI). Note that return on investment could also be calculated as profit

Figure 23

KEY ROI FACTORS

"Margin" = $\dfrac{\text{Profit}}{\text{Sales}}$

(i.e., what percentage profit do you make on sales)

"Turnover" = $\dfrac{\text{Sales}}{\text{Total Investment}}$

(i.e., the amount of sales to your total investment level)

divided by total investment. This short form is derived by a simple mathematical function in which the sales figures in the basic formula cancel each other.

While the answer obtained is the same, the short form ignores the fact that return on investment is influenced by two relationships:

1. Profit to sales, and

2. Total investment to sales.

Both of these relationships must be analyzed to localize any source of change in return on investment. Each company should attempt to increase sales while simultaneously employing its resources in such a manner that it consistently increases its profit on total investment. The basic formula emphasizes this dual movement.

Before we go any further, maybe you would like to go back and reread what we have covered. If you understand the basics, it is all downhill from here.

Relationship of operating ratios

As simple as the basic ROI formula appears to be, it takes into consideration all the various items that go into a balance sheet and income statement.

Figure 25 presents a graphic outline of the relationship of these items to return on investment and to each other.

Application of basic formula

Let's take a specific example to illustrate the use of the formula. The operations data

Figure 24

BASIC ROI FORMULA

ROI = Margin × Turnover

or substituting

ROI = $\dfrac{\text{Profit}}{\text{Sales}}$ × $\dfrac{\text{Sales}}{\text{Total Investment}}$

Figure 25

RELATIONSHIP OF OPERATING RATIOS

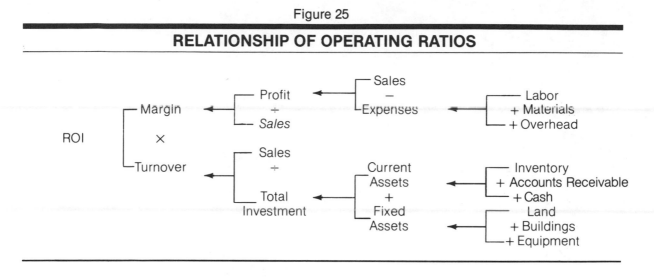

in Figure 26 have been taken from the income statements and balance sheets of two divisions of the "PDQ Specialties Co."

Now let's calculate the ROI's for each division (Figure 27).

Implications for decision making
Note that Divisions A and B made the same profits ($100,000). Also, they had the same amount of money invested in fixed assets ($400,000). Yet, the return on investment for Division A is significantly higher than that earned by Division B. How could this be?

We see from Division B's balance sheet that it has considerably more money tied up in current assets—in other words, inventory, accounts receivable, and cash. Now,

Figure 26

INCOME STATEMENT DATA

	Division A	Division B
Sales	$1,000,000	$1,000,000
Less Cost of Sales	900,000	900,000
Profit	$ 100,000	$ 100,000

BALANCE SHEET DATA

	Division A	Division B
Fixed Assets	$400,000	$400,000
Current Assets	200,000	400,000
Total Investment	$600,000	$800,000

Figure 27

ROI'S FOR DIVISIONS A & B

ROI =	$\dfrac{\text{Profit}}{\text{Sales}}$	×	$\dfrac{\text{Sales}}{\text{Total Investment}}$		

Division A

ROI =	$\dfrac{\$100,000}{\$1,000,000}$	×	$\dfrac{\$1,000,000}{\$600,000}$	=	16.6%

Division B

ROI =	$\dfrac{\$100,000}{\$1,000,000}$	×	$\dfrac{\$1,000,000}{\$800,000}$	=	12.5%

there are two possible explanations. Either Division B is poorly run and has not properly managed its current assets, or Division B is in a considerably different business which requires significantly more inventory and involves slower-paying customers than Division A.

Whatever the case, it should be clear that to compare the two divisions in terms of profit level alone would be misleading. Only when we examine how efficiently they use their resources (i.e., by using ROI analysis) can we properly compare the two businesses and make competent management decisions.

Methods of improving ROI

Given this background, we can now consider how we might go about improving the efficiency and earning power of your business. Again, we must examine the two main components of ROI, margin and turnover. There are two ways to improve each item.

Margin:
Increase sales revenue more than expenses—i.e., charge considerably more for only slightly more of a product. A good example is the trend of some chewing gum manufacturers—only a little more product for twice the previous price.

Cut expenses more than sales—i.e., charge the same amount for less of the product. The shrinking candy bar at the same price is a classic example.

Turnover:
Increase sales relatively more than total investment—i.e., improve utilitization and efficiency of present assets or replace old assets with considerably more efficient new assets.

Reduce total investment relatively faster than sales—i.e., try to cut inventory levels and sell off or reduce other unproductive assets.

Return on investment analysis provides the manager with an excellent tool to compare various operating entities both within and outside his own industry and firm. Take a few moments to compute your own company or division's ROI. Then walk around your business and ask yourself the question, "Does this asset help or hurt my overall return?" You will probably find it quite a revealing exercise.

Profit Variance Analysis

Every month—or certainly every quarter—you have a Profit & Loss statement prepared. Obviously, it shows one of three things: profits are up, down, or about the same. But, how do you analyze why profits have changed? Actually, major internal changes can be taking place in your business that don't even show up in your P&L until it's too late. Here's how to do your own "profit variance analysis"—a vital technique that not one businessperson in ten knows about, and even precious few accountants.

First, let's define our terms. We are only going to be looking at gross profit, i.e., net sales minus cost-of-goods-sold. Changes in gross profit from one period to the next may be due to any one or a combination of the following variances:

Sales
• Sales price. If your sales price per unit goes up or down, it will affect gross profit. This is called "sales price variance."
• Sales volume. Here too, if the quantity of what you sell varies, gross profit will change. This is "sales volume variance."

Goods sold
• Cost of goods sold. Here we are looking at variances in overall cost of goods sold caused by costs going up or down. Obviously, this "cost price variance" affects gross profits.
• Volume of goods sold. Finally, there can be changes in total costs caused by the volume of goods sold. This is "cost volume variance." (Not to be confused with "sales volume" variance.)

The four factors above can be further analyzed and combined into what is called an

---

Figure 28

A TYPICAL COMPANY (SELECTED STATISTICS)

	Last year	This year	Change
Number of units sold....................	100,000	60,000	(− 40,000)
Sales price per unit.....................	$10.00	$20.00	$10.00
Cost per unit...........................	$6.50	$11.83	$5.33
		Condensed P & L	
Net sales.............................	$1,000,000	$1,200,000	$200,000
Cost of sales..........................	650,000	710,000[1]	60,000[1]
Gross Profit...........................	$ 350,000	$ 490,000	$140,000

[1]Data have been rounded.

Figure 29

SALES PRICE/SALES VOLUME VARIANCES

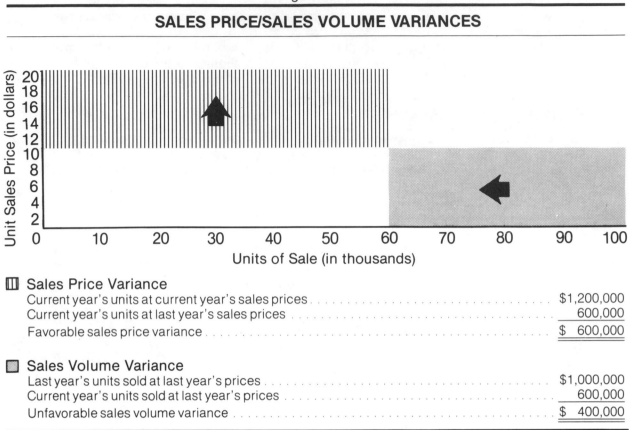

Units of Sale (in thousands)

⊞ **Sales Price Variance**

Current year's units at current year's sales prices	$1,200,000
Current year's units at last year's sales prices	600,000
Favorable sales price variance	$ 600,000

▦ **Sales Volume Variance**

Last year's units sold at last year's prices	$1,000,000
Current year's units sold at last year's prices	600,000
Unfavorable sales volume variance	$ 400,000

overall "sales mix variance" and a "final sales volume variance." Let's take an actual example to help clarify this. Please note the following statistics from the records of A Typical Company (see Figure 28):

Variance computation

• Sales price variance. The sales price variance indicates the change in sales dollars due to changes in sales price from one period to another. It is computed as shown in Figure 29. Note that in this computation, the current units are kept constant and sales prices are variable. The increased sales price contributed $600,000 to sales revenue (and therefore to gross profit) despite a 40,000-unit decrease. This reflects a favorable sales price variance.

• Sales volume variance. The sales volume variance discloses changes in sales dollars due to changes in the number of units sold from one year to another. It is computed as shown in Figure 29. Note that last year's sales prices are kept constant and that units sold are variable in this computation. With no change in sales price, sales would have decreased $400,000 because of the decrease in volume. This decrease in revenue would have an unfavorable effect on gross profit.

• Cost-price variance. The cost-price variance explains changes in the cost of goods sold from one period to another because of changes in cost. It is computed as shown in Figure 30. Note that current units are kept constant and costs are variable in this computation. The increase in the unit cost for goods sold caused a $320,000 increase in the cost of goods sold. This obviously has an unfavorable impact on gross profit.

• Cost-volume variance. The cost-volume variance points out changes in the cost of goods sold from one period to another due to changes in the number of units sold, i.e., volume. It is computed as shown in Figure 30. Note that last year's cost is kept constant and the units sold are variable in this computation. Because of the 40,000 decrease in units sold this year, the cost of goods sold would have been $260,000 less in the current period than it would have been in the last period. This has a favorable impact on gross profit.

The $140,000 increase in gross profit of A Typical Company between the current year and last year may be attributed to the variances computed above. Figure 31 is a recapitulation of these computations.

Analysis by product line
In the illustrations of variances in this section, the data were assumed to be for a one-product firm or a multiproduct company for which an average selling price and an average cost of goods had been computed. You can use the same basic techniques that were applied above to compute variances on a product line basis. That is, instead of using totals (in the case of a one-product firm) or an average (for a multiproduct firm), you use the sales and cost information for each product. This method will allow

Figure 30

COST PRICE/COST VOLUME VARIANCE

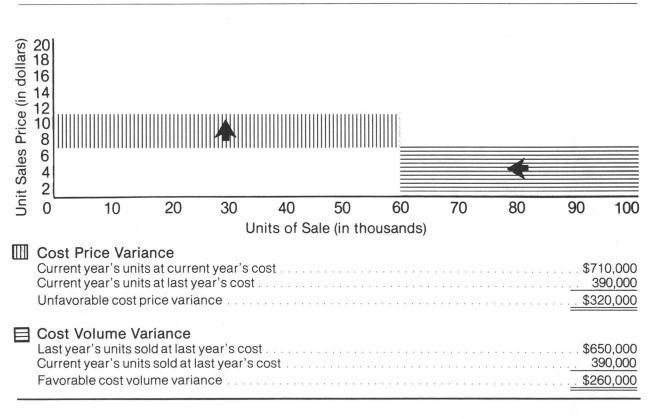

Cost Price Variance

Current year's units at current year's cost	$710,000
Current year's units at last year's cost	390,000
Unfavorable cost price variance	$320,000

Cost Volume Variance

Last year's units sold at last year's cost	$650,000
Current year's units sold at last year's cost	390,000
Favorable cost volume variance	$260,000

Figure 31

COMPUTATION OF NET PROFIT VARIANCE

	Sales	Cost of Goods Sold	Gross Profit
Current year	$1,200,000	$710,000	$490,000
Last year	1,000,000	650,000	350,000
Difference	$ 200,000	$ 60,000	$140,000
Changes attributable to—			
Sales price variance	$600,000		$600,000
Sales volume variance	(−400,000)		(−400,000)
Cost price variance		$(−320,000)	(−320,000)
Cost volume variance		260,000	260,000
Total	$200,000	$(− 60,000)	$140,000

---

you to analyze the contribution that each product makes toward the total gross profit and also the reasons for the variations in gross profit of each product that occur from period to period.

Sales mix and final sales volume variance

In addition to the four variances computed thus far, many large, multiproduct companies also compute two additional variances on a companywide basis—i.e., with all product lines lumped together. Here the overall change in selling prices, costs, and gross profits results in what is called the "sales mix variance." Similarly, the overall change in total sales dollars attributable to changes in the number of units sold of each product is called the "final sales volume variance."

To calculate these final two variances, you must first determine the overall average gross profit percentage rate earned on all types of units sold last year and for the current year. Once this is done, you are ready to compute the two variances. Let's take a simple example:

	Last Year	This Year
Total sales volume	$4,000	$7,500
Total direct costs	1,000	2,100
Gross margin	$3,000	$5,400

As we can see, the gross margin percentage is 75% for last year and 72% ($5,400 divided by $7,500) for the current year.

• Sales mix variance. To compute the sales mix variance, you compare total current year's sales ($7,500) at last year's gross margin rate (75%) to current year's sales at current year's gross margin rate (72%). In this case, the variance ($225) is unfavorable, since the margin is declining. (In effect, it shows that at current sales volume, you are making $225 less from margin changes alone than you could have at last year's margins.)

• Final sales volume variance. Here, we compare last year's sales ($4,000) at last year's gross margin rate (75%) with current sales ($7,500) at last year's gross margin rate (75%). The result ($2,625) is favorable, since sales volume increased. In other words, at last year's margin, you would have made $2,625 more this year due to sales volume increases alone.

Controlling Accounts Receivable

Credit control is one of the most fundamental aspects of managing a business. Too often, however, managers relegate this function to others. This inattention can be especially dangerous if there are economic changes that impact directly on the cost, control, and management of credit sales.

How much are accounts receivable costing you?

When one business advances goods or services to another on credit, it is effectively loaning short-term working capital. Naturally, there is a cost associated with such capital that increases as (1) interest rates rise and/or (2) customers take longer to pay. The combination of these two factors can reduce profits, adversely affect cash flow, and in extreme cases, can even endanger the business. Here is a simple example of how this works:

The John Doe Tool Company borrows to finance its receivables and allows 30 days credit terms to customers. Last year it had sales of $5 million and had average accounts receivable outstanding of $410,000. The cost of money last year was 10%, making the cost to maintain this level of credit $41,000. This year, while sales remained constant, the borrowing cost rose to 15%, and average accounts receivable expanded to $640,000. The result was that the cost of extending credit to customers more than doubled to $96,000 per year ($640,000 × 15%)—an increase of over $55,000 that would have a direct impact on profits.

How to use the days credit formula

An easy way to track the health of credit sales is to monitor the average number of days customers take to pay ("days credit"), as in Figure 32.

Applying this formula, the Doe Company controller determined how long customers were stretching their payments.

The Doe Company calculation showed that while last year customers were sticking to the 30 days credit allowed them, this year they were taking an average of 17 extra days. While nothing could be done about the higher interest rates, this laxness in collecting the receivables incurred nearly $35,000 of the $55,000 overall increase in financing costs ($640,000 − $410,000 × 15% = $34,500). And, of course, this says nothing about the attendant cash flow problems.

Tightening up

On a routine basis, every manager should track: (1) the number of days credit he has outstanding using the formula above, and (2) the absolute cost of maintaining the current level of receivables. In addition, new accounts should be closely scrutinized. A standard operating procedure for evaluating a new credit candidate should include the following:

- Ask for and check all supplier and bank references.

- Independently check suppliers in your same type of business regarding the creditworthiness of the new account.

- Ask for the customer's recent audited financial statements.

85

Figure 32

DAYS CREDIT FORMULA

$$\frac{\text{Average accounts receivable outstanding}}{\text{Annual sales level}} \times 365 = \text{Average days taken by customers to settle accounts}$$

DOE COMPANY DAYS CREDIT

Last year	This year
$\dfrac{\$410,000}{\$5,000,000} \times 365 = 30$ days	$\dfrac{\$640,000}{\$5,000,000} \times 365 = 47$ days

---

- Set credit limits and terms and monitor the account in the first few months.

- Refer to Dun & Bradstreet where possible or applicable.

How to Collect Accounts Receivable

A past due account represents potential stolen merchandise.

It's as simple as that. Credit is the backbone of businesses, and as companies expand, they often overextend themselves into bankruptcy. Here's a detailed plan of action to get your cash in—fast!

How much does credit cost?

You sell $1,000 worth of widgets on credit to XYZ Manufacturing Company. You've done business with XYZ in the past, and although you've sometimes had to send two or three invoices, eventually the bills have been paid. Your profit margin on the widgets is 5%.

Several months go by, and the amount is still outstanding. When you pursue the collection, you discover that XYZ has gone out of business.

At a profit margin of 5%, you must sell $20,000 of widgets to offset the $1,000 you can't collect.

Figure 33 shows just how much uncollected accounts can cost you.

How to invoice for fast payment

The logical place to start in collecting accounts receivable is with the invoice. The invoice should be mailed the same day the goods are shipped or delivered.

Make your invoices clear and easy to read. Include the date ordered, the person who placed the order, the date shipped or delivered, a description of the goods, the unit price, and the total amount. Underline any discount for prompt payment.

Finally, make it easy for the customer to communicate with you. Enclose a return envelope. Print the telephone number and your bookkeeper's name conspicuously on the invoice.

Figure 33

COST OF BAD DEBTS

Profit Margin	Additional Sales Needed per $100 of Uncollected Accounts
5%	$2,000
10%	1,000
15%	666
20%	500
25%	400
30%	333

Following up stale accounts

The cardinal rule for collections is consistency. Develop a system and adhere to it. Your customers will learn what to expect from you and will respond to an established plan of action. Here's one system that you can either use or modify for use in your company.

First: Send a "memory-jogger" on the tenth day after payment is due. ("Have you overlooked our statement?") At this point, well-intentioned customers may call to report that the original invoice was misplaced, or to ask for clarification of some items. Attend to their questions immediately, and the payment will usually follow promptly.

Second: Thirty days after the payment was due, telephone the customer and politely—but firmly—request immediate payment. The goal of this first telephone call is to get a commitment from the customer as to the exact date when the payment will be made.

Third: Record the payment date commitment on a calendar and telephone again on that date if payment has not been received. You will build credibility and create a no-nonsense impression by your immediate action. Do not wait even 24 hours after the agreed-upon date.

Fourth: Repeat the third step as many times as reasonable under the circumstances. But don't carry it on indefinitely. If it looks as though collection is doubtful, tell the customer that his credit has been suspended but will be reinstated if payment is received by a certain date.

Fifth: If no payment has been received by the target date, notify the customer in writing that credit has been suspended and the account will be turned over for legal collection unless payment is received.

Sixth: On the final deadline date, turn the account over to a collection agency, your collection department, or an attorney. Establish a reputation for toughness!

Tested ways to expedite delinquent accounts

• Know your debtor. What will make him respond? Does he have other sources of supply, or will a credit suspension with your company have serious effects on his merchandise flow? Will he be swayed by the threat of damage to a good reputation? Does he have a history of settling in small claims court? Find out everything you can, and tailor your approach accordingly.

• Charge interest. Make your interest rate for delinquency as high as the law allows.

87

You reap a twofold gain: your outstanding cash has not been sitting idle, and your customer will be motivated to stop the interest clock through prompt payment.

• Offer installment payment plans. Collecting small sums regularly is better than not collecting large sums at all. Establish an installment payment plan agreement in writing and have your customer sign a copy of it.

• Vary your collection approaches. If you find yourself dealing with someone who refuses to be available to you, don't give up. Use different envelopes without return addresses; have your secretary place the call; call person-to-person from out of town. Go see him. A confrontation at his home or on the golf course can be unnerving.

• Compromise. Discount the bill for immediate payment. Take back unused merchandise and resell it. Trade the outstanding amount for his goods or merchandise.

• Keep a journal of your progress—or lack of it—directly on the customer's ledger card. You'll have a permanent credit profile which will alert you to potential problems and strategies.

CHAPTER SEVEN

Basic Accounting Techniques

What Is Accounting?

Accounting has often been called the "language of business." Every businessman uses accounting terms and concepts to describe the events that make up the existence of his business. The underlying purpose of accounting is to provide financial information about the business. This information is needed by the businessman himself, to help him plan and control the activities of his organization. It is also needed by others—banks, lessors, investors, creditors, or the public, who have supplied money to the business or who have some other interest that will be served by information about its financial position and operating results. The material contained in this chapter will help you to become conversant with this extremely important language.

The Balance Sheet and Income Statements

Financial statements are the end products of the accounting process. They reveal a clear picture of the profitability and financial status of a business.

The two most important financial statements of any business are the balance sheet and the income statement. These statements are summaries of all pertinent accounting information.

A balance sheet shows the financial position of a business at a given point in time, for example on the last day of the fiscal year. Some businesses prepare a balance sheet every month, some on a quarterly basis, but all businesses must prepare a balance at the end of the business year. This balance sheet contains a list of the assets and liabilities of a business as well as a description of the owner's equity.

An income statement describes profits and losses over a period of time. All businesses must prepare income statements at least once a year to satisfy the IRS. Of course, as with the balance sheet, some firms prepare income statements more than once during the year because they can provide managers with reliable indication of the company's progress.

How to read a balance sheet

Every time you sell products or services on credit, you are acting as a banker. Even though you may conduct periodic credit checks on your customers through Dun & Bradstreet and your bank, if one company becomes a major customer purchasing, say, 5% or more of your total sales, you should make your own analysis of that customer's financial condition. Many companies will not release their income statements, but you can invariably obtain a balance sheet, and this is where your analysis should center. Remember, too, that the condition of suppliers may also be important, particularly if you are buying long lead time items.

No customer or supplier is immune from financial difficulty, nor are bankers infallible judges of corporate solvency. Here's a list of often overlooked points you should check to decide if a company is in a solid financial position.

Date. The balance sheet is a static snapshot of the financial condition of a company on one particular day of the year. Therefore, always try to obtain the most recent statement available—of the past month or quarter if possible.

Auditor's option. Many companies have their year-end financial statements audited by a Certified Public Accountant. The auditor prepares a statement describing the manner in which he conducted the audit and expresses his opinion as to the manner of preparation, consistency with prior periods, and fairness of valuation. Often an auditor will state that his opinion is "subject to" occurrence of some event or a particular accounting principle. In this case he is bringing some special item to your attention, and you should determine whether the qualification is serious. When no auditor's opinion is attached, remember that the figures have been prepared by company management and may be inaccurate or even deliberately misleading.

Footnotes. You can generally detect a company in trouble by carefully reading the footnotes to its balance sheet. This most often overlooked area should be the starting point of your analysis—not an afterthought. Important items to check are:

- Contingent liabilities. Debts that a company may owe do not show up on its balance sheet but could have an adverse impact on the condition of the firm.

- Lease obligations. Obligations for payments under leases are fixed obligations of the company and hence a form of debt. Such fixed commitments may not show up on the balance sheet, however, and leasing used to be referred to as "off the balance sheet financing." Check this area carefully.

- Reserve for contingencies. Many companies will set up a reserve account if they anticipate major losses from a setback, such as a product that failed, bad debts, or a fire. Check the reason for any reserve and assess whether it appears adequate to cover the potential loss.

- Financial arrangements. The balance sheet will tell you how much debt a company has. It will not give you such details as when sinking fund payments must be made, how much remains on a line of credit, or the interest rate the company is paying. For these details, you should consult the footnotes.

- Capitalized items. Companies have the option of showing certain items as assets when, in fact, they may represent only intangibles. Examples that you should check include organizational expenses, goodwill, research and development expenses, and preopening expenses. To test the company's financial condition, eliminate intangibles from the balance sheet by deduction from net stockholders equity (otherwise known as "net worth"). If this results in a deficit net worth or reduces total assets by more than 25 percent, further investigation is merited.

Other problem areas

• Cash. Be aware of a large cash balance. If bank debt under current liabilities is equal to or greater than cash, the company may be engaged in window dressing to give the appearance of greater liquidity than it actually has.

• Receivables. A large portion of the receivables may be uncollectable. Prudent management will establish a reserve for bad debts. Make sure it appears reasonable.

• Inventories. Another significant asset, inventories may be worthless at liquidation. Valuation of finished goods inventory at cost rather than net selling price is more conservative. Also, check the footnotes to see if the company uses the FIFO (first in, first out) or LIFO (last in, first out) inventory accounting system. FIFO is less conservative than LIFO but either is acceptable.

• Net worth. This is the most widely used indicator of a company's financial condition. It represents the difference between the value of assets and liabilities. However, you should look into the computation of net worth. It is made up of two primary items: (1) capital and surplus, being the money paid in by the company's stockholders, and (2) retained earnings (or deficit), being the accumulated result of the company's operations. A deficit indicates that losses have exceeded profits. If comparison with the previous year reveals an increased deficit, then the company may still be losing money.

Reading the balance sheet as a means of evaluating a company's financial condition may have its limitations owing to problems with valuating certain assets. However, your own analysis along with professional advice should help prevent losses.

How to read an income statement

The interaction of an income statement and a balance sheet can be confusing. Basically, a balance sheet shows what assets a business has at a certain point in time and who has claim to them, giving the basic accounting equation: Assets equals Liabilities plus Owners Equity. This means that all the assets of any business are claimed by either: (1) the creditors, such as tradesmen, bond holders, or banks (liabilities), or (2) the owners, who have a right to whatever is left over (owners equity).

Whereas a balance sheet is a static snapshot of assets and liabilities, the income statement is a dynamic summary of the profits and losses of the business over a period of time. Figure 1 shows this important difference.

As you can see from the figure, an income statement bridges the time period be-

91

Figure 1

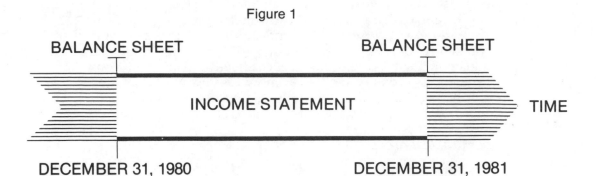

tween the two balance sheets. Any changes in the overall condition of a business from one period to another must be explained by the intervening income statement. Suppose that the XYZ Corporation has a balance sheet at the end of 1981 as shown in Figure 2. Its $10,000 in assets are represented by $2,000 owed the bank, $3,000 in capital that the owners contributed, and $5,000 from past earnings that were retained in the business. As shown on its income statement, 1981 was a profitable year and the company netted $7,800 after taxes. Now to update the old balance sheet.

We can see from XYZ's income statement that all profits for 1981 were retained in the business. Total assets must, therefore, have gone up in 1981. To keep this new balance sheet in balance, an adjustment must now be made to its right side. This is done by taking the retained earnings as of the previous year ($5,000) and adding the profits retained form the current year's operations ($7,800), yielding an updated retained earnings figure as of December 31, 1981, of $12,800. The basic accounting formula is now satisfied, and total assets equal liabilities plus owners equity.

The major elements of an income statement

Accountants have many formats for presenting income statements, but the one in

Figure 2

BALANCE SHEET	INCOME STATEMENT	BALANCE SHEET
XYZ Corporation as of December 31, 1980	XYZ Corporation Calendar Year 1981	XYZ Corporation as of December 31, 1981

ASSETS		LIABILITIES				ASSETS		LIABILITIES	
Cash	$2,500	Bank loan	$2,000	Sales	$100,000	Cash	$9,000	Bank loan	$2,000
Inventory	7,500			Cost of goods sold	80,000	Inventory	8,800		
				Gross profit	20,000				
				Overhead	10,000				
		OWNERS EQUITY						OWNERS EQUITY	
		Paid in capital	$3,000	Profit before tax	10,000			Paid in capital	$3,000
				Taxes @ 22%	2,200				
		Retained earnings	5,000	Profit after tax	7,800			Retained earnings	12,800
				Dividends	0				
Total	$10,000	Total	$10,000			Total	$17,800	Total	$17,800
				Retained earnings	$7,800				

Figure 3 is representative. The important thing is to obtain audited statements with all footnotes. Here is an explanation of the three major components of an income statement:

1. Revenues

Gross sales. This component is the total invoice price of goods shipped, excluding sales taxes or excise duties, charged to the customer. Always check the footnotes to see how sales are "recognized." Significant differences can result depending on whether the company is on a cash or accrual basis, if installment reporting is used, or if goods are shipped on consignment.

Returns, allowances, and discounts. Returns and allowances are sometimes deducted directly from gross sales. Discounts refer to reductions taken by customers for prompt payments, such as 2/10 net 30 days.

2. Expenses

Cost of goods sold. The final amount of COGS is dependent on the inventory convention used. Companies on the "full cost" system sometimes engage in a practice at year's end known as "selling to inventory." This can materially distort profits. A switch to the LIFO system, depreciation policies, and capitalization procedures can significantly affect COGS and profits. Details on all these points should be checked in the footnotes, and any questions should be referred to your accountant.

Selling and general and administrative. These expenses should be itemized, but sometimes they are combined. If not itemized,

Figure 3

ABC CORPORATION INCOME STATEMENT

ABC Corporation Income Statement—Year ended December 31, 1981			Expense ratios (% of net sales)	Profit ratios (% of net sales)
Gross sales		$300,000		
less: Returns & allowances	2,000			
Discounts	4,000			
Net sales		294,000	100.0%	100.0%
less: Cost of goods sold		175,000	59.5%	
Gross profit		119,000		40.5%
less: Selling, general, & administrative	65,000		22.1%	
Depreciation	20,000		6.8%	
Operating profit		34,000		11.6%
less: Interest expense		9,000	3.1%	
Profit before tax		25,000		8.5%
less: taxes		5,500	1.9%	
Profit after tax		$19,500	6.6%	6.6%

check the footnotes for any significant pension expenses, deferred compensation arrangements, bad debts, or unusually high officers' salaries.

Interest expense. This item can be a clue to how much debt the company owes if a balance sheet is not available.

3. Profits

Gross, operating, and profit before tax. Gross profit is the difference when cost of goods sold is subtracted from net sales. Operating profit is the amount the business earns before any financing expense. PBT, the amount of profit on which taxes are computed, is the final amount left after all expenses have been met.

Profit after tax. Many business managers are confused to find that profits before and after tax are sometimes similar; in other words, little tax was paid even though there were healthy profits. Often the explanation is that there were significant investment credits or a healthy loss carryforward. Check the footnotes for details.

What the income statement shows

The significance of a company's income accounts can only be determined by comparing the current figures with: (1) figures of the same company prepared in prior years, or (2) figures available for other companies engaged in a similar business. The easiest way to make these comparisons is to reduce the figures to a set of expense and profitability ratios. These can then be analyzed to reveal significant discrepancies, trends, or problem areas.

Never rely on a balance sheet alone when evaluating a company. Only an income statement can tell and give you the results of current operations and help pinpoint possible problem areas. A strong balance sheet is certainly a point in a company's favor, but its income statement is usually much more indicative of its future prospects.

Financial Ratio Analysis Checklist

Every businessman must be able to check the condition of his business quickly and accurately. Many businessmen, however, examine only raw figures, such as the amount of cash on hand, the dollar amount of accounts payable, and so on. This type of analysis can be highly misleading because it neglects the financial interaction between the various sources and uses of capital. For example, it is of little use to know the amount of your current assets if you do not also examine the level of current liabilities. Ratio analysis provides a number of comparative indicators that you can track from month to month to monitor your company's financial condition, efficiency, and profitability.

1. *Ratios measuring liquidity*

Current assets to current liabilities. The "current ratio" is the most commonly used index of financial strength. It measures the ability of the business to pay its current obligations. A current ratio of at least two is considered prudent in most businesses; less than one is unsound.

Cash, marketable securities, and receivables to current liabilities. Called the "acid test," this is the most severe test of a business's ability to pay its current debts. It eliminates inventory and considers only liquid assets whose value is fairly certain. A rule of thumb is to keep this ratio at least one to one.

2. *Debt ratios*

These ratios consider the ability of the business to meet its long-term obligations as well as the current liabilities measured above.

Total debt to total assets. This ratio measures the relative proportion of the firm's assets that have been contributed from borrowed sources. Certain firms, such as leasing companies, often operate with over 90% borrowed funds. For most businesses, however, a figure from 10% to 40% debt is usually considered a prudent maximum.

Current debt to total debt. This ratio measures the proportion of the company's debt that matures and must be paid within one year. Undue reliance must never be placed on short-term sources of debt, and care must be taken to ensure that a disproportionate amount of debt does not come due in any given year.

3. *Turnover ratios*

Sales to receivables. This ratio indicates how well the business is collecting its accounts. In times of tight money, it is a critical ratio to monitor.

Sales to inventory. This relationship approximates the number of times inventory "turns over" during the sales period. Because inventory ties up a substantial portion of most companies' funds, it is important to keep this ratio as high as possible, without the danger of running out of stock and losing sales.

Sales to fixed assets. This ratio measures how effectively the existing plant and equipment are being utilized. It should be kept as high as possible.

4. *Profitability ratios*

Profit (before interest and taxes) to sales. This common ratio is often called "profit margin." It measures the relative efficiency of operations, although it can be distorted by changes in prices or sales volume.

Profit (after tax) to net worth. Normally called "return on equity," this ratio measures the return to the owners of the business after all taxes and interest have been paid.

The above represent just a few of many financial ratios that are commonly used. Some businesses also monitor certain physical-financial ratios, such as:

- Working capital per unit of product.

- Sales volume per unit of product.

- Fixed costs per unit of product.

- Total capital per unit of product.

Try to identify the critical factors that are unique to your particular business. By periodically tracking only a few key ratios, you can have a fail-safe early warning system to spot any deteriorating conditions. If you would like to see how your company compares with others in your industry, Dun & Bradstreet publishes a 200-page book, *Key Business Ratios,* which contains statistics from the Census of Business on 800 lines of business activities. Write Dun & Bradstreet, 99 Church St., New York, NY 10007, Attention: Public Relations Department.

Elements of Cost Accounting

Almost every manager fears that certain costs may get out of hand without his knowledge. Yet any time a business grows beyond the point where one individual can supervise each and every expenditure, a major element of cost control has been lost. This is why many companies never reach full potential. Management effectively stifles growth by devoting too much time to watching minute expenses and not enough time determining which products are most profitable and promoting their sale. In any business the key to staying on top—and growing—is an effective cost accounting system.

What is meant by cost accounting

When a businessman says something costs him a dollar to produce, what does he really mean? Is he talking about the material cost, the materials plus labor, or all the direct costs to produce the item plus some allocation for overhead? To avoid confusion, it is important to understand how various costs are defined. Figure 4 shows a cost breakdown for a typical manufactured item that has a "full cost" of $1. Similar groupings of costs could be used for service or retail firms.

Elements of full cost

As you can see from Figure 4, costs break down into the general categories of ma-

Figure 4

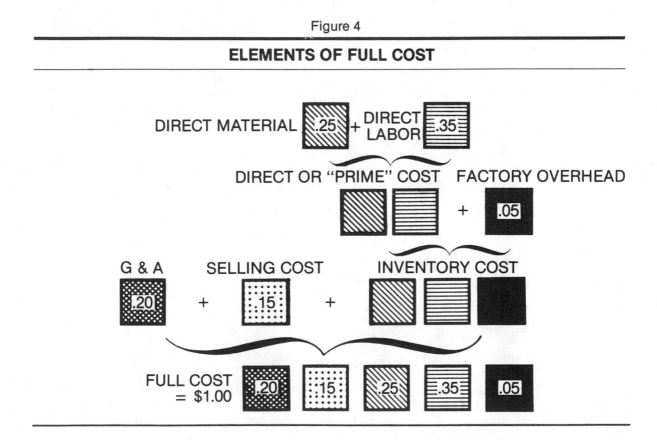

96

terial, labor, and various types of overhead costs. Here are examples of each type:

- Direct material cost includes raw materials that become part of the final product. Not included are supplies, such as tool bits and lubricating oil, that are used in production but do not become part of the final product.

- Direct labor cost includes those labor costs that can be traced directly to the production of the product. A direct relationship exists between the number of units produced and direct material and direct labor costs.

- Factory overhead is all manufacturing costs except direct materials and labor. This includes expenses of the factory, such as janitors, tool room keepers, supplies, heat, water, lights, maintenance, depreciation, taxes, etc. The sum of direct materials and labor and factory overhead yields the cost at which completed goods are carried in inventory. In financial accounting, when the items are eventually sold, this amount is called "cost of goods sold."

- Selling cost includes the costs incurred to get the goods from the factory to the customer. Included are such expenses as shipping and salesmen's commissions.

- General and administrative cost is a catchall category to reflect expenses not covered above. This category includes officers' salaries, research and development, accounting, legal, and public relations costs.

The difference between cost accounting
and financial accounting

Although interrelated, cost accounting and financial accounting differ considerably and are used for dissimilar purposes.

Financial accounting. This is the familiar type of accounting that involves an income statement and a balance sheet. As the term "financial accounting" implies, its primary use is summarizing all the financial information concerning a firm at a particular time. It is based on rather rigid principles, relies on past history and information, and is of special interest to outsiders, such as lenders or investors. Chart 1 in Figure 5 shows an example of financial accounting.

Cost accounting. Primarily for internal use of a firm, it is not bound by rigid accounting principles, and its main purpose is to help management make decisions about the future. Note on Chart 2 in Figure 5 that cost accounting breaks down by product line the aggregate figures provided by Chart 1 so each cost element can be analyzed in detail.

How cost accounting is used

Cost accounting allows management to easily and quickly pinpoint problem areas. Here are several examples:

- Which product to produce? The fact that Product C is in trouble is immediately visible from Chart 2. Its manufacturing costs are out of line, and it may have to be dropped. It is able to carry $3,000 of factory overhead, and this is a point in its favor. Nevertheless, if some plant capacity devoted to Product C could be di-

Figure 5

FINANCIAL AND COST ACCOUNTING

Chart 1
Financial Accounting System

XYZ Company
Statement for Month Ended Nov. 30, 1981

Sales		$50,000
Cost of goods sold:		
Direct materials	15,000	
Direct labor	10,000	
Factory overhead	10,000	35,000
Gross profit on sales		15,000
Selling expense		5,000
General & administrative		5,000
Net profit before tax		$5,000

Chart 2
Cost Accounting Approach

XYZ Company
Statement for Month Ended Nov. 30, 1981

	PRODUCT A		PRODUCT B		PRODUCT C	
Sales		25,000		15,000		10,000
Manufacturing costs						
Direct materials	7,500		3,500		4,000	
Direct labor	3,500		3,500		4,000	
Factory overhead	4,000	15,000	3,000	10,000	3,000	10,000
Gross profit (loss)		10,000		5,000		0
Selling expense		2,500		1,500		1,000
General & administrative		2,500		1,250		1,250
Net profit (loss)		$5,000		$2,250		($2,250)
Units completed and sold		1,000		500		500
Selling price per unit		$25.00		$30.00		$20.00
Full cost per unit		20.00		25.50		24.50
Gross profit (loss) per unit		$5.00		$4.50		($4.50)

---

verted to Products A or B, it obviously would be profitable to do so.

• What price to charge? Pricing is a crucial management decision based on many factors, such as competition, state of the economy, regulation, or seasonality. However, management must also have accurate knowledge of its costs, or errors can result.

• Cost control. Once each of the elements of cost to produce an item is known, "standards" can be established. For example, if the average cost of direct materials for Product A is $7.50 per unit, then $7.50 per unit can be set as the direct materials standard. Thereafter, rather than analyze Product A's costs, only deviations from its standard costs would be examined.

Every manager must know the approximate full cost of everything he produces and sells. Without this knowledge, it is impossible to know where money is being made or lost in a business. However, before proceeding further, ask yourself these questions:

- *Do I need a formal system?* If you're right on top of every item of expense in your firm, including close supervision of the labor force, an informal system may be sufficient. If, however, you are at all removed from the productive process, a limited system of cost accounting may be needed to adequately control your business.

- *Is my product (or service) mass-produced or custom-made?* If your production level is fairly steady and your products are uniform, the simpler "process costing" system will be more appropriate. Here total costs incurred by the firm in a period are divided by the number of units produced to arrive at the full cost. To keep on top of a custom-made or changing product, you will need a "job costing" system that accumulates costs for each individual item being produced.

- *What costs should I accumulate and control?* In most businesses, 80% of the costs are caused by only 20% of the expense items. You should worry most about accumulating costs, setting standards, and controlling the crucial 20%.

How to Prepare a Budget

No business action is more fundamental than preparing a budget. Yet a surprisingly small percentage of business managers actually use a budget to help plan and control their operations. They feel that if they know what their sales volume is and if their bank account tells them how much money they have, there is nothing to worry about. Unfortunately, many businesspeople are finding that there is indeed more to worry about. For example, what happens to cash balances if a big order goes out late or raw materials shoot up 15% in price? No business manager will get very far with his banker if he uses a seat-of-the-pants approach to dealing with these working capital problems. Budgets are not simply nice to have anymore—they may be your lifeboat to financial safety.

How to begin

There are many different kinds of budgets, such as sales budgets, production budgets, and expense budgets. The most important one to the average business manager is a cash budget. Let's prepare a hypothetical cash budget for the manager of the Wooley Woolen Factory who is considering a new sweater line. First, estimate sales levels from the new line for the next year. Then, the breakdown between cash and credit sales can be estimated and the length of time to collect the receivables computed. For example, January sales are projected at $20,000. Of this amount, $2,000 is expected to be cash sales and the remainder on credit. Fifty percent of the $18,000 ac-

Figure 6

WORKSHEET

Wooley Woolen Factory—Preliminary Worksheet for New Sweater Line

	Jan.	Feb.	March	April	May	June	July	Aug.	Sept.	Oct.	Nov.	Dec.
Total Sales	$20,000	$20,000	$10,000	$5,000	—	—	$5,000	$10,000	$30,000	$20,000	$20,000	$20,000
Cash sales	2,000	2,000	1,000	500	—	—	500	1,000	3,000	2,000	2,000	2,000
A/R Collection												
50% (present month)	9,000	9,000	4,500	2,250	—	—	2,250	4,500	13,500	9,000	9,000	9,000
40% (next month)	—	7,200	7,200	3,600	1,800	—	—	1,800	3,600	10,800	7,200	7,200
10% (third month)	—	—	1,800	1,800	900	450	—	—	450	900	2,700	1,800
Total Cash In	$11,000	$18,200	$14,500	$8,150	$2,700	$450	$2,750	$7,300	$20,550	$22,700	$20,900	$20,000
Purchases												
(30% of sales)	6,000	6,000	3,000	1,500	—	—	1,500	3,000	9,000	6,000	6,000	6,000
Cash Out for Purchases (Disbursements made 30 days after purchase)	—	6,000	6,000	3,000	1,500	—	—	1,500	3,000	9,000	6,000	6,000

counts receivable ($9,000) is expected to be collected in the current month, 40% in the next month, and the rest in three months. These figures are noted by arrows. The cash and collection figures for subsequent months follow the same general pattern. (See worksheet, Figure 6.)

Purchases of raw materials are also heavily dependent on sales levels. In the case of Wooley Woolen, raw materials cost about 30% of sales, and suppliers allow Wooley Woolen 30-day payment terms. As a result, although $6,000 of supplies were purchased in January, the cash was not actually disbursed until the following month.

The final cash budget

Now that the major sources and uses of cash are available from the worksheet,

Figure 7

FINAL CASH BUDGET

Wooley Woolen Factory—Final Cash Budget

	Jan.	Feb.	March	April	May	June	July	Aug.	Sept.	Oct.	Nov.	Dec.
Estimated Receipts												
Cash Sales	$2,000	$2,000	$1,000	$500	—	—	$500	$1,000	$3,000	$2,000	$2,000	$2,000
A/R Collection	9,000	16,200	13,500	7,650	2,700	450	2,250	6,300	17,550	20,700	18,900	18,000
Total Cash In	$11,000	$18,200	$14,500	$8,150	$2,700	$450	$2,750	$7,300	$20,550	$22,700	$20,900	$20,000
Estimated Disbursements												
Purchases	—	6,000	6,000	3,000	1,500	—	—	1,500	3,000	9,000	6,000	6,000
Wages	1,500	1,500	1,500	1,500	1,500	1,500	1,500	1,500	1,500	1,500	1,500	1,500
Rent	1,000	1,000	1,000	1,000	1,000	1,000	1,000	1,000	1,000	1,000	1,000	1,000
Other	500	500	500	500	500	500	500	500	500	500	500	500
Total Cash Out	$3,000	$9,000	$9,000	$6,000	$4,500	$3,000	$3,000	$4,500	$6,000	$12,000	$9,000	$9,000
Net Gain (Loss) In Cash	8,000	9,200	5,500	2,150	(1,800)	(2,550)	(250)	2,800	14,550	10,700	11,900	11,000
Cumulative Total	$8,000	$17,200	$22,700	$24,850	$23,050	$20,500	$20,250	$23,050	$37,600	$48,300	$60,200	$71,200

Figure 8

CASH BUDGET

Original Estimate of Working Capital Needs

	Month					
	1	2	3	4	5	6
Receipts	—	—	$100,000	$100,000	$100,000	$100,000
Disbursements						
Materials	75,000	—	—	—	—	—
Labor	25,000	25,000	25,000	25,000	25,000	—
Total	100,000	25,000	25,000	25,000	25,000	—
Total Gain (Loss) In Cash	(100,000)	(25,000)	75,000	75,000	75,000	100,000
		peak working capital requirement				
Cumulative total	$100,000	($125,000)	($50,000)	$25,000	$100,000	$200,000

Revised Estimate of Working Capital Needs

	Month					
	1	2	3	4	5	6
Receipts	—	$50,000	$100,000	$100,000	$100,000	$50,000
Disbursements						
Materials	—	—	25,000	25,000	25,000	—
Labor	25,000	25,000	25,000	25,000	25,000	—
Total	25,000	25,000	50,000	50,000	50,000	—
Total Gain (Loss) In Cash	(25,000)	25,000	50,000	50,000	50,000	50,000
	peak working capital requirement					
Cumulative total	($25,000)	—	$50,000	$100,000	$150,000	$200,000

Wooley Woolen's manager can prepare his final cash budget.

The basic figures for receipts and purchases were taken from the worksheet. In addition, disbursements for salaries, rent, and other expenses were also accounted for. The result shows the net gain or loss in cash for each month and the cumulative total. (See Figure 7.)

Case history of cash budgeting in action

A small company in the Midwest was notified that it was the low bidder on a subcontract from an aircraft manufacturer to produce part of an engine assembly. The contract called for initial deliveries of parts in two months, with completion of the

101

contract three months later. To meet the deadline, the company first thought it would have to borrow $125,000 for extra working capital. However, by preparing and analyzing a cash budget, it was able to reduce working capital needs to $25,000 and successfully complete the contract. (See Figure 8.)

Note that in the original plan all inventory was to be purchased and paid for in the first month. But by buying supplies only as needed and negotiating 60-day terms with suppliers, the company cut the working capital dramatically. The company also negotiated a progress payment of $50,000 from the aircraft manufacturer, which eased working capital requirements considerably. As a result of both of these actions, the working capital requirements were reduced from $125,000 to $25,000—a figure that the company had no difficulty obtaining. Without a careful look at a cash budget and searching for ways to reduce borrowing needs, the company could very easily have been forced to pass up a lucrative contract.

How a cash budget is used

There are two main uses for a budget—for planning and for control.

> • Planning. Budgeting is the only way that cash requirements can be estimated in advance. For example, your banker will be far more disposed to lend money if you tell him you need $50,000 in two months, and show him that the loan will be liquidated three months after that, than if you say, "I can't meet Friday's payroll!"

> • Control. While never 100% accurate, budgets give a standard against which actual performance can be measured and controlled. For example, if cash receipts are below forecast, either sales are off or collections are down, or both. The slippage is immediately apparent and remedial action can be taken. Similarly, disbursements that are out of line will also be readily visible.

Limitations and pitfalls

Like most management techniques, budgets are no panacea, and they can be used improperly. Watch for these points:

> 1. Budget period. Ordinarily, the budget should be prepared for at least as long as the time required to complete the natural cash cycle from purchase of raw materials (cash out) to ultimate collection of money from sale of the finished goods (cash in). In the case of a sweater manufacturer who produces an inventory for sale next winter, the cycle could be as long as a year. In other cases, only a few weeks or months will suffice. Revise budgets periodically and don't budget too far ahead, or the projections become meaningless.

> 2. Tyranny. Budgets are to be used only as guides. They should not be used to tyrannize employees if the fault for shortcomings lies beyond their control.

> 3. Flexibility. Opportunities can arise and conditions change. Budgets are aids to administration, not substitutes for business judgment.

> 4. Birth pains. Anything new can be difficult to introduce.

There will be resistance to any attempt to tie things down with a budget. Do not expect the budgeting process to proceed smoothly. Any time an employee must commit himself to specifics, such as certain sales levels or holding the line on expenses, he also gives up autonomy. Cooperation will come grudgingly and slowly until the benefits of the system are apparent.

Cost Recovery Methods—Major Changes from the 1981 Tax Act

One of the greatest changes for business taxpayers is in the area of depreciation. The 1981 Tax Act replaces the term with a new concept called "cost recovery." No longer will taxpayers squabble with the IRS concerning "useful lives" of assets. In fact, the new system (called the "Accelerated Cost Recovery System" or ACRS) drastically changes (and simplifies) almost all aspects of recovering an asset's cost.

Straight-line vs. Accelerated Cost Recovery

Before diving into the specifics of cost recovery, let's first consider the basics. As we will see shortly, cost recovery deductions can be computed using either the straight line method or an accelerated method, i.e., 150%, 175%, or 200% declining balance.

> Straight-line. Straight-line (S.L.) is the simplest cost recovery method. Using S.L., the amount subject to cost recovery is deducted in equal installments over the cost recovery period. Figure 9 shows an example based on $1,000 subject to cost recovery over a five year cost recovery period.

> Declining balance. The cost recovery allowance using an accelerated method is found by taking the straight line amount and multiplying it times the appropriate acceleration factor (i.e., 150%, 175%, or 200%). The balance subject to cost recovery actually declines over time, since the previous amount of cost recovery is subtracted each year. Hence the name. The following example, based on a $1,000 asset and 150% declining balance, makes the concept clear.

As you can see, using declining balance, the full $1,000 would not be recovered in five years. For this reason, a switch to the straight-line method is normally made at some point in time. In this case, it would be advantageous to switch in the third year. At that point, $490 of cost still remains to be recovered. Switching to S.L. would allow (490 ÷ 3) or $163.33 to be recovered each year rather than the amounts shown ($147, $103, $72).

Figure 11 is a graphic illustration of straight-line vs. the 150% declining balance method.

Recovery property categories

The 1981 Tax Act places all "recovery property" (i.e., property subject to cost recovery) into five categories. The ones of interest to most business people are as follows:

> *Three-year property.* Autos, light trucks, as well as machinery/equipment used in connection with R&D.

> *Five-year property.* Most recovery property will fall into this

103

Figure 9

STRAIGHT LINE DEPRECIATION

Year	Calculation	Depreciation Expense
1	(1/5 × $1,000)	$ 200
2	(1/5 × 1,000)	200
3	(1/5 × 1,000)	200
4	(1/5 × 1,000)	200
5	(1/5 × 1,000)	200
Total allowable depreciation		$1,000

class. It includes any property not classified as three-year or fifteen-year property.

Fifteen-Year Real Property. Generally, this category includes all improvements to real property (real estate.)

As you can see, virtually all business property is given an arbitrary five-year recovery period, except autos and light trucks, which are three-years. Also, estimated salvage value does not have to be deducted from initial cost for purposes of cost recovery, as it was under prior law.

Recovery allowances under ACRS

The method of recovery for cost of an asset placed into service after December 31, 1980, and before January 1, 1985, is based on a 150% declining balance method, converting to straight-line when most advantageous to rapid cost recovery. Translated into plain English, here are the percentages of an asset's costs you can recover each year. Note that these percentages will change to allow even more rapid recovery for assets placed in service in 1985 and thereafter.

Note that under ACRS the so called "half-year" conversion applies. Property placed in service in the first year is arbitrarily assumed to be used one-half year; however, in the year property is disposed of, no recovery deduction is allowed for that year.

Turning now to real estate, taxpayers may *elect* to use straight-line recovery over the 15-year recovery period. Otherwise, 175% declining balance may be used (200%

Figure 10

150% DECLINING BALANCE COST RECOVERY

Year	Amount Subject to Cost Recovery	Calculation	Cost Recovery Deduction	
1	$1,000	($1000 × ⅕) × 150%	$ 300	
2	700	(700 × ⅕) × 150%	210	
3	490	(490 × ⅕) × 150%	147	163.33*
4	343	(343 × ⅕) × 150%	103	163.33*
5	240	(240 × ⅕) × 150%	72	163.33*
			$ 832	1000.00

*Switch to straight-line.

declining balance if low-income property), later switching to straight line when advantageous to maximize deductions. The half year conversion does *not* apply in the case of real property. Also, breaking down property into "components" and depreciating each separately is no longer allowed. Finally, as under prior law, land is not subject to cost recovery.

Figure 11

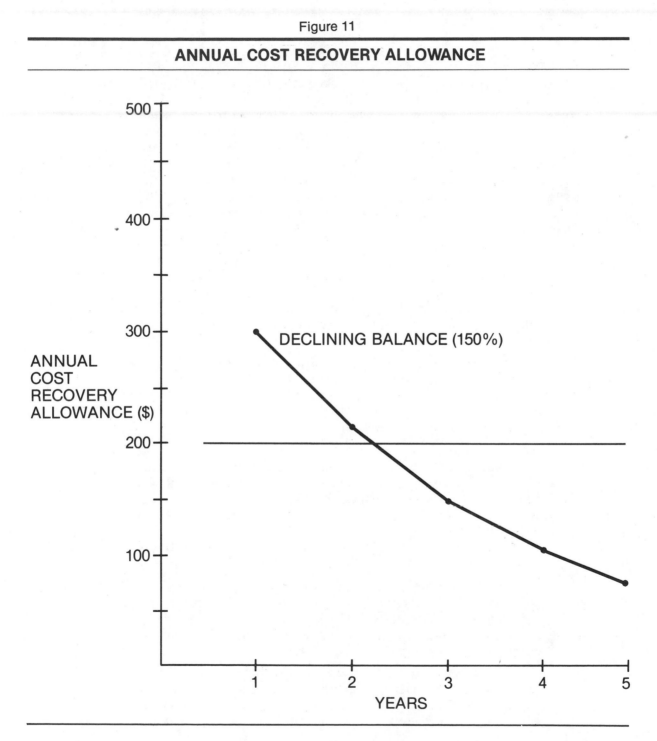

ANNUAL COST RECOVERY ALLOWANCE

DECLINING BALANCE (150%)

ANNUAL COST RECOVERY ALLOWANCE ($)

YEARS

Cost recovery recapture

As you recover the cost of an asset through cost recovery, you lower its cost basis. If you sell that same asset for a price that is higher than the adjusted cost basis, you are considered to have sold it at a gain. Generally, gain that is realized because of cost recovery is said to have been "recaptured," and that gain will be taxed as ordinary income. The IRS, however, treats cost recovery recapture on the sale of personal property and real estate in different ways. Let's look first at the treatment of personal property, using numbers to keep the issue clear.

Personal property. Gain from previous cost-recovery deduction (i.e., you sell the used property for more than its adjusted cost basis) is taxed as ordinary income. This applies to personal property depreciation taken after 1962. (Prior to 1962, gain on depreciation was taxed at lower capital gains rates.)

Suppose you have a machine that was purchased in 1981 for $8,500 and you took $3,000 cost recovery on it before selling it in 1983 for $7,000. The adjusted basis at time of sale (purchase price less cost recovery) was $5,500, so gain on the sale amounted to $1,500. Since the gain ($1,500) is less than the cost recovery ($3,000), the whole gain is considered "recaptured and is taxed as ordinary income.

But if you sold the same machine for $9,000, the gain would be $3,500 (sales price less basis of $5,500) and the $3,000 attributable to cost recovery would be recaptured and taxed as ordinary income, while the extra $500 would be taxed at capital gain rates.

Real property. The rule in regard to "real property," or real estate, is that all cost recovery is recaptured and taxed as ordinary income if the property is held for less than one year. The rule for property held for more than one year varies, depending on the years in which depreciation or cost recovery was taken, and whether the property is residential or commercial real estate.

> • 1964-1969. Depreciation taken during these years is recaptured according to an IRS schedule that determines the proper taxable part of the excess of accelerated depreciation over straight line depreciation.

> • After 1970. If you sell property on which accelerated depreciation was taken in or after 1970, all the excess accelerated depreciation over straight line depreciation is usually recaptured. For example, suppose you own property for three years and take $2,000 accelerated depreciation. Had you elected to take straight line, let us say that the depreciation would have been only $1,200 over that same three year period. So, if you then sell the property, $800 of the depreciation is recaptured and is then taxed as ordinary income.

> • Post 1980 commercial property. *All* gain due to previous cost recovery deductions will be recaptured as ordinary income. Note a critical point. The above risk is a significant departure from previous law and makes the use of accelerated cost recovery on commercial property general inadvisable.

> • Post 1980 residential property. Gain to the extent that accelerated cost recovery deductions exceed the recovery that would have resulted from straight line is taxed as ordinary income. Note that the result of the new 1981 Tax Act is to make in-

vestment in residential real estate considerably more attractive than commercial property.

Having recapture taxed as ordinary income can be a costly experience. Therefore, it would be pleasant to avoid depreciation and/or cost recovery recapture if possible. Here are a few ways to do it.

1. Do not use accelerated cost recovery on commercial property acquired after 1980.

2. Hold onto real estate for at least a year. All cost recovery is recaptured (be it straight line or accelerated) if the property sold is held less than 12 months. It all gets taxed as ordinary income. But if you hold on for more than one year, you only recapture the difference between straight line and accelerated depreciation unless it's commercial real estate. There is an exception to this in the area of residential rental property. You should check with your tax adviser if you need details on this matter.

3. Sell the corporation's stock, not the assets. Instead of selling a corporation's assets, which would be subject to expensive recapture, sell the corporation's stock. That way you avoid recapture.

4. Borrow on the property instead of selling it. Suppose you need money and you have property to sell. If you sell it, you may get hit by a large cost recovery recapture, but if you borrow on the property—refinance it—you will not pay for cost recovery recapture.

5. Give the property to a member of the family. If you want to sell a property that will be subject to heavy recapture, consider giving it to your son or daughter. They will still have to pay the recapture, but their ordinary tax rate is probably considerably less than yours.

6. Use straight line cost recovery. This option is painfully obvious, but seldom used since you lose the "time value" of current tax deductions from accelerated cost recovery.

These are just a few suggestions for avoiding expensive cost recovery recapture. Whether you or your tax adviser can find a way to get around recapture or not, be aware that the effect of recapture can be significant, especially if it catches you unaware.

LIFO vs. FIFO: Managing Your Inventory

How much tax you pay is determined, to a large extent, by the particular inventory valuation method you choose. Unknown to many businesspeople, there is considerable latitude to either increase or reduce stated profits by the selection of certain inventory accounting methods—all perfectly acceptable to the IRS and in complete accordance with guidelines known as GAAP (Generally Accepted Accounting Principles).

Cost of goods sold

Look at the income statement of almost any business, and you will see that one item usually stands out as a prime determinant of the company's profit—cost of goods sold. (See Figure 12.)

As this typical income statement shows, the cost of goods sold figure of $650,000 is by far the most significant expense item. It is computed by taking the inventory on hand at the beginning of the year, adding the amount of purchases during the year, and then subtracting the inventory at the end of the year. This yields the amount of inventory that was used up during the year and must, therefore, be subtracted as an expense from the sales revenue figure.

Valuation of inventory

Thus far, everything is quite straightforward. The problem arises, however, when computing two critical factors in the cost of goods sold formula—the values of the inventory at the beginning and at the end of the year. Here's why: Many businesses find it impossible or impractical to segregate their inventory, and, as a result, stocks are commingled, regardless of when they were acquired. As an example, a manufacturing business may keep a certain grade of steel on hand. The company uses and replenishes the stock as needed throughout the year without physically identifying which particular lot was used. At the end of the year, however, the accountant has a dilemma —should he assume that the inventory was consumed in the order it was acquired and that what is left is the most recently purchased stock? Or, should he consider that the latest inventory purchased was used first and that it is actually the older stock that is still on hand?

Well, in actual fact, the accountant generally doesn't know or care how the inventory was physically used—what he is more concerned about is adopting a bookkeeping convention that will place a reasonably accurate value on the inventory and can be followed consistently from year to year.

LIFO vs. FIFO

In order to value inventory consistently year after year, two main accounting systems are generally used:

> • Last-In, First-Out (LIFO) assumes that the more recently acquired inventory was used first and that remaining stocks consist of older material.

> • First-In, First-Out (FIFO) assumes that there is an orderly flow of inventory and that the first material purchased is the first consumed.

Here's the reason for the different systems. When prices are stable, both LIFO and FIFO yield the same results. But in times of inflation or shortages when prices are rising, LIFO yields a lower net profit figure because the cost of goods sold under LIFO assumes that the most recently bought (and the most expensive) inventory has been used. FIFO, on the other hand, yields a higher profit since it is assumed that older stock (bought at lower prices) has been used. Keep in mind, however, that when using either LIFO or FIFO, it makes no difference which physical items in inventory are actually consumed. The FIFO and LIFO methods are merely bookkeeping conventions for determining the value of inventory. Let's consider an example that will clarify the situation.

As you can see from Figure 13, all numbers to arrive at gross profit are the same, except for the valuation of the closing inventory. Under the LIFO system, it is assumed

Figure 12

INCOME STATEMENT

XYZ Company—Year Ended 12/31/80

	Sales revenue		$1,000,000
Less:	Cost of goods sold:		
	Inventory, January 1	$400,000	
	Purchases	600,000	
Less:	Inventory, December 31	350,000	650,000
	Gross profit		350,000
Less:	Overhead		225,000
Less:	Interest		25,000
	Profit (before tax)		$ 100,000

---

that the most recently purchased (last-in) inventory was the first to be consumed (first-out). Therefore, what remains as of December 31 is the stock that was on hand at the first of the year valued at $10 per unit times 40,000 units, or $400,000. In contrast, FIFO assumes that the original inventory (first-in) was the first consumed (first-out) and that the ending stocks consist of the most recently acquired material, valued at $12 per unit or $480,000. Hence, the value placed on the closing inventory is lower under the LIFO system, which results in a higher cost of goods sold and lower profit figure than FIFO. The LIFO system, therefore, yields a considerable tax deferment and will continue to do so each succeeding year in which material costs continue to rise, so long as the closing inventory in terms of units doesn't drop below the quantity on hand in the beginning of the year LIFO was adopted.

Advantages of LIFO

Inflation has a tremendous effect on corporate profits. Every time inflation goes up 1%, the income taxes of some companies potentially go up by nearly one-half that

Figure 13

INCOME STATEMENT—LIFO VS. FIFO

XYZ Company—Year Ended 12/31/80

		LIFO		FIFO	
	Sales revenue		$1,000,000		$1,000,000
Less:	Cost of goods sold:				
	Inventory, January 1: 40,000 units @ $10	400,000		400,000	
	Purchases: 50,000 units @ $12	600,000		600,000	
	Inventory,December 31:				
	40,000 units @ $10	(400,000)			
	40,000 units @ $12			(480,000)	
			600,000		520,000
	Gross profit (before overhead, interest and taxes)		$ 400,000		$ 480,000

---

much (assuming a 46% tax bracket). Hence, it can be a large drain on corporate profits. LIFO eliminates these so-called "inventory profits," which can be so deceptive of true performance, by directly linking the current sales price of merchandise with the current cost to produce it. Hence, it is the taxpayer's defense against an undeserved tax on "paper profits" as opposed to real ones. Here are several other points to consider:

- If desired, you may designate that only certain raw material items be place on the LIFO system while others can be left on FIFO.

- Work in process and finished goods inventory (as well as their individual components of materials, labor, and overhead) can be selectively placed on LIFO, if desired.

- Where there is a wide variety of similar products, a "dollar value" method of LIFO can be used whereby inventory value is based on price indices published by the Department of Commerce. In addition, some manufacturers create their own price change index for certain commodities.

How to adopt the LIFO method

You do not have to elect the LIFO method until after your tax year is over. You then file for use of LIFO on Treasury Form 970 and, once granted, you must continue to use the LIFO system in subsequent years, unless the IRS again authorizes a change. Once LIFO is adopted, the IRS generally requires that it be used for both book as well as tax accounting, although new regulations (January 16, 1981) allow FIFO reports for internal management purposes and for interim statements (i.e. less than 12 months). Also, the 1981 Tax Act makes LIFO significantly more attractive for small businesses. In particular, any business with $2,000,000 or less in gross receipts need only use a single LIFO "pool." This greatly simplifies LIFO computations and reduces cost.

As we have seen, often a company can increase or decrease its taxable profits by selecting an appropriate inventory valuation method. However, both the IRS and accountants insist that you consistently follow whatever method is chosen.

Any company with large inventories should give serious consideration to a switch to LIFO. The only significant disadvantage to LIFO is that if inventory prices fall, profits may be overstated. But, with inflation and the burden of taxes on the inventory profits of companies that do not use LIFO, the switch may not be a choice. It may become a practical necessity.

CHAPTER EIGHT

Sources of Money for Your Business

Debt or Equity Funds— What's Best for You?

The question of whether to finance expansion by selling stock or borrowing is a common one. In general, most businessmen should put off selling equity as long as possible in order to have a better chance of selling shares later at a higher price. However, tight credit conditions plus the insistence of many bankers that more equity funds be put in some companies' balance sheets has forced many businessmen to reassess the equity alternative. There are no easy answers to financing problems, but there are certain tools available to help you understand the relative costs of your alternatives. One of the most common techniques is called "EBIT analysis."

Comparative cost of debt and equity

Whenever a business obtains funds from outside sources, there is an explicit cost to the shareholders. If debt is used, the interest charges reduce total earnings and hence "earnings per share" (EPS). Selling stock, on the other hand, does not "cost" anything in terms of reducing earnings, but since a larger number of shares become outstanding, the EPS are proportionately reduced. Hence one analytical way to compare debt and equity alternatives is to analyze the impact of each on EPS.

Consider the following example. You wish to expand your plant and need $200,000. The bank has agreed to lend the money, but they insist on an interest rate of 15% per year. An investor group has also approached you with an offer to buy 4,000 shares at $50.00 per share (20 times this year's estimated earnings of $2.50 per share). Which alternative would you choose?

EBIT analysis

Either way, you will obtain the needed $200,000. But which has a cheaper explicit

111

cost in terms of its impact on EPS? The way to calculate this is by first determining "earnings before interest and taxes" (EBIT). Let's assume that amount is $530,000 and that you also have present interest charges of $50,000 per year. Here is how to proceed with your analysis.

As you can see from Figure 1, even though 4,000 more shares are outstanding, the EPS are slightly higher with the equity alternative. You certainly should not decide to sell stock based on this analysis alone, especially since the EPS in both cases are relatively close. It does illustrate, however, that in many cases selling equity can be advantageous to debt, other factors being equal. Before making a final decision, though, consider the following:

> *Risk.* If you borrow, when must the money be repaid? Don't finance projects with long-term payouts with short-term money. You may be caught by not being able to roll the debt over at maturity. In addition, interest rates could rise. With equity you will always have better cash flow since the money does not have to be repaid.

> *Flexibility.* What are the terms with both debt and equity? Will any restrictive covenants limit your flexibility?

> *Control.* Is there any chance you might lose control if the company sells stock?

> *Timing.* Are interest rates expected to rise or fall? Should you finance this project with equity and a later one with debt when interest rates are hopefully lower? Alternatively, could you sell the shares at a higher price by waiting until later?

> *Leverage.* Most companies should carry only a certain amount of debt. Beyond this point, cash flow is constrained and they become overly susceptible to economic downturns. If your company is leveraged too high, it may be preferable to sell equity even though its explicit cost in terms of EPS is high.

Consider your financing alternatives carefully. In these days of extremely high in-

Figure 1

EBIT ANALYSIS

	Debt	Equity
Present earnings before interest and taxes (EBIT)	$530,000	$530,000
Less: Present interest expense	50,000	50,000
Less: New interest on $200,000 at 15%	30,000	—
Earnings before taxes	$450,000	$480,000
Less: Taxes at 46%	207,000	220,800
Profit after tax	$243,000	$259,200
Common shares outstanding	100,000	104,000
Earnings per share (EPS)	$2.43	$2.49

terest rates, don't lock yourself into an overly expensive debt burden. But don't sell away part of your company either, unless it can definitely be shown to be the preferred alternative. Try using the EBIT technique—it might help you to avoid making a costly mistake!

A Borrower's Checklist:
How to Get the Money You Need

Every businessperson needs to borrow money from time to time. The key to effortless financing is the old Boy Scout motto—Be Prepared! Your bank is in the business of loaning money, and there will rarely be any problem if you've done your homework. Carefully consider the following borrower's checklist before you make a loan application:

Why does the applicant need the money?
When your business needs money, it is a sign of one of two things:

> *Success.* Hence, the need to finance expansion, seasonal sales, inventory, or increase working capital.

> *Failure.* Losing money due to poor management, production problems, sagging sales, deficiencies, etc.

It is your job to convince the loan officer that your need for money is based on success, not failure.

What security does the applicant offer?
Banks normally try to minimize the risk of loss by requiring collateral to secure the loan. Here are several ways to assure your bank that the loan is safe:

> *Endorser, co-maker, or guarantor.* Someone else who will be liable if you default.

> *Lease assignment.* The bank will hold as collateral a lease you have with a third party on property you own.

> *Warehouse receipts.* The bank will loan money against merchandise kept in a public warehouse.

> *Trust receipts.* Used as a legal document for "floor planning" that applies to serial numbered merchandise (such as machines, refrigerators, cars, etc.). You agree to: (1) acknowledge receipt of the merchandise; (2) keep the merchandise in trust for the bank; (3) pay the bank as you sell the merchandise.

> *Stocks, bonds, or life insurance.* The bank holds the foregoing as collateral and lends you money against their cash or current market value.

> *Accounts receivable.* You assign accounts receivable to the bank, which collects them for you.

> *Real estate.* Common collateral for longer-term loans.

> *Chattel mortgages.* A direct lien on specified physical assets such as a machine, vehicle, etc.

What is the character of the applicant?

This is the most important question of all! Collateral is small comfort if the banker questions your integrity. Address this one head on:

> Provide a list of references with whom you've had business dealings.

> Provide a list of any previous borrowings and your payment record.

To protect your good name and make the process easier next time, take these steps:

> If you might be late with a payment, notify your loan officer ahead of time.

> Once the loan is paid, keep sending periodic financial statements.

> Visit with your loan officer occasionally. Keep him informed how you and your business are doing.

Key financial ratios

Here are a few key ratios that almost every lender will want to see:

> *Current ratio* ("current assets" divided by "current liabilities"). Indicates your ability to repay debt and margin of working capital.

> *Debt to equity* ("debt" divided by "shareholder's equity"). Shows if the business is already highly leveraged.

> *Sales to receivables* ("annual sales" divided by "outstanding receivables"). Shows how well receivables are being collected.

> *Operating ratio* ("net income" divided by "sales"). Shows the profit margin of the business.

> *Return on capital* ("net profit" divided by "total capital employed"). Shows how efficiently the business utilizes its capital investment.

> *Inventory turnover* ("cost of goods sold" divided by "inventory at end of period"). Shows how fast inventory turns over.

How to Get a Loan from the SBA

Many business managers who are refused a business loan by a bank never think of turning to the Small Business Administration (SBA). The fact is that by law, the SBA cannot make a loan until you have been turned down by private sources, such as a bank. Here are the facts concerning the many types of SBA loans and how you may qualify.

Types of loans

Traditionally, the SBA has made loans directly to small businesses, but the recent demand for financial assistance has seriously depleted SBA loan funds. As a result, the SBA now emphasizes maximum banking industry participation in each loan. The agency does this by guaranteeing loans made by banks to small businesses or by participating with banks in such loans. Additionally, in 1977 the SBA introduced a program to help provide a contract line of credit for certain businesses. Here again, the SBA

Figure 2

TYPES OF SBA LOANS

Types of Loans	Loan Limit	Loan Purpose	Maximum Loan Maturity	Maximum Interest Rates	Maximum SBA Participation	Collateral	Pre-payment Fee
Direct Loan	$350,000	• Business construction, expansion, or conversion	10 years (up to 20 for construction portion)	Fluctuates with market conditions	lesser of 90% or $500,000	Mortgage on land, buildings, machinery and equipment, automotive equipment, furniture and fixtures, warehouse receipts on inventory, accounts receivable, personal guarantees, assignments of life insurance, etc.	0
Guaranteed Loan	$500,000	• Purchase of machinery, equipment, facilities, supplies or materials • Working capital		Maturity less than 7 years—2¼% over published NY prime rate. Maturity over 7 years—2¾% over published NY prime rate	Up to 90% guaranteed		0
Participating Loan	$350,000			1% below guaranteed rate	75%		0

does not actually lend its funds, but guarantees funds extended by banks. Each of these types of loans is explained in Figure 2. Besides those listed, the agency can also make several special types of loans, such as economic opportunity loans to help disadvantaged persons, disaster loans, and economic displacement loans, to help offset the effects of legislation, such as the Occupational Safety and Health Act.

Who qualifies for an SBA loan?

For purposes of making loans, the SBA defines a small business as one meeting these general size standards:

• Wholesale. Annual sales less than $9.5 million to $22 million, depending on the industry.

• Retail. Annual sales less than $2 million to $7.5 million, depending on the industry.

• Service. Annual sales less than $2 million to $8 million, depending on the industry.

• Construction. Annual sales of not more than $9.5 million averaged over a three-year period. (Special trade construction limits also exist.)

• Manufacturing. Generally up to 1,500 employees, depending on the industry.

How to proceed

If you wait until you are desperate for funds, chances are you may be unsuccessful in obtaining a loan in time. The key to dealing with the government is to have all the necessary paperwork prepared and to allow enough time.

• Prepare a balance sheet and income statement for the previous year and current period.

• Prepare a personal financial statement for any stockholder owning 20% or more of the business.

• State the amount of money needed and explain the purpose of the loan.

• List collateral to be offered for the loan and estimate the current market value.

115

• Take the above materials to your banker and ask for a direct loan. If denied, ask if the bank will participate with the SBA or make an SBA guaranteed loan. In most cases of participation or guaranteed loans, the bank deals directly with the SBA on your behalf.

• If SBA participation for a guaranteed loan cannot be obtained, write or visit the nearest SBA office. To expedite matters, present your financial information when you first contact the Small Business Administration. The process can take as long as several months.

Leasing: An Often Overlooked Source of Funds

Leasing is one of the most important sources of long-term capital. But surprisingly, leasing is often overlooked entirely as an alternative form of financing.

Types of leases

There are two general types of leases:

Operating—Cancelable payments for use of an asset or service with no acquisition or ownership rights. An example would be telephone service.

Capital. Noncancelable commitment to make a series of payments over a fixed time period for use of an asset. The sum of the payments is generally sufficient for the lessor to: (1) recover the equipment cost; (2) pay for interest cost on capital involved; (3) compensate for risk of obsolescence; (4) recover administrative expenses and provide a profit. A frequent result of capital leases is transfer of ownership to the lessee.

Capital leases

Since a financial lease represents a fixed commitment over time, it is, strictly speaking, a form of debt. Because it doesn't always appear on the balance sheet as a liability, however, it has been referred to as "off the balance sheet financing." (It may, however, be listed as a footnote.) Literally thousands of companies are involved in leasing everything from cattle and brood sows to computers and complete chemical plants.

Capital leases are of two types:

• Sale-leaseback—Used to free up capital invested in fixed assets such as land or machinery already owned by the business. The assets are sold to a financial institution and then leased back over time. Purely a financial transaction—the asset doesn't move, only its legal title.

• Direct acquisition lease—Used to acquire specific assets needed in the business. The lessor may be an equipment manufacturer, a leasing specialist, or a financial house.

Advantages of capital leases

Leasing offers several advantages to the businessperson:

• Frees working capital for more productive use (money not tied up in low yielding fixed assets).

• Finances 100% of the cost of assets involved (versus 75 to 80% through other methods).

• Generally leaves normal bank lines of credit undisturbed.

116

• Doesn't require pledging other assets as collateral.

• Allows tax write-offs of certain assets, such as land, that normally can't be expensed (operating lease only).

• Simplifies tax accounting. The entire lease fee is generally deductible. Saves the trouble of cost recovery calculations, recapture, interest deductions, etc. (operating lease only).

• Transfer of investment credits. The 1981 Tax Act now allows corporations to effectively sell investment tax credits through capital leases. Although the rules are complex, this provision is a major advantage to companies unable to fully utilize tax credits.

Disadvantages of leasing

• Higher cost. Generally more expensive than outright purchase and usually more expensive than any other form of financing.
• Loss of salvage value. At expiration of the lease, the residual value of the equipment usually belongs to the lessor. However, some lease agreements allow the lessee to purchase the asset at its market value at the time of lease expiration.

• Capital gain. In a sale-leaseback transaction, if the tax basis of the asset is below its sale price, there may be a capital gain tax to pay on the difference.

Questions to ask before signing a lease
Whether it is a sale-leaseback or a direct acquisition lease, you should always check the following points before signing:

• Investment credit—Who receives the benefit? (It can be passed on to you for a significant tax savings.)

• Insurance—Who pays?

• Maintenance—Who provides and pays?

• Purchase option at end of lease?

• Repossession—On what basis?

• Restrictive covenants—Check your present lending agreement for a prohibition against capital leases.

• Deductibility of lease fees—Check with your accountant or lawyer to be sure there are no terms in the lease that could jeopardize deductibility.

Personal tax breaks—lease to your company
Many businesspeople have found it advantageous to lease assets to their companies themselves, either directly or through a sale-leaseback arrangement. For example, you may own a valuable piece of property which your business could use. Rather than sell it, you can retain title to the property and lease it to the company. You will be able to take a deduction for the depreciation and interest costs, and the company will be able to deduct the lease payments to you. Be sure, however, to have your accountant check the limitation on deductibility of interest. Also, there are some complicated rules relating to "tax preference items" that may apply.

Lease arrangements such as this are not limited to real estate. For example, you can keep patents, equipment, and any other asset you may own outside the business by leasing. It is important, however, to insure that the lease payments hold up as "reasonable" under IRS scrutiny.

Leasing can be done through equipment manufacturers, third-party leasing specialists, or financial houses. In addition, your bank probably has a specialized leasing department or can refer you to an affiliated bank that does. Finally, you should check with your accountant to be sure that any leasing arrangement fits your financial requirements.

Venture Capital: "Secret" Source of Funds

There are three standard ways for a business to obtain funds. For short-term needs, it can rent money at a local bank. For longer-term requirements, it can lease money by issuing bonds. For permanent funds, it can buy capital by issuing stock to investors. When the first two debt alternatives are unavailable, "venture capital" financing can often be a solution.

What is venture capital?

Venture capital (V.C.) has traditionally been the seed capital injected into a new company by investors who become part owners in exchange for the risks they assume.

In fact, today most venture capital firms prefer to invest in a company once it is off the ground, during its so-called second- or third-round financings.

Whenever the investment is made, however, venture capitalists generally take risks and expect returns higher than most other sources of financing.

And although venture capital usually involves smaller firms, occasionally extremely large firms are financed. In fact, the largest venture capital deal in history was that of Federal Express—some $70 million of start-up capital to purchase their fleet of courier jets!

Where is V.C. obtained?

• Wealthy individuals. High tax brackets and the opportunity to deduct most losses against ordinary income make wealthy individuals a prime source of V.C. Generally, these individuals are inclined to take greater risks and to desire less involvement in a business than the institutional sources described below.

• SBICs. Small business investment companies are government-chartered venture capital firms formed specifically to increase the availability of V.C. The more than 600 SBICs break down into those that are controlled by large financial institutions and those that are independent. Many large banks and insurance companies, for example, have captive SBICs that provide equity funds to supplement the debt funds these institutions normally provide. Independent SBICs are sometimes owned by a few individuals or a group of institutions, and some are even publicly held. However, SBICs are normally limited to minority investments, and may not take an active role in management unless covenants of the original purchase agreement are violated.

• Private V.C. firms. These firms are usually related to family fortunes. Notable examples would be the New Court Securities (Rothschilds), Bessemer Securities (Phipps), and Venrock Associates (Rockefellers). These firms maintain the reputation of the family name and desire to make major contributions to society, technology, or industry. Because they can afford to screen opportunities, these V.C. firms tend to prefer large investments (over $100,000) in highly selective situations.

• Corporate V.C. activities. Many large corporations engage in V.C. activities. The investments are usually made in related but noncompeting fields to cultivate potential customers or acquisition candidates. This source is generally not well publicized.

What does a V.C. firm look for?

A venture capital firm divides its analysis of any proposed investment into two main categories—management and business proposition. Here is a checklist of some of the major points it is looking for:

Management

• Self-discipline and motivation. Ability to work hard and deal with prosperity as well as adversity.

• Management expertise and balance. Venture capitalists have seen too many people more adept at raising money than at building a solid business. They shun promoters and look for a management team capable of handling all facets of the proposed business.

• Integrity and reliability. Is there any question?

• Candor and flexibility. Is the candidate realistic about the risks involved? Is he flexible enough to respond to new situations? Are his goals realistic and compatible with the investors'?

• Financial stake. Are the managers staking their financial fortunes on the venture by investing their own funds, however limited?

Business

• Growth potential. Venture capitalists are not interested in static situations. They like to see a tenfold return on their money in five to seven years.

• How can the V.C. liquidate? The venture capitalist is interested in prospects for recovering his investment if he decides to pull out.

• Unique business. A proprietary product or unique service is generally preferred. V.C. firms tend to specialize in certain types of businesses.

• Probability of success and downside risk. Even after careful analysis, over 50% of V.C. investments are complete losses.

• Size of investment required. Each V.C. firm has certain amounts above and below which it prefers not to invest. Most firms prefer to make larger investments since the investigation for a $10,000 proposed investment can take as long as one for $100,000. Individuals tend toward smaller investments.

How to proceed

The first step to take for V.C. financing is to prepare a business plan. The following is a list of topics that should be covered in the plan.

1. Summary.

2. Table of contents.

3. Background and history.

4. Description of product/service.

5. Market:

Who is the customer?

119

How large is the market?
What portion of the market do you hope to penetrate?

6. Competition:

Who are they?
How does their product/service differ?

7. Marketing strategy:

Price.
Method of promotion.
Channels of distribution.

8. Production:

How will the product/service be produced?
How long will production take—one year, three years, five years?

9. Financial:

Past and present balance sheets and income statements.
Future cash flow budgets.
Use of proceeds of the financing.

10. Ownership and management:

Who owns the company?
Short resume of each member of management team.

Sources for further information

The Small Business Administration publishes a complete list of SBICs on a quarterly basis. Write SBA, Investment Division, 1441 Second Street NW, Washington, DC 20416.

An excellent book on venture capital is *Sourceguide for Borrowing Capital* by Leonard E. Smollen, Mark Rollinson, and Stanley M. Rubel. This book describes the maze of federal, state, and local business development programs so that businessmen can easily understand and effectively utilize these sources of capital for their businesses. The book is available in many large libraries, or write Capital Publishing Company, P.O. Box 348, Wellesley Hills, MA 02181 ($49.50 plus mailing).

CHAPTER NINE

Additional Financial Topics

Ten Questions You Should Ask Your Accountant Each Year

Your outside accountant is much more than an auditor. Besides being a valuable source of information with respect to planning, taxation, and control systems, he can help you with many operational problems. However, your accountant must be asked relevant questions before he can supply the services you need. Here are ten questions you should ask every year:

1. What will be our need for funds over the coming year? With tight money and high borrowing costs, it is essential that you know by month, week, or even by day what your cash needs will be.

Review pro forma cash statements and help assess the impact of unexpected fluctuations in sales, receivables, inventory, and interest rates.

Outline the pros and cons of such alternate sources of funds as leasing, factoring, debentures, and equity.

2. Have payroll tax returns and deposits and estimated business income tax deposits been made on time?

Payroll: If $500 or more, federal withholding must be deposited at least monthly in a federal depository bank. In addition, the Internal Revenue Service and most states require the filing of quarterly informational returns. Failure to file a quarterly return usually results in penalties as well as interest charges.

Business income tax: Federal and state governments require deposit of business income taxes throughout the year in anticipation of year-end taxes. Estimates must be paid quarterly and failure to comply results in penalties of up to 20% in the case of the federal government.

3. Can the state of accounts receivable (A/R) be improved? It costs money to be a banker for your customers and any excess funds tied up in A/R can be costly.

Compute your average collection period (A/R divided by average daily sales).

Compare the collection period to normal credit terms and industry norms.

Set up and/or review collection procedures and files.

4. Should we adopt a pension plan? This may be the time to consider a pension or profit-sharing plan. The big advantage of such plans is that pretax dollars go into a fund to be distributed at a future time when, presumably, personal tax brackets will be lower. Also ask about tax-saving features of other plans, such as disability insurance and life insurance.

5. Are all necessary records required by federal and state governments and other authorities available? Payroll statements, general ledgers, journals, cash books, and so on must be kept for varying lengths of time for different authorities.

6. Can the business be split into two or more taxable entities? Does the nature of your business allow it to be split into different taxable entities—perhaps a corporation, a partnership, or sole proprietorship? A Subchapter S corporation might also be used. The resulting split in taxable income may result in substantial tax savings.

7. If incorporated, have all required state annual reports been filed? All states require that corporations file annual reports in addition to state income tax returns.

The reports include a year-end balance sheet and possibly an income statement, as well as information on capital stock, directors, and officers.

The reports become a part of the public record and are often used by credit agencies.

If your company does business in other than its state of incorporation, you may be required to file a tax return in that state as well.

Failure to file properly may mean revocation of your corporate charter and it may mean possible personal liability for corporate debts.

8. Are present accounting systems adequate for future growth?

You may wish to revise present accounting procedures and/or investigate minicomputers and time-sharing service bureaus to reduce clerical efforts and obtain:

Timely information. Statements should be available within ten days of month's end.

Complete information. Basic financial statements supplemented with aged listing of accounts receivable, accounts payable, and pertinent ratios.

Flexibility. The accounting systems should be capable of growing with the business.

9. Do we need certified financial statements? Unless required by lenders, investors, or other outsiders, certified statements can be an unnecessary expense. Your accountant can review your internal controls and furnish unaudited statements that should be just as useful for management purposes.

10. Are assets being adequately protected? Be sure your accountant checks:

Cash control. It is better to have A/R (accounts receivable) and A/P (accounts payable) handled by different people. Also, be sure all receipts are deposited daily to minimize possible juggling of figures.

Inventory. Is there any evidence of undue shrinkage?

Fixed assets. Is full advantage being taken of the 10% investment tax credit? Are the new cost recovery rules being properly used to minimize taxes?

Intangibles. Are taxes being minimized by adequate write-off of organizational expenses, start-up costs, R&D (including the 1981 Tax Act R&D credit), and so on?

Fiscal vs. Calendar Year—Which Can Save You More Money?

Most smaller companies are on a calendar year (ending December 31), while many larger companies use tax years ending in other months. Let's take a closer look at the facts a business manager should know.

First, there are actually three types of accounting years from which you can choose:

Calendar year. Required for any taxpayer who does not elect a fiscal year and used by most individuals, partnerships, and corporations.

Fiscal year. Any 12-month period ending on the last day of any month except December.

> *52-53 week year.* A fiscal year, but varying between 52 and 53 weeks and always ending on the same day of the week.

Now, the obvious question is why use anything other than a standard calendar year? Here are three reasons a new corporation or partnership should carefully consider its "reporting year" options.

Subchapter S corporation

If you choose to be taxed as a "Sub S," where the shareholders pay tax by including a pro rata share of the corporation's income in their personal tax return in lieu of paying tax at the corporate level, you have an opportunity to postpone tax for as long as 14 months. Here is how:

> Assume that you report your personal income on a calendar-year basis.

> You are a stockholder of a "Sub S" corporation which began business February 1, 1981 and will have a fiscal tax year ending January 31, 1982.

> On December 31, 1981 your personal tax year ends, but you do not have to report your portion of the Subchapter S corporation's income (except to the extent that income was paid out as dividends) because its accounting year does not end for one more month. In other words, you can defer your share of the corporation's income into your 1982 calendar tax year. Actually, since final payment of your 1982 personal taxes is not due until April 15, 1983, you can effectively stay over 14 months ahead of most of your "Sub S" tax liabilities. However, check with your accountant to be sure that the proper reports are filed with the Internal Revenue Service.

Graduated tax rates

For the tax years beginning in 1983, ordinary corporations pay only 15% federal tax on income up to $25,000, 18% on the next $25,000, 30% on the next $25,000, 40% on the next $25,000, and 46% on income above $100,000. In the case of a new corporation, you may wish to choose your first fiscal year so that it cuts off as you approach the next highest income bracket.

Budgeting and control

Certain businesses wish to budget and measure performance on strict weekly cycles. For example, you may wish to close your books on the last Saturday of May each year. A 52-53 week year will permit this type of accounting.

What if you already have an established tax year? Should you change? Can you? Whether you should is, of course, up to you and your accountant. Certainly you can, so long as there is a good business reason and the IRS doesn't feel you are only trying to avoid tax.

The procedure to change is to send Form 1128 to the Commissioner of Internal Revenue, Washington, DC 20224. If you are a corporation, no IRS approval is needed so long as:

> The corporation hasn't changed its accounting tax year in the last ten years.

> The corporation isn't showing a tax loss for the current year.

124

The annualized taxable income this year is projected to be at least 80% of last year's income.

The corporation doesn't change its "status"—i.e., become a personal holding company.

The corporation does not elect Subchapter S status in the year following election.

Cash vs. Accrual Accounting

Almost every day businessmen run up against accounting problems. Unfortunately, many managers feel that the subject is too technical for them to understand. In actual fact, armed with only a few basic concepts, there is no reason why you shouldn't manage this important function as competently and confidently as any other part of your business.

Choice of accounting method

One of the most fundamental decisions a manager must make concerns the choice of an accounting method because it determines how and when income and expenses will be computed for his business. Depending on the system you choose, it is often possible to defer certain income items and accelerate expenses in order to reduce taxable income. Here is a list of the eight most common systems:

- Cash.
- Accrual.
- Hybrid.
- Installment.
- Long-term contract.
- Completed contract.
- Deferred payment sales.
- Crop.

The two most popular accounting systems used by businesses are the cash and accrual methods.

Cash method

The cash receipts and disbursements method of accounting is used primarily by businesses where inventories are not a significant revenue-generating factor. These would include many professional firms and individuals whose income consists primarily of salaries, fees, or commissions, as well as certain service, financial, and real estate businesses.

> • *Recognition of income.* Under the cash method, a business does not recognize income until the cash or property is actually received. Sometimes additional income is said to have been "constructively" received and hence is taxable. Examples would be interest coupons accrued on bonds that have not been redeemed or checks from customers that have been received but not cashed.

• *Recognition of expenses.* Deductions for any expenses actually paid are generally allowed (with interest expenses being a notable exception) in the year paid, even though they may actually relate to a different tax year. Hence, under the cash method, expenses can be prepaid or supplies purchased ahead to reduce taxes, so long as they don't materially distort income.

Advantages of the cash method

• Income is not taxable until cash is actually (or constructively) received.

• Taxable income can be reduced by prepaying certain expenses.

• Accounting is simplified, although adequate accounting records must be maintained.

Disadvantages of the cash method

• Unless income is carefully managed, it can bunch up and not reflect the true financial condition of the firm.

• If the business is sold or liquidated, careful attention must be given to the accounts receivable and payable to ensure that income is not accelerated or deductions lost.

Accrual method

This method is used by practically all manufacturing, retail, or service businesses where the production, purchase, or sale of merchandise represents a significant portion of income. The accrual method generally provides a more accurate representation of the true condition of a business at any point in time.

• Recognition of income. Under this method of accounting, income is "accrued" and taxed not when actually received, but when one has the right to receive it. To illustrate, under the accrual concept, a business realizes taxable income when it sells, ships, or invoices an item. Under the cash concept, on the other hand, income would not be recognized until payment is actually received.

• Recognition of expenses. Expenses are considered accrued and deductible when they are payable, not when they are actually paid.

Advantages of the accrual method

• Income and expenses tend to be more closely matched than in the cash method and more acurately reflect the true financial condition of the firm.

• Taxable income is not subject to gross distortion due to accelerated or lagging payables and receivables.

Hybrid method

The hybrid method of accounting is, as the name implies, a combination of two or more of the other recognized methods. It can be used, for example, by a businessman who would prefer the accuracy of the accrual method, but finds the bookkeeping too burdensome. He can use the accrual method to record such major income expense items as sales and purchases while keeping the remainder of the business on a cash basis. The chief beneficiaries of the hybrid accounting method are smaller businesses.

How to change your accounting method

To adopt a new method, even when proper and allowed by regulation, you must file Form 3115 with the IRS and obtain approval. Normally, the form must be filed within 180 days after the start of the year for which the change in accounting method is desired.

Too important for accountants alone

As you can see, accounting policy is not a humdrum science best left to men in green eyeshades. It is a dynamic area of business where decisions can influence the amount of tax you pay as well as have a significant impact on your financial statements and those who read them, such as bankers, creditors, stockholders, and suppliers.

Does Your Financial Year Fit Your Business?

With current economic conditions as they are, it is more important than ever to accurately communicate with lenders and outside shareholders concerning your sales and profits. Many businessmen are hampered by accounting years that distort or confuse true financial performance. Here is what you should know to insure that your business is not inadvertently caught up in the crisis of confidence affecting many companies today.

Many businesses are on a January 1 to December 31 calendar year simply because it coincides with the normal tax year. Other companies adopt a fiscal year (any 12-month period ending the last day of any month but December) for reasons such as conformity with industry practice or because sales are slack and personnel are available to take physical inventory. However, no matter what accounting year is used, it's likely that little thought was given to whether the year accurately reflects the company's profits from quarter to quarter.

A business can have sales that rise and fall according to a seasonal pattern. Profits can also vary. As shown in Figures 1 and 2, cumulative earnings are substantially different, depending on when the company starts its accounting year. If, for example, it opens its books January 1, the company will show two quarters when cumulative earnings are negative. A fiscal year starting October 1 will show one negative quarter and one nearly so. A fiscal year beginning in April or July, on the other hand, would be far more appropriate.

How to change your financial year

If you are in a similar position and wish to change your business calendar, it is permissible to do so under existing federal tax law. However, a tax return covering the fractional year between the close of the old period and the beginning of the new is required. Application to change is made on IRS Form 1128 on or before the fifteenth day of the second calendar month following the close of the short tax year. The change will normally be approved by the IRS if in their view it does not distort income and reduce taxes.

Special rule

Corporations need no approval if: (1) the corporation has not changed its accoun-

---

Figure 1

QUARTERLY SALES AND CUMULATIVE EARNINGS

These comparisons are for one company with the same quarterly sales and quarterly earnings but different starting dates for the fiscal year. Quarterly Sales and Cumulative Earnings are in thousands of dollars.

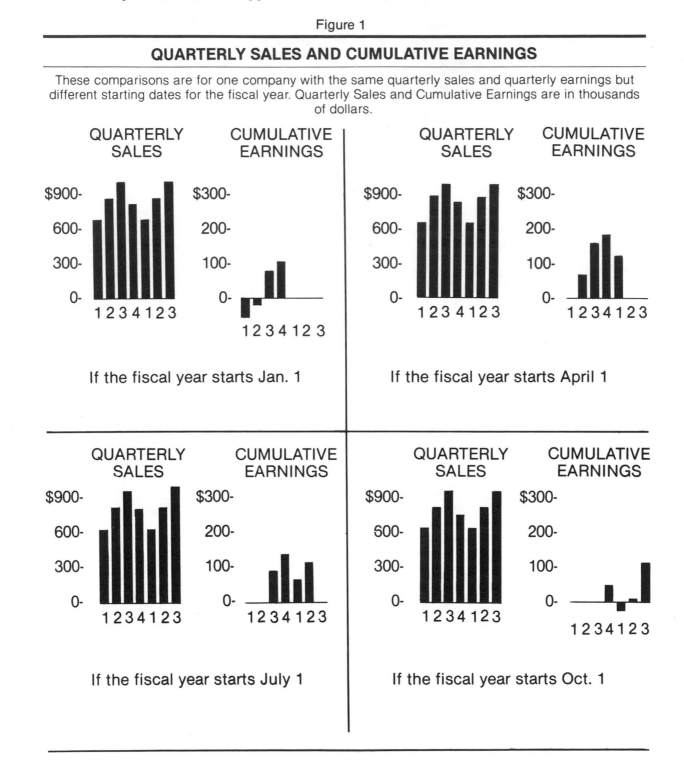

If the fiscal year starts Jan. 1

If the fiscal year starts April 1

If the fiscal year starts July 1

If the fiscal year starts Oct. 1

Figure 2

PROFITS FOR YEAR

1st calendar quarter	$ – 63,000
2nd calendar quarter	+ 46,000
3rd calendar quarter	+ 89,000
4th calendar quarter	+ 28,000
Total profit per year	$100,000

ting year for ten years, (2) the short tax year shows no operating loss, or (3) annualized taxable income is at least 80% of the taxable income for the previous full tax year, (4) corporation doesn't change its "status," (5) corporation does not elect Sub S in the year following election.

Money Market Instruments: How to Maximize Return on Excess Cash

Many companies occasionally have more cash than they need in the near future. For convenience and security these idle funds are often put to work in short-term investments, such as Treasury bills. You should be aware, however, that several other

Figure 3

MONEY MARKET SECURITIES

	Description	Denominations	Maturity	Security	Secondary Market
United States Treasury Bills	Direct obligations of U.S. Government: 3 & 6 months bills auctioned weekly; 1 year bills auctioned monthly	$10,000 to $1 million	Up to one year	Excellent	Excellent
Money Market Certificates	Obligation of issuing bank or S & L but government insured to $40,000 per buyer	$10,000 and up	6 months	Excellent	Can be redeemed, but at penalty
Negotiable Time Certificates of Deposit	Negotiable time deposits in a commercial bank	$100,000 to $1 million	30 days to one year	Dependent on Issuer	Good if well-known issuer
Commercial Paper	Promissory notes of industrial and finance institutions	$25,000 to $5 million	5 to 270 days	Dependent on Issuer	Limited
Bankers' Acceptances	Time drafts drawn on and "accepted" by a banking institution	$25,000 to $1 million	Up to 6 months	Very Good	Fair
Federal Agency Issues	Obligations of federal agencies but not government guaranteed	$1,000 to $1 million	Variable to one year and beyond	Very Good	Good
Short-term Tax-Exempts	Notes of local municipalities or states, some federally guaranteed	$25,000 to $100,000	Variable, usually 6 months to one year	Dependent on Issuer	Good

money-market instruments also exist. (See Figure 3.) Check with your bank to see which of these instruments could be best for your business.

Treasury bills. ''T-bills'' constitute direct obligations of the United States Government and are about the safest and most liquid investment available. These and other government securities can be bought from commercial banks and brokerage firms for a fee or directly from the Federal Reserve.

Money market certificates. These instruments, offered at commercial banks since June 1978, have a yield keyed to the T-bill rates.

Negotiable time certificates of deposit. Basically, a CD is a bank's IOU for a time deposit but with the distinction of being negotiable (i.e., it can be bought and sold before maturity). This gives the corporate treasurer the advantage of somewhat higher yields than T-bills along with good liquidity.

Commercial paper. Unsecured promissory notes issued by industrial and finance companies. Commercial paper has proved a highly popular outlet for short-term funds for many companies.

Bankers' acceptances. A negotiable draft drawn on a commercial bank used to finance commercial transactions. It offers bank creditworthiness, fair liquidity, and usually a higher yield than T-bills and commercial paper.

Federal agency issues. Several U.S. government agencies are allowed to borrow directly from the public. Although these securities are not guaranteed by the federal government, it is considered highly unlikely that they would be permitted to default on an obligation. Because of the slightly higher risk, these securities carry higher yields than T-bills.

Short-term tax-exempts. Obligations of states and municipalities as well as of local branches of such federal agencies as the Public Housing Authority and the Housing and Home Finance Agency.

Taxation

Before deciding whether a particular investment provides a good yield, be sure to check its tax status. T-bills and all federal agency issues except securities of the Federal National Mortgage Association (''Fannie Mae'') are subject to federal taxes but exempt from state and local taxes. Money-market certificates and Fannie Mae issues are taxed at all three levels of government, while tax-exempts are normally free from such taxes. A word of warning about tax-free securities: If an individual or a corporation buys tax-exempt securities rather than paying off its interest-bearing debt, interest on an equivalent amount of the interest-bearing debt may be disallowed.

Cost-Cutting Checklist

Sales are necessary for business; profits are necessary for survival. What keeps a sales dollar from becoming a profit dollar? One thing—expenses. In tough times most businessmen concentrate on increasing sales when it might be more productive to concentrate on cutting costs. A $100 increase in sales may increase profits by $10, but only a $10 decrease in costs is equivalent to a $100 increase in sales, since reduced costs flow directly to the "bottom line" as additional profits. Put your effort where you get the most profit leverage—in cutting costs. Here are some ways to reduce expenses in your company:

Productivity. More output per employee and per dollar invested means lower costs. To remain competitive, start programs now for higher productivity among your work force.

• Upgrade employees. The government will pick up much of the tab to train and upgrade skills of your employees. For more information, contact your state employment office.

• Solicit ideas. No one can save you more money than your employees if the proper incentive and recognition are given by top management. Suggestion programs and an "open door" policy can save thousands.

Payroll.

• Overtime. Slash overtime by: (1) adding shifts, (2) staggering working hours, (3) hiring part-timers for peak loads, (4) personally inspecting all overtime records to be sure the work was necessary. Also, cut mandatory overtime payments under the Wage-Hour Law by qualifying supervisors and foremen as "exempt" employees with varying workweeks on a "guaranteed wage" plan and granting compensatory time off in slack periods in lieu of cash overtime payments.

• Special employees. Whenever possible, hire employees who are less expensive in terms of salary, benefits, recruitment, and payroll taxes than your regular work force. Keep close track of everyone who performs services for you. Many such persons may be classified as "independent contractors" which means you can avoid needless payroll taxes.

• Unemployment taxes. To successfully cut expenses in this area: (1) Learn how the "experience rating" works in your state. There are four types of plans: (a) reserve ratio, (b) benefit wage ratio, (c) benefit ratio, and (d) payroll stabilization. (2) If at all possible, avoid layoffs that will increase your rating. (3) Be sure your experience rating is correct. A small error could cost hundreds or thousands of dollars. (4) Take aggressive action to insure that all claims paid from your account are fully justified. Appeal any that are questionable.

• Worker's compensation. Take the following steps: (1) Review your policy and compare it to several other insurers (there are both mutual and stock companies as well as state-run funds) to determine the lowest net premium. (2) Insist on preemployment physicals to avoid undetected disabilities. (3) Use the insurance company's safety engineers. They are experienced, expert, and usually free. (4) Review your experience rating to be sure it is correct.

Purchasing.

• Discounts. Take advantage whenever possible. For example, if you pass up "2/10 net 30" terms, you are paying 36.5% per year for use of a supplier's money! Use blanket orders. Buy everything you need in one bulk discount but have it delivered and pay for it only as you need it.

• Economic order quantity. See the next chapter to determine the proper EOQ for major inventory items. Also, conduct a "make or buy" analysis on purchased items to see if you can possibly make them cheaper.

• Suppliers fair. Advertise what you want to buy rather than sell, or even set up a "suppliers fair" where potential vendors can come to see what you need. And shop around! It is convenient to go to a known vendor, but he could be considerably more expensive.

Advertising.

• Keyed media. Find some way to "key" media to tell which are most effective—eliminate the least effective. Drop some of the out-of-town Yellow Pages listings if they have not been productive. Test the pulling power of slightly smaller newspaper ads.

• Accounts receivable. Take an aggressive stance with late payers. Being a banker to your customers means you have to borrow more at your bank and pay high interest charges.

• Production. Value analysis looks for new techniques, materials, and procedures to do the same job at a significant cost savings. Always ask the following "value analysis" questions about everything you make, buy, or sell: What does it do? What does it cost? What else would do the job cheaper but as efficiently?

Little-Known Ways to Cut Postal Expenses

Behold the humble postage stamp. Amazingly, it can cost you thousands of wasted dollars each year!

Use these little-known—but proven—tips to cut costs and increase your mailing efficiency.

You have a consultant at the Post Office

The best (and least-known) tip of all: Get to know your Postal Service customer service representative. CSRs are liaisons between the post office and the business mailing world. This valuable, free service will save you countless hours, dollars, and aspirin tablets.

The Postal Service publishes various bulletins (at little or no cost) for specialized mailing needs. Ask your CSR which publications are best for your operation.

Use the Postal Service's special equipment (which they will provide at no charge). Canvas bags for bulk mailings, steel racks to hold the bags, large canvas carts on wheels, trays—all of this equipment will not only make your operation more convenient but will cut processing time.

Classification of certain types of mail is open to interpretation. If you can't determine the exact classification, ask your CSR for help. And if you feel that you're entitled to a different classification that would lower your costs, protest and appeal to your Postal Services Center.

Mail at the right rate for the job

Mailing at the cheapest rate isn't always the best rate. Mail at whatever rate is right for the job. Here is where your customer service representative can really help out. The *Postal Manual* is updated weekly and is virtually impossible to wade through without assistance. Your CSR is trained to lead you through the morass of constantly changing regulations.

First-class mail can be presorted by ZIP code for a substantial discount, if you have at least 500 pieces. See your CSR for details.

Use the distinctive green diamond border, reserved exclusively for first-class mailings, on your oversized pieces for instant identification.

Although the "air mail" designation is obsolete (all nonlocal mail is sent by air), envelopes with "Air Mail" printed on them give your mail a look of priority and urgency.

Second-class mail is reserved for newspapers and other periodical publications that are mailed at least quarterly. If your company mails bulletins or newsletters, second class will be only a fraction of first or third class.

Two hundred identical pieces mailed at the same time qualifies you for reduced third-class (bulk mail) rates.

Special fourth-class book rates (at up to 60% savings) apply, in general, to books of 24 pages or more.

Invoices must be sent first class (except those related to a third- or fourth-class parcel; those may be enclosed).

There's a surcharge if your mail does not meet certain dimensional standards. Your CSR can give you details.

Make special postal services work for you

Certified mail costs one-third of registered mail and is just as effective unless the package has insurable value or irreplaceable contents.

Registered mail is the only class of mail that is traceable. The constant tracking involved causes it to move more slowly, but if you have irreplaceable documents traveling through the mails, it's definitely worth the extra cost and delay.

Special delivery does not give any priority in transportation but does add immediate delivery upon receipt at the addressee's post office. It should never be used on Friday. (Chances are the mail would reach its destination by Monday without special delivery.)

Priority mail routes heavier pieces (13 ounces to 70 pounds) at first-class speeds for a surprisingly low cost.

Streamline internal procedures

Speed your mail 20% by "traying"—placing it in trays with postage and addresses facing in the same direction. (The Postal Service will provide the trays.)

Presort your mail into "local" and "out of town" for faster delivery. Saves the post office one step—two, if the mail is metered and so marked.

Metered mail must be deposited the day it is postmarked, or you run the risk of getting it all back for remetering. If you'll be mailing after the last pickup, change the meter date.

Parcel post packages may not be deposited in, or left beside, street mailboxes. You must take them to the post office.

Direct-mailing houses will process your large or bulk mailings for you. Look in the Yellow Pages under "Mailing."

A penny saved . . .

Get a 90% rebate from the post office on unused or spoiled metered envelopes and tapes.

Is your postage scale accurate? Nine pennies should weigh exactly one ounce. Check it once a month—more often if your scale is subject to frequent temperature changes.

Train anyone who will be using the postage meter. That machine is cranking out money.

If you repeatedly mail bulky, heavy reports, consider microfilm. "Recently we switched . . . to mailing only microfiche and cut our postage costs by so much it is almost unbelievable," says Robert Foster, traffic manager for an international corporation. "We placed a microfiche reader in our overseas offices, at a cost of $189 each . . . our first month's savings more than paid for all of the readers and the cost of microfilming."

Pick up the booklets *Express Mail* and *Express Mail Directory* at the post office for details on next-day delivery at one-third to one-half the cost of other overnight courier services.

If you mail several pieces a day to the same address—a branch office, for example—address and seal individual envelopes but group them in one large, strong envelope for mailing. Similarly, group same-destination small parcels into one large, strong carton.

Check your postage meter periodically to make sure imprints are legible. The post office won't accept faint postmarks.

Print long reports on both sides of the paper. You'll cut postage costs in half (and save on printing, too).

CHAPTER TEN

Inventory Control

The EOQ Concept—How to Manage Your Inventory

One basic problem in almost every business is inventory. Small wonder so many businessmen find themselves asking, "Why the devil are we always out of stock on this item?" or, the other extreme, "What happens if we get stuck with all this inventory?" So go the laments and frustrations of trying to simultaneously maintain a steady work flow, provide customers with adequate service, and still keep investment in inventory stocks down to reasonable levels. Whether you are a restaurateur buying lettuce or a manufacturer ordering component parts, there is a technique you should understand. It is called "economic order quality" (EOQ) analysis, and it will help you determine: (1) when an inventory item should be ordered, and (2) how large the order should be.

Elements of inventory cost

There are two cost factors that affect the decision of how much inventory to order. The first is the cost of investment in the inventory ("carrying cost"). The second is the cost of placing inventory replenishment orders ("ordering cost"). The economic order quantity is that order quantity that minimizes the combined cost of ordering and carrying any inventory item.

Let's take a simplified example: The Ace Manufacturing Company purchases a certain metal flange at $10 apiece. Expected usage of the flange is 6,000 a year, with 1,500 purchased every three months. With some help from its accountant, the company can determine its inventory cost as follows:

> *Carrying cost.* By determining an annual carrying cost (as a percentage of total dollars invested in inventory), Ace management can quickly determine the total carrying cost for this item

135

Figure 1

ANNUAL CARRYING COST

Spoilage and theft	2%	
Obsolescence	3	(risk of product or design obsolescence)
Storage and insurance	8	
Opportunity cost	12	(the amount that could be earned if the cash invested in inventory were to be put to work elsewhere.)
Total annual carrying cost	25%	(Note: US Department of Commerce studies estimate that a 25 percent annual carrying cost is a typical minimum cost for small manufacturers.)

based on different order levels. (See Figure 1.) For example, if orders are placed for 1,000 units, there will be an average inventory on hand of $5,000 (500 units times $10 per unit). Based on the 25% annual carrying cost, this amounts to $1,250. When the annual carrying cost is computed at other order sizes and plotted graphically, management can see that it is a straight-line function of order size. (See the first graph in Figure 3.)

Ordering cost. The management of Ace estimates that the paperwork, handling, inspection, and other costs associated with placing an order for flanges come to about $30 per order. They can now determine the annual cost of ordering associated with different order sizes as in Figure 2.

When each of these annual ordering costs is plotted at the different volume levels, the second graph in Figure 3, a downward curve, results.

The economic order quantity

The total inventory cost to Ace for the flanges can now be determined by graphically adding the carrying and ordering cost charts. The results are shown in Figure 4. The low point of the total inventory cost curve occurs where the carrying cost and ordering cost lines intersect. By visual inspection, we can determine that the EOQ is ap-

Figure 2

ANNUAL ORDERING COST

Order size (units)	100	500	1,000	1,500
Number of orders placed per year	60	12	6	4
Cost per order	× $30	× $30	× $30	× $30
Annual ordering cost	$1,800	$360	$180	$120

proximately 400 units. In other words, if Ace changes its order quantity for flanges from 1,500 to 400, it could save about $1,000 per year in total expenses on this one inventory item.

Mathematical technique

You can eliminate the graph and determine the EOQ on any inventory item by a simple formula, as in Figure 5.

In this example, where annual usage is 6,000 units, ordering cost is $30, cost per unit is $10, and the annual carrying cost is 25%, the exact EOQ would be 380 units. The EOQ can be off by a factor of two and still cause only a 6% change in total cost. So as long as Ace orders somewhere between 1/2 × 380 units = 190 units and 2 × 380 units = 760 units, they will be within the EOQ "ballpark."

Quantity discounts

Some businessmen fear losing volume discounts if they reduce the size of their orders. Figure 6 shows the incremental cost advantage of purchasing at the EOQ lot size as compared to large orders at a 2% price discount. Even though larger orders would yield a discount, it is more economical to purchase the small quantity. In times of material shortages and rising prices, it may be safer to hold larger stocks and avoid

Figure 3

ANNUAL CARRYING AND ORDERING COST

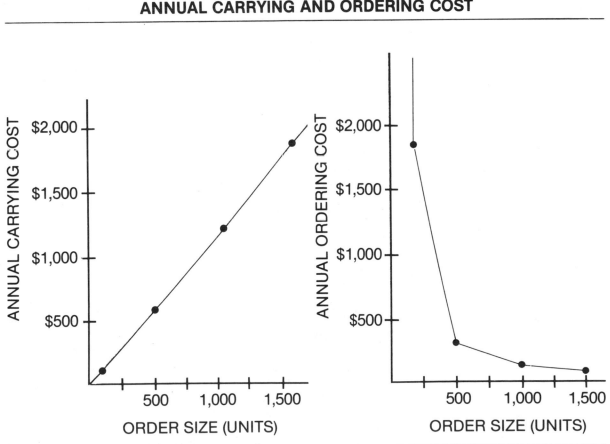

Figure 4

TOTAL ANNUAL COST OF
ORDERING AND CARRYING INVENTORY

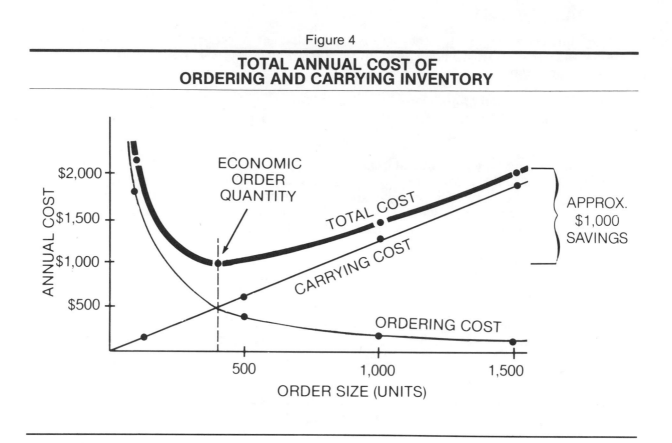

paying higher prices later. But prices can sometimes fall dramatically after an inflationary period—don't be caught at that point with excess inventory and high carrying costs.

Can your company use EOQ?

Not all inventory items lend themselves to employing the EOQ formula. Use this checklist to determine if EOQ is appropriate:

• The inventory item should be one periodically replenished in batches, either purchased from outside vendors or manufactured internally.

• Sale or usage rates should be fairly steady and predictable.

Figure 5

MATHEMATICAL EOQ FORMULA

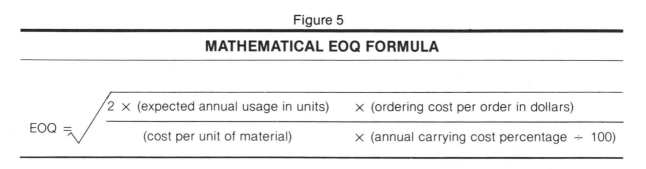

$$EOQ = \sqrt{\frac{2 \times \text{(expected annual usage in units)} \times \text{(ordering cost per order in dollars)}}{\text{(cost per unit of material)} \times \text{(annual carrying cost percentage} \div 100)}}$$

Figure 6

INCREMENTAL COST ANALYSIS TO DETERMINE NET ADVANTAGE WHEN 2% PRICE DISCOUNT FOR 2.000 OR MORE UNITS IS OFFERED

	Lots of 380, price $10.00 per unit	Lots of 2,000, price $9.80 per unit (2% discount)
Purchase cost, one year's supply (6,000 units)	$60,000	$58,800
Ordering cost	480	90
Inventory carrying cost (average inventory × unit cost × 25%)	475	2,450
	$60,955	$61,340

- Inventory of the item should represent a significant dollar investment to make it worth the analysis. It is estimated, for example, that less than 20% of the items inventoried by the average company represents over 80% of their total inventory investment. Concentrate on the 20% first. This is often accomplished by using the so-called ABC technique.

ABC Analysis: Save More by Focusing Inventory Controls

Inventory controls are vital. But they can be expensive—often meaning more paperwork, more formal procedures, and more overhead cost. Use of ABC analysis lets you save more on your inventory controls by focusing them where they will do the most good—on the few items that in all probability make up most of your inventory costs.

Using the ABC system

Split your inventory items into three broad groups. Figure 7 shows how the breakdown worked for one typical company, both in terms of total inventory percentage and total inventory investment.

How to classify your inventory

The exact method you use to classify your inventory depends on the nature of your business, but most manufacturing businesses use the following method of classification:

- Determine the cost of each part in inventory. For parts you produce, charge materials, labor, and overhead.

- Estimate the average number of each part you need to inventory. Multiply the cost for each part by this number. Add all the figures to get your total inventory investment, and find what share each part has.

139

Figure 7

ABC SYSTEM

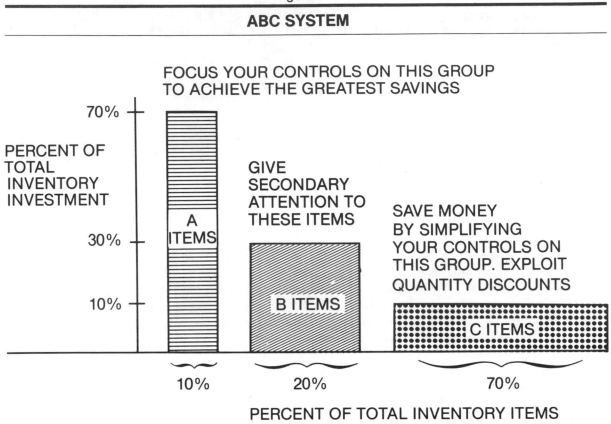

A sample ABC Analysis worksheet is shown in Figure 8. The two columns on the right have been used to classify the full list of parts into the A, B, and C categories. These three items are typical of the relationships between the number of items and investment levels for a typical company's inventory.

Figure 8

ABC ANALYSIS

Part Number	Cost per Part	Average Number in Inventory	Total Investment in This Part	% of Total Inventory Items	% of Total Inventory Investment	Category
258: Motor	$20.00	50	$1,000	1%	10%	A
1091: Bearing	$ 1.60	250	$ 400	5%	4%	B
3372: 5/8 Screws (in gross)	$ 0.20	500 gross	$ 100	10%	1%	C
Totals		5,000 items		5,000 items	$10,000	

Controlling the A items. Achieve the smallest reasonable stock level of these items by:

• Rechecking your estimates of usage of these parts. Overestimates waste money.

• Reducing the size of your buffer stocks by having more frequent checks on usage and stock levels.

• Trying to negotiate faster delivery times in order to reduce the stock cover needed for reorder time.

• Insuring that receiving and flow through the factory of these items are as fast as possible.

You can apply similar principles to B items, but clearly they don't require quite as much attention.

Special handling for C items. Because C items represent only a small portion of your investment, it's generally better to place just a few big orders for these items during the year. This way you can obtain quantity discounts, reduce your order-processing costs, and save clerical costs by looser control.

Getting the most from the ABC system

ABC analysis makes a great partner with the EOQ method of inventory management. The ABC method will show you the items to focus on when applying control techniques like EOQ. ABC works best if everyone helps. Your employees will probably be as interested as you to find how much money is tied up in a few items. Get them to help in controlling A items. Publicize the method. Let them know which items you are trying to control. It's a good way to get your employees involved in the vital problem of inventory control.

CHAPTER ELEVEN

Introduction To Marketing

Marketing Myths:
Misconceptions to Avoid[1]

A company's marketing methods can destine its products for overwhelming success—or equally overwhelming failure. While it's true that there is virtually no way to predict with 100% accuracy how your product or industry will do in the marketplace, you do have more control than you think. The simple awareness of marketing misconceptions can help you avoid disastrous mistakes.

Fifty years ago, a Boston millionaire unintentionally sentenced his heirs to poverty by stipulating in his will that his entire estate be invested exclusively in electric streetcar utilities.

Like the electric streetcar business, every major company was once a growth company. But where growth slowed or stopped, it did so not because the market became saturated, but because there was some lack of management foresight.

- The railroads got in trouble because they limited their business to the rails rather than "transportation," ignoring a need for expanded freight haulage by truck and air.

- Hollywood barely escaped total devastation from television; it thought it was in the movie business rather than entertainment.

- Dry cleaning, a growth industry in an age of wool garments, now faces decline because of synthetic fibers.

- The corner grocery store of the 1930's never recovered from the competition of the supermarket.

[1]Portions of this section are condensed from Theodore Levitt's "Marketing Myopia," *Harvard Business Review,* September-October 1975.

> • Electric utilities are supposedly a "no-substitute" industry. Yet solar energy and chemical fuel cells may well spell their end.

In each case, the industry's strength lay in the apparently unchallenged superiority of its product; it was a runaway substitute for the product it had replaced.

Warning signals

There is really no such thing as a growth industry—only companies organized and operated to create and capitalize on growth opportunities. Do you wonder what you can do to keep your company growing, even after the obvious opportunities have been exhausted? Here are four basic assumptions that can lead you astray:

Scientific improvements. Top management can become transfixed by the profit possibilities of technical research and development. The greatest danger facing some new electronics companies is not that they do not pay enough attention to R&D, but that they pay too much attention to it. In some cases, their success has been shaped in the virtually guaranteed market of military subsidies. Consequently, expansion is sometimes devoid of marketing effort.

These managements have developed the philosophy that continued growth is a matter of continued product innovation and improvement; the company grows under the illusion that a superior product will sell itself. Once its management has created a superior product, it continues to be oriented toward the product rather than toward the people who consume it.

What gets shortchanged are the realities of the market. Consumers are unpredictable, varied, fickle, short-sighted, stubborn, and generally bothersome. The engineers/managers don't say this, but deep down, it's what many believe.

Population myth. Every manager likes to believe that profits are assured by an expanding and more affluent population. If consumers are multiplying and also buying more of your product or service, you don't have to think very hard or imaginatively. As a result, you will not give much thought to how to expand your market. For several decades, the oil industry did little to create a demand for its product. That industry's efforts were traditionally focused on improving production efficiency, rather than on improving the generic product or its marketing. Today, aside from the obvious supply problems, the oil industry is asking for trouble from outsiders who might come out with a solar energy system that is more ecologically sound and more reliable.

No competition. There is no guarantee against product obsolescence. If your company's own research does not make it obsolete, another's will. Unless your company is especially lucky, it can easily go down in a sea of red figures—just as many of the railroads and the corner grocery stores have. The best way for your company to be lucky is for you to know what makes it successful.

Mass production. In some respects, Henry Ford was the most brilliant marketer in American history. He fashioned a production system designed to fit market needs. However, his real genius was not in production but in marketing. He actually invented the assembly line because he had concluded that he could sell millions of cars at $500. Mass production was the result, not the cause, of his low prices. We can all take a lesson from this approach: We are not in business to create a better production line but to satisfy customer needs.

Produce consumer services, not things

What can be learned from these four warnings? An industry is a customer-satisfying process, not a goods-producing process. There is a crucial difference between marketing and selling. Selling focuses on the needs of the seller to convert the product into cash, and marketing focuses on satisfying the needs of the buyer, through the product and through everything associated with creating, delivering, and finally consuming it.

A company begins with the customer and his needs, not with a patent, a raw material, or a selling skill. Given the customer's needs, the industry develops backwards, from the physical delivery of customer satisfactions, to creating the things by which these satisfactions are achieved, to finding the raw materials necessary for making those products. To be successful, a company must concentrate on its customers. Customer orientation involves the following:

- The entire corporation must view itself as a customer-creating, customer-satisfying organism.

- Your industry must be consumer-oriented, not product-oriented.

- The company should not produce products, but provide customer-creating value satisfactions.

- This idea must pervade every aspect of the organization.

- You must set your company's style, its direction, and its goals.

Preventing Marketing Disasters[2]

Reliance upon marketing myths and old wives' tales can mean your undoing, but sometimes even the experts can lead you astray. These days, instead of gypsies and tea-leaf readers we have "futurologists"—experts in predicting what is going to happen in the future. Overreliance on these contemporary soothsayers, who often combine sophisticated computers with their crystal balls, can lead to modern marketing disasters.

Every business manager is concerned about the future. Whenever a supposed expert predicts that certain markets will open up, we all take note. However, forecasts based on technology must be tempered with common sense. Too often there can be a need, but no market, or a market, but no customer, or a customer, but no salesman available to sell the product.

Market forecasters frequently fail to understand these miscalculations about such highly publicized opportunities as pollution control, educational technology, urban transportation, and the leisure market.

A need, but no market

A popular prescription for guaranteed success in business is "find a need and then fill it." However, prospective caterers to an obvious need may find the road to commercial success blocked by custom, tradition, or just plain stubbornness.

Before any business manager hurries to satisfy an obvious need, he should first consider that accustomed habits can be difficult to change. For example, in a world of starving people, we are told that the sea can provide 30% of our nutritional needs. Yet food habits are among the most difficult to change, and there are numerous discouraging examples of companies that created new, low-priced, high-protein foods for the undernourished masses of India and South America who refused to

---

[2]Portions of this section were condensed from: Theodore Levitt's "The New Markets—Think Before You Leap," *Harvard Business Review,* May-June 1969.

145

abandon their traditional diets. Thousands continue to starve in India amid a large roving supply of edible beef.

Thirty years ago, smoke from the steel mills of Pittsburgh blotted out the sun. The need for pollution control was obvious, but there was no market even though means to control the smog were available. Numerous examples of a need, but no market, abound in today's business world.

A market, but no customer

There are many exciting prospects in such fields as education, mass transit, and medical care, but the existence of a market does not mean that anyone can afford to buy the product. For example, General Electric and Time Inc. teamed up and spent $10 million to develop electronic teaching materials only to discover that no school system was affluent enough to afford them. Similarly, there is a huge market for pollution control equipment, but the difficulty has been to persuade various towns and cities along a river bank or a shoreline to share the cost of buying it. Before any business manager commits resources to a new market, he should first assure himself that there is someone on the receiving end willing—and able—to buy the product or service.

A customer, but no salesman

Few problems in business get so much attention as the salesman problem—how to recruit, train, pay, evaluate, and retain them. The simple fact is that although your product may be excellent and the customer willing to buy, if you cannot get enough effective salesmen into the field, the product may flop.

In these cases, you may need to attack the problem from the other end. Instead of spending more money hiring and training salesmen, you need to use a "controlled sales proposition"—a fully controlled, carefully executed, standard sales pitch. For example, instead of using a highly paid super-talker, try a salesman of lesser skills who uses an attache case-sized projector to show slides or a movie to explain clearly and effectively the details of what is being offered. Similarly, telephones can be used to give the customer a prerecorded explanation of an item that interests him. Just be sure that before gearing up to produce a new product or service, the people and the means are available to sell it.

Case example of a potential disaster—the illusory leisure market

Few markets have been more confidently anticipated by futurologists than the so-called leisure market. Certainly sales of skis, boats, and camping equipment have grown at a rapid rate for the past few years. With the four-day/forty-hour work week, Monday holidays, and rising income, the trend toward increased recreation time and bigger leisure markets seemed assured. Business managers everywhere climbed on this safe and growing bandwagon. Yet it now appears that the experts were predicting the wrong actions for the wrong reasons:

- The U.S. population actually works more today than it did in the 1930s. In 1939 the average factory worker was on the job 37.7 hours per week; the figure is now about 40.6 hours.

- Less time at work does not mean more leisure time. It may take an hour to get to work today from the suburbs as opposed to ten minutes in a streetcar in the 1930s.

- Spending on leisure goods and services is more dependent on

146

affluence than on free time. As inflation cuts into disposable income, leisure-related spending is quickly cut back. During the Great Depression there were 12 million unemployed who had plenty of free time, but they were certainly no market for leisure goods. If real incomes decline, there may be no need and few salesmen necessary to serve this market that so recently was described by experts as a solid growth area of the future.

We generalize to simplify our business life. Similarly, we are drawn to experts who seem to have clear answers and strategies for the future. However, today more than ever, it is apparent that the essential difference between those who get to the top and those who don't is not the ability to expound management principles and textbook formulas, but the ability to determine what the problem really is. Intuition and common sense are generally of more use to the average business manager than reliance on supposed experts and their forecasts of the future.

Product Life Cycle— A Vital Marketing Concept

We can all think of industries that qualify for that mystical title "growth industry." And, of course, within those industries there are numerous growth products. But products are like people—they have life cycles. From introduction to demise, a product exists in different environments. Unless management recognizes and responds to its products' evolutionary cycles, the shadow of market decline and obsolescence is never far away.

Life cycle stages

A product's life cycle can normally be divided into six stages: (1) introduction, (2) growth, (3) maturity, (4) saturation, (5) decline, (6) obsolescence (see Figure 1).

The time required to go from introduction to obsolescence can vary considerably among products. A fashion or apparel fad may last only a few weeks from start to finish, while other products, such as the automobile or telephone, may continue for several decades before they become obsolete. Even the duration between the stages can vary considerably. But inevitably, decline and abandonment set in for one or more reasons:

> *Superior marketing by a competitor*—a good example would be Procter & Gamble's coup when the American Dental Association endorsed the decay-prevention claims of Crest toothpaste.

> *Superior or less expensive product introduced*—for example, transistor radio for tube type, or plastic substituted for wood or metal parts.

> *Lack of need*—such as coal stokers for indoor furnaces.

It is important for management to analyze the life cycle stages of each of its products. This is because the competitive environment and resultant marketing strategies necessary to prolong "life" and profitability will normally vary depending on the stage.

Introduction. During the first stage of a product's life cycle, demand must normally be "created" and the consumer educated as to the superior merits of the product. As a result, this stage is characterized by high prices, high promotional costs, low sales volume, and minimal profits. In general there are few competitors at this point, and the key success factors are: (1) accurate market research to pinpoint probable consumers, (2) product design and adaptation, and (3) promotional expertise.

Growth. Because of the high risk of failure in the introductory phase, many companies have a conscious "second bite" strategy. They will settle for their piece of the apple after someone else has taken the risk and proven the viability of the product. Hence, this stage is characterized by the entry of competitors and a scramble for competitive position. Advertising shifts to "buy my brand" rather than "try this product." Sales and profit increase rapidly, but prices and margin per unit begin to decline. Distribution and promotional support to lock up market share are essential during this phase.

Maturity. At this point, marginal competitors are "shaken out," and a highly volatile competitive situation emerges between the survivors. While sales continue to rise, competition is so intense that overall profits begin to decline. The ability to adapt to the volatile competitive situation and to innovate with new uses or "models" of the product is essential during this phase.

Saturation. During this phase, total sales peak and replacement sales become a significant factor. Automobiles are still considered to be in this stage. Sales begin to be more responsive to basic economic forces, such as recession or inflation, than to promotional expenditures. With sales peaking and profits dropping further, production efficiencies become a vital competitive factor.

Decline and obsolescence. It now becomes a question of how long to "milk" the

Figure 1

PRODUCT LIFE CYCLE STAGES

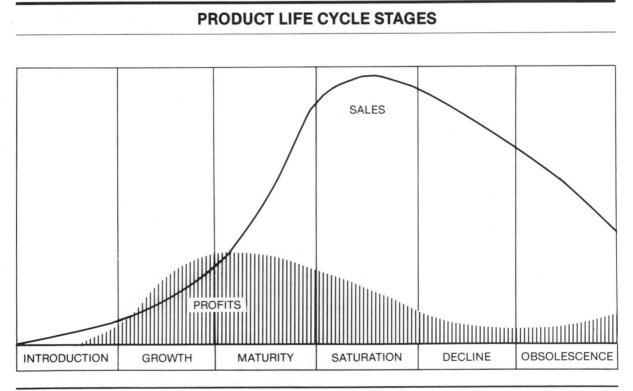

product before dropping it completely. Although margins are lowest during this phase, competition has lessened and promotional expenditures can be reduced or eliminated. With proper management, this phase can be highly profitable, although perhaps short-lived.

A classic example—electronic calculators

In 1971 the first hand-held models were introduced, costing over $300 each. Several Japanese companies captured an estimated 65% of the U.S. market. However, once the market potential had been demonstrated, several American manufacturers decided to enter the market themselves. Sales prices dropped to an average of $100 per unit. Numerous assemblers and marginal producers were forced out of the market. Fully integrated American companies then moved ahead to become dominant forces. A fierce competitive battle is now raging between these companies and prices continue to drop, approaching $5-$30 per unit. A proliferation of features and models is now being developed for specific users.

How to manage your product's life cycle

How do your products fit the life cycle model? Don't be overly concerned if they appear fairly mature, because a product's "life" can be extended by revitalizing it through new packing, repricing, or design modifications. For example, Jell-O and Scotch tape—two classically mature products—have extended their lives by constantly innovating with new uses and applications. If you have a sick product, however, don't invest scarce money and management time in it that could be devoted to a healthy one. Often, knowing when to abandon old products is as important as introducing new ones!

Basic Overview of Market Research

Product life cycle isn't just some isolated and abstract business concept. Customer buying patterns are the primary determinants of the product life cycle. Thus the life cycle helps you to keep in touch with your market—the people "out there" who pay real cash for your product. But life cycle is only a reflection of market conditions. A good manager's essential market information comes from market research.

What is market research?

Market research is a methodical search for a comprehensive, accurate, and useful description of your market. It should help you to answer any of the following questions:

1. Market potential and characteristics. How large is the estimated market in terms of units and dollars? What growth rate can be expected? What are the potential profits in the market? What share of the market can be expected? Where are potential customers located (industry, geography, etc.)?

2. Consumer attitudes and needs. Who will buy this product? Why? What are the main perceived advantages and disadvantages of the product? How often will the product be bought?

3. Price information. At what price are competitive products being offered? At what price should our product be sold?

4. Product information. What are the prime characteristics of

competitive products? How will our product be perceived by the consumer?

5. Promotion. What media should be used to help sell the product (i.e., radio, TV, print, etc.)? What points should be stressed that will be most effective in selling the product?

6. Place (channels of distribution). What distribution channels should be used to sell the product? How can the product most efficiently be moved from the producer to the consumer?

You may not need the answers to all of these questions, so be clear about what you do want before the research gets underway. You save time and money by knowing what you want before you go after it.

Why should you do market research?
There are three outstanding reasons for investing time and resources in marketing research:

- The information you get back helps you to perceive, evaluate, and, hopefully, profit from learning about new money-making opportunities.

- The information aids in spotting problems in current programs and in determining whether previous goals are being met.

- Marketing research provides information that must be used in making vital decisions and in formulating alternative action plans.

When should you do marketing research?
Countless variables will determine the proper timing for a given individual's need for market research, but it would not be facetious to say that you'll use it when you need it. Marketing research takes time and it can be expensive. But how much more is risked when important corporate decisions are made without access to vital information? Chances are good that you will call for market research when you can't afford to risk making a decision without it.

Market Research Techniques

Segmentation analyses
One technique used to obtain a useful picture of your market is market segmentation. Whatever your business, from plumbing to politics, it's likely that you have assorted customers who subscribe to your particular product or service for a variety of different reasons. This is the key to successful marketing—identify the particular characteristics or "consumer profile" of every conceivable customer and then, to the extent economically feasible, mount a market campaign tailored to his specific needs.

Market segmentation is a relatively recent and revolutionary concept. Traditionally, American business saw the keys to profit based on a single uniform product, mass produced, and mass distributed. As Ford once put it: "They can buy any color automobile they want—as long as it is black." But as competition increased and consumer tastes proliferated, the key to profit shifted from mass production skills to the skill of determining exactly what the customer wanted—and then giving it to him. Companies such as General Motors and Procter & Gamble have followed this credo and profited immensely. They introduced quality, style, and image in their products, and this has led to the profusion of brands, models, colors, and options that distinguish today's marketplace.

Segmentation categories

How do you start this process of splitting up your market into manageable pieces? The traditional variables of market segmentation fall into two main categories: demographic and geographic. In recent years, however, two additional methods of segmentation have proven successful: psychographic and consumer-behavioral. (See Figure 2.)

Examples of segmentation

We can best illustrate the use of these variables by taking a number of examples.

Demographic. Every day, whether we realize it or not, we are barraged with advertisements focused at a certain age group, sex, or occupation. However, sometimes demographic segmentation can backfire, as Rheingold Beer found out in New York. Rheingold promoted the fact that Puerto Ricans, Italians, Greeks, Poles, and other ethnic groups drank Rheingold more than any other beer. It did not work, and subsequent research revealed the problem—no one ethnic group wanted to be identified so closely with another. Creative segmentation is fine, but back it up with market research before, not after, the fact.

Geographic. Different areas of the country have different tastes. And, of course, the consumption characteristics of city dwellers can be distinguished from those of country folk. A small grocer knows his primary trading area to be perhaps only a few blocks, while a national manufacturer may classify his customers by region of the country or by state, county, or township. For example, few people would want to invest heavily in a scheme to sell cowboy hats to the general population of New York City.

Psychographic. This is a relatively recent and highly interesting market classification method. One of the most famous studies was of the psychological characteristics of Chevrolet versus Ford owners. It was found that the Ford owners were independent, impulsive, and masculine, while Chevrolet owners were conservative, thrifty, and prestige-conscious. No doubt these particular labels have shifted today, but the

---

Figure 2

MARKET SEGMENTATION CATEGORIES

Demographic	Geographic	Psychographic	Consumer-Behavioral
Age	Country	Leader or follower	Rate of usage
Sex	Region	High or low achiever	Benefits sought:
Income	State	Extrovert or introvert	(i.e., economy,
Occupation	Size of population	Compulsive or placid	reliability,
Religion	Climate	Independent or	comfort, etc.)
Race	Density of	dependent	Method of usage
Education	population	Conservative or liberal	Frequency of usage
Social class		Dominant or submissive	

---

entire range of American cars can be segmented according to the dominant psychographic characteristic to which each one appeals. Knowledge of these factors is crucial to successful styling and effective advertising. And, of course, the cigarette companies are masters at psychographic segmentation. Who really is the Marlboro man?

Consumer-behavioral. Another relatively recent entrant, behavioral segmentation, has proven successful for a large number of companies. The key here is to know why the customer bought and how he uses your product. For example, we find Schaefer going after the "more-than-one" beer drinker, Ultra-Brite after those who need sex appeal, and the soap companies after so many behavioral segments in the laundry room that there can't be any more left.

But excessive segmentation can be dangerous too. With a neat bit of unsegmenting, the Gillette Company sensed in the mid-1960s that in spite of being distinctively designed and promoted, men's and women's deodorants were often being used by the whole family. Right Guard quickly became the leading family deodorant! The same is true of Johnson's baby shampoo, which is now being pitched to Dad, Mom, and the teens.

Can you begin to conceive of various market segments for your product that you have not previously considered? Remember, however, that creating different versions of a product does not constitute market segmentation. Marketing starts with the customer and his constantly shifting needs, not with what you have on hand and would like to sell.

Sources of market research information

Market research information comes from two types of sources, primary and secondary. A primary source would be a direct survey or interview with consumers. Secondary sources are usually printed sources of information, such as books, surveys, catalogues, or trade magazines, that have been prepared for reasons other than your specific marketing problem.

Secondary sources

Odd as it may sound, you begin your market research with the secondary sources. The main reason is that it's generally more efficient to consult already published data in order to gather as much information as possible before you conduct any special field studies or interviews. Other reasons: it is usually easier and less expensive; is usually quicker; may be all you need to solve your problem; should help to clarify your problem; and helps in planning for primary research.

Secondary sources are vital. Too often business and marketing judgments are made in the dark or on the basis of intuition simply because the decision maker doesn't know where—and how—to quickly obtain relevant facts and figures. Remember: An important difference between business managers who make good decisions and those who don't is the quality of their information. You don't have to be a part of a large company with a market research staff to have the information you need for decision making.

Basic sources

Here is a basic list of reference sources, available at any city library. This list is by no means complete, but it should indicate that no business manager need make ill-considered decisions for lack of information.

Basic bibliographies:
Business Information Sources (Lorna M. Daniells). This is the best basic reference

guide to all types of business information. ($14.95—University of California Press.)

Business Reference Sources (Lorna M. Daniells). A compact working guide, this booklet was originally intended for students at the Harvard Business School but is an excellent reference source for most businesspeople. It is available for $6.50 from Baker Library, Harvard Business School, Boston, MA 02163.

Directories:

Guide to American Directories (B. Klein Publications). This guide provides an annotated listing of more than 6,000 major industrial, business, and professional directories.

Million Dollar Directory (Dun & Bradstreet, annual). This directory lists over 47,000 U.S. companies with net worths of $1 million or more. Gives officers, products, sales figures, and number of employees.

Poor's Register of Corporations, Directors and Executives (Standard and Poors). Similar to *Million Dollar Directory.*

Thomas Register of American Manufacturers (annual). This standard reference of 12 volumes lists manufacturers by specific product; three volumes are devoted to selected company catalogues.

Guide to Venture Capital Sources (Stanley M. Rubel, biennial). This directory lists over 600 venture capital firms and indicates how to deal with them.

Market Research:

A Guide to Consumer Markets (Conference Board, annual). This excellent source contains statistics and graphs on population, employment, income, expenditures, production, and prices.

Survey of Current Business (U.S. Department of Commerce, monthly). A useful source of market research regarding current business conditions.

Market Guide (Editor and Publisher Co., Inc., annual). This compendium of marketing information covers over 1,500 local communities in the United States and Canada.

Survey of Buying Power (published in the July and October issues of *Sales and Marketing Management* magazine, annual). Estimates population, retail sales, and buying income for each city, county, and state in the United States.

Data on specific industries:

Trade associations. There are over 6,000 national trade and professional associations which compile innumerable statistics and reports. For addresses and a listing of their publications, consult the *National Trade and Professional Associations of the U.S. and Canada and Labor Unions* (Columbia Books, Inc.).

Trade journals. Most trade publications have special editions containing specialized information. Consult the *F & S Index United States* (Predicasts, Inc., weekly), which lists by specific company and SIC code articles and reports in all major trade journals and business periodicals. For a list of journals and their addresses, see the *Standard Periodical Directory* (Oxbridge Publishing Company).

Government Sources:

Statistical Abstract of the United States (U.S. Census Bureau). This comprehensive compilation includes U.S. industrial, social, and economic statistics.

Census statistics. Of most interest to the business manager are the censuses of: population (1980), business (1977), manufacturers (1977), *County and City Data Book,* and *County Business Patterns.*

Monthly periodicals For an excellent source of basic tables and charts on the U.S.

economy, consult *Economic Indicators* (published by the U.S. Council of Economic Advisors).

Free Market Research from the Government

Effective management knows that profitable markets for the company's products must be pinpointed to achieve maximum sales. Any "hit-or-miss" marketing campaign is usually doomed to failure in today's competitive marketplace.

But isn't market research expensive? Not when you know where the resources are and how to use them. In fact, many companies conduct highly sophisticated market surveys with only a modest outlay. One important key is to unlock the comprehensive and readily usable information available from "secondary sources," such as the Bureau of the Census.

Consumer vs. industrial goods

In order to efficiently utilize Census Bureau statistics, it is important to understand the basic definitions of market classifications. Generally, all commodities fall into two broad categories: consumer goods and industrial goods.

The distinction between the two classes is the use to which the commodity is put. Consumer goods—manufactured products used by individuals and families—are generally classified into two groupings: "durables," such as passenger cars and appliances, and "nondurables," such as food, clothing, and tobacco. Industrial goods are products used in manufacturing consumer goods and other industrial goods, in supplying services, or in facilitating the operation of an enterprise.

Type of information available

The marketer of consumer goods is primarily interested in population and income characteristics of individuals and families. In contrast, the marketer of industrial goods is more interested in sales and employment statistics of business firms that might use his product. A similar dichotomy exists for personal versus business services, such as hotels, laundries, or secretarial services. In some instances, however, certain products have both a consumer and industrial use (e.g., electric light bulbs), in which case both the consumer and the industrial market may be of interest to a manufacturer and/or distributor.

Census data

The *Census of the United States* at present incorporates over eight different censuses. Together with other bulletins and reports issued by the Census Bureau, they constitute the single most fruitful source of data for market research. Here are some of the censuses of most importance to the businessman:

Census of Population. This census reports the count of population by state, county, city, metropolitan area, and, in large cities, by census tract. Census tracts are fixed geographical areas of about 4,000 residents that were established with the intention of being maintained over a long period of time—very convenient in marketing surveys as constant indices from one census to another. The *Census of Population* covers such population characteristics as age, sex, race, mother tongue, citizenship, education, families and their composition, employment status, place of work, occupation, and income.

Census of Business. This census was taken for 1977 and is divided into three parts: (1) retail trade, (2) wholesale trade, and (3) selected services. The statistics cover total sales, number of employees, payrolls, and number of establishments for each principal type of business. The enumerations are made by state, county, metropolitan area, and city.

Census of Housing. Made in conjunction with the *Census of Population,* this census enumerates types of structure, year built, equipment (including clothes washer, air conditioners, etc.), water source, sewage disposal, fuel used, rent paid, value, number of persons per room, occupancy and tenure, race of occupants, conditions of dwelling, size, and mortgage status. This census gives reports by city block for those cities with over 50,000 population.

Census of Manufacturers. This census gives data on the number and size of establishments, the legal form of ownership, payrolls, man-hours, sales by customer class, inventories, selected costs and book value of assets, capital expenditures, metalworking operations, fuels and electric energy consumed, and value added by manufacturer. The census covers all establishments in over 430 manufacturing industries.

You can use census data to solve the following marketing problems:

- Determine market potential.

- Distribute advertising appropriations.

- Select a retail location.

- Set sales quotas.

- Select media.

- Analyze interindustry demand.

Here's how to get started. Write the Government Printing Office, Washington, D.C. 20402, and ask for the *Bureau of Census Catalog* ($15.00/year for four quarterly issues). You will find that the Census Bureau keeps all the information remarkably current.

Primary research

Secondary sources are invaluable for calculations that are based on broad statistics, but there are some things that secondary sources simply cannot provide. For example, a secondary source may be able to tell you how many tons of soap were produced last year, but it cannot tell you why Mrs. Johnson bought brand X instead of brand Y. To understand Mrs. Johnson's reasoning or to find out how many bars of brand X she bought this week, you have to ask her. When you ask the consumer directly, you are doing primary research.

How to do your own consumer surveys

The key to successful marketing is learning why customers are (or are not) satisfied with what you sell. Remember, customers don't buy products, they buy satisfaction. If you hesitate to make decisions because buyers seem illogical and unpredictable, remember that their actions would be logical if you knew their real needs. Here are some research-it-yourself methods so you can get the kind of primary information you need without paying high prices for it:

Interviews

Use interviews when you have relatively complex questions you need answered, when the type of people you want to question are easy for an interviewer to meet, and when an interviewer's assessment of the respondent (e.g., age, social class, or income) is important.

Suppose you are a supermarket operator who wants to increase business. You must determine four things before you begin interview research:

Whom to ask: If you feel your store is doing pretty well and you just want more of the same type of customer, you'll probably want to interview existing customers. But if you have a small slice of the market and want new customers, you face the larger task of researching consumers in general. You might do this by interviewing customers who shop at one or two of your main competitors.

If you are a manufacturer, you must choose between asking immediate buyers (the distributors) and ultimate buyers (the consumers or end-users).

Accurate research only comes from a fairly large sample (more than 100 people) that is representative of all the people you wish to interview.

How to ask: You should begin with a statement of why you are conducting the study (for example, to improve service). Be careful not to offend people. "What line of goods do you normally buy?" is much more tactful than "Do you always buy the cheapest lines?" Ask open-ended questions (those that cannot be answered by "yes" or "no") to invite clarification and comment.

Keep the total number of questions below 30, when possible, and don't have more than 10 items on a checklist.

What to ask: It is vital to define ahead of time what you want ot learn from your research. Typically, you will want to know the motives of the people who buy your product. For example, you'll want to know if attitudes depend on such buyer characteristics as income, sex, or social level. You may want to know how much television they watch or how long they've used your product. The motives of people who have just switched products can also be very significant.

Here are some useful questions to consider asking women customers in your supermarket:

- Which supermarket does the respondent regularly patronize?

- How long has she used it?

- Why did she first use it (e.g., advertising, location, friend recommended it)?

- Why is this her regular store?

- Show her a checklist of reasons to place in order of importance (e.g., prices, opening hours, quality of meat and dairy goods).

- What other supermarkets has she tried?

- What did she like or dislike about them?

- What are the range of age, income, and family size of the respondent? This information will help you in defining your market segment.

How to interpret the data: It's best to look at answers as a percentage of people answering the question. Looking at answers within subgroups or segments is useful, too. With small numbers in the sample, only differences greater than 15 percentage points will mean much, and you should treat interview research as a broad guide only, to be used along with your intuition.

Questionnaires

Mail questionnaires are generally less costly than interview research and are used in the following situations:

- When you want relatively simple answers from a large number of people.

- When you need answers from a small number of specialists who wouldn't have time to see an interviewer and who are scattered geographically.

You can regard questionnaires as postal interviews and apply most of the rules given above. However, a big problem with questionnaires is that the rate of response is often quite low, and those who reply may not be typical.

Panel Tests

For some products, you can get useful data by testing with a small panel of potential users. (These are sometimes called "focus groups.") Ask them to use the product and note their reactions to whatever features they feel are important (appearance, ease of operation, flavor, and so on). Ask them to guess the price.

Two or three panels of three to seven people each will often provide much useful information. Sometimes you can recruit panel members from among your employees, their families, or customers you know well. However, because they may be biased in your favor, it is usually better to use outsiders, if possible.

CHAPTER TWELVE

The Marketing Mix

Having looked at how to get basic information on your market from primary and secondary sources, you're now in a better position to decide how to sell your product or service most effectively by using what is called the "marketing mix."

The marketing mix is the interplay of the four basic and interrelated elements of a marketing program, the four P's: product, price, promotion, and place. They will be examined, one at a time, but it is of primary importance that you realize that they are interdependent. A change in one element usually brings on a change in the others. Proper orchestration of these elements is the key to a sound marketing program.

Product

The product you sell is the very heart of your business, so you must be clear in your mind about what it is you are really selling. The best way to define your product is to define it from the point of view of the consumer. Suppose you sell lamps. Are you selling a necessity, i.e., a light-producing device to prevent your customer from stumbling in the dark, or are you selling economic status symbols for your customer's living room?

The customer's perception (which you can control to a degree) determines the true nature of your product, and you must be sensitive to this perception when you define your "product policy"—the degree of quality you will build into the product, its appearance, and its physical characteristics. But the needs of the marketplace often change, so in addition to defining your product (or service) as it exists now, you should periodically reassess the product to see if you need to update what you sell or reposition it in the marketplace.

Positioning your product

Positioning a product is a matter of aiming at a particular segment of a market. Ever wonder why Schlitz beer is for gusto-grabbers and Michelob is for weekenders? Why

Nyquil, the nighttime cold medicine, claims to fight your sniffles only after dark while Contac works all through the day? Or why certain aspirin tablets get to your bloodstream faster while others kill more pain? It's all part of "positioning"—a way to promote your product with a different image to differentiate it from the competition. For example, there are many soaps on the market today, but they all seem to have a slightly different position. Lava is a tough soap; Camay is a gentle, feminine soap. Dial will allow you to get into a crowded elevator with confidence; and Dove will moisturize your skin. Each product occupies a different "position" and each appeals to a different segment of the market. You distinguish your product by promotion rather than by its inherent characteristics.

While this concept is controversial (and, some feel, overrated), its skillful use has allowed an impressive number of relatively small companies to successfully outspecialize many industrial giants. To understand what positioning is all about, a look back in time will be helpful.

The 1950s was the product era. All you needed was a superior product and enough money to tell people about it. However, the late 1950s brought a technological revolution, and manufacturers found that as soon as a new product was introduced, a "new and improved" competitor followed immediately behind. So marketing strategies that stressed a product's superior attributes declined in effectiveness in that decade.

Next came the 1960s, the image era. Successful companies found that reputation and image could be more important in selling their product than specific product features. Classic examples of successful images are the Hathaway man, the Cadillac purchaser, or the Marlboro man. But just as the differences between products became confused in the consumer's mind in the 1950s, competing images soon became confused and ineffective as well.

The positioning era officially began in the 1970s when Avis boldly announced that it was only number two in the car rental industry. Prior to that time it was considered bad taste (and poor strategy) to mention competitive products. However, in desperation after 13 straight years of losses, Avis took the chance and acknowledged that Hertz was ahead but stressed that "Avis tries harder." By admitting its shortcomings but stressing its strengths, Avis soon moved into the black.

The need for a position

It is estimated that today's average American receives well over 200 commercial stimuli per day. As a defense mechanism against this volume of advertising, the human mind screens and rejects much of the information it receives. In general, it tends to filter out all information that does not match its prior knowledge. For example, when an advertisement said, "NCR means computers," the mind rejected it. IBM means computers; NCR meant cash registers. For a competitor to somehow gain a foothold in this market, he has to relate to IBM's dominant position—for example, Honeywell's strategy of describing itself as "the other computer company." The attempt by RCA and GE to compete head-on with IBM was doomed to failure. When there is a dominant force in a business, a competitor is often far better off relating his product to the industry leader rather than trying to establish his own independent beachhead.

The Seven-Up theme is a good case in point. Colas are the dominant force in the soft drink industry. There's not much room left for competing brands. But no product is invincible—consider the "Un-Cola" theme that Seven-Up devised. This reverse twist may seem silly—until you take a closer look. "Wet and Wild" was fine for the image era, but the Un-Cola made good sense as a positioning strategy. Sales jumped 10% in the first year of the campaign. The brilliance of the theme can be

160

understood when you realize that two out of three soft drinks consumed in this country are cola beverages. By linking itself to the dominant position of cola drinks and at the same time stressing its difference, Un-Cola firmly established its identity in the consumer's mind as an alternative to cola drinks (and hence an alternative to most of its competition).

It is sometimes possible to undercut the competition by taking a niche that no one else wants. Probably the best example was Volkswagen's positioning against sleek, good-looking cars with its "ugly but reliable bug" theme. Like Avis, admitting to a shortcoming often stimulates a positive reaction. Another example is Smucker's —"With a name like Smucker's, it has to be good."

Most businessmen think their product (or service) is superior to their competitors' and promote it as such. However, the din from so many rivals all claiming to be the best only serves to confuse and make the customer skeptical. Rather than being drowned out by the competition, you may be able to reposition your product to fill a specific need other competitors don't emphasize. What is required is to forget the literal definition of your product and focus on what it does for the customer. You will probably discover numerous niches that can be both secure for the product and profitable for you.

Positioning can be a powerful marketing tool. Although for clarity we've used well-known consumer products as examples, the same principles apply to any business. You don't necessarily have to crash head-on with a competitor to compete effectively. A slight shift in your product's position might make a dramatic difference in sales and profits.

How to analyze ideas for new products

When existing products are reaching the maturity stage of their life cycles, you should be thinking of new products to introduce into your line. Figure 1, "Factor and Subfactor Ratings for a New Product," illustrates some criteria with which you can analyze your ideas for new products and rank them in order of priority.

Pricing

Once you decide that a new product is viable, you must still decide how much you are going to charge for it. Ford automobiles are good products and they have a definite share of the market, but they wouldn't sell at $20,000 each and Ford would collapse at $100 each. The optimal price for long-term profits generally requires careful analysis.

Certainly, pricing strategy isn't just the province of huge corporations. Every business manager from a hardware dealer to a beauty parlor operator faces the problem of how to price his or her product or service. Of course, there are rules of thumb in every industry, and there is always the old standby—charge what the market will bear.

Pricing is one of the most important strategic decisions a businessperson can make, and if arbitrary criteria are used, there may be undesirable results. Here is how to approach this difficult problem.

Cost structure of the business

Before an effective pricing strategy can be devised, every manager must know his firm's cost structure. One useful way to determine a cost structure is to classify costs as variable or fixed. Variable costs change almost in direct relation to changes in sales or output. These include direct labor costs and most materials. Fixed costs, such as

Figure 1

FACTOR AND SUBFACTOR RATINGS FOR A NEW PRODUCT

	VERY GOOD	GOOD	AVERAGE	POOR	VERY POOR
MARKETABILITY					
Relation to distribution channels	Can reach major markets by distributing through present channels.	Can reach major markets by distributing mostly through present channels, partly through new channels.	Will have to distribute equally between new and present channels, in order to reach major markets.	Will have to distribute mostly through new channels in order to reach major markets.	Will have to distribute entirely through new channels in order to reach major markets.
Relation to present product lines	Complements a present line which needs more products to fill it.	Complements a present line that does not need, but can handle, another product.	Can be fitted into a present line.	Can be fitted into a present line but does not fill it entirely.	Does not fit in with any present product line.
Quality/price relationship	Priced below all competing products of similar quality.	Priced below most competing products of similar quality.	Approximately the same price as competing products of similar quality.	Priced above many competing products of similar quality.	Priced above all competing products of similar quality.
Number of sizes and grades	Few staple sizes and grades.	Several sizes and grades, but customers will be satisfied with few staples.	Several sizes and grades, but can satisfy customer wants with small inventory of nonstaples.	Several sizes and grades, each of which will have to be stocked in equal amounts.	Many sizes and grades, which will necessitate heavy inventories.
Merchandis-ability	Has product characteristics over and above those of competing products that lend themselves to the kind of promotion, advertising, and display that the given company does best.	Has promotable characteristics that will compare favorably with the characteristics of competing products.	Has promotable characteristics that are equal to those of other products.	Has a few characteristics that are promotable, but generally does not measure up to characteristics of competing products.	Has no characteristics at all that are equal to competitors' or that lend themselves to imaginative promotion.

PRODUCTIVE ABILITY

	VERY GOOD	GOOD	AVERAGE	POOR	VERY POOR
Equipment necessary	Can be produced with equipment that is presently idle.	Can be produced with present equipment, but production will have to be scheduled with other products.	Can be produced largely with present equipment, but the company will have to purchase some additional equipment.	Company will have to buy a good deal of new equipment, but some present equipment can be used.	Company will have to buy all new equipment.
Production knowledge and personnel necessary	Present knowledge and personnel will be able to produce new product.	With very few minor exceptions, present knowledge and personnel will be able to produce new product.	With some exceptions, present knowledge and personnel will be able to produce new product.	A ratio of approximately 50-50 will prevail between the needs for new knowledge and personnel and for present knowledge and personnel.	Mostly new knowledge and personnel are needed to produce the new product.
Raw materials' availability	Company can purchase raw materials from its best supplier(s) exclusively.	Company can purchase major portion of raw materials from its best supplier(s), and remainder from any one of a number of companies.	Company can purchase approximately half of raw materials from its best supplier(s), and other half from any one of a number of companies.	Company must purchase most of raw materials from any one of a number of companies other than its best supplier(s).	Company must purchase most or all of raw materials from a certain few companies other than its best supplier(s).

GROWTH POTENTIAL

	VERY GOOD	GOOD	AVERAGE	POOR	VERY POOR
Place in market	New type of product that will fill a need presently not being filled.	Product that will substantially improve on products presently on the market.	Product that will have certain new characteristics that will appeal to a substantial segment of the market.	Product that will have minor improvements over products presently on the market.	Product similar to those presently on the market and which adds nothing new.
Expected competitive situation—value added	Very high value added so as to substantially restrict number of competitors.	High enough value added so that, unless other competitors is extremely well suited to other firms, they will not want to invest in additional facilities.	High enough value added so that, unless other companies are as strong in market as this firm, it will not be profitable for them to compete.	Lower value added so as to allow large, medium, and some smaller companies to compete.	Very low value added so that all companies can profitably enter market.
Expected availability of end users	Number of end users will increase substantially.	Number of end users will increase moderately	Number of end users will increase slightly, if at all.	Number of end users will decrease moderately.	Number of end users will decrease substantially.
Effects on sales of present products	Should aid in sales of present products.	May help sales of present products; definitely will not be harmful to present sales	Should have no effect on present sales.	May hinder present sales some; definitely will not aid present sales.	Will reduce sales of presently profitable products.

(continued)

163

FACTOR AND SUBFACTOR RATINGS FOR A NEW PRODUCT (continued)

	VERY GOOD	GOOD	AVERAGE	POOR	VERY POOR
DURABILITY *Stability*	Basic product which can always expect to have uses.	Product which will have uses long enough to earn back initial investment, plus at least 10 years of additional profits.	Product which will have uses long enough to earn back initial investment plus several (from 5 to 10) years of additional profits.	Product which will have uses long enough to earn back initial investment, plus 1 to 5 years of additional profits.	Product which will probably be obsolete in near future.
Breadth of market	A national market, a wide variety of consumers, and a potential foreign market.	A national market and a wide variety of consumers.	Either a national market or a wide variety of consumers.	A regional market and a restricted variety of consumers.	A specialized market in a small marketing area.
Resistance to cyclical fluctuations	Will sell readily in inflation or depression.	Effects of cyclical changes will be moderate, and will be felt after changes in economic outlook.	Sales will rise and fall with the economy.	Effects of cyclical changes will be heavy and will be felt before changes in economic outlook.	Cyclical changes will cause extreme fluctuations in demand.
Resistance seasonal fluctuations	Steady sales throughout the year.	Steady sales except under unusual circumstances.	Seasonal fluctuations, but inventory and personnel problems can be absorbed.	Heavy seasonal fluctuations that will cause considerable inventory and personnel problems.	Severe seasonal fluctuations that will necessitate layoffs and heavy inventories.
Exclusiveness of design	Can be protected by a patent with no loopholes.	Can be patented, but the patent might be circumvented.	Cannot be patented, but has certain salient characteristics that cannot be copied very well.	Cannot be patented, and can be copied by larger, more knowledgeable companies.	Cannot be patented, and can be copied by anyone.

From John T. O'Meara, Jr., "Selecting Profitable Products," Harvard Business Review, January-February 1961.

rent or administrative expenses, tend to remain constant, regardless of your output.

Once the costs have been segregated, a breakeven chart (see Chapter 6) can be prepared and the impact of various selling prices on profits can be easily calculated. Firms with high fixed costs and low variable costs, such as airlines or oil refineries, are highly volume sensitive. A change of 1% in an airline's passenger load factor, for example, can make a 25% difference in overall profits. Therefore, whenever demand falls off, these types of firms are willing to cut prices just to keep their planes (or pipelines) full.

Firms with low fixed costs and high variable costs, such as supermarkets, guard service companies, or fuel oil distributors, are highly price sensitive. For these types of firms, a 1% change in price can make a 10% or 20% change in profits. As you can see, it is very important to understand your cost structure and how your company's profits vary at different sales volumes.

The nature of the product

The type of product you are trying to sell also influences the price you will charge. For example, a man who makes steel cable may stockpile his product for a while and wait for an improved market, but a man who produces avocados cannot. The avocado farmer may charge a stiff price when the season opens and his particular product is a novelty. Later, he must settle for what he can on the matter of price when his product threatens to rot in the sun. There is also a difference between products that are easy to imitate and those that are virtually unique. If your product is easily imitated, you will have only a short introductory stage in which you can extract large profit margins. If it is difficult to copy, you may have more latitude in setting your price. These kinds of considerations must be recognized as you look for the right pricing strategy.

Price life cycle

You will recall that products have a predictable life cycle. Well, prices go through a life cycle too. In a product's introductory stage, the price is usually higher because there is less competition and the consumer is often willing to pay more for a novelty. For example, when digital wristwatches and hand calculators first came on the market, they were novelties and sold for a high price. Later, when these products had reached maturity and many companies were manufacturing them, prices fell drastically. The same item (or an improved model, for that matter) now sells at a significantly lower price. The point here is that you should be sure you know where a given product is in its life cycle when you determine the price.

Competitive situation

Competition obviously affects a pricing strategy. The question, however, is why some products have high profit margins while others have low profit margins. The answer hinges on the "differentiation" of the product. If the product is nondifferentiated (i.e., all products are similar), the market is generally highly competitive and profit margins are low. In some cases, the prices even have to be supported by government subsidies. Some examples of nondifferentiated products would be gasoline, lumber, and agricultural products, such as milk and eggs.

At the other extreme are highly differentiated products, such as Polaroid film and cameras, the latest style of clothing, and many drugs. In fact, the drug companies are in a desperate battle to try to prevent their undifferentiated (and high profit margin) name-brand drugs from becoming "generic" or nondifferentiated.

If you have a product that tends to be difficult to differentiate, try to reposition it away from immediate competition. One classic solution is to rename it (Excedrin instead of aspirin); another is to emphasize some particular feature (the little nose bridge, rather than what Ocusol does for your eyes). You should be able to think of many ways to differentiate your product to lessen competition and successfully allow its profit margin to be maintained or even raised.

Without a degree of differentiation between your product and its competitors you lose a good deal of price flexibility. Without differentiation you dare not raise your price for fear of being abandoned by the consumer. You're locked into what is called an elastic market.

Price elasticity

"Price elasticity of demand" is a high-sounding economic term used to describe a very simple concept—how sales of an item respond to a small change in price. If a big price increase results in only a small decrease in unit sales, the market is said to be "inelastic." Conversely, where sales drop significantly as a result of a price increase, the market is termed "elastic."

Clearly, the object of raising prices is to increase dollar sales volume and profits by holding unit sales relatively stable at the increased price. But you must avoid a price raise that will drop sales volume below the point where the price rise compensates for the loss. Two illustrations may be helpful here.

The Ajax Jewelry Company increased its retail prices by 20% across the board and discovered that unit sales only dropped by 1% as a direct result. Actual sales revenue and income increased substantially. Here, the market was relatively inelastic, the customers were not price sensitive, and the small loss in unit sales was more than offset by the 99% of stable business paying 20% more for the same items.

The Morning Fresh Bakery, on the other hand, raised bread prices by 5% only to discover that unit sales rapidly dropped off by 30%. The result was disastrous. The market was highly elastic, and the consumer was clearly price sensitive.

If you belong to an industry association, consult them. They may have made recent elasticity studies on your products or product lines that could be helpful. In any case, before finalizing a price adjustment, you should consider the following points in relation to your particular product and business and the price sensitivity of your particular customers:

- How strong is the competition? Would a price hike put you out on a limb or bring you more in line with competitors' price levels?

- Is your product intended for a luxury, high-price market (not generally sensitive to price) or for a standard product or "commodity" market (highly price sensitive)?

- Do you compete primarily on the basis of price or on other marketing aspects, such as promotion, advertising, location, reputation, innovation, or quality?

- Is there anything distinctive or unique about your product that reduces competition or the importance of price competition?

Legal considerations

Naturally, there are limits to the ways in which you may seek to increase profit margins through pricing. For example, you can't sell your product to Smith's Department Store down the block for $5.00 and then turn around and sell the same product to Jones's Department Store around the corner for $7.00. This kind of price discrimination is out because the Robinson-Patman Act forbids the selling of the same product at different prices to different buyers who compete with each other, except in certain limited situations. Although the law is gradually changing, many states still have fair trade laws that limit pricing flexibility. Finally, according to the Sherman Act, no group of producers or sellers may conspire to maintain or fix prices except in fair trade situations.

Strategic goals for the firm

Every firm should have specific short-term and long-term goals. To become quickly established in the market, for example, one company may choose to charge extremely low prices in the hopes that large sales volume plus gradual price rises over a period of time will be the most profitable long-term strategy. Other companies may choose to charge high prices initially and "milk" the product. Over a period of time they might gradually lower prices. Study the "Pricing Strategy Checklist," Figure 2, and choose the strategy most appropriate for your product or service.

Promotion

You now have a feel for what it is you want to sell and at what price you want to sell it, but how are you going to promote the product? In the broadest sense, promotion is the communication between the producer and the consumer.

First you must decide what it is you intend to tell the consumer about your product (i.e., different, less expensive, better). Second, you must decide how to get the message across; and then finally you might want to find out if the promotion worked by checking results through surveys and other established means.

Most businessmen are experts when it comes to producing the goods, but companies fail to reach their full potential when it comes to the marketing side—selling the goods.

Why is this so? One major reason is that production is "in here" while marketing is "out there." It's relatively easy to control the production process; you can literally see what has gone wrong. Marketing is another matter entirely. As a result, few companies are selective or systematic in their marketing approach—they tend to see many markets and want to sell to all of them—often with disastrous results!

Differentiation

As discussed earlier, one of the first steps in understanding your competitive situation and formulating an effective marketing strategy is to determine how your product is differentiated. By this we mean whether the consumer sees your brand as significantly different from other similar or competing products. For example, at one extreme, milk, meat, or eggs are prime examples of almost completely nondifferentiated products. Eggs are eggs. They come bigger and smaller, but they're still eggs. Thanks to strict government regulations and cooperative chickens, one carton of eggs is about the same as another. Many other commodity products, such as lumber, metals, and gasoline, also fall in this nondifferentiated category.

It is possible, however, to take a relatively nondifferentiated product and make it differentiated (in the consumer's mind) through massive doses of advertising. "All aspirin is not alike. Bayer's is different—it's purer." Hundreds of millions of dollars are spent trying to make us think Brand X really is different from (and therefore better than) Brand Y. You may be able through skillful advertising to differentiate your product if it tends to be nondifferentiated.

At the opposite extreme, we have products that are highly differentiated. Good ex-

167

amples would be Rolls-Royce or Cadillac automobiles, the skills of a specialized brain surgeon, or a rare French perfume.

Push or pull

Once you have a rough idea where your product falls on the differentiation spectrum, we are ready to consider the next question—would it be more efficient to "push" or "pull" your product through the distribution channels? By push we mean using a direct marketing method to literally push your product toward the customer. Examples of this would be all forms of direct sales, such as by door-to-door salesmen, insurance agents, securities brokers, or manufacturer's representatives. By pull we mean advertising or other forms of promotion to literally pull the customer to your product. Examples of this would be promotional flyers, television advertising, leaflets, or brochures.

Generally speaking, the pull approach is more efficient than the push simply because of the high cost associated with using direct salesmen. As a result, companies that use push are constantly seeking ways to supplement it with pull. For example, rather than have an agent "cold call" from door-to-door (push), insurance companies constantly advertise and send out promotion pieces (pull), often offering free gifts, just to find out who might be interested in buying insurance. The agent then has a better chance of success when he calls on a customer who has already expressed some interest.

The final decision of whether to use push or pull is dependent on two additional factors: product and pricing.

Certain products must be pushed or pulled. A complicated and specialized machine requiring a skilled salesman cannot be sold on television (pull). Likewise, it would be economically impossible to sell Band-Aids from door to door (push). Consequently, before deciding on your marketing strategy, you must consider the product itself. Must it, because of its very nature, be sold one way or the other? Also, what is the price margin of the product? If you don't have a high dollar contribution from the item, it will not financially support the services of a direct sales force.

Thus far, we have considered the nature of the product, its profit margin, and differentiation. If you sell a relatively nondifferentiated, low-margin product, would you advertise it heavily or not?

The answer is no. It would be wasteful and perhaps disastrous financially. Let's go back to our egg example. Since eggs are basically a commodity, it would do little good to advertise because the consumer wouldn't take much notice. But, even more important, there is extreme price competition in selling a commodity simply because the consumer won't pay more to get a different type of egg (because there aren't different types). As a result, there is relatively little profit margin to allow for advertising.

But when you do have a product that merits some advertising, be sure you are clear about what you would like the advertising to do for you. It isn't good enough to say that you would like your advertising dollar to increase profits, bring more people into the store, or convey what good guys you are in the community. You want to be more specific.

What advertising can do

       1. Raise immediate sales by:
       Announcing special promotions like sales.
       Dispensing coupons that may be redeemed with purchases.
       Urging people to come into your store.
       Interesting people in distributing your product.

2. Increase consumer awareness of your company through:
Telling people where you are located.
Extolling special product features.
Listing new products.
Publicizing special changes like price or packaging.
Emphasizing the company's service record.
Demonstrating the proper use of the product.
Comparison with competing products.

Advertising is designed to convey these messages. Just be sure you're communicating the information you want and to the right people. In order to further specify what you want your advertising dollar to accomplish, you might say that you would like to see 40% more children aware of new speed wheels bicycle tires within the next nine months. This is what you're after. After the advertising campaign you could use a survey to see if you accomplished your goal.

Media choices

Assuming you know what you want to say and to whom you want to say it, you are then faced with the choice of medium. Of all the media available, which one or combination suits your market best? To help you evaluate the various media, here is a list of their various characteristics.

1. Newspapers:
More Americans still read them.
They lend a factual air to your advertisement due to their overall news.
They are local and allow you to hit specific geographic target markets.
You can change your ads easily or submit them on relatively short notice.
They are good for dispensing discount coupons.

2. Magazines:
They allow you to reach select audiences because they are often specialty magazines.
They can be even more select with special geographic or demographic editions.
High quality of printing from your advertisement.
They are read more carefully and are kept around the house longer than most newspapers.

3. Television:
Has enormous mass coverage. Over 95% of Americans own a television set.
Filmed ads may have greater impact and are good for demonstrating the operation of your product.
Production and air time costs can be high.
Not easy to change ads and ads can rarely be done on short notice.

4. Radio:
Since most stations have specific audiences, you can reach specialty groups.

Figure 2

PRICING STRATEGY CHECKLIST[1]

STRATEGY/OBJECTIVE	WHEN GENERALLY USED	PROCEDURE	ADVANTAGES	DISADVANTAGES
Skim the cream of the market for high short-term profit (without regard for long term)	No comparable competitive products	Determine preliminary customer reaction. Charge premium price for product distinctiveness in short run, without considering long-run position. Some buyers will pay more because of higher present value to them. Then, gradually reduce price to tap successive market levels (i.e., skimming the cream of a market that is relatively insensitive to price. Finally, tap more sensitive segments).	Cushions against cost overruns	Assumes that a market exists at high price
	Dramatically improved product or new product innovation		Requires smaller investment	Results in ill will in early buyers when price is **later reduced**
	Large numbers of buyers		Provides funds quickly to cover new product **promotions and initial** development costs	Attracts competition
	Little danger of competitor entry due to high price, patent control, high R&D costs, high promotion costs, and/or raw material control		Limits demand until production is ready	Likely to underestimate ability of competitors to copy product
			Suggests higher value in buyer's mind	Discourages some buyers from trying the product (connotes high profits)
	Uncertain costs		Emphasizes value rather than cost as a guide to pricing	May cause long-run inefficiencies
	Short life cycle		Allows initial feeling out of demand before full-scale production	
	Inelastic demand			
Slide down demand curve to become established as efficient manufacturer at optimum volume before competitors become entrenched, without sacrificing long-term objectives (e.g., obtain satisfactory share of market)	By established companies launching innovations	Tap successive layers of demand at highest prices possible. Then slide down demand curve faster and further than forced to in view of potential competition. Rate of price change is slow enough to add significant volume at each successive price level, but fast enough to prevent large competitor from becoming established on a low-cost volume basis.	Emphasizes value rather than cost as a guide to pricing	Requires broad knowledge of competitive product developments
	Durable goods		Provides rapid return on investment	Requires much documented experience
	Slight barriers to entry by competition		Provides slight cushion against cost overruns	Results in ill will in early buyers when price is reduced
	Medium life span			Discourages some buyers from buying at initial high price

Objective	Conditions	Method	Advantages	Disadvantages
Compete at the market price to encourage others to produce and promote the product to stimulate primary demand	Several comparable products Growing market Medium to long product life span Known costs	Start with final price and work back to cost. Use customer surveys and studies of competitors' prices to approximate final price. Deduct selling margins. Adjust product, production, and selling methods to sell at this price and still make necessary profit margins.	Requires less analysis and research Existing market requires less promotion efforts Causes no ill will in early buyers since price will not be lowered soon	Limited flexibility Limited cushion for error Slower recovery of investment Must rely on other differentiating tools
Market penetration to stimulate market growth and capture and hold a satisfactory market share at a profit through low prices. Become strongly entrenched to generate profits over long term	Long product life span Mass market Easy market entry Demand is highly sensitive to price Unit costs of production and distribution decrease rapidly as quantity of output increases Newer product No "elite" market willing to pay premium for newest and best	Charge low prices to create a mass market resulting in cost advantages derived from larger volume. Look at lower end of demand curve to get price low enough to attract a large customer base. Also review past and competitor prices.	Discourages actual and potential competitor inroads because of apparent low profit margins Emphasizes value more than cost in pricing Allows maximum exposure and penetration in minimum time May maximize long-term profits if competition is minimized	Assumes volume is always responsive to price reductions, which isn't always true Relies somewhat on glamour and psychological pricing, which doesn't always work May create more business than production capacity available Requires significant investment Small errors often result in large losses
Preemptive pricing, to keep competitors out of market or eliminate existing ones	Used more often in consumer markets Manufacturers may use this approach on one or two products, with other prices meeting or higher than those of competitors	Price at low levels so that market is unattractive to possible competitors. Set prices as close as possible to total unit cost, pass advantage to buyers via lower prices. If costs decline rapidly with increases in volume, can start price below cost. (Can use price approaching variable costs.)	Discourages potential competitors because of apparent low profit margins Limits competitive activity and expensive requirements to meet them	Must offer other polices which permit lower price (limited credit, delivery, or promotions) Small errors can result in large losses Long-term payback period

¹Portions of chart reprinted with permission from *The Marketing Problem Solver* by Cochrane Chase and Kenneth L. Barasch, ©1976.

Messages can be changed on short notice.
Relatively low-cost advertising.

5. Trade publications:
The main advantage of this medium is that you can reach a very special market (i.e., golfers, Teamsters, or restaurateurs).
Good for industrial advertising.

6. Outdoor advertising:
Best used as a supplement to advertising in other media.
Good technique for reminding consumer of your product but not so good for explanations.
Obviously good for ground transportation user market.

7. Direct mail:
This gives you maximum selectivity of audience since each ad is mailed to an individual.
It is generally costly in relation to other means.
It has low prestige because of popular dislike of junk mail.

This list does not pretend to give you definitive answers about the advantages and disadvantages of each major medium. Talk to an advertising agency for further details.

Place (Channels of Distribution)

The fourth key element of the marketing mix is "place," i.e., where your product has to go to get to market. This element of channels of distribution is a vital part of the overall marketing mix. Clearly, even if you have the world's greatest product on sale at a low price and you're spending millions to promote it, you'll be out of business unless you can get that product to the consumer in an efficient manner.

What is a distribution channel?
A channel of distribution is a link between the manufacturer and the consumer. It is the means by which the product gets to the buyer. Often the product is channeled through middlemen (wholesalers, retailers, and so on) and these middlemen take over control of, or title to, the product. It is this transfer of control or ownership—more than the physical transfer from a plant to a warehouse—that defines a distribution channel.

Preliminary considerations
Before you choose a distribution system, be clear in your mind about these three things:

1. What exactly must be done to get your product to your buyer? (Transportation, storage, speed, etc.)

2. What channels of distribution can do this for you and how well can each one do it?

3. How much will each distribution system cost in the long run? Be sure to calculate long-run costs because it isn't often easy to switch distribution methods. Check with your legal adviser and accountant before taking action on a distribution plan.

Basic alternatives

Since the selling of industrial goods can differ significantly from the selling of consumer goods, we will divide our discussion of channels between the two types of goods. However, this distinction is not always so clear in the real world.

Industrial goods are those goods that are manufactured to aid in the production of other goods or services. For example, turbine generators, belts, machine lathes, and kilns are industrial goods. Industrial firms usually use one of the following distribution methods (see Figure 3).

• Direct sales. Company employees sell directly to the buyer. The producer must have a sales staff.

• Manufacturer's representatives (agents). These agents are independent of the company and may supply many different products within a defined market.

• Distributors. Generally, a distributor is an independent company offering a whole line of related products.

Which method is best? Generally, situations that would call for the use of a direct sales force are:

• Established firms with funds to support sales staff.

• The product demands a high level of technical skill in sales effort, installation, or maintenance.

• Sales territories are already stable. The market is already established.

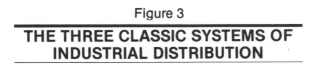

Figure 3

THE THREE CLASSIC SYSTEMS OF INDUSTRIAL DISTRIBUTION

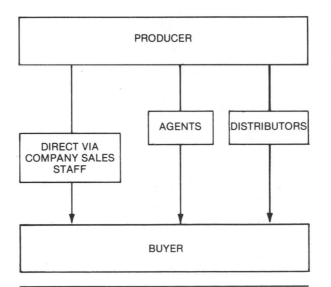

Conditions usually associated with the use of manufacturer's representatives are:

- Company lacks funds for its own sales force.
- Company is limited to a single product line.
- Company is little known.
- Regular sales force is otherwise occupied.

Distributors are necessary in industrial sales when:

- Customers are accustomed to dealing with distributors.

- Little-known company needs the use of the reputation of an established distributor.

- Company is new to the territory.

Figure 4

ADVANTAGES AND DISADVANTAGES OF THE THREE BASIC INDUSTRIAL CHANNELS OF DISTRIBUTION

	Advantages	Disadvantages
Direct Sales	• Your own salesmen sell only your product. • Good control of prices. • You control level of service to your buyers. • Good feedback from your market. • Possibility of giving discounts for dealing direct.	• High cost of retaining a sales force. • More effort needed to open new territories. • Takes time to build sales force and train personnel. • Must add specialists for delivery, credit management, etc.
Manufacturer's Representatives	• Lowers cost of sales personnel. • Lowers time spent on training and recruiting salesmen. • Rep is already established in his territory. • Good price control.	• May represent others as well. • May purposely restrict your contact with your buyer. • Minimum feedback on your market. • Less control over sales end.
Distributors	• Little cost incurred until sales are made. • Localized warehousing of stock. • Already has an established sales force. • Can handle complaints. • Good knowledge of local market.	• Less enthusiasm about selling your product. • May have to grant special discounts to keep him happy. • Less control of pricing. • Insulates you from your customers and the end user. • Increased advertising obligations.

• Company cannot satisfy the buyer without the distributor.

A chart summarizing the advantages and disadvantages of the three basic industrial channels of distribution is found at Figure 4.

For nonindustrial or consumer goods, the three principal means of nonindustrial distribution are: direct to consumer; manufacturer to retailer to consumer; and manufacturer to wholesaler to retailer to consumer (see Figure 5). The conditions under which each would be most appropriate are as follows:

1. Direct: If you intend to sell directly to the end user of your product, you may need to set up, for example, a mail order system that will ensure that your product goes directly from you to the consumer's home. Or else you set up a door-to-door sales force ("Avon calling") and deal one-to-one with your consumer. This cuts out the middleman and offers good customer contact, but it only works for certain products. It does not, for example, lend itself to selling sofas—for obvious reasons.

2. Retailers: If your own salesmen will not be dealing directly with the consumer, you may find that your consumer is best served by a retailer. Retailing is the most common distribution channel used in the United States today. But before you pick the needed retailer(s), consider the following:

Do you want a discount house, a department store, or a high-class specialty house?

Will your retailers be ten miles away from the factory or one thousand?

Figure 5

THREE PRINCIPAL MEANS OF NONINDUSTRIAL DISTRIBUTION

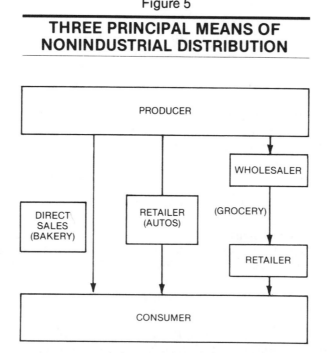

Will your product sell best in a city, in a suburb, or in a rural area?

Would you prefer to have your retailers located near schools, shopping centers, office buildings, sports arenas, or some other specific area?

How many stores will be selling your product in a given area? Even if you can envision the perfect retail conditions for your product, you still have to find out which of them are possible and which are not possible. Finding the right retail distribution channel may boil down to finding the most advantageous compromise on a number of factors.

3. Wholesalers: Once you establish the appropriate retail conditions for your product, you must decide if you want to deal with retailers through a wholesaler. To recapitulate, the idea behind your distribution strategy is to meet the needs of the consumer most effectively. If retailers seem to do it best, fine, but now how can you keep the retailers interested in selling your product? In choosing a wholesaler, the overall question is, can he meet the needs of your retailer(s)?

Type of distribution

1. Intensive distribution. Dropping your product in every available store front window is called "intensive distribution." This kind of distribution works well for low-priced, high-volume items like fingernail clippers, razor blades, and chewing gum. Generally, the profit margin on intensive distribution items is small.

2. Selective distribution. In this case you elect to have your product available only in certain "select" outlets. This system of distribution usually works best for products of high perceived value. In other words, the customer will go out of his way to buy them. The following must be considered in the area of selective distribution: store location; reputation of the store; clientele; and other products on sale in the store.

Selective distribution works well when the customer needs more than the simple exchange of cash for goods. He selects the store and the product because of: wide selection; informed and reassuring sales staff; credit arrangements; delivery capacity; and warranty and repair service.

Examples of products that should be distributed on a selective basis are music equipment, women's dresses, and camera equipment.

3. Exclusive distribution. Sometimes high-priced and high-quality products are distributed "exclusively" to one store in an area. Often these products have a small market (for example, Rolls-Royce cars, pianos, or imported crystal), but the buyers will go to considerable trouble to make their purchases.

To meet the needs of your retailers, the wholesaler must: be close enough to the retailer to allow for ease and speed of resupply; have acceptable space for inventory;

have a good reputation for reliability; and have reasonable prices.

Generally, the number of wholesalers will depend on your production capabilities and your type of distribution effort. If you intend an intensive distribution, you will need more wholesalers to supply all your retailers. Similarly, a selective and exclusive distribution effort will require fewer wholesalers.

What needs are being met by your distribution channels?

Your very first consideration in the area of distribution should be for the end user of your product, the person (or company) who will finally lay out the cash. Most consumers, be they individuals or companies, will only buy your product under certain conditions, even if they want it and can use it to their advantage. The middleman you want is the one who can best answer these consumer questions.

What does the buyer want?
- Is the price right?
- Can it be obtained today?
- Is there a guarantee?
- Can it be fixed if it breaks?
- Is this the right product for me?

What does the middleman want?
- A good profit margin on his resale.
- Reliability from the producer.
- Some promotion of the product.
- Easy system of supply.

What do you want from the middleman?
- Good coverage of your potential market.
- Assumption of maximum distribution responsibilities.
- Good service to the buyer.
- Good information about buyer satisfaction, market conditions, and so on.

Criteria for choosing individual outlets

Assuming you already know the number, type, and location of the outlets you will need for your product, there still remains the problem of picking the specific retailers or wholesalers you wish to do business with. Here are some points you should consider in choosing your individual outlets.

- Credit. Can the outlet pay for what you sell them? Most businessmen agree that this is the most important consideration in choosing your specific channels of distribution.
- Service available to buyers.
- Facilities (especially important for retailers).
- Percent of market outlet can cover.
- Quality of management.

177

- Level of inventory carried.

- Degree of adherence to manufacturer's suggested price.

- Skill and quality of sales force.

- Other products carried that might influence the sale of your products.

Your relationship with your distributor

Your business relationship with your distributor can be based on a handshake or on a carefully worded written contract. It can be as detailed or as general and liberal as you like, but it should include some understanding of these four areas:

- Territorial rights.

- Specific obligations of each party.

- Terms of sales.

- Price and discount structure.

Of course, you should consult your attorney before finalizing any written agreements with your channels of distribution.

CHAPTER THIRTEEN

Personnel and Labor Relations

Your employees are one of your most valuable resources. Yet effective employee management is one of the most difficult aspects of running a business. Mastering personnel administrative skills is as much an art as a science.

Sound management policies, combined with positive labor relations, will stimulate employee satisfaction and productivity. This, in turn, will generate higher company profits.

This chapter reveals important guidelines to develop and enhance your personnel policies.

How to Find the Right Person for Any Job

People, people, people. Your greatest asset—and your greatest worry! Why do some organizations have such great people? Because they start right and evaluate job applicants just as carefully and methodically as they do a major supplier. "What am I going to get for my money?" is even more appropriate with potential employees as it is with vendors.

Interviewing is a skill that few of us possess. Here are some pointers to help you get maximum leverage in your next job interview.

1. Know exactly what you're looking for.

A written job description drawn up before you begin your search can save considerable time and frustration. Not only will it clarify what types of skills and experience are required, but it will aid the person you eventually hire by alerting him to the parameters of the position. (Note that we said "written description." The discipline and time are well worth it.)

Make a list of "essential" and "preferred" qualifications. These could include education, employment background, job responsibilities, mechanical skills (such as typing), personality traits, etc. The "essential" list should be the absolute minimum qualifications; if an applicant lacks one or more, he will be immediately rejected. The "preferred" list contains the qualities that are not essential to job success but would enhance the success potential.

2. Recruit selectively.

Next, consider carefully the "help wanted" ad route versus using an employment agency. For example, before you run an ad in the newspaper, make sure you have the time and staff to answer the ads and screen out unsuitable prospects. It may be more time- and cost-efficient to turn your list of "essentials" and "preferreds" over to an agency with instructions to call only about applicants with the essential requirements.

3. Stay in control of the interview.

When you get to the interview stage, take a few minutes at the beginning to break the ice with the candidate. This is more than hospitality; the more comfortable and secure the applicant feels, the more honest and straightforward he or she will be. The odds increase that you will hear more of the candid truth and less of what he thinks you want to hear.

Establish your control of the interview by saying, "First, I'd like to hear about your background and plans for the future. I'd also like to ask some questions about your strengths and weaknesses. Then I'll be happy to answer any questions you may have about the job."

Save the details about the position for later. First, it does no good to paint a glorious picture of advancement opportunity and salary potential if you're dealing with a candidate you'll eventually reject. Second, by revealing your preferences and requirements, you're alerting the applicant to things you'll want to hear.

4. Keep quiet.

Silence can be an effective tool for drawing out information the applicant may not have intended to mention. For instance:

You: "I see you moved here from Buffalo last month. Why did you leave Buffalo after seven years?"

Applicant: "My family lives here, and I was ready for a change."

You: "Tell me more."

Applicant: "I felt that I had progressed as far as I could in that position."

You: (Silence)

Applicant: "And there, uh, was a new supervisor that I had, uh, a personality conflict with."

Ah! Now you can pursue the conflict. It may be that the applicant had legitimate reasons for feeling the supervisor was unreasonable. Or the previous supervisor may have been too lenient, and the applicant found he couldn't "skate by" any longer. Whatever the reasons, you now have an avenue to explore that the applicant didn't intend to bring up.

5. Read between the lines.

Listening to what the applicant doesn't say can be as helpful as what he does say. Be especially alert for "speech delay patterns," otherwise known as stalling. For example:

You: "I notice on your resume that you have marketing experience with a national home-product corporation."

Applicant: "Yes, uh, yes, that's right."

You: "What were your job responsibilities?"

Applicant: "Well, now, let me think. I was responsible for marketing this home product on a territorial basis."

What does the applicant have to stop and think about? Does he not remember what his job responsibilities were (probably not), or does he have to think of a way to make them sound more important than they really were (probably)? Press him a little further, and you might find out that what he actually did was sell vacuum cleaners door-to-door.

Consider "truth-stretching" in context. There's a difference between an applicant who claims he was in charge of a marketing department (but really sold vacuum cleaners door-to-door) and one who claims the same experience but was really second in command.

Unfortunately, there is no way to guarantee job success for any position in any company. However, intelligent interviewing can increase the odds that the people you hire will be assets, rather than liabilities, to your company.

How to Avoid Trouble with Antidiscrimination Laws

Businesspeople often unknowingly engage in discriminatory practices. Court interpretations have gone considerably beyond the letter of the federal statutes, and many states have new, stiff employment practice laws. To avoid a compliance suit and possible penalties, review each of these potential problems and take the appropriate corrective steps.

Employment application

The law states that you cannot discriminate on the basis of race, color, religion, national origin, sex, age, or handicap. Here is what you can—and cannot—ask on the employment application and interview.

Name. You may, of course, ask an applicant's name, including the maiden name, but you may not ask an applicant's original name if it was changed with the approval of a court.

Native tongue. You cannot ask the applicant's native language, but you may ask if the applicant speaks any foreign languages.

Nationality. You may ask if the applicant is a U.S. citizen. However, you cannot ask whether he or she is native born or a naturalized citizen or the applicant's country of origin.

Age. You may not require the applicant to state his or her age or submit a birth certificate.

Race and religion. You may not ask an applicant's religion or require the applicant to provide a photograph before hiring.

Clubs and military service. You may ask an applicant only about those clubs and organizations that would not reveal race, color, creed, sex, or country of origin. You may ask for information about former military service as long as the questions are fairly general.

Testing

A second broad area of difficulty concerns pre-employment and prepromotional tests. The overall requirements as stated by the Equal Employment Opportunity Commission (EEOC) and the Supreme Court are that any employment test must predict potential job performance and success. You may wish to review the criteria

181

issued by the American Psychological Association, 1200 17th Street, NW, Washington, DC 20036 ("Uniform Guidelines for Employee Selection Procedures").

Personnel policies

Although your application blank and testing procedures may be nondiscriminatory, certain personnel policies could cause you trouble. Here are the most common problems and how to avoid them:

Age. It is illegal to run a help-wanted ad stipulating that a job is open to a "young lady" or a man "age 22 to 30," and you cannot refuse to hire an older person just because he may have only a few years of potential service remaining. However, you may require an applicant to pass a medical examination to be sure he or she is fit for the job.

Sex. Both male and female employees must receive equal pay if they do equal work, and policies such as double pay on Sundays and holidays must apply across the board. Be sure that equal pay includes benefits. The law says you cannot refuse to hire a woman just because most women wouldn't like or couldn't do the job. You must consider the individual applicant on his or her merits alone. However, you can stipulate that certain job-related standards be met, such as education, weight, height, etc., but if these standards exclude most members of one sex, you must be certain that they are essential to the performance of the job.

Handicap. A recent addition to the law prohibits discrimination against handicapped persons, provided the handicap would not interfere with the ability to perform the job. Note that it is not just physically disabled persons who are protected; in certain situations, alcoholism and drug addiction have been deemed handicaps for purposes of this law.

State laws and formal reporting requirements

Even though you comply with a state requirement, the EEOC may rule that you violate a federal law. This is especially true concerning "equal rights for women" where the laws of some states have not kept up with recent amendments to the federal Civil Rights Act. To be safe, check both the state and federal requirements. If your business does work for the federal government or works on a government subcontract, you may have to have an affirmative action program and/or make a formal nondiscrimination report if: (1) your contract is over $50,000, and, (2) you have 15 or more employees. For further information, contact the U.S. Department of Labor, Office of Federal Contract Compliance, 200 Constitution Avenue, NW, Washington, DC 20210.

If you run into a problem

If you find that one of your practices is discriminatory, correct it immediately and announce the new policy to employees. Keep a record of all changes you make to document your intent to comply if questioned by the EEOC. If you are faced with a suit and the plaintiff has a strong case, try to settle out of court as rapidly as possible. Go to court as a last resort and retain a specialist in these matters to represent you. Discrimination suits are often emotional, and a substantial judgment could be awarded if you lose. Finally, encourage minority employees to apply for higher jobs.

Get Employee Commitment: "Management by Objectives"

A laborer was asked to dig a three-foot hole beside a building. After he completed the job, his foreman asked him to dig another a few feet away. The foreman then requested a third hole and a fourth. Finally, the man threw down his pick and shovel and shouted, "I quit!" Although he was well paid, he refused to aimlessly dig holes in the ground. As soon as the foreman told him that the purpose was to locate a broken drainage pipe, the man went back to work and willingly dug until the pipe was located.

A new era of management

Most employees today are just like the laborer above. They seek fulfillment, self-expression, and "meaning" in their work. As a result, the era of the "hard-nosed manager" and "management by pressure" is giving way to management by objectives. MBO is probably the dominant management philosophy of this decade and has been used successfully by an impressive number of companies throughout the world.

What is MBO?

MBO is based on two simple, but powerful, concepts:

• The clearer the idea employees have of where a business is going, the better the chance it has of getting there.

• Real progress can only be measured in relation to what one is striving toward. When these concepts are put into action, MBO consists of three concrete steps:

• Superiors and subordinates jointly agree on the overall goals of the organization.

• Each manager's major area of responsibility is delineated, and his specific performance objectives are jointly agreed upon.

• These objectives serve as guides for operating the unit and assessing the performance of its members.

Efficiency vs. effectiveness

Traditional management philosophies focus on efficiency; MBO is based on effectiveness. Most managers encourage "workmanship" and "doing a good job." But the danger is that the manager will confuse efficiency in digging holes (doing things right) with effectiveness in solving drainage problems (doing right things). Successful management, therefore, goes beyond setting production quotas or standards of workmanship. It is the art of obtaining organizational commitment to the overall goals of the company. Without this focus on the "big picture," effort throughout the company can become misdirected; and friction, frustration, and conflict will inevitably result.

Job descriptions

Does your business have job descriptions? If they contain such behavioral words as "administers," "maintains," "organizes," "plans," "schedules," etc., you can be sure that they are not very useful as an operating guide. Only when a job description emphasizes output does it become effective. It might deal with sales and costs and the authority to increase or decrease staff, use overtime, change products or services, rearrange work flow, or modify production patterns. It does little good to tell a man what he will administer and to whom he will report if he does not have objectives. Objectives tell him what he is working toward and how his progress will be evaluated.

Setting objectives

The first step in setting objectives is to clarify the company's overall goals. Typically, these are stated in terms of sales and profitability, although sometimes such factors as market standing, productivity, and social responsibility are also mentioned.

The second step is to determine all the key factors that contribute toward meeting these overall goals. They could include optimum business areas; profitability by line of business; productivity; financial and physical resources; management resources; and employee performance and attitude.

Mistakes to avoid when setting objectives

Many executives make these mistakes when setting objectives for their subordinates:

- Goals are set too low to challenge the individuals (underload).

- Goals are set too high (overload).

- Goals are not measurable.

- Too many goals are set.

- The time period for achieving the goals is too long or too short.

- The emphasis on goal attainment is out of balance.

- The real obstacles to achieving specific goals are ignored.

- Intermediate target dates by which to measure the subordinates' progress are not set.

- Subordinates are not allowed to seize new opportunities or targets in lieu of stated goals.

Once determined, specific objectives are usually arranged in hierarchical fashion. Figure 1 illustrates this principle.

Success with MBO

The strength—and weakness—of MBO is that it appears to be simple to introduce.

Figure 1

TYPICAL HIERARCHY OF OBJECTIVES

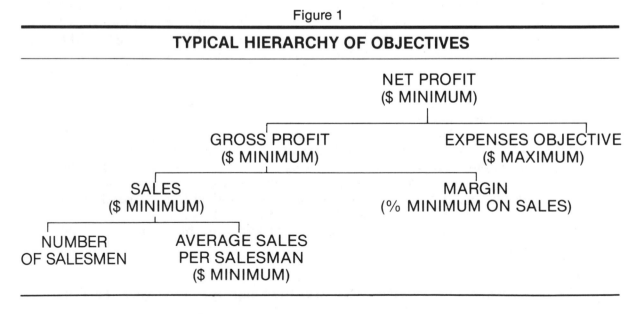

To ensure success, several factors must be present: (1) Top management must be intimately involved and dedicated to making the program work. (2) Subordinates must be confident that they will be evaluated on how well they meet their objectives. (3) Objectives must be jointly set by superiors and subordinates. (4) The MBO program must not become clogged with paperwork.

MBO is not a panacea to "pin things down." If anything, it introduces flexibility up and down the line. Hence, a climate conducive to creativity and expression by subordinates must be encouraged.

Flexitime: Increase Worker Morale and Productivity

Employee discontent (manifested by absenteeism, tardiness, decreased productivity, and high turnover) could be one of the major "hidden costs" of your business. This discontent arises, in part, from an employee's lack of personal identification with the firm and his perceived absence of control over his environment.

Faced with these problems, German firms in the late 1960s pioneered the concept known as *gleitende arbeitszeit,* or "gliding time." This management tool has since spread to the United States, where it is most commonly referred to as Flexitime.

What is Flexitime?

Basically, the concept is simple. Fixed times of arrival and departure are replaced by a working day that is composed of two different types of time: core time and flexible time.

• Core time is the number of hours designated during which all employees must be present.

• Flexible time is all the time designated before and after the core time within

Figure 2

STANDARD WORKDAY VS. FLEXITIME

CORE TIME ☰   FLEXITIME ⊞

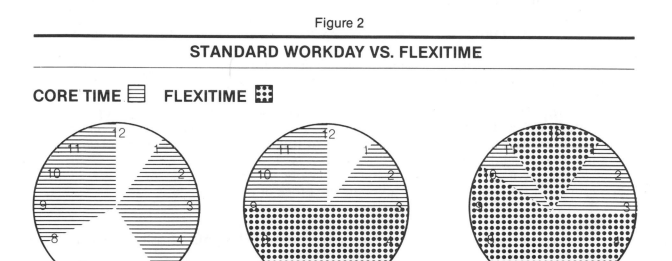

Standard workday, not on flexitime.

Flexitime workday with fixed lunch. Employees may work from 6 a.m. to 3 p.m., 9 a.m. to 6 p.m., or any combination in between.

Flexitime workday with flexible hours at beginning, middle, and end of day.

---

which the employees may choose their times of arrival and departure from the office or plant.

The two requirements of Flexitime are (1) The employee must be present during core time, and (2) he must account for the total number of required hours each day. Beyond this, the precise working hours can be selected in accordance with the wishes and individual circumstances of each worker.

Figure 2 illustrates how Flexitime can be used in an office where "regular hours" are 8 a.m. to 5 p.m., with the hour of 12 noon to 1 p.m. designated as the luncheon hour.

With Flexitime, the employee determines his own arrival and departure times. If the lunch break is a fixed period, then obviously the time of his arrival determines the time he leaves. If the lunch break is a flexible period, then within this period the employee can choose the time of lunch. Thus, the time he leaves work is dependent not only on the time of arrival but also on the length of his lunch break.

The daily format can be adapted to the span of a week, or even a month, where carryover of debit and/or credit hours is permitted. This enables the employee to cope with fluctuating work loads without working overtime. The employee's only concern is to account for the contracted number of hours each week and to be present during core time.

Within any of these systems, lunch breaks can either be fixed or converted into flexible hours. The preferable system depends upon the amount and timing of core time needed, based on individual circumstances.

Advantages of Flexitime

The advantages of Flexitime are typically divided into those benefiting management and those benefiting employees. (See Figure 3.)

Factors to consider

Before implementing Flexitime in your company, you should consider the following complicating factors:

Additional record keeping to maintain accurate account of varied working hours will be required.

Supervisors will not be available to subordinates during part of an extended workday. Therefore, management must do a thorough job of planning and scheduling work flow.

Overhead costs may increase for lights, heat, etc. because of the need to keep the workplace open for an extended day. (Note that overall energy consumption will be neutralized by the decline in fuel consumption realized through reduced travel time on less congested highways.)

Management personnel may be required to work earlier or later than previously, to ensure that someone is on duty all hours the office or plant is open.

How to begin

This outline of suggested steps will help determine if Flexitime is feasible for your operation.

1. Form a feasibility study group. This group, consisting of 3-5 persons, should represent an overview of the operation of the company. Select representatives from personnel, planning, production, sales, etc.

2. Define your objectives. Identify and describe the unique characteristics and problems of your company in terms of personnel and work load.

3. Define your work force. Include total number of employees, number of supervisors, and kinds of jobs. This will provide you with a basis for determining the

degree of flexibility possible.

4. Identify special work groups who will require special schedules and work adjustments if Flexitime is installed. These include switchboard operators, cleaning and maintenance crews, etc.

5. Examine work load. Identify peak periods involving influx of outside calls, person-to-person contact with the public, and mail. Determine how work loads vary from department to department, and from time to time. (Do peak periods occur every day, week, month, or seasonally?)

6. Involve the union. Solicit the views of any union representing a substantial number of employees.

If, after analyzing the data collected, it appears that Flexitime is feasible and desirable, you are ready to implement the system, which involves two further steps:

Figure 3

ADVANTAGES OF FLEXITIME

MANAGEMENT

Short-term absences reduced as employees handle many personal affairs before or after their selected workday.

Quicker starts as employees arriving at different times quickly and quietly settle down to work without usual morning conversations.

A quiet time is possible for thought and concentration as not all employees are present for the same hours.

Services may be increased to the public if Flexitime allows the organization to be open longer hours.

Workers become job oriented rather than time oriented as time now becomes an element the worker can control.

Cross-training and cooperation among employees improves as they share skills and know-how in order to "fill in" during another worker's absence.

Productivity increases for all of the above reasons, and reports of 1-5% gains from organizations utilizing Flexitime are common.

Supervisory skills improve as the supervisor's absence during part of the workday requires him to more effectively plan and communicate daily assignments.

EMPLOYEES

Individuals can set personal pace and adjust work hours according to own rhythm. As a result, "night people" and "morning people" work with greater enthusiasm, concentration, and enjoyment.

Rush hour frustrations are reduced as workers utilize the highways, buses, subways, and trains at other than peak periods. Travel time and costs are reduced.

Family, community, and social activities increase as employees are better able to schedule participation.

Education may be continued as schedules result in access to classes previously unavailable.

Recreation facilities can be utilized during less crowded hours. More daylight hours are available for swimming, tennis, golf, etc.

Shopping can be done when stores are less crowded.

Car pools are easier to form as individuals who have been prevented from car-pooling because of working hours find this problem eliminated.

Determine core time

Core time is that portion of the day when all employees must be at work. The larger the core time, the smaller the flexible time bands will be. Too large a core time will negate the purpose of flexible hours. On the other hand, too small a core time could result in inefficiency. Productivity gains can be significantly affected by your attention to this key detail.

Typically, core time takes up four to five hours of the day. Some questions that may guide you are:

Does your organization or some of its departments have contact with the public on a regular volume basis? If so—

Are there peak periods of work load generated by phone, mail, or public contact that can be identified?

Are certain times of the week or month heavier than others?

What are the minimum manning levels required to do the job during peak work load periods? During other periods?

Are there daily or periodic deadlines to be met?

When are meetings typically held? Can they be adjusted to fall within the core time?

Solicit employee input

Although it is rare that the majority of employees are not receptive to a Flexitime plan, it is important to determine to the extent possible the impact the plan will have on business operations. Therefore, try to gauge your workers' feelings by a survey, including such questions as:

- Does the idea of Flexitime appeal to you?

- Given the option, would you prefer to start work at a different time?

- Given a choice, when would you prefer to begin working?

- Would you prefer a longer or shorter lunch period than you have now?

- What length of time would you take for lunch?

Remember that Flexitime is not a panacea for all management ills. However, it may prove a useful, productive tool if these basic steps are followed:

1. Analyze the situations and special problems of your organization.

2. Plan your program carefully.

3. Educate and communicate with the work force.

Also, check legal and regulatory considerations when designing your Flexitime plan. Test your proposed model against regulations concerning number of hours worked consecutively, shift differentials, overtime, etc. (Contact your Department of Labor office for federal regulations.)

Great Expectations: How to Develop Top-Notch Subordinates[1]

In *My Fair Lady,* Professor Higgins, like the sculptor Pygmalion in Greek mythology, transforms another person through his effort and will. And in the world of management, many executives play Pygmalion-like roles in developing able subordinates and stimulating them to superior performance. But like Professor Higgins,

---

[1]Condensed from J. Sterling Livingston's "Pygmalion in Management," *Harvard Business Review.*

most managers unintentionally treat their subordinates so that their performance is lower than they are capable of achieving.

Why do some managers succeed? And how do they differ from managers who fail to develop top-notch subordinates?

Managerial expectations

Managers' expectations subtly affect their subordinates. If expectations are high, productivity is likely to be excellent. If they are low, then productivity is likely to be poor. Scientific research now reveals that:

• Subordinates do what they believe they are expected to do by those above them in the organization.

• What a manager expects of his subordinates and the way he treats them largely determines their performance and career progress.

• A unique characteristic of superior managers is their ability to create high performance expectations that subordinates fulfill.

• Less effective managers fail to develop similar expectations, and, as a consequence, the productivity of their subordinates suffers.

Placebo effect

The healing professions have long recognized that a doctor's expectations can have a formidable influence on a patient's physical or mental health. The negative results from a pessimistic prognosis have often been observed. In short, a physician's expectations can greatly influence a patient's response to medical treatment. This is referred to as the "placebo effect" and works in the business world as well.

For example, branch bank managers whose lending authority had been reduced because of high rates became progressively less effective. They turned to making only "safe" loans that resulted in loss of business to competing banks and a relative decline in both deposits and profits at their own branches. To reverse that decline, they then "reached" for loans and became almost irrational in accepting questionable credit risks, in the hope of avoiding further damage to their egos and careers. Thus, they did what they believed they were expected to do.

Power of expectations

An experiment conducted in a life insurance company illustrates the power a manager's expectations have over subordinates' performance:

• Salesmen who are treated by their managers as supersalesmen try to live up to that image.

• Salesmen with poor productivity records who are treated by their managers as having no chance of success fulfill that image.

Why is it difficult for unsuccessful subordinates to maintain their self-image and self-esteem? Responding to low managerial expectations, they try to avoid situations leading to greater failure. (For example, they might reduce the number of sales calls or avoid trying to close sales where rejection is a possibility.) Managers cannot avoid the depressing cycle of events that flows from low expectations merely by hiding their feelings from subordinates. If a manager believes a subordinate will perform poorly, it is virtually impossible for him to mask his expectations, because the message usually is communicated unintentionally, without conscious action on his part.

Indeed, a manager often communicates most when he believes he is communicating least. For instance, when he says nothing, when he becomes "cold" and "uncommunicative," it is usually a sign that he is displeased by a subordinate or believes he is "hopeless." The silent treatment communicates negative feelings even more effectively, at times, than a tongue-lashing does. What seems to be critical in the communication of expectations is not what the boss says, so much as the way he behaves. Indifferent and noncommittal treatment, more often than not, is the kind of treatment that communicates low expectations and leads to poor performance.

Secret of superiority

Something takes place in the minds of superior managers that does not occur in the less effective. Superior managers have greater confidence than other managers in their own ability to develop their subordinates' talent. Surprisingly, their high expectations are based primarily on what they think about themselves—about their ability to select, train, and motivate their subordinates. And this subtly influences their beliefs, expectations, and treatment of subordinates.

If you are confident that you can develop and stimulate your subordinates to high levels of performance, you will expect a lot and treat them with confidence that they will meet your expectations. But if you doubt your abilities, then you will expect less and treat them with less confidence.

In other words, the superior manager's record of success and his confidence in his ability give credibility to his high expectations. Consequently, his subordinates accept his expectations as realistic and try hard to achieve them.

Impossible dreams

Managerial expectations must be realistic before they can be translated into performance. They must be made of more substantial material than the power of positive thinking.

Subordinates will not be motivated to reach high levels of productivity unless they consider the boss's high expectations realistic and achievable. If they are encouraged to strive for unattainable goals, they eventually give up trying and settle for results that are lower than they are capable of achieving.

Considerable research documents that the relationship of motivation to expectancy takes the form of a bell-shaped curve (see Figure 4).

The degree of motivation and effort rises until the expectancy of success is midway between being virtually certain and virtually impossible. Then it begins to fall, even though the boss's expectation of success continues to rise. No response is aroused when a goal is seen as either virtually certain or impossible to attain. The experience of a large electrical manufacturing company illustrates this point. Production actually declined if quotas were set too high, because the workers simply stopped trying to meet them.

Your most valuable resource

Industry has not developed effective first-time managers fast enough to meet its needs. As a consequence, many companies are underdeveloping their most valuable resource—talented young men and women. They are incurring heavy attrition costs and contributing to the negative attitudes young people often have about careers in business.

For you—an executive concerned with the productivity of your organization and the careers of your young employees—the challenge is clear: speed the development of managers who will treat subordinates in ways that lead to high performance and career satisfaction. The manager not only shapes the expectations and productivity of

190

others, but also influences their attitudes toward their jobs and themselves. If the manager is unskilled, he leaves scars on the careers of the young men and women, cuts deeply into their self-esteem, and distorts their image of themselves as human beings. But if he is skillful and has high expectations of his subordinates, their self-confidence will grow, their capabilities will develop, and their productivity will be high.

How to Save Under the Wage-Hour Law

If your company is typical, your employees alternate between overtime in rush periods and underwork in slack periods. Most business managers would prefer to even out these hours or give compensatory time off, but the federal Fair Labor Standards ("Wage-Hour") Act is very specific: All work over 40 hours per week must be paid at time-and-a-half rates. However, certain employees on salary can be exempt from overtime provisions of the law. The key to saving payroll dollars is to know which employees can be switched to salary and whether a switch would be profitable.

Employees may be exempted from the overtime provisions of the law if they: (1) are classified as executives, administrators, or professionals; (2) perform certain duties; and (3) are paid a minimum salary. The requirements are outlined in the chart of guidelines (see Figure 5), and all of them must be met to receive the exemption.

Should you change your employees' status?

By examining Figure 5, you may discover that several of your employees could be

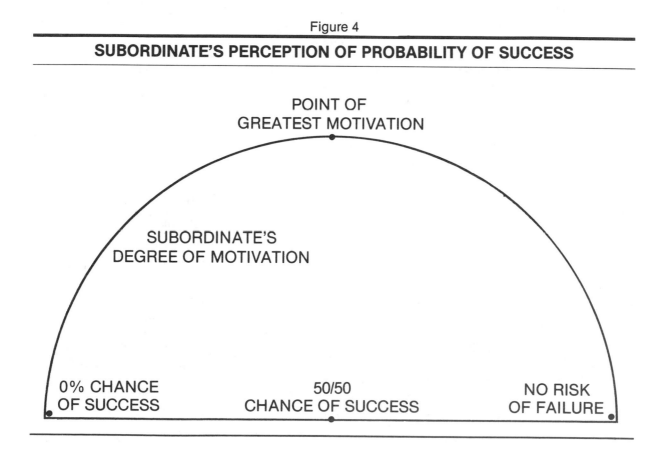

Figure 4

SUBORDINATE'S PERCEPTION OF PROBABILITY OF SUCCESS

POINT OF
GREATEST MOTIVATION

SUBORDINATE'S
DEGREE OF MOTIVATION

0% CHANCE
OF SUCCESS

50/50
CHANCE OF SUCCESS

NO RISK
OF FAILURE

salaried and exempt from the Wage-Hour Law. Or you may find that with a slight shift in duties, they will qualify.

The question is whether it is worth raising their salaries to the minimum required for exemption. Here's how to examine each employee's status:

• Estimate the amount of overtime you will probably have to pay the employee over the next year.

• Compare this figure with the increase in wages that you would have to pay as salary to bring the employee up to the required level for exemption.

Besides the economics of whether it makes sense to change an employee's status, you should also consider the possible effect of any special increase on the other employees. In addition, try to determine if there will be an effect on customary wage differentials you may wish to maintain.

How salary is handled

An employee is considered salaried if he receives a certain amount each pay period that is not subject to reduction based on the number of hours worked. In other words, a salaried employee must receive a full wage for any week he or she works. But there are important exceptions to this rule. If an exempt employee takes off for a full day on personal business, you are not required to pay for that day. If an exempt employee is sick for a whole week, you don't have to pay unless you have a sick pay plan. You only pay if part of a week is worked.

Because you pay a salary does not mean you cannot also use a commission percent

Figure 5

GUIDELINES TO EXEMPTION UNDER WAGE-HOUR ACT

Require-ments	Executive	Administrative	Professional
Minimum salary per week	$225 (effective 2/13/83, $250)	$225 (effective 2/13/83, $250)	$250 (effective 2/13/83, $280)
Types of duties	1. Managerial. 2. Directs the work of two or more employees (or equivalent). 3. May hire and fire, or recommendations carry weight. 4. Exercises discretionary powers.	1. Primary duty is office or non-manual work directly related to general business operations. 2. Exercises discretion and independent judgment. 3. Directly assists owner, executive, or other administrative employees, or performs work along specialized or technical lines requiring special training, experience, or knowledge.	1. Primary duty requires advanced knowledge customarily acquired by advanced study. 2. Work requires discretion and independent judgment. 3. Work is intellectual, varied, and results not standardized.
Restrictions	May not work more than 20% of time (40% if retail or service establishment) on tasks not directly related to executive duties. (Does not apply if paid $250 or more per week and primary duty is supervision or in sole charge of an independent establishment, or own 20% or more interest in business.)	May not work more than 20% of time (40% if retail or service establishment) on tasks not directly related to executive duties. (Does not apply if paid $250 or more per week and primary duty includes discretion and independent judgment.)	May not work more than 20% of time on tasks not directly related to professional duties. (Does not apply if paid $250 or more per week and primary duties are of the type listed above.)

of profit or other similar method of payment as long as the salary portion of the compensation meets the minimum requirements. For example, if you pay a store manager a weekly salary of $200 plus 3% of sales, the salary would not meet the requirement of $225 per week, even if the manager actually makes much more than that as a result of the bonus program.

How to proceed

For more information, obtain a copy of the booklet, *Regulations, Part 541: Defining the Terms "Executive," "Administrative," "Professional" and "Outside Salesman"* from the Wage-Hour Division of your local Department of Labor. Or write the Government Printing Office, Washington, DC 20402 and ask for Wage-Hour Publication 1281. If you question whether or not an employee is exempt, protect yourself from the cost of back pay and overtime by obtaining a written ruling. Send full particulars to the Department of Labor, Wage-Hour Division, 200 Constitution Avenue NW, Washington, DC 20210.

How to Cut Your Unemployment Taxes

Many business managers are experiencing enormous increases in their unemployment insurance tax rates. Remember that if any of your former employees collect unemployment benefits, the state charges your unemployment tax account. Obviously, the more charges, the higher your future rate will be. Here's how to keep your rate as low as possible.

In a typical state, an employer may pay $42 per employee per year for unemployment taxes. If just a few ex-workers draw on his account, that amount can easily jump to several hundred dollars per employee—a substantial increase. Many employers are shocked to learn that an employee who they thought had quit of his own accord or was fired for a good reason can collect benefits for one reason or another. Here's why:

• Change in job conditions. If an employee is transferred from the day shift to the night shift (or vice versa) and then quits, unemployment benefits can be collected because job conditions were changed. To avoid this, first learn whether or not the employee will work nights. If so, the departure would have been voluntary, and no benefits could be collected.

• Employer's convenience. An employee who was constantly tipsy or late to work was finally told he had to go as soon as a replacement could be found. In this situation the employee can collect because the departure was timed to suit the employer's convenience. The employee would not be able to collect if, after giving the employee an ultimatum, you immediately dismissed him when he disregarded your warning.

• Language difficulties. If a foreign employee was fired because he smoked in an area clearly marked "no smoking" where explosive solvents were kept, he can collect on the argument that his dismissal was based on instructions he couldn't understand. Be sure directions and procedures can be clearly understood by all employees.

Here are five easy steps that can cut your unemployment taxes:

1. Be specific. If you fire an employee, make sure he knows why. Document the dismissal with a memorandum to your employment file. When you receive notice that he has filed for benefits, give specific reasons for the dismissal. In most states, an employee may be disqualified for benefits for the following reasons:

193

- Misconduct (cheating, stealing, absence, insubordination, etc.).

- Quitting.

- Refusal to work.

- Inability to work.

2. Amend your employment application blank. Ask such questions as:

- Will you agree to work on any shift, as assigned?

- Will you work on weekends or holidays, if required?

Do not ask if the applicant has ever filed for unemployment. This is a violation of the antidiscrimination laws.

3. Know who is collecting from your account. Past employees who you can prove are clearly unqualified may be collecting. Check with your local employment office frequently.

4. Watch the calendar. If a new employee doesn't make the grade, let him go before three months elapse. If he cannot obtain another job, suggest that he file for unemployment because most states will not count you as the most recent employer, since the employee didn't work a full quarter on your payroll. As a result, any benefits he collects for the following 12 months cannot be charged against you.

5. Pay attention to your employment account. Review your rate notice annually, and if you can make a voluntary contribution, do so. This may make you eligible for a lower rate. In most states, voluntary contribution instructions are sent with the rate notice; otherwise, check with your local employment office for the forms.

It's the indirect taxes—unemployment taxes, worker's compensation, Social Security—that can add up! Start to cut your payroll costs now. A few hundred dollars savings per employee may make a substantial difference to your business.

Employee vs. Independent Contractor

Quite often an employer can save payroll taxes, overtime costs, and benefits by classifying certain workers as independent contractors. The common law says:

- If the employer has the right to control an individual's work not only as to what is done but also how it is done, that person is an employee. It doesn't matter that the employee has considerable freedom of action and discretion, as long as the employer has right of control.

- If the employer has the right to control the final result but not the means or methods for doing it, then the worker is an independent contractor.

As you can see, there is a fine line between the two. Figure 6 is a handy guide compiled from numerous court decisions.

Some operations in your business could possibly be turned over to outsiders at a lower net cost. Examples would be delivery services, building and equipment maintenance, office cleaning, and bookkeeping services. Or you might wish to set up certain existing employees in business for themselves and give them a long-term con-

Figure 6

EMPLOYEE VS. INDEPENDENT CONTRACTOR

	Employee	Independent Contractor
Employer's right to dismiss individual	Free right to discharge.	Right to discharge limited by contractual relationship, written or implied.
Payment	Periodically or by the hour.	By the job.
Tenure	Permanent relationship intended.	More limited relationship intended.
Employment conditions	Employer furnishes place to work, tools, and equipment.	Substantial investment by the worker in tools, equipment, etc., giving opportunity for profit or loss.
	Work done personally. May not employ assistants without permission from employer.	Worker has right to employ others to assist him.
Employment restrictions	Outside employment by worker may be restricted.	None. Services offered to the general public.
		Recognized trade or calling.

tract to handle these services.

The possibilities are numerous, but before making a change, consider two points: (1) A worker may be classified as an independent contractor for federal purposes but as an employee under state law. Check with your employment office. (2) The Internal Revenue Service is alert to any change in a worker's status. Substantial potential liabilities for Social Security and income tax withholding can build up unless you have a "reasonable basis" for treating an individual as an independent contractor.

What to Do if Faced with Unionization

At some point, most business managers will face the prospect of having their work forces unionized. Many managers will react by firing union leaders and sympathizers, but this can be dangerous. If unfair labor practices can be proved against you, the National Labor Relations Board (NLRB) can certify a union as the workers' exclusive bargaining agent, even though an election was not held or a majority vote obtained. Here is what you may—and may not—do when dealing with this delicate situation.

What the employer may do:

> • Tell employees that if a majority of them select the union, the company will have to deal with it on all their daily problems involving wages, hours, and other conditions of employment.

> • Tell employees that you and other members of management are always willing to discuss any subject of interest to them.

> • Tell the employees about the benefits they now enjoy—all of

195

which may have been obtained without union representation. Avoid promises or threats, either direct or veiled.

• Tell employees how their wages, benefits, and working conditions compare favorably with other companies in the area, whether unionized or not.

• Tell employees some of the disadvantages of belonging to a union—such as the expense of initiation fees, monthly dues, fines, strike assessments, and membership rules. Quote from the specific union's constitution and bylaws granting the union power to impose punishment and discipline on its members.

• Tell employees that there is a possibility that a union will call a strike or work stoppage even though many employees may not want to strike and even though the employer is willing to bargain or has been bargaining with the union. Inform employees that any strike will cost them money in lost wages.

• Tell employees that in negotiating with the union the company does not have to agree to all the union's terms and certainly not to any terms that are not in the economic interest of the business.

• Tell employees that merely signing a union authorization card or application for membership does not mean that they must vote for the union in an election. If the situation warrants, advise employees that the union may use the signed authorization cards to obtain bargaining rights without an NLRB election.

• Enforce rules that solicitation of membership or discussion of union affairs must be outside working time so that it will not interfere with work. However, an employee can solicit and discuss the union on his own time, even on company premises, when it does not interrupt work.

• Express a personal preference for one union over the other if two or more unions are organizing.

• Lay off, discipline, and discharge for cause so long as such action follows customary practice and is not done with regard to union membership.

What the employer may not do:

• Don't promise or grant employees a pay increase, promotion, betterment, benefit, or special favor if they stay out of the union or vote against it. Customary wage increases must be granted as scheduled.

• Don't threaten loss of jobs, reduction of income, discontinuance of privileges or benefits presently enjoyed, or use intimidating language that may be designed to influence an employee in the exercise of his right to belong to a union. Don't threaten or actually discharge, discipline, or lay off an employee because of his activities in behalf of a union. And don't discriminate against employees actively supporting the union by intentionally assign-

196

ing undesirable work to the union employee or transfer employees prejudicially because of union affiliation.

• Don't threaten to close or move the plant or to drastically reduce operations if a union is selected as a representative.

• Don't spy on union meetings. (Parking across the street from a union hall to watch employees entering the hall would be suspect.) Don't ask employees about the internal affairs of unions, such as meetings. (Some employees may, of their own accord, tell you of such matters. It is not an unfair labor practice to listen, but you must not ask questions to obtain additional information.)

• Don't engage in any partiality favoring nonunion employees over employees active in behalf of the union or discipline or penalize employees actively supporting a union for an infraction that nonunion employees are permitted to commit without being similarly disciplined.

• Don't intentionally assign work or transfer employees so that those active in behalf of the union are separated from those you believe are not interested in supporting a union.

• Don't ask employees for an expression of their thoughts about a union or its officers, and don't ask employees how they intend to vote in a union election or ask them the identity of the instigator or leader of employees favoring the union.

• Don't ask employees at time of hiring or thereafter whether they belong to a union or have signed a union application or authorization card.

• Don't make a statement that you will not deal with a union.

• Don't make speeches to massed assemblies of employees on company time within the 24-hour period before the opening of polls for a representation election. And do not speak to an employee or small group of employees in your office about the union campaign. The best place to talk to them about the union is at their work stations where other employees are present.

CHAPTER FOURTEEN

Legal Fundamentals

Annual Legal Checklist

You may become so preoccupied with the specific details of running your business that you put off touching base with your attorney. To be sure the legal affairs of your business are in order, you should check these points with counsel at least once in every year:

1. Corporate housekeeping:

State of incorporation. State corporation laws are constantly changing, and the business climate of another state may be better. Also check the tax advantages of Delaware's new General Corporate Law.

Purposes and bylaws. There may be changes in your business that necessitate a revision of your corporate charter and its by-laws. You may wish to change your fiscal year, indemnify officers and directors, or call stockholders meetings out of state. In a close company you may wish to operate by consent rather than by holding director's meetings.

Capitalization. Stock splits, acquisitions, need for new capital, and stock options are several factors that could result in a need to revise your capital structure. Consider issuing a preferred stock instead of common stock or straight debt. If lenders desire equity participation, debentures with warrants can offer tax advantages over convertibles.

Records and meetings. Minutes of shareholders and directors meetings can have important tax and legal consequences. Be sure they are in order, and be sure that an annual meeting is held and

199

that all officers and directors of the corporation are duly elected.

2. Tax law changes:

Legal organizational form. Is your present form of doing business appropriate?

Personal holding company. If more than 50% of the stock of your corporation is held by five or fewer individuals and 60% or more of corporate income is from passive sources, such as rents, dividends, or interest, you could be classified as a personal holding company and be taxed at a 70% rate on all undistributed income.

Sale-leaseback. If you are contemplating a personal sale-leaseback with your corporation, watch that you don't receive unexpected dividends or ordinary income instead of capital gains, and make sure that losses are not disallowed. Any transaction between a corporation and its stockholders must always be closely checked for the "form versus substance" rule and tax technicalities. Sections 1239 and 267, among others, of the Internal Revenue Code must be consulted.

3. Employment laws and requirements. Review your employment policies to be sure that they comply with federal and state statutes concerning such matters as wages, working conditions, hours, and nondiscrimination. Be sure that any covenants you have entered into not to compete have been properly drawn up and are valid.

4. State laws. Be sure you are validly registered in all states where you do business, or certain contracts may be invalid. Check to see if doing business under a "multistate tax compact" could save you money. Compile a list and review the expiration dates of all local licenses and permits.

5. Liability exposure:

Directors and officers. Review indemnification agreements and their enforceability in view of recent developments. See if "D&O" insurance is needed.

Corporate. If you are considering a private placement, check that the provisions of Rule 146 and other securities regulations are met. Also, recent changes in product liability laws should be reviewed.

6. Benefits and compensation. Review stock option, bonus, pension, and profitsharing plans to be sure they conform to the law. All pension plans must be amended to conform to the recently enacted pension law. Be sure that the coverage and dollar limits of your insurance are adequate. Also check that salaries paid to stockholder-employees are sufficiently reasonable to avoid double taxation.

7. Continuity of business:

Buy-sell agreements. Check whether stockholders should enter either a buy-sell or redemption agreement. Be sure that any formula valuation is up to date.

Control. If appropriate, review shareholder control devices, such as restrictions on stock transfers, voting trusts, and deadlock provisions.

Antitrust Laws and the Average Business

Does antitrust legislation have any relevance to the average business? You probably feel that it doesn't if your company is not a huge conglomerate and doesn't engage in monopolistic practices. But you may be surprised to learn that you probably come in contact with antitrust questions more often than you realize—not that your business will ever violate the statutes, but there are numerous situations where unfair pressure can be placed on you by a competitor or supplier. A basic knowledge of what is—and is not—allowed is essential to recognizing an unlawful situation and taking action to protect your company. Know your legal rights and obligations to avoid difficulty and to protect yourself from unfair practices.

The case of enforced price levels

Almost every business manager is familiar with the following situation: John Jones runs a small company and occasionally drops the prices on certain items to generate extra business. Several of his competitors have complained that he is hurting their sales, but Jones continues this practice. Finally, his major supplier tells him, "John, we've been doing business for a long time, but if you don't quit cutting prices, I'm afraid we'll have to drop your account. Too many of our other customers have complained. I'm sure you understand our position." Jones is obviously perplexed and concerned, but he also resents the intrusion into running his business. In fact, he even suspects that it is illegal. Is it? Let's take a look at the basic antitrust statutes.

The antitrust laws in perspective

• The Sherman Act. In broadest terms, this 1890 statute forbids any contract, combination, or conspiracy that restrains trade. This includes "horizontal" arrangements (i.e., between competitors), such as fixing prices or allocating territories and customers, and "vertical" relationships (i.e., between a seller and his customer). Except for fair trade laws in certain states that involve only brand name products, any resale price maintenance agreement is illegal. Although a supplier may suggest resale prices, it is illegal to solicit promises or demand that the prices be maintained.

• The Clayton Act and Robinson-Patman Amendment. In 1914 the Clayton Act was passed to restrict tie-ins and exclusive dealing arrangements as well as to clarify the legality of certain types of mergers and acquisitions. A portion of the Clayton Act concerning pricing was later amended in 1936 by the Robinson-Patman Amendment. These laws attempt to ensure that costs of supplies are the same for every competitor at a given distribution level, regardless of his size or affiliation. In other words, General Motors must normally sell its AC spark plugs at the same price to a small gasoline station as to a large discounter or to one of its own dealers.

• The Federal Trade Commission Act. This act created the Federal Trade Commission and gave it exceptionally broad authority to stop all unfair competitive methods and deceptive trade practices. The Department of Justice usually enforces the Sherman Act, which can involve criminal penalties, and the FTC enforces the Clayton Act, the Robinson-Patman Amendment, and the FTC Act, which involve civil penalties.

To further point out the different situations in which these statutes apply, let's take a short true/false quiz.

True or false:

Small businesses don't have to worry about antimonopoly laws since a monopoly, by definition, is a multimillion dollar corporation.

FALSE. A monopoly is not defined by dollar volume of sales. It's the share of the market controlled that counts. And if you have 60% or more of your market's share, no matter how small your business, you could be on the brink of a problem. Here's why:

Suppose you are the wholesale manufacturer of an antipollution device required by law to be installed in all diesel engines. As the only local manufacturer, you have 75% of your area's market. A company with a poor credit history and a sagging sales record places a large order with you. Are you obligated to fill it?

You could be. To do otherwise might be to illegally restrain trade, since your customer may not have an immediate alternative source of supply. The bottom line: A company that has a monopoly on its product does not have the right to choose its customers. (You can, however, stipulate more stringent credit terms.)

True or false:

If a new business moves into your neighborhood and undercuts your prices, you are justified in having a "one-time-only" below-cost sale to regain your customers.

FALSE. Let's suppose you have a greenhouse operation which you have built into a success over the years, and you have just opened your second outlet. In moves a new competitor, who, in an attempt to establish accounts, sells his merchandise at prices barely above cost. Can you contact the florists near the location of your new store to let them know you're having an "unadvertised special" and sell your inventory below cost, if necessary, in the hope of regaining their business?

You're treading on thin ice if you do. First of all, you might be violating the Robinson-Patman law against geographic price discrimination, which prohibits price reductions only to certain customers or in certain territorial areas. Secondly, a price cut designed to injure a competitor may leave you open to charges of anticompetitive violations. In other words, you can't deliberately lose money just so a competitor won't make money.

Other invitations for trouble on price cutting: (1) offering volume discounts to large buyers if you can't prove that you're only passing along your own savings; and, (2) providing marketing or promotional services (such as counter displays) to some customers and not to others.

True or false:

If you are conversing with a group of competitors, say at a trade convention, it's only natural—and it can't hurt—to "talk shop," discussing prices, territories, or customers, for example.

TRUE and FALSE. It may be only natural, but it certainly can be harmful.

One of the most common (and well-intentioned) antitrust violations involves the natural tendency of businesspeople in similar fields to discuss markets, regulations, and prices. It isn't even necessary to reach an agreement ("We should all raise our prices 5% next year—cost of living, and all"); if subsequent pricing trends parallel that discussion even generally, the courts could conclude that price-fixing occurred.

Ignorance is not a defense, nor is the fact that the discussions didn't actually lead to controlled pricing. The fact is, discussion of prices under such circumstances is illegal.

There are other taboo subjects as well. Illegal group boycotts occur when competitors agree not to buy from a particular supplier or sell to a particular buyer. Allocations of territories or customers could be construed as illegal noncompetition covenants.

It is clear that any meeting with your competitors can have long-range ramifications, no matter how innocent it may seem at the time. Take special care to avoid even the appearance of price- or territory-fixing discussions.

True or false:
You, as a manufacturer, are within your rights to refuse to sell to a distributor who doesn't comply with your territorial or list-price requirements.

FALSE. You cannot force a buyer to sell at a given price. A recent case involved a distributor (the XYZ Company), which, through mutual consent with its supplier (the ABC Company), sold ABC's goods at any price it wished within XYZ's home state. When XYZ sold the product outside of the home state at less than list prices, however, ABC terminated the distributorship.

XYZ brought charges, claiming that the manufacturer was trying to impose unlawful territorial and price restrictions that, in violation of the Sherman Act, limited XYZ's ability to compete. XYZ won the case.

There are situations, however, where territorial restriction is not automatically illegal. Fast-food chains, for example, may require their franchisees to sell in one location only. But any restriction that limits competition is against the law.

True or false:
If you have a "hot" seller that is in great demand, it is smart salesmanship to restrict its purchase to only those customers who buy other products simultaneously.

FALSE. Courts are usually stern with business owners who use "tie-in" sales to manipulate customers, for example.

It's the Christmas season, and you have an exclusive on the toy industry's hottest product this year—a new fashion doll whose name every eight-year-old girl is whispering in Santa's ear. The modestly-priced doll has 39 changes of costume. Can you require purchasers of the doll to also buy a healthy costume inventory?

Not unless you're prepared to deal with cries of "unfair!" Such a strategy reduces competition among costume distributors and restricts the buyer's freedom of choice. In short, it is illegal to use one product's strength to force a customer to buy something he may not want—or at any rate, may not want to buy from you.

The antitrust laws change constantly, and these examples are not intended to be comprehensive. But an awareness of the broad categories of illegal activities can help you avoid them in your own business and recognize a potential violation by your suppliers. Of course, any specific problems or questions should be discussed with your attorney right away.

John Jones's problem
As you can see, the action by John Jones's supplier is definitely illegal. If the supplier carries through with the threat to drop his account and if Jones can prove that he

lost money as a result, he can sue for treble damages. However, a brief letter from Jones's attorney citing the violation would probably straighten out the situation very quickly. But what if deliveries from the supplier mysteriously become delayed? Again, Jones can sue for treble damages if he can prove injury and that the delays are a reprisal for price cutting.

Basic Securities Laws

Certain common business activities are covered by various federal and state laws concerning securities. If you sell or exchange stock, issue debentures, or even buy out another shareholder's interest, various federal and state securities laws come into play.

The economic disaster of the early 1930s prompted Congress to take a close look at the securities industry. Its study, which uncovered numerous abuses, resulted in the Securities Act of 1933. This act requires adequate disclosure of securities sold to the public to ensure that the purchaser has full knowledge to determine for himself how good (or bad) the investment might be. One year later, the Securities Exchange Act of 1934 set up the Securities and Exchange Commission (SEC). In addition to these federal statutes, every state has now enacted its own securities laws, the so-called "blue sky" laws.

Specific aspects of securities laws important to business managers

The securities laws are highly complex, but there are certain aspects of particular importance to business managers that can be broken down into the following categories:

Antifraud. Suppose that you make a deal to buy out your partner knowing that you can sell the business to a third party at a handsome gain. This could be a violation of the antifraud provisions of federal and blue sky statutes. Specifically, Rule 10b of the 1934 act requires disclosure of any material information before the purchase or sale of any stock—even of a closely held company.

Exempted securities. In order to be sold, most securities have to be registered with the SEC—a complicated, expensive process. But there are three important exceptions:

> 1. Private offering exemption. The basic intent of Congress in the 1933 act was to protect the general public from unscrupulous operators. Congress did not intend to encumber legitimate fund-raising transactions involving investors who could decide for themselves whether or not an investment has merit. As a result, the SEC adopted Rule 146, which helps to define the private offering exemption. It provides that a company can sell its securities without registering with the SEC if the following tests are met:
>
> • Type of investors: only investors who are experienced and sophisticated in business matters and who can bear the economic risk of loss may be approached to purchase the securities.
>
> • Manner of offering: all transactions must be by "direct communications." The purchaser must be able to ask questions about the securities and receive answers from the offerer.
>
> • Number of purchasers: there can be no more than 35 pur-

chasers. If one person buys more than $150,000 of the securities, he will not be included in the 35.

2. Intrastate exemption. Congress did not intend to regulate local financing when securities were sold entirely within one state. The mechanics of the intrastate exemption are governed by SEC Rule 147 which stipulates the following:

• Doing business within the state: to qualify for an exemption, the issuer must be organized and have its principal office in the state of the offering, must have at least 80% of its assets and revenues within the state, and must use at least 80% of the net proceeds of the offering for operations in the state.

• Residency of purchasers: all purchasers must be resident in the state of the offering, and for nine months any resale of the securities may be made only to other state residents. Any violation of this provision, however slight, nullifies the entire exemption and opens the door to liability for failure to register.

3. Small offering exemption. According to SEC Rule 240, an offering of up to $100,000 of corporate stock may be made without registration as long as certain conditions are met:

• Manner of offering: no securities may be offered through advertising or general solicitation, and no agent may be paid to find prospective buyers.

• Number of stockholders: immediately before and after the sale, there can be no more than 100 owners of the stock. Also, resale of the stock is restricted.

Regulation A. Congress did not want the 1933 act to unduly hamper smaller businesses, so the SEC adopted Regulation A which permits a company to raise up to $1,500,000 without going through the full SEC registration process. This allows a small company to go public and have a traded stock without much of the elaborate documentation and paperwork of a regular public offering.

Remember that the antifraud provisions always apply whether or not the offering is exempt from the SEC registration. Never approach unsophisticated investors to buy your stock unless you have an intrastate or Rule 240 exemption. Always retain a competent attorney to advise you.

Product Liability: What You Should Know

"Product Liability" is the liability that a manufacturer and seller have to the user of a product for personal injury or property damage resulting from use of the goods. The product liability law and its application have changed dramatically in the last decade and today this area represents one of the least understood and potentially most severe of all business liabilities.

Historical context

Early business transactions usually involved buyers and sellers dealing face to face and bargaining for advantage. As a result, the concept of *caveat emptor* ("buyer beware") developed where the buyer purchased at his own peril and the seller rejected responsibility for his product.

As social attitudes changed, manufacturers began to be held responsible for injury caused by goods they sold. Today, whether you are a manufacturer, processor, distributor, or merchant, you now face unprecedented questions of product liability.

Sources of liability

There are several ways in which a seller can become liable for the goods he sells:

• Statute. Where any statutes regulating the production or sale of a product can be shown to have been violated, the offender can be held legally accountable for any injury caused. A well-known statute would be the Pure Food and Drug Act.

• Negligence. The seller can be held liable for injuries if there was failure to properly design, inspect, test, disclose known defects or risks, or properly instruct in the use of a product. Automobile manufacturers and dealers have faced numerous suits on grounds of negligence.

• Misrepresentation. If the seller advertises a product and makes misrepresentations concerning its character or quality, he can be held liable for any injury caused as a result of the misrepresentation.

Warranty liability

In addition to the above sources of liability, there is a fourth broad category known as "warranty" liability. In the broadest sense, a warranty is the legal assumption of responsibility by the seller for the quality, character, and suitability of the goods sold. There are two main types of warranties—express and implied.

• Express warranty. Any oral or written representation on the part of the seller, which is accepted by the buyer and relied upon by him in purchasing, becomes a part of the sales contract and is known as an "express" warranty. For example, such statements as "100% pure" or "safe for indoor use" constitute legally binding express warranties by the seller. Descriptions, such as diagrams, pictures, blueprints, and technical specifications, also constitute warranties where they form part of the basis of the sales transaction.

• Implied warranties. Two warranties are imposed by the Uniform Commercial Code, irrespective of the seller's intentions and regardless of the fact that he has made no promises or representations concerning the product.

• Merchantability. This warranty is the implied assurance of every seller that his product is of reasonable quality and fit for the usual and ordinary purpose for which the goods are intended.

• Particular purpose. This warranty arises when a product is used for a special purpose, and the buyer relies upon the manufacturer's skill and judgment in furnishing or selecting the product.

Disclaimers

A seller can attempt to restrict or eliminate warranty liabilities, but strict rules apply to all disclaimers. It is not sufficient to state that "no warranties are made, either express or implied." Conspicuous and precise language must be used. Even with proper language and format, however, the courts often look askance at warranty limitations.

Strict liability

This is the most controversial and recently developed theory of recovery in product liability. In many states, anyone who sells a product in a defective condition (including such things as improper packaging, warnings, or directions) or one that is considered "unreasonably dangerous" is liable for any physical harm caused to the ultimate user or to his property. The theory is that the manufacturer is better able than the consumer to bear any burden of injury. Strict liability applies even though the manufacturer exercised all possible care in the production, and no warranties were made. Lack of privity or warranty disclaimers are not available as defenses.

What should you do?
Make sure products conform to all trade and legal standards.
Have potentially dangerous products safety tested by an independent agency.
Identify and label all dangerous parts of a product.
Check that all instructions and manuals give clear directions and warnings.
Review advertising and sales literature for unintended warranties.
Consider product liability insurance and "hold harmless" agreements between yourself and others in your chain of distribution.
In 1960 there were fewer than 50,000 product liability suits in the courts. By 1970 the number had jumped to 500,000 and is soon expected to pass 1,000,000. For more information, contact the U.S. Consumer Product Safety Commission, 5401 Westwood Ave., Bethesda, MD 20207, or one of its many regional offices.

Annual Meeting Checklist

Most companies, whether large or small, are required to hold an annual meeting to report to stockholders. Here is a checklist you should consult before your next stockholder meeting.

Preparation for the meeting
While some of these points may not be applicable to your particular situation, you should consider:

• Agenda. Prepare all items to be discussed and resolutions to be ratified, including the proposed slate of directors.

• Stockholders of record. Prepare a list of stockholders. Usually, the record date of the stockholder list must be between 10 and 60 days prior to the annual meeting.

• Notice of meeting. Generally, the directors must call the meeting if a time and date are not listed in the bylaws or certificate of incorporation. Notify all stockholders of the date, time, and place.

• Proxy statement. Prepare all proxies and proxy statements and distribute to stockholders in accordance with notice provisions.

• Annual report. Usually, the annual report is presented at the same time as the proxy statement.

• Corporate records. Gather all documents (bylaws, certificate of incorporation, financial records, etc.) necessary to answer any stockholder's inquiry. In addition, it is usually advisable to have the company's counsel and accountant present to answer any questions that may arise.

Actions requiring stockholder approval
The annual meeting gives stockholders the opportunitjy to ratify certain actions re-

quiring their approval. While the exact requirements vary by state, here is a list of corporate undertakings generally requiring such approval:

• Corporate charter and bylaws. Almost all states require stockholder approval to amend the certificate of incorporation. Unless otherwise provided, similar approval may also be needed for changes in the bylaws.

• No-par value shares. No-par value shares may be issued in most states. However, stockholder approval is often required to set a price for such shares and to allocate the proceeds between the "paid-in capital" and the "surplus" accounts.

• Stock options. Favorable stock options may normally be given to outsiders in the normal course of business, without specific stockholder approval. (An example would be an equity "kicker" in connection with a debt issue.) When the option is to existing officers or employees, however, many states require stockholders to approve the details to prevent insider dealings and corporate abuse.

• Officers and directors. In some states, loans may be made by the corporation to officers and directors only when approved by the stockholders. Also, many states require stockholder approval before the corporation can grant indemnification to officers and directors for mismanagement, conflict of interest, etc.

• Merger or disposal of major assets. Most states require stockholder approval for such actions, often by more than a simple majority vote. In addition, certain large acquisitions must be approved in some states.

• Guarantees. Normally, if the corporation makes any guarantee "not in the furtherance of normal business" (such as guaranteeing a debt of a director or officer), stockholder approval is required.

• Elections. The directors must generally be elected by the stockholders. In addition, ratification of accountants is usually considered a stockholder prerogative.

After the meeting

• Minutes. Prepare minutes for corporate records and stockholders.

• Press releases. Usually distributed after the meeting.

• Amendments. Follow up on filing all appropriate amendments (contracts, bylaws, charter, etc.) with the appropriate authorities.

Appraisal Rights—
Little-Known Facts

Many business managers do not realize that the laws of most states provide that whenever a corporation makes a major change in its business, nonassenting shareholders have the right to sell their shares back to the corporation. If a price cannot be agreed upon, the dissenters can generally insist on an objective appraisal of the fair market value of the shares—hence the term "appraisal rights."

The theory behind appraisal rights is that a person buys stock in a company with the anticipation that it will be operated as it was in the past. If the company subsequently decides to make major changes in its operation and organization, shareholders who disagree with the changes should have the right to recover their money. The exact definition of which damages are major varies widely state by state. However, any action involving a merger, consolidation, sale of a major asset, dissolution, or, in some cases, change in corporate charter, generally involves appraisal rights.

How do appraisal rights work?

Because the purchase of their shares may impose a severe burden on the corporation, the nonassenting stockholders must adhere to the letter of the law in exercising their right to sell. For example, most state statutes provide that the dissenter must notify the company prior to the meeting when the proposed change will be voted on. As a result, the corporation is aware of its repurchase obligation in the event that the proposed change is adopted. After the dissent has been filed, but before the shares are finally sold, the stockholder normally has no further right to vote on corporate affairs. Most statutes also provide that if the corporation subsequently decides to abandon the proposed action, the dissenters lose their right to "put" their stock to the company.

What should the business manager do?

Most business managers don't think about appraisal rights until they are confronted with the prospect of purchasing a block of stock if a proposed change is approved. While minority shareholders may lack the votes to affect company policy, they can be a formidable force in certain important situations. As a first step, every business manager should ask his attorney to summarize the appraisal rights laws of his state of incorporation. And equally important, he should be aware that even though he may own only a small percentage of some other company, he may have the right to sell his shares at fair market value if its management makes certain major changes which he feels are unwarranted.

Buy-Sell Agreements

Most close companies want to avoid shares falling into unwanted hands. To prevent this, participants in any new venture generally have an agreement that sets forth how a shareholder's stock will be handled should he die or wish to depart the business. This is commonly called a buy-sell agreement. It states how the shares will be bought and sold in the event that certain things happen. Here are the major points to understand:

Redemption vs. cross-purchase

The first decision to make when setting up a buy-sell agreement is whether the shares should be purchased by the corporation (called a "redemption" agreement) or by the remaining shareholders ("cross-purchase" agreement). In making this important decision, these factors should be considered:

1. Source of funds. Under a redemption agreement the shares are purchased with corporate money, whereas a cross-purchase agreement involves the use of the shareholders' personal funds. In certain states a corporation may not be allowed to purchase shares under a redemption agreement if it does not have sufficient capital surplus at the time.

2. Cost basis. When the corporation redeems the stock of a deceased shareholder, the cost basis of the remaining shareholders' stock remains the same while its value increases. Hence, a latent capital gain liability is built up. With cross-purchase the basis of the stock is stepped up to the purchase price and no tax liability is incurred.

3. Control. With redemption the proportionate interests of each remaining

shareholder remain the same. With cross-purchase the number of shares that each survivor can or must buy can be varied as desired.

4. Attribution. When only a portion of a deceased shareholder's stock is redeemed by the corporation, the proceeds may be treated as a taxable dividend to the estate instead of a purchase. With cross-purchase this is no problem since the corporation is not a party to the transaction.

Funding

To assure that enough money will be available to purchase the shares, buy-sell agreements are often funded by life insurance. If a redemption agreement is used, the corporation takes out a policy on each shareholder and names itself as beneficiary. With cross-purchase each shareholder carries life insurance on every other shareholder. With more than three or four major shareholders, cross-purchase can become too unwieldy to fund with insurance.

Setting the price

This is the final trouble spot—how to set the price at which the shares will be bought and sold. There are four possibilities:

- Fixed price. With this most common method, a fixed price is set and periodically changed to reflect the current status of the business.

- Appraisal. The price of the stock is set by an independent appraisal at the time of sale.

- Earnings. A multiple of net profits is set that determines the share price.

- Book value. The price is based on some multiple of the net worth of the company.

Bankruptcy: Don't Go Down With Your Debtors

Bankruptcy has its roots in the law of the Roman Empire and has been a part of English jurisprudence since 1542. Laws relating to bankruptcy have been enacted or amended in the United States after every major economic depression. The current Bankruptcy Code, which took effect October 1, 1979, provides for both involuntary (instigated at the request of creditors) and voluntary (instigated by the debtor) bankruptcy under Chapters 7 and 11. Chapter 7 bankruptcy deals with liquidation (when a company literally goes out of business), while Chapter 11 deals with reorganization (where the company generally stays in business, but consolidates its assets to pay its creditors so that it may "start fresh").

Basically, the Bankruptcy Code provides various methods to accomplish three things:

- Relieve debtors of their debts entirely.

- Postpone the time debtors have to pay creditors.

- Protect some rights of creditors.

Proceedings

To initiate bankruptcy is a relatively simple procedure. A petition is filed with the local federal court on standard forms, and the schedules must be sworn to under oath. If filed by the debtor (voluntary bankruptcy), the document must contain four items:

1. List of creditors, secured and unsecured.

2. List of property claimed to be "exempt."

3. Statement of affairs of the bankrupt.

4. List of assets.

Involuntary petitions filed by creditors seek to have the court adjudge the debtor bankrupt. In particular, the petition must demonstrate that the debtor is not generally paying his debts when due.

Bankruptcy court

The new Code abolished the concept of a "referee" in bankruptcy. The court official with jurisdiction is now called the Bankruptcy Judge. A pilot program underway in several districts around the country uses the concept of a "U.S. Trustee," whose function is more administrative than judicial. The U.S. Trustee handles the paperwork, presides over the initial meeting of creditors, and generally performs the routine tasks that are associated with a bankruptcy procedure. This pilot program will be evaluated in 1984, and, if it is proven successful, may be instituted across the country.

Judgment of bankruptcy

After the proceedings are initiated, the steps are the same whether the petition was voluntary or involuntary. The court notifies each creditor of the proceedings, the date of filing claims, and the date of the first meeting of the creditors with the debtor. The law provides that the Bankruptcy Judge may appoint an "interim trustee" (comparable to the position of the "receiver" in the old Bankruptcy Act) to take charge of the assets and, generally, run the debtor's business until a permanent trustee is appointed. The interim trustee is appointed from a panel selected from the debtor's community; in some cases, as explained in the paragraph above, the U.S. Trustee fills this function.

Trustee in bankruptcy

At the first meeting of creditors, a "trustee" is elected by a majority in number and amount of the claims. (Usually, the interim trustee will also be the permanent trustee.) The trustee, under supervision of the court, then disposes of all nonexempt property for the benefit of the creditors.

Who may file for bankruptcy

Any person, partnership, or corporation may file a voluntary bankruptcy, except railroads, banks, insurance companies, and savings and loan associations. Farmers and nonbusiness (charitable and nonprofit, for instance) corporations may not be forced into involuntary bankruptcy by creditors.

Importance to the businessman

Too often, the first notice that a businessman has that a certain debtor may be in trouble is when he is notified by the court of bankruptcy proceedings. At the time of notice, it is important that the businessman determine whether or not he has a claim against the debtor and whether he is entitled to any "dividend" (payment by trustee to creditors). Otherwise, his claim may be counted as "dischargeable" and nothing will be received.

Claims

To qualify as a claim, it must be filed with the court within six months of the date first set by the Bankruptcy Judge for the first meeting of creditors. Most such claims are for ordinary trade credit or instruments in writing such as contracts or rental agreements.

Nondischargeable claims

Certain claims cannot be discharged in bankruptcy: taxes due any governmental body, claims by employees under employment contracts, debts created by fraud, and wages earned within three months of filing the bankruptcy petition.

Priority of claims

The first priority of claims is to secured creditors who collect their debts to the extent of the security interest they hold. Note, however, that unsecured creditors are last on the list of persons to be paid. They don't get their money until the attorney and trustee fees, taxes, and court costs have been paid. In short, they get what's left, if anything.

How to minimize losses

1. A good offense is the best defense. Keep close watch on all delinquent accounts. Bankruptcies don't just happen—they are caused.

2. Obtain a list of creditors. If you learn that a major account has filed for bankruptcy, immediately contact the debtor or the federal court where the proceeding was filed to obtain a full list of creditors.

3. Try to get appointed to the creditors' committee. Appoint an attorney to represent the committee.

4. Proof of claim. Verify that your debt is listed correctly on the court's schedule of debts. If not, file a proof of claim.

5. Work together. One of the toughest jobs is to get major creditors to work collectively. Together you must agree whether to accept a proposed settlement or to ask that the business be liquidated. No plan of settlement can ever be fully equitable to all parties.

How to Maintain Control of Your Company

Most businessmen associate 51% stock ownership with "control" of a company. As a successful business grows, however, major amounts of equity capital must sometimes be raised with the result that the original founders are often diluted below 51%. This need be no cause for alarm. There are numerous ways to exercise rock-solid control of a company with substantially less than majority stock ownership. It does, however, require careful and deliberate planning.

Two situations affect corporate control that every businessman should recognize: sale of new stock by the company, and sale by a stockholder of stock already issued.

In the former case, the company has several options, since new stock being issued can be restricted to the extent allowed by statute. In the latter case, however, where the stock has already been sold, unless the company exercised its prerogative to restrict the stock in some way at the time of sale, there is little the company can later say about the disposition of the stock. Hence, it is vital to plan before shares are sold. Otherwise, you may literally lose control of your destiny.

Sale of new stock by the company

As mentioned, you have quite a bit of latitude here to protect yourself. Long before you might fall below 51% ownership of the common shares, there are several alternatives you should consider:

• Different classes of stock. By far the simplest and most popular method is to segregate the classes of stock. For example, certain stock may be sold as nonvoting shares, while you keep control of the majority of voting stock. Another possibility is to designate the shares as Class A, Class B, and so on, with each class having the right to elect a certain number of directors. If you control the Class A stock, you take care to have Class A entitled to elect the majority of directors.

• Voting agreements. Although you must be mindful of applicable state statutes, it is often possible to sell stock with the stipulation that the new shareholders agree to certain conditions, such as voting only for certain directors. In other cases the company can require an "irrevocable proxy" from new shareholders and have it so legended on the face of the share certificates.

• Staggered elections. One very popular control technique is to amend the bylaws to require that the election of directors be staggered over time. This obviates the threat of a takeover, since only a limited number of directors may be elected at any one time.

• Veto power. Although it might stifle certain corporate actions, many states will allow bylaws requiring all fundamental corporate acts to be unanimous. In effect, even as a minority shareholding director, you would still have veto power over any undesired changes.

Sale by shareholders

The second broad area of concern regarding corporate control is what happens to shares after they are issued. Most owners of somewhat closely held firms do not want shares to be freely transferable for two main reasons:

• To avoid purchase of shares by certain individuals or groups (such as competitors) who might grant them certain rights (such as inspecting corporate records).

• To ensure that the new shareholders and present owners have compatible interests (for example, outside shareholders might wish low salaries and high dividends as opposed to a policy of high salaries, maximum depreciation rates, and low dividends by shareholders who are also members of management).

There are a number of ways to impose restrictions on transfer of securities. Here are the main ones:

• Right of first refusal. The corporation or any of its officers and directors may be given refusal rights on all shares available for sale. This method is generally the simplest and most popular way to prevent shares from falling into undesirable hands.

• Restricted transferees. The stock may be restricted so that it can be sold only to certain persons or classes of individuals, such as family, back to the corporation, or other employees.

• Option to buy out. Upon certain events (such as the death or incapacity of a shareholder), the corporation, officers, directors, or other shareholders may exercise an option to buy out the shares in question.

Legal note

Two points should be observed:

• It is difficult to generalize concerning corporate control because the statutes of each state vary widely in this area. We have tried to give you some guidelines, but, of course, you should check specifics with your attorney.

• Some measures restricting control may invalidate a Sub S election. Remember, Sub S corporations can have only one class of stock outstanding.

Annual Report Checklist

Almost every business has some outside investors. For some companies, they are the shareholders who own part of the equity of the business. Other companies, even if they are 100% owned by management, also have interested "investors"—usually the local commercial bank. But whoever your investors are, they can be instrumental to growth and sometimes even to survival. Keep them informed at least once a year of the following via a chat with your banker or a written report to stockholders.

1. Business activity:

a) Products and/or services. Describe each in as much detail as possible and try to include photographs or samples. Note how the products and/or services may have changed over the past year.

b) Organization. Illustrate how the company is organized. List where subsidiaries or divisions operate and what they produce. Also, note major properties owned and important lease arrangements.

c) Success factors. What does it take to be successful in your business—production expertise, marketing abilities, ability to motivate people, or some other special competence? Without releasing confidential information, discuss the keys to success and how you plan to improve your company's capabilities.

2. Management. Note who runs the firm. Name each officer and director and list his background, age, length of service, outside relationships, if any, and duties in the firm.

3. Financial. The financial highlights should always include an easy-to-read, one-page summary. Use charts or graphs to make trends easier to interpret. Always compare present results with past performance, if possible. When practical, statements should be audited. Be sure to address the following:

a) Sales and profits. Show absolute figures and percent of change over past few years.

b) Retained earnings. Show what proportion of profits is retained in the business and what part is paid as dividends.

c) Accounting conventions. Discuss depreciation, capitalization, bad debt write-offs, and other financial policies that can significantly affect performance.

4. Marketing:

a) Pricing. Discuss the impact of inflation on company pricing policies. Have higher prices for your products resulted in customer resistance and consequent loss of sales?

b) Advertising. Show how the various media (TV, radio, newspapers, direct mail, etc.) are being used for promotion. Discuss their effectiveness and your future plans.

c) Distribution. Describe how your products and/or services are delivered to the consumer. Have there been changes? Are you investigating more efficient distribution methods?

5. Employees. Discuss the number of employees, their efficiency, morale, and the situation concerning a union. In particular, list:

a) Employee plans. Briefly outline any pension, stock option, or profitsharing plans the company has.

b) Health and safety. What has been the effect of OSHA requirements? Has the business been inspected? Were there any violations? What is being done to remedy the situation?

6. Future prospects and objectives. Future goals should seem aggressive, yet they must be credible. If possible, show last year's projections and how well (or poorly) they were met. Address such important points as:

- Expected sales and earnings.

- New products to be developed and marketed.

- Growth in number of employees and size of facilities.

- Expected market share and position in the industry.

- Pending legal proceedings that may materially affect the company.

Final notes

Always discuss the bad with the good. Rosy forecasts alone can only damage your credibility. When possible, show how outside factors in the local and national economy have affected your business. Finally, always disclose as much as possible without jeopardizing your competitive situation. The more your investors can understand the business and its problems and prospects, the more they will be able to assist you.

Corporate Director's Liability Checklist

If you are now a director or you are considering becoming a director of a corporation, know your responsibilities. Ignorance of the law could prove disastrous.

Don't confuse your loyalties

Corporations are creatures of the state. As a director, you have a fiduciary responsibility, not as an agent for the stockholders, as commonly supposed, but to the corporation as an entity (and to the state that sanctioned it).

Ultra vires acts

To ensure that you do not participate in any acts beyond the corporation's power (*ultra vires* acts) for which you could be personally responsible, consult with your attorney concerning applicable state statutes. In addition, check the certificate of incorporation and the bylaws of the corporation to be sure you understand your rights and responsibilities. In particular, check these points:

- Dividends. In most states you can legally pay a dividend only after certain conditions are met. Be sure to check the statutes.

- Compensation. If possible, all matters of compensation where the board may benefit (like salary, bonus, pension, profit sharing plans, and stock options) should be ratified by the majority of shareholders. As long as you adhere to reasonable guidelines, you should incur no liability.

- Employees. Directors can be personally liable if they indiscriminately fire any employees who have contracts, such as an officer with a management contract or certain union workers.

- Taxes. A critical item. If you are a director as well as a ''responsible officer,'' you are personally liable for any payroll deductions either not withheld or used for any other purpose. You may be personally liable for a 100% penalty because you have no discretion to use such funds for corporate purposes.

- Annual reports. Even if you are the sole stockholder, you must still file an annual report in most states. Not doing so can involve personal liability.

- Signature. If you have signature authority, always sign the name of the corporation, then the word ''by,'' and put your name and title. If you leave out the word ''by,'' you may have personally bound yourself.

Corporate opportunity doctrine

- Conflict of interest. If there is any possibility that you might personally profit from a corporate action to which you are a party, make full disclosure and get the facts into the record. Then make sure that the matter was supported by a sufficient vote of the disinterested directors. Also, be sure the bylaws contain an ''exculpatory'' clause permitting such transactions.

- Inside information. According to a recent court ruling, inside information belongs to the corporation, not to its officers or directors. Remember your fiduciary responsibilities to all shareholders, and there will be no problems.

Outside dealings

- Personal loans to the corporation. Although usury laws do not apply in many states, you should take care that the interest rate charged is considered reasonable by the stockholders.

- Borrowing from the corporation may be hazardous. In the event of default, you may be personally liable if you voted funds for a loan to a fellow director.

Don't be a dummy director

- ''See no evil . . .'' It used to be if you saw no evil, you couldn't be held responsible. No more. If you accept the responsibility of being a director, you may be personally liable for corporate acts, even if you were absent from a director's meeting. Don't lend your good name to a corporation as director unless you plan to actually participate in corporate affairs.

- Professional advice. Always insist on qualified outside advice to ensure ''due care'' whenever you feel a professional opinion is needed.

- Dissent. If you object to a corporate action, your dissent should be carefully noted in the corporate minutes. To minimize your liability, you should continue to exert influence on the corporation to change its course.

216

CHAPTER FIFTEEN

Tax Techniques

Introduction

Value of tax savings

Too many business managers get caught up in the day-to-day operation of their businesses and are content to let the accountant look after the taxes. Sometimes this works out just fine, but other times the manager is choosing to ignore or surrender responsibility for one of the most significant sources of income, tax savings.

A manager will stay up all night to save a few dollars in costs on his operation, but he is unwilling to spend even a few minutes looking at the more lucrative possibilities for saving taxes in his business. The absurdity of this attitude toward taxes is vividly illustrated in Figure 1, which compares tax savings with dollars saved in costs.

Sources of tax-free income

The following are a few of the more important sources of tax-free income.

- Children's income. Normally taxed to the child, not the parent.

- Damages for personal injury.

- Employee death benefits, up to $5,000.

- Discount on tax-exempt bonds.

- Dividends and interest—up to the exclusion amount ($200 in 1981 only; then reverts to $100).

- Gifts.

- Home—gain realized on sale of principal residence if you buy or build another house of comparable value.

- Health insurance gains not deducted previously.

- Inheritances.

- Insurance proceeds from accidents, generally.

- Insurance proceeds for additional living expenses.

- Interest from insurance that is included in payments to surviving spouse up to $1,000 per year.

- Interest on tax-exempt bonds (state or local).

- Life insurance proceeds.

- Lifetime exclusion of up to $1000 for interest in qualified tax exempt savings certificates issues after Sept. 1981 and before 1983.

- Loans.

- Salary advances from your employer that you will repay.

- Social Security benefits.

- Stock dividends paid in stock.

- Utility dividends reinvested in company stock (only for certain utilities and for periods between 19823-1985 inclusive).

- Worker's Compensation set payments.

In addition to the above sources of tax-free income, your business can also be a source of tax-free income. This is especially possible for stockholder-employees in a close corporation.

How to Get Money Out of your Business

If you are a stockholder-employee of a closely held corporation, you naturally want to reduce your tax expenses as much as possible. You'd like to avoid having income taxed twice—first at the corporate level and then as a dividend at the personal level. Here is a checklist of ways to extract cash from a going corporation, while minimizing tax liability.

Stockholder-employee benefits

- Medical expenses reimbursements. So long as the arrangement does not

Figure 1

TAX VS. COST SAVINGS

Before taxes profit margin on sales	Amount of sales needed to equal $1,000 savings in cost	Amount of sales needed to equal a $1,000 saving in taxes @ 46%
3%	$33,333	$72,463
5	20,000	43,478
10	10,000	21,739
15	6,667	14,493
30	3,333	7,246

---

discriminate in favor of highly paid executives or shareholder-employees, medical expenses for employees and their families may be paid directly by the corporation or through an insurance company with the corporation paying the premium.

In addition, health and accident premiums may be paid for the benefit of employees. If the plan is an insured medical reimbursement plan and meets certain criteria, the payments are deductible by the corporation and tax-free to the employee. (Note: To be safe, check with your attorney and be sure your plan is in writing.)

• Meals, lodging, and entertainment. The cost of meals and lodging for overnight travel away from home is deductible by the corporation and nontaxable to the stockholder-employee as long as a valid business purpose exists and the expenses are substantiated.

Similarly, most entertainment expenses are also deductible as long as they are reasonable and substantiated.

• Life insurance. A corporation can provide up to $50,000 of group term life insurance tax-free to employee-stockholders. Premiums on insurance in excess of $50,000 are treated as taxable compensation to the employee. In most cases, however, the tax imputation is considerably less than the actual cost of the insurance.

• Pension and profit-sharing plans. This source is probably the single most important source of "wealth building" for a shareholder-employee.

Subject to certain rules, a corporation can pay substantial amounts into a pension trust. The payments are deductible by the corporation and nontaxable to the employee until he begins drawing the funds when he retires and is presumably in a lower tax bracket.

Such plans can tie benefits to wage levels and Social Security benefits, thus offering advantages to highly paid shareholder-employees.

Taxable payments to stockholder-employees

• Salary. The corporation may deduct the payment of a reasonable salary to a stockholder-employee. Try to determine the salary that costs the least in combined corporate and personal taxes.

High salaries must have a justifiable business purpose, or the IRS may hold part of the salary as a "constructive dividend" and deny the corporate deduction while still taxing the individual.

• Rent or lease payments. The stockholder-employee can lease or rent real estate or equipment to the corporation at reasonable rates. This may be useful if the stockholder is already making a maximum reasonable salary. Excess payments are again subject to treatment as constructive dividends.

Other ways to get cash

• Borrowing from the corporation. A stockholder can borrow cash from the corporation, but there should be a note evidencing the debt and stipulating a fixed repayment schedule. An interesting tax planning opportunity is for the loan to be interest-free to the stockholder. See your tax adviser for details.

• Payments that exceed earnings from a deficit corporation. If a corporation has no accumulated earnings and profits and pays out dividends in excess of earnings for the current fiscal year, the excess is treated as a tax-free return of capital rather than as a dividend.

Pay out dividends equal to two years' earnings every other year, and only the portion equivalent to the current year's earnings will be taxed as a dividend.

• Subchapter S election. A Subchapter S election generally avoids federal taxation at the corporate level. There must be 25 or fewer shareholders and only one class of stock. Not more than 20% of gross income can be from "passive" sources (i.e., rents, interest, etc.).

All corporate earnings may then be distributed to shareholders and will be taxed only once—at the personal level. Family taxes may be reduced if stock ownership is spread among family members who are in low tax brackets.

In light of the value of a tax dollar and the wealth of sources for such savings, it is vital for an alert business manager to be aware of his tax possibilities, if not an expert on them. The key to being a good manager is understanding what is going on and knowing where to get more information if necessary. But now the question arises as to how far you dare go with tax savings.

When does it pay to push your luck?

Tax avoidance is both lawful and ethical. It is making the best use of legal procedures to reduce the amount of tax you have to pay. On the other hand, tax evasion is not legal. Tax evasion is the willful misrepresentation of fact or the concealment of information to evade lawful tax. There may be some doubt in your mind as to the propriety of certain tax deductions if you seek to avoid tax, but if you are evading tax, there will be no question in your mind about what you are doing.

Tax issues are often complicated. It isn't surprising that tax courts hear hundreds of cases each year in hopes of straightening out some of the questions. Therefore it is understandable if you (even with the aid of your accountant) are unsure of the legality of certain deductions. If you have no clear guidelines on the correct procedure in regard to some of your deductions, go ahead and take the deduction. If your accountant doesn't know how clear an issue is, have him say so in writing to protect yourself in case the IRS disagrees with your judgment.

In deciding how far you should push your luck, you must consider how much you stand to gain and how much you could lose. If you have a reasonable deduction, try for it. If the IRS says no, you've still had use of that money over the time it took them to get around to your case. Furthermore, be clear that such things as honest disagreements do occur in some areas of tax. Even if they go against you, you don't have to feel like a criminal. And of course, if you get no challenge from the IRS, you will have made yourself some money.

Usually, you don't risk much by taking chances on deductions. The IRS may make you pay back the sum with interest, but you probably decided beforehand that the possible loss in interest costs was worth gambling for the possible saving. This idea of pushing your luck does not mean you can make statements you know to be false, because falsehoods can lead to questions of fraud and tax evasion. The penalties in these areas can be stiff indeed.

T & E Expenses—Key Facts to Avoid Problems

For any business travel to be deductible, the IRS imposes two main requirements. First, the travel must be reasonable, have a necessary business purpose, and be "away from home." Second, the amount of the deduction cannot be lavish and must be documented.

"Home" is defined as the taxpayer's place of employment, regardless of where his family residence is located. You do not receive a deduction for commuting to and from work, but you would for any other business travel, even if it is in the city where you live.

The cost of meals on a business trip is also deductible, but only if you stay away from home overnight. Of course, if the traveler manages to combine meals and business conversation with clients, then the cost would be deductible whether you stay overnight or not.

The amount of time spent on business during your domestic travels will determine the extent of the deductions involved. Here's how the Internal Revenue Service looks at it:

If your trip is all business, then all reasonable expenses for food, lodging, and transportation are deductible.

If the trip is primarily—but not all—business, you may deduct the business related expenses and the transportation costs.

A trip that is mostly pleasure, with a little business thrown in, is not deductible except for the expenses directly related to business. You may not deduct transportation costs.

You must be able to document your travel expenses if you wish to use the travel deductions. Documentation is a receipt, a bill marked paid, or some other verifiable document proving the expense. Here are the items for which you will need documentation:

• The number of days you spend away from home overnight and the exact dates you were away.

• Where you went—city, state, or town.

• Business reason for the trip. What you hoped to gain by the travel.

• Amount spent on lodging, transportation, and food. If you like, you may use a general category for such things as meals and gas and oil, as long as the total amount is reasonable and substantiated.

Automobile expenses—itemized deductions vs. standard mileage deductions

To the extent that auto travel is related to business, the following expenses may be itemized and are deductible:

• Auto operation. This includes gas, oil, maintenance, washing and polishing, garaging, auto club membership, etc.

• State and local assessments. This includes any use taxes, registration fees, sales taxes, and license fees.

• Cost recovery. The full cost of the car may be recovered over its useful life. The 1981 Tax Act allows a useful life as short as three years. Based on a three-year life, you can also use 150% accelerated cost recovery.

• Insurance. All insurance premiums including liability, fire and theft, and collision are deductible.

• Theft and casualty losses. To the extent not reimbursed by insurance, you may deduct all such expenses without regard to the business use limitations described below.

If a car is used for both business and personal travel, the expenses may be allocated by determining the number of business and personal miles and then prorating them. For example, if eight out of ten miles driven are for business, then 80% of expenses may be deducted. But whatever percentage is used, it must be a fair representation of actual business related expenses and proper records to substantiate the deductions must be kept.

Rather than itemize expenses, owners may use a mileage allowance of 20¢ per mile for the first 15,000 miles and 11¢ a mile thereafter. The previous rate was 18½¢ and 10¢, respectively.

This allowance may be taken no matter what age or type of car you drive. However, the mileage rate may not be used when the owner previously itemized and used an accelerated depreciation method or took the allowance for additional first-year depreciation.

If you have a new car, it may be a good idea to itemize using the straight-line depreciation method while the car is new and later shift to the mileage allowance system. However, once the car is fully depreciated, you may only take a flat 11¢ per mile allowance.

Be sure to compute the deductions both ways each year and use the one that gives more tax savings. You may switch back and forth as often as you like.

For example, John Johnson has a new car which cost $7,000. He drives it 25,000 miles a year, of which 20,000 are for business. Estimated trade-in value of the car is $1,000 after three years. Figure 2 shows the way the trade-off would work using both methods.

While the car is new, it is more advantageous to itemize. However, in the fourth year after the depreciation allowance runs out, the standard rate method will yield higher deductions. Under both methods, an investment credit (based upon the useful life of the automobile, and available only on the business portion) may be claimed up to the limitation of the taxpayer's income tax liability, and sales tax and interest may be claimed in their entirety.

An employee doesn't have to account for specific auto expenses if his company reimburses him for using his car on a straight mileage basis which is not more than 20¢ per mile, according to the IRS. So you can use the 20¢ per mile reimbursement rule to give an officer or employee a tax-free raise. This can be done because an employee, officer, or officer-stockholder does not pay tax on excess compensation

Figure 2

ITEMIZED METHOD

Straight-line
     depreciation (3 years) $2,000
Gas 2,500
Oil and lube 100
Tires 300
Repairs 500
Insurance 350
                             $5,750

4/5 business use = $4,600 deductible

STANDARD RATE METHOD

15,000 miles × $.20 . . . . $3,000
5,000 miles × $.11 550
20,000 business miles $3,550

= $3,550 deductible

---

paid out on the 20¢ per mile reimbursement. Thus, if you want to increase a company officer's salary without arousing IRS suspicions about an unreasonable salary, have him use his own car on company business if he can operate it at a personal cost of less than 20¢ per mile.

In addition to car expenses, an employer may pay an employee a daily allowance in lieu of subsistence without requiring detailed substantiation of the expenses other than time, place, and purpose of travel. The allowance was formerly $36 per day and is now generally $44 per day. Any executive who owns more than 10% of his company's stock cannot use the per diem reimbursement. If you happen to fall into this category, you must continue to give a full account of all food, lodging, and similar expenses.

Entertainment expenses

Entertainment of business associates can be a deductible expense if it meets any of the following tests:

• The entertainment is directly related to business; i.e., although you combined business and pleasure, the primary activity was business. For example, a "clients only" cocktail party.

• Entertainment associated with business is deductible if you can show that it took place the same day as the business meeting and that the business was the real reason for getting together. To be associated with business the entertainment must directly precede or follow business.

• "Quiet business meal" is a term applied to those situations where you either have a quiet meal with a business associate or buy him or her a drink in an establishment that has a minimum of distractions. The idea here is that you get together in a place that is conducive to conversation. Taking a businessman to the fights does not qualify here.

Generally, expenses incurred attending business seminars or conventions are deductible, unless the IRS feels there was more pleasure than business at the convention. If the IRS says the convention was primarily for pleasure, travel costs will not be deductible but costs directly related to business will be. Expenses for wives or husbands who are not directly affiliated with the business are not deductible unless the spouse's presence serves a bona fide business purpose. From now on, the deductibility of attending foreign conventions is severely curtailed. If you anticipate going overseas for such a convention, check with your accountant before leaving. You must produce stringent documentation of all expenses and the actual time you were in attendance.

Goodwill entertaining at a restaurant may be deducted as a "quiet business meal" and theater tickets may be deducted as "associated with" business if the business was conducted on the day the curtain went up.

Like travel expenditures, entertainment costs are not deductible in virtually any category unless you can document them according to IRS specifications. Generally, you must have receipts or be able to document the following:

• The date of your entertainment expenditure.

• The location and type of entertainment.

• The precise cost of the entertainment. (Taxi money and other incidental costs may be listed on a daily basis by their various classifications instead of by individual incident.)

• The purpose of the entertainment, the nature of the business discussion, and the benefit you anticipate from the entertainment.

• The business relationship of your guest to you. You should show his firm, his name, and his title.

Business gifts

You may make gifts to business associates, but you may claim no more than $25.00 tax deduction per person per year. A gift to a member of a businessman's family is considered a gift to him. Promotional items under $4.00, like pens or paperweights, advertising displays, and awards to employees (under $100.00) for service, are not considered gifts.

If you want your $25.00 deduction for a business gift you must be able to document the following:

• The identification of the recipient: his name, title, and firm.

• The reason for giving the gift or else what you hoped to gain by it.

• The nature of the gift. A brief description of it would suffice.

• When the gift was given.

• How much it cost.

Suppose a business client comes to town and you just happen to have tickets for a performance that night by his favorite singer. Can you give him the tickets and put it down to entertainment or do you have to use up your gift deduction by calling the tickets a gift? If you do not accompany him to the performance, but you do spend time with him that afternoon talking business, you may call the tickets "entertainment associated with business" and save the gift deduction for Christmas.

What if the IRS disallows your deductions?

The reason for being careful about keeping travel and entertainment records is that the IRS may hit you with a double tax if it disallows your deductions. Your company can lose the deduction and you, who received reimbursement for the expense, will be taxed for the receipt of additional income, perhaps in the form of a dividend. For this reason it is worthwhile to plan ahead for your travel and entertainment expenditures by having standard procedures for recording the expenses and being sure they are always followed.

The Investment Credit: Major Source of Tax Savings

The investment credit ranks as one of the most important sources of tax savings for the average business. But surprisingly, many businesses overlook the substantial taxes this device can save.

The investment credit grants up to a 10% dollar-for-dollar credit against federal income taxes for investment in certain qualified business assets. This credit is worth more to you than an expense deductible from gross income because the credit is applied directly to your yearly tax bill.

The credit is generally available only on property that is placed in service in the year the tax credit is claimed and that meets three tests: (1) The investment must be in property that is depreciable, (2) the property must have a useful life of at least three years,

(3) the property must be both tangible and personal. (See Figure 3 for further details.)

Restrictions in credit allowed

• New property. The cost of all qualified new property is eligible for investment credit. There is no limit on new property; i.e., if you purchase a new asset for $180,000, you may compute your investment credit on that entire figure. However, there is a limit on the amount of credit that can be claimed in any one year.

• Used property. There is a $125,000 yearly cost limit for investment credit on used property. If you purchase $150,000 worth of qualified used property in one year, you may compute your credit on only $125,000 of cost. Excess cost may not be carried over to another year. Naturally, if you acquire different used properties that collectively cost more than the $125,000 limit, you would choose to take the investment credit on the properties with the longest asset recovery period in order to maximize your credit.

• Recovery period. The portion of an otherwise qualified investment on which the credit may be computed depends on its expected life. The 10% credit is allowable on the total cost of property with a recovery period of at least five years. Property with a recovery period at least three years is allowed a 10% credit on 60% of its cost, or 6% net credit; and property with a useful life of less than three years does not qualify for the credit.

Annual credit limitation

You may claim investment credit on as much qualified new property as you want, but there is a limit to the amount of credit you can claim for both new and used prop-

Figure 3

QUALIFICATION OF PROPERTY FOR INVESTMENT CREDIT

Qualifies

Tangible personal property. Office equipment and furnishings; manufacturing and production equipment; automobiles, trucks, boats, and planes.

Integral part of production process. Printing presses, railroad tracks, and oil pipelines.

Livestock (except horses).

Single purpose livestock and horticultural structures. Structures used to breed chickens, hogs, produce milk from dairy cattle, etc.

Certain rehabilitation expenditures on buildings which have been in service for over 30 years. Work must begin at least 30 years after the date the building was first placed in service. Residential buildings do not qualify.

Does not qualify

Land and any improvements such as grading, sidewalks, etc.

Buildings and most structural components.

Patents, copyrights, licenses, and other intangibles.

Inventory.

erty in any one year. The amount of credit in one year cannot exceed the lesser of your total tax liability, or the first $25,000 of tax liability plus a percentage of the liability over $25,000. The 1978 Revenue Act increased the percentages over the next several tax years as follows:

1978 and prior	50%
1979	60%
1980	70%
1981	80%
1982	90%

• Recapture. If you dispose of an asset before the end of its estimated useful life, any excess credit you took must be added to your current tax. For example, if you acquired a qualified asset for $100,000 with an estimated life of five years, you could take 10% × $100,000 = $10,000 as a tax credit. If the asset only lasts four years, the credit to which you should have been entitled is only 80% × ($100,000 × 10%) = $8,000 = $2,000 tax due in the year you dispose of the asset. Before selling property on which you have claimed an investment credit, check with your accountant to find out if the sale will trigger recapture rules.

• Depreciation base. Note that even though your effective cost for new equipment is only 90% of its actual cost (Uncle Sam paid the remainder by reducing your taxes), the amount that can be recovered under the new cost recovery system of the 1981 Tax Act is still unchanged: you can still use a full 100% of the purchase price as the depreciable cost.

Investment credit strategy

Here are five ways by means of which you can maximize your investment credit benefits:

1. Leasing transactions. Under certain conditions, individuals or partnerships may lease equipment to corporations and retain the ITC at the lessor level. An example of this would be where a businessman leases equipment to his own corporation in order to obtain tax benefits. However, watch for strict rules here—your accountant can't help you.

2. Used equipment. If you sell old property and replace it within 60 days with other used equipment, your investment credit is computed on the cost of the purchased used replacement less the basis of the old property. But if you wait 61 days before buying the replacement, your credit is computed on the full price of the replacement property. Or you could buy the replacement, use it alongside the old property for 61 days, and then sell the old property. This way, too, you can compute credit on the basis of the full cost of the replacement.

3. Leasing. The lessor of new equipment gets the investment credit when he buys the equipment. Therefore, if you intend to lease new equipment, always try to get the lessor to pass the credit on to you or at least persuade him to reduce the cost of the lease.

4. Stimulate sales. If you sell qualified equipment, use the investment credit as a sales device by reminding customers that they get an automatic tax credit. With the credit and accelerated cost recovery deduction, the customer will recover a large part of his investment in the first year.

5. Incorporation. If you plan to incorporate and you also plan to acquire qualified property, buy the property before you incorporate so you can use the investment

credit against your personal income tax return. Later, after incorporation, you can transfer your property to the corporation without incurring recapture penalties.

Tax-Wise Handling of Seven Critical Elections

Taxpayers have a variety of elections which they can make under the Internal Revenue Code and IRS regulations. Some are binding for only one year, others until revoked. In certain cases, IRS approval is needed to make the election; in others, it is at the taxpayer's discretion. Here is a rundown and brief explanation of the elections most important to the businessman:

Bad debts

Specific charge-off vs. reserve method. Bad debts may be deducted by one of two methods. The specific charge-off method allows the taxpayer to deduct bad debts in the year in which they become worthless. Under the reserve method, bad debts are not deducted directly from income but are instead charged against a bad debt reserve.

Election. An accrual-basis taxpayer can select either method when he files his first return which claims bad debts. The same method must be used in subsequent years unless approval to change is obtained. A cash-basis taxpayer does not need a bad debt election, since only actual cash collections are reported.

Changing method. You may automatically change from charge-off to the reserve method, conditional on compliance with several factors that are outlined in Rev. Proc. 64-51.

Depreciation

Here, the taxpayer has two elections: (1) which recovery period to use (how many years), and (2) whether to use an accelerated cost recovery method.

The 1981 Tax Act introduced a new concept called ACRS—Accelerated Cost Recovery System. Under this system, asset costs are "recovered" over various statutory lives unrelated to (and usually shorter than) those previously allowed.

Asset recovery method: The taxpayer may choose between two general methods: (1) straight line, and (2) "statutory" declining balance. Straight line needs no explanation here. The statutory declining balance is 150% of straight line for personal property; 175% of straight line for real property.

New expense deduction

Beginning in 1982, certain taxpayers may elect to expense up to $5,000 of eligible personal property. The only qualification is that the property would otherwise qualify for the investment credit. Note that this election knocks out investment credit on the property.

Installment sales

Dealers in personal property may report sales on the installment basis, that is, proportionately as collections are made. No permission is needed to go from the accrual basis to the installment basis. Real estate sales also qualify.

Inventory valuation

The taxpayer can elect one of two methods for valuing inventory used in his business: (1) cost, or (2) cost or market, whichever is lower.

Measurement of "cost." To measure cost, three general methods may be used: (1) specific identification, (2) first-in, first-out (FIFO), or, (3) last-in, first-out (LIFO). While retailers can use the "retail" method, manufacturers must use the full absorption cost method when the inventory consists of several kinds, sizes, and grades. Application to change methods is made on Form 3115 and must be filed within 180 days after the start of the tax year. All elections can be changed only with IRS permission.

LIFO. If the last-in, first-out method is chosen, IRS approval must be obtained. Application to use LIFO is made on Form 970 filed with the return for the first year the method is to be used.

Accounting methods

Cash, accrual, or any other method that clearly reflects income may be used. Where inventories are involved, the cash method may not be used. Application to change accounting methods is made by filing Form 3115.

Long-term contracts

The taxpayer has the option of reporting on the "percentage completion" or the "completed contract" basis. No consent is required to use either method. However, use of either method must be consistent and cannot be changed without IRS consent.

Subchapter S

Election is made by filing Form 2553 along with consents from each shareholder. The election may be made at any time during the corporation's previous tax year, or during the first 75 days of the year for which a change to Sub-S is desired. The election is effective for all later years, unless revoked.

Tax attorneys and CPAs furnish competent tax advice. But they can never have complete knowledge of your business and must be asked competent questions in order to be efficient and effective. Know your tax options before you seek professional help. You probably won't have the answers—but at least you will be asking the right questions.

How Tax Shelters Work

Too often investors do not understand how tax shelters work or the meaning of such terms as "soft dollars," "flow through," or "depreciation shield." The result is that they make unwise investments—or avoid shelters altogether when they could have been used effectively to legally reduce taxes.

Figure 4

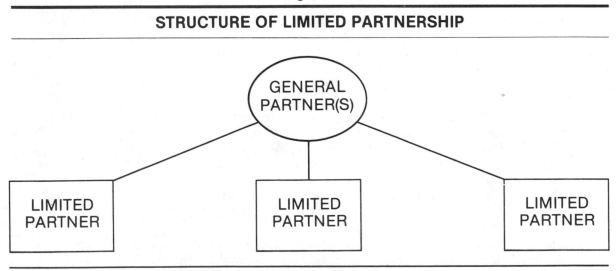

STRUCTURE OF LIMITED PARTNERSHIP

A married taxpayer with taxable income above $60,000 pays a minimum marginal tax rate of 49% (1982). If taxpayers in that bracket can somehow reduce taxable income by $1, they can save about 50¢. By investing in a particular venture, the investor takes deductions that reduce taxable income (and taxes). The most popular tax shelter is a limited partnership (see Figure 4).

The limited partnership

The limited partnership structure is used for most tax shelters because partnerships are not taxed directly—all profits and losses "flow through" to the partners, and any tax due is paid individually by them. The principal disadvantage is that the partners are usually jointly liable for any debts or other liabilities of the business. This drawback is overcome by the use of a limited partnership—the investor can participate in profits, but his liability is limited to the amount of his investment. The general partners run the day-to-day operations of the venture. They may be a corporation or a group of individuals, but they do not enjoy limited liability.

Sources of tax deductions

The most common limited partnership tax shelter involves the ownership of real estate. The tax deductions for limited partners may be taken in the following ways:

• *Depreciation.* Often called a "depreciation shield" because it can be used to offset income, depreciation (now called "cost recovery") is a key ingredient of most tax shelters. Let's take a hypothetical example. Suppose you are a 10% investor in the purchase of a new $1,000,000 apartment complex. (For our purposes, we will assume that the land—which is not depreciable—has been leased. Therefore, the full $1,000,000 cost of the apartment building is depreciable.) By borrowing 90% of the purchase price ($900,000) in the form of a nonrecourse mortgage (i.e., no one is personally liable for the loan), each 10% partner would only have to put up $10,000 of the $100,000 in equity money. Yet the basis for depreciation would still be the full price of $1,000,000. Using the accelerated cost recovery system (175% of straight line over 15 years), the first year's depreciation would come to a total of $116,687, assuming the property was purchased in the first month of the year. This would mean a total tax deduction of $11,668 on your investment of $10,000, yielding a tax saving (if you are in the 50% bracket) of $5,834. Such tax savings are often called "soft dollars."

You effectively get $6,000 of your investment back and have your "hard dollar" investment in the project reduced to only $4,000. Furthermore, you would continue to receive cost recovery deductions in future years and still own 10% of the project. Although cost recovery reduces your taxable basis in the partnership, a tax must be paid on the gain when the property is finally sold. Part or all of this gain may be taxed at ordinary income tax rates because of cost recovery "recapture" rules. There is still a significant advantage, however, in that taxes may effectively be deferred for many years, allowing you to use the tax money saved for investment and other productive purposes.

• Operating losses. If there are actual operating losses (as opposed to those resulting from interest on borrowings or cost recovery deductions), they are also deductible by the partners. Limited partners in real estate investments can deduct losses in excess of their investment if the partnership and financing are appropriately structured.

• Interest. Using the example above in which $900,000 was borrowed, almost $144,000 of interest deductions would result in the first year alone based on a 16%, 25-year mortgage. To the extent that these deductions were not offset by operating revenue, they should be deductible pro rata by the partners, assuming a full year's operation. However, there are also important interest expense limitations to consider.

Tax shelters are not immoral—the laws facilitating them were purposely designed to facilitate investment in higher risk and socially necessary ventures. But they are also not for the unsophisticated; for example, many tax professionals consider it potentially disastrous to use the accelerated cost recovery system for nonresidential property acquired after 1980. Always retain a competent tax adviser.

Trusts: Not Just for the Rich

Trusts are just for the rich and superrich, right? Well, not exactly. In fact, trusts are relatively easy to set up and are a convenient way for almost any person with modest resources to shelter a portion of his income from tax. But no one is going to come to you with the inside knowledge. You must take the initiative.

How to give a tax-free college "scholarship" to your children

Your daughter is three and your son is eight. Within ten years, your son will be starting college. You've been setting aside a little money for the children's education, and now your fund has $10,000 and earns 8%, or $800 per annum, in interest.

But you're in a 40% bracket, including state and local taxes. So $320 of your income from this account goes right back to Uncle Sam, and much of the remainder gets eaten up by inflation. A real treadmill!

What would you say if:

• Most, if not all of the interest from the fund could accumulate completely tax free for your children's education; and

• You would still retain effective control of the original investment.

Impossible? Not at all! Here's how it would work for your older child.

Clifford trust

Using what is known as a "short-term" or "Clifford" trust, you would turn the $10,000 over to a trustee, naming your son as beneficiary of all income from the trust.

The trust will hold the $10,000 and credit any interest income to your son's account. Your son (not you, his father) will be liable for tax on $800 per year of interest income, but he has a personal exemption of $1,000, so he pays no tax at all. You, as his father, still get a dependency exemption for all the years the trust is accumulating money so long as you contribute at least half of your son's support and he is under 19 or a full-time student.

Off to college

When your son goes to college in ten years, over $11,589 (thanks to compounding) of tax-free money will be ready for him. And the original $10,000 reverts free and clear to you. It can then be used for your daughter's education or in any other way you desire.

Note that in this situation you do not have to pay any gift tax (husband and wife may make tax-free gifts of up to $3,000 each year to each child), and that your basic financial situation is unaffected. Be sure, however, to consider the following:

• Retain competent legal counsel to set up the trust.

• Make sure the trust is irrevocable for at least ten years and one day.

230

- Protect yourself against emergencies by putting a clause in the trust agreement that you may borrow the cash/securities when secured by adequate collateral.

- Do not specify the purpose of the funds in the trust.

- Keep the accumulating interest and the original investment segregated.

- Never commingle your personal assets with the trust assets.

Finally, in some situations, a father may be considered "required" to put his children through college as part of his duty of support. In these cases, using trust income for the education may make it taxable to the father. Where the age of majority is 18, this should be no problem. If the age of majority is 21, however, it may be better not to use the son's income for college expenses until age 21.

Other possibilities for Clifford trusts

Short-term trusts are highly effective whenever there is an appreciable difference between the tax brackets of the grantor (in the above example, the father) and the beneficiary (the son). You could also use the Clifford trust to accomplish any of the following:

- Accumulate savings for your spouse or some other member of the family.

- Provide support for a parent or some other dependent without the necessity of first passing income through your higher tax bracket.

- Accumulate funds within the trust for estate liquidity purposes.

Other types of trusts

There are many other types of trusts available for flexible financial planning. For example, with life insurance trusts, you assign your life insurance policies to a trustee under a formal written agreement. During your lifetime, you have complete control over both the policies and the trust arrangement. At the time of your death, however, the trustee will collect the proceeds of the policies, invest the principal, and distribute the income and principal in accordance with your written instructions. Thus, your spouse and children are relieved of the burden of investment decisions, and you can be assured that there will be adequate funds on hand for emergencies.

Another broad classification of trusts, known as testamentary trusts, is created by will and becomes effective at death. They offer the same flexibility and variety of benefits as living trusts. Income can be paid to one or more beneficiaries, accumulated, or "sprinkled" among a group of beneficiaries at the discretion of the trustee. Principal can be paid in specified sums at various ages or times, upon occurrence of certain events, or at the discretion of the trustee.

Who should be trustee?

Today, more and more people are capable of making intelligent business decisions. Yet there are many who, even though they possess the resources, do not always have the time, talent, or temperament necessary to successfully manage investment portfolios. That is why many individuals choose to name a financial institution as trustee. Experience, impartiality, financial responsibility, availability, and permanence: it's imperative that whoever serves as trustee possess these qualifications.

What You Need to Know About Capital Transactions

Gains and losses in capital transactions receive different tax treatment depending upon the nature of the capital assets, how long they have been held, and who holds them. The difference in the tax treatment because of these three factors leads to some frustrating complexity, but most businesspeople can obtain a useful understanding of capital transactions if they take the subject one step at a time, starting with definitions of the basic terms.

Basic definitions

What are capital assets? A capital asset is anything you own, with the following exceptions:

- Depreciable property used in your business.

- Inventory (property intended for sale).

- Real estate used in your business.

- Accounts receivable.

- Some short-term government discount obligations.

- Some copyrights, literary work, U.S. government publications, etc.

Naturally, there are exceptions to the exceptions listed above. Although depreciable business real estate and property are considered noncapital assets, such properties, when used for more than a certain time, may be taxed as if they were capital assets if there is a gain on their sale. This kind of business property is known as "Section 1231" property.

What is a capital transaction? Generally, a capital transaction is a sale or exchange of capital assets. Usually, this results in capital gains or losses. In addition, the results of the following types of transactions will also sometimes be treated as capital gains or losses:

- Corporate liquidation.

- Distributions from pre-1974 employee participation in pension, stock bonus, or profitsharing plans.

- Involuntary conversion of property used in trade or business.

- Worthless securities.

- Default by nonbusiness debtors.

- Certain stock redemption payments.

Section 1231 property

Normally, gain on the sale or exchange of property used in business (noncapital assets) would be treated as ordinary income. As noted, however, there is a special category known as Section 1231 property. Under this section, property used in business for more than 12 months may be treated as a capital asset if there is gain upon exchange or sale. As a result, the property is subject to the lower capital gain tax. Here are some further stipulations in regard to Section 1231 property.

- Gain on the sale of business property held for less than 12 months is treated as ordinary income.

- Loss on the sale of business property—no matter how long it is held—is regarded as ordinary loss.

- Gains on casualty or theft insurance settlements are normally taxed as long-term capital gains. Losses, on the other hand, are deductible from ordinary income.

• Gain on the sale of Section 1231 property realized as a result of depreciation will be subject to depreciation recapture rules. Generally, the recapture provisions call for the gain to be treated as ordinary income.

You can save tax money by making sure that you don't sell Section 1231 property at a loss in the same year you realize a gain from the sale of another Section 1231 property. Section 1231 property gains and losses in a given year must be netted so the gain offsets the loss. But gain is capital gain and loss is ordinary loss. Thus, you could be offsetting a capital gain with a 100% deductible loss. This would cost you an unnecessarily high amount of tax dollars. The strategy here is take the gain in one year and the loss in another.

How net capital gains and losses are computed and taxed

Short-term capital gains and losses result from the sale of property held for 12 months or less. Long-term capital gains and losses result from the sale of property that is held for more than 12 months. To find your net capital gains and losses, you separate the year's transactions into two categories. You offset all long-term gains against all long-term losses in order to compute your annual long-term gain (or loss). Similarly, short-term gains are offset by short-term losses to give you your net short-term result.

Once the net amounts of the capital gains or losses are known and categorized (short term or long term), the final factor is whether the capital gain or loss pertains to a corporation or an individual. Figure 5 summarizes the tax treatment of all possible capital gain or loss situations.

Year-End
Tax Planning Checklist

Too many businessmen don't think about tax strategies until their returns are prepared, two or three months after the books are closed. A few simple moves to shift your income and expenses would minimize your tax liability and could save you hundreds, or even thousands, of tax dollars.

To take maximum advantage of the lower tax rate, profits should be spread as evenly as possible from year to year. For example, a lower total tax will probably result from two years with $40,000 income each than from one with $20,000 and one with $60,000. If you just signed a big contract which you know will net an unusual amount of income next year, start planning now to shift income strategically to avoid being taxed at a higher rate.

When planning your year-end strategies, take into consideration the corporate rates, which for tax years beginning in 1983 will be 17% on the first $25,000 of taxable income; 18% on the next $25,000; 30% on the third $25,000; 40% on the fourth $25,000; and 46% on taxable income over $100,000. Capital gains rates will change substantially as well.

How to accelerate or defer business income

1. Open account vs. consignment sales. To speed up income, switch to open sales; title then passes and income is recognized when the goods are turned over to a common carrier. To defer income, sell on consignment; that way, income is not recognized until the purchaser sells the merchandise.

2. Outright sale vs. approval. Outright sale with right of return results in immediate

recognition of income. By switching to approval sales, income is not recognized until the goods are accepted and approved.

3. Collection policy. If on a cash basis, defer income by slowing up on billings and collections. Conversely, if collections are increased, income is greater. Speed up payments by giving discounts.

4. Installment sales. If you sell merchandise on the installment plan, you can spread the profit over the collection period while taking expense deductions in the current period. To speed up income, you can sell the installment obligations to a third party. Note that you can switch to installment reporting without IRS permission. There are some limitations on who may use installment reporting; check with your accountant.

Figure 5

TAXATION OF CAPITAL GAINS AND LOSSES

Capital Gain and Loss Situation	Individual	Corporation
Net long-term gain	40% of net long-term gain is taxed at the regular individual rate.	Pays normal corporate tax on ordinary income plus net long-term gain OR pays normal tax on ordinary income plus 28% tax on gain.
Net long-term loss	May deduct 50% of loss from ordinary income, up to $3,000. All excess loss may be carried forward until it is used up.	May not deduct capital losses from current income, but may carry back loss three years to offset previous capital gains or five years forward to offset gains.
Net short-term gain	Fully taxed as ordinary income.	Fully taxed as ordinary income.
Net short-term loss	Deduct full amount from other income up to $3,000. Excess can be carried to succeeding years.	Carry back/forward to offset gains.
Net long-term gain and net short-term gain	Add 40% of long-term gain and 100% of short-term gain to your ordinary income and it will be taxed at the rate of your other income.	Add all short-term and long-term gain or ordinary income OR add short-term gain to ordinary income and compute long-term gain at the alternative 28% rate.
Net long-term gain and net short-term loss	Deduct the short-term loss from the long-term gain. If the remainder is a loss, deduct it from ordinary income up to $3,000. Carry over to later years if necessary. If remainder is a gain, add 40% to other income.	Deduct the short-term loss from the long-term gain. If loss exceeds gain, it can be carried back/forward to offset capital gains in other years. It may not be deducted. If gain exceeds loss, excess gain can be added to ordinary income. OR be taxed at alternative 28% rate.
Net short-term gain and net long-term loss	Deduct the long-term loss from the short-term gain. If gain is greater, add remainder to other income. If loss is greater, remaining net long-term loss is deductible under normal rules for net long-term loss.	Deduct the loss from the gain and if gain exceeds loss, gain is added to ordinary income. If loss exceeds gain, loss cannot be deducted, but it can be carried back/forward to offset gain in other years.
Net long-term loss and net short-term loss	Losses may be applied to offset up to $3,000 in the following manner: (a) apply short-term loss and then the long-term loss; (b) carryovers retain their identity as short-term or long-term losses in later years.	May not deduct capital losses, but may carry them back/forward to offset capital gains.

5. Long-term contracts. If the contract will not be completed in the taxable year in which it was entered, you can postpone recognition of income and expenses until the contract is completed ("completed contract" method). Alternatively, you can report on the "percentage of completion" method and pick up income and expenses as you go. Certain restrictions apply to manufacturing contracts. Once adopted, a change to or from either method requires IRS approval.

6. Equipment trade-in. If the trade-in value of a piece of used equipment is higher than its tax basis, sell it outright to a third party to capture the gain. Conversely, to avoid recognition of the gain, trade the equipment in.

How to shift business expenses

7. Acquire assets. If you plan to buy needed equipment, time the purchase to give you expenses when you need them. By acquiring assets and placing them in service before the end of the year (even if you buy on time), you get a double benefit: (1) cost recovery deductions as if you owned the equipment for half the year, and (2) 10% investment credit, which means you effectively pay only 90% of the asset's cost.

8. Repairs and supplies. To accelerate expenses, make needed repairs, remodel if needed, and buy supplies now. Hold off if you want the expenses next year. (The acceleration of deduction technique for supplies only works if you are on a cash basis.)

9. Prepayments. If on a cash basis, pay all bills by December 31 for a deduction this year. To defer the expenses, wait until January. Certain expenses can also be prepaid, such as office expenses, advertising, travel expenses, as well as next year's real estate taxes and state income tax. Interest usually cannot be prepaid. Note: Payment by check at the end of the year will give a current deduction, even if the check doesn't clear until next year. Prepayments cannot materially distort income.

10. Advertising. So long as it does not materially distort income, you can plan and prepay for advertising programs this year even though the programs will not go into effect until next year. The expense can then be applied to this year even though you will not benefit from the advertising until next year. (Cash basis taxpayers only.)

11. Bad debts. If a debt is questionable, press hard to prove it is worthless for a deduction this year. Otherwise, wait until next year.

12. Inventory. IRS regulations allow certain obsolete and damaged goods to be valued at a bona fide sales price less the direct costs of disposition. The burden of proof is on the taxpayer, so if you can't substantiate the deduction, hold off.

13. Equipment. To get a current deduction, junk or abandon any worthless equipment before December 31. However, watch for investment credit recapture problems.

Other considerations

Contested liability. If someone claims that your firm owes them a given sum of money, but you disagree, you have a contested liability. If you refuse to pay it, you cannot take a current deduction for it, but you may pay the amount into an escrow account and take the tax break in the current year. Later, if the settlement gives you a refund from the money you put into escrow, this refund is treated as ordinary income in the year received. Similar tactics may be applied to a contested tax bill, allowing you to make use of a tax problem to save tax dollars elsewhere.

Effect on money use. When you accelerate deductions and defer income, you temporarily lose the use of the money involved. However, if you defer deductions and accelerate income and taxes, you improve your cash flow.

Inventory policy. To reduce income, switch to the last-in, first-out (LIFO) inventory accounting method. First-in, first-out (FIFO) generally results in higher income. Note: These changes cannot be made at will. Get further details from your tax consultant. Also, some businessmen have the impression that loading up on inventory at the end of the year will reduce income and taxes. This is not true. All that happens is cash is exchanged for another asset—inventory.

Personal tax planning

It will always be to your advantage to take the time to coordinate your business tax strategy with your personal tax strategy. Secondly, establishing an effective personal tax strategy may necessitate a change in your spending habits. The idea is to time your deductible expenditures so you have an option in regard to the year in which you claim tax deductions. This option will allow you to be flexible enough to accommodate changes in your own income from year to year as well as changes in tax rates.

Timing cash payments. According to the IRS, an expense is not deductible until it is paid and it is considered to be paid on the day you put your check in the mail. Therefore, if you can arrange to have some of the year's predictable expenses fall due in December, you can either pay them in December and take the tax deduction that year, or wait until January to pay them so you can take the deduction in the following year. Similarly, it might be possible to arrange to have certain annual incoming monies delayed until early the following year, allowing you to defer tax until the subsequent year. (Consult with your tax adviser concerning so-called "constructive receipt rules.)

Charitable contributions. In general, you should plan your strategy in regard to charitable contributions later in the year when you will be able to judge if the year will produce high or low income. You get your personal deduction for contributions when the check is mailed, not when you promise to pay. However, a recent IRS ruling allows a current deduction for contributions charged to a credit card, even though the bills aren't paid until the next year. If you donate long-term property, appreciation is included in determining the amount of contribution. Short-term property is deductible only on the basis of its cost. Appreciation isn't counted on short-term property.

Personal property taxes and real estate. Sometimes you can prepay taxes on personal property and real estate and in this way control the time of your deduction. This isn't always permissible so you should be sure it is an allowable procedure with your local government before you include it in your strategy. A deposit on future tax is not a deductible expense when it is paid.

Prepayment of state income tax. You may deduct current year state income tax from current year federal tax if you report the state tax and prepay it on a tentative state return before the end of the current year. This is a good tactic when you have an unusually high income in one year because the deduction goes in the same year as the federal return that reports the higher gross income. The taxable income is therefore reduced by the deduction for the state tax.

Medical expenses. Try to shift medical expenses so that the bulk of the expenses fall into every other tax year. The point is this: you can only deduct the part of your total medical expense that exceeds 3% of your adjusted gross income. (Included in your medical expenses is the part of the total cost of drugs and medicines that exceeds 1% of your adjusted gross income.) So if your adjusted gross income this year is $20,000, and your total medical expenses this year are $800, you may only deduct $200 for this year [$800 − (.03 × $20,000) = $200]. If you have the same income and medical expenses next year, your total deduction over the two years will be $400. However, if you could somehow shift $300 of this year's medical expense into next year, you would have no deduction for this year, but you would get a $500 deduction next year ($800 + $300 = $1,100 − 3% of $20,000 = $500) and thus obtain an extra $100 deduction over the two years.

To shift medical expenses into the next year, you should schedule nonemergency treatment like checkups, minor surgery, and dental work for December and then delay paying the bills until January.

Half the cost of medical insurance premiums that you personally pay is deductible up to $150. The 3% limit does not apply to this half, but the other half of the premium cost is included in the 3% limit. Therefore, if you carry a policy that costs at least $300, half of that is deductible.

If you pay for a medical examination that is required for your job, you can deduct its cost as a business related expense. The 3% limit does not apply unless treatment is prescribed after the examination. The cost of the treatment is subject to the limit.

If you pay for more than half the support of a parent, you may usually deduct any medical expense you pay for that parent. For this reason it makes sense to have the parent assign his medical expenses to your half of his support costs and pay the other half with his own income.

Miscellaneous deductions. The following are some deductible expenses that should be scheduled for payment in December to give you the maximum flexibility in determining the more advantageous tax year for them. They are expenses for: investment advice, safe deposit box rental, tax counsel, purchase of uniforms needed in your work, business association dues, and other business related expenses that cannot be charged off through your work.

Offset capital gains and losses. If you have capital gains or losses this year, think about selling other property that will offset this year's gain or loss.

Itemize one year, take "zero bracket" amount the next. You have an option each year of taking the zero bracket amount on adjusted gross income or itemizing your deductions. By alternating the itemizing system and the standard deduction (which allows deductions up to $2,300 in the case of a single person), you can save additional tax dollars. Here is how it can work: If you itemize $4,000 this year and $4,000 the next, you get a two-year total of $8,000 in deductions. But if you shift $3,000 out of one year and into the next, you may itemize $7,000 in one year and utilize the $2,300 zero bracket amount in the other year, a total of $9,300 in deduction benefits. You gain $1,300 in deductions that, when multiplied by your tax rate, gives you the money saved over the two years.

Gifts. If you want to make a gift to a family member, think about taking advantage of the $10,000 annual gift tax exclusion. This means you may give a gift of up to $3,000 each year without paying gift tax. If you plan to pass your estate on to your children, you can start this year and avoid a large estate tax later on. If your wife also makes a gift, the limit for the exclusion is doubled to $10,000, but remember, a gift by check to a family member should clear the bank by December 31.

These are just a few suggestions for personal tax planning. Depending upon your individual tax situation, there may be many more ways in which you can reduce your yearly tax liability.

How to Handle Operating Loss Carryback/Forward

If a taxpayer has an operating loss, that loss may be carried back three years to offset previous highly taxed income. This may yield a tax refund. If the loss is not used up in offsetting income of the previous three years, it may be carried forward to offset future income for 15 years for losses incurred in tax years after 1975. If, after being carried forward 15 years, the loss is still not used up, the excess loss is wasted and may no longer be used to offset income.

This carryback/forward rule may allow you to gain a substantial tax saving by shifting income into the coming year to create a loss in the current year. This loss may then be used to offset past income and to gain a tax refund.

For example, suppose your business paid $6,000 tax on an income of $40,000 in 1978, but now in the year 1981 you anticipate only breaking even. However, you can foresee that in 1982 your fortunes will rebound somewhat and your tax rate will be 17%. Here's how you save money. By deferring income into 1982 and by accelerating cost recovery, you create a current 1981 loss of $6,000. You may now carryback that loss to 1978 and get a refund of a maximum of $6,000. In 1982 you then pay 17% tax on the monies that were deferred into that year, but it still totals out to an incremental tax saving.

It's an unpleasant thought, but there's always the chance that a business will suffer losses that are too great to be absorbed by either the three-year carryback or the seven-year carryforward. What then? Well, here's one way you might be able to use up the excess loss in offsetting future income, despite restrictions.

Just to pick a figure, suppose you still have $5,000 of loss left over after the fifteenth future year of carryforward that will be wasted. You notice, however, that in the following year you anticipate $500 per month income from rental of some equipment. You may want to approach the renter and offer a $1,000 discount on the annual rent if he'll pay it for the whole year in advance. If he agrees, that $5,000 comes into the current year's income and allows you to utilize the $5,000 loss carryforward that otherwise would have been lost. The net tax savings, if your business is taxed at 46%, is $5,000 × 46% = $2,300. Of course you gave up $1,000 as a rental discount, but you are still well ahead.

Tax-Free (Section 1031) Exchanges

Tax-free exchanges are treated under Section 1031 of the Internal Revenue Code. Basically the regulations state that no gain or loss will be recognized on property held for business or investment purposes if it is exchanged for other property of like kind. In practice, what this means is that if you swap real estate that you own for other similar property, you can effectively defer any tax you would have owed on gains had you sold the property outright. Hence the term "tax-free exchange."

For example, ten years ago you purchased a piece of land for your business for $10,000. Today it has a market value of $60,000 and you want to get rid of it so you can move your business to a new location. The new location you want happens to be owned by Mr. Smith and it, too, let us say, has a present market value of $60,000. If you sell your old property outright, you must pay capital gains tax on $50,000, which amounts to a maximum of $14,000 tax. But if Smith will agree to a direct exchange of properties, you may indefinitely defer payment of the capital gains tax. Of course, should you decide to sell your new property outright years later, you would then have to pay the capital gains tax.

But what if Mr. Smith isn't interested in swapping for your property? Suppose he wants cash? Then you must bring in a third party. Here is how it is done by real estate professionals, step by step:

Step 1. You find a person who wishes to buy your property and have him sign an agreement to purchase the property from a third party at the agreed price.

Step 2. With this agreement in hand, you locate a seller of suitable replacement property that you would like to own. The definition of "like kind property" is quite broad. For example, you could exchange improved city real estate for an unimproved farm, an apartment house for a building lot, or a leasehold of 30 or more years for raw land.

Step 3. You and the seller agree to exchange your properties. Any difference in price can be balanced with cash, notes, or other considerations. (Of course, the person receiving the additional consideration, be it cash, a mortgage reduction, or something else, must pay tax on this additional consideration.)

Step 4. At the closing, you convey your property to the seller and he conveys his property to you. Assuming all other considerations are properly handled, you have met the requirements of a direct exchange and have legally postponed any capital gains tax.

Step 5. One final step remains. The seller does not want your property. The problem is solved, however, because you arranged for him to convey it to your original buyer immediately after the exchange. Everyone is happy, and the circle is complete. The seller merely acted as a conduit in the transaction.

Section 1031 exchanges offer the sophisticated businessman and investor a valuable and straightforward technique to achieve nonrecognition of otherwise taxable gain. Unless you do not intend to reinvest the proceeds of the sale in real estate, always consider an exchange instead of a sale. In any transaction of this type, however, you should retain the services of competent professionals to assist you.

The Tax-Saving Possibilities of Charitable Contributions

You can save a substantial amount of tax dollars when you make a donation to a qualified charity by donating property instead of cash. Appreciated property, which would yield a long-term capital gain if sold, can be donated for a deduction equal to the fair market value at time of donation. This will be explained in depth shortly, but first we should review the basic rules that apply to charitable contributions.

An individual may donate up to 50% of his adjusted gross income to a church or public charity and get a full deduction on his donation. But if the donation is appreciated property that would otherwise qualify for long-term capital gains, the limit for the deduction is 30% of the adjusted gross income. Also, if the donation is made to a private charity, the deduction is limited to a donation of 20% of the adjusted gross income. A carryover of five years is permitted for any contribution to a public charity.

A corporation may deduct a donation up to a limit of 10% of its taxable income for 1982 and later, and it too may use a five-year carryover period for excess donation.

The type of donation
The type of property contributed determines the tax treatment of a donation.

• Cash. You may deduct the amount of cash contributed.

• Property subject to cost recovery. You may deduct the fair market value of property subject to cost recovery minus any portion of the asset previously expensed. A recapture of an investment credit is also a possiblity.

• Long-term capital assets to public charity. A donation to a public charity of a

239

capital asset held more than 12 months may be deducted according to its current fair market value. The fair market value would include any and all appreciation in value.

• Long-term capital assets to private charity. If you choose to donate appreciated long-term assets to a private charity, you may deduct the cost basis plus 60% of any appreciation in value.

• Short-term capital assets. A donation of capital assets held for investment for less than 12 months may be deducted according to its cost basis or its fair market value —whichever is less.

• Other contributions. If you hold a flea market sale for the benefit of a charity, or donate personal, tangible property, preferred stock received as a nontaxable dividend, or make any other type of contribution, check with your tax adviser about the allowable deductions. These items can invoke some complicated restrictions.

An examination of the nature and treatment of charitable donations reveals that the best kind of donation from a tax standpoint is the contribution of long-term capital assets to a public charity. Here's how you can save tax dollars on such a donation:

Suppose you want to donate $2,000 cash to your church. You are in the 30% income tax bracket. You get a deduction of $2,000, which reduces your taxes by $2,000 × .30 = $600. But if instead you give property worth $2,000, which you bought six years ago for $800, you get the tax deduction of $2,000 and you avoid a capital gain tax of ($1,200 gain × 40% capital gain taxable portion × 30% tax rate) = $144.

In regard to charitable donations, note that:

• You must keep records of contributions, and if the contribution of property exceeds $200, you must attach a note to your tax return giving details of the contribution (to whom, where located, etc.).

You may not deduct for personal services rendered the charity or for the use of property.

• Gifts to charities reduce your income tax and also reduce your taxable estate.

Small items that add up

Sometimes you can make a respectable tax saving at the end of the year by adding up all the little charitable contributions you made during the year. For example:

• The cost of materials used to make an item that is donated to charity is deductible whether the item is a Stroganoff casserole and the deductible ingredient is meat, or the item is a picnic table made of 35 board feet of redwood.

• Household goods donated for the church bazaar are deductible, and if the charity won't appraise them upon receipt, figure them at estimated value.

• If you go to a charity ball, you may deduct the portion of the ticket not related to food and drink; tickets for charity lotteries or bingo are not deductible at all.

• If you wear a special uniform while performing a charitable service and that uniform can't be worn elsewhere, you may deduct the cost of the uniform.

• If you drive your car for a charitable purpose you may deduct 9¢ per mile.

Get into the habit of keeping records on this kind of charitable contribution and add them up at the end of the year. Every little bit helps.

You May Save Money by Income Averaging

If you have income this year that is substantially greater than your income in the previous four years, you may be able to use income averaging to reduce your income tax liability. Subject to conditions described below, an individual may use income averaging if a yearly income is more than $3,000 greater than 120% of his average income over the four previous years. This system, originally designed to aid artists and inventors who might spend years on a project before realizing any income from it, allows an individual to put the unusually high income into a lower bracket for computation. It does not allow you to spread out tax payments over a number of years.

Who can use it?

Only individuals may use income averaging. Corporations, estates, and trusts are not allowed to use it. If you were not a resident or citizen of the United States during any of the four years you will use to determine your income average, you may not use income averaging. Generally, if you did not provide at least 50% of your support during the years upon which you will base your income average (as in years spent in school), you may not use it. This provision is designed to prevent new college graduates who land high-paying jobs from using their student days for income averaging.

Definitions

For ease of further discussion, definition of the following words is needed.

• "Computation year" is the year you receive the income you hope to average.

• "Base period years" means the four preceding years upon which you base your income average.

• "Taxable income" means adjusted gross income less exemptions and excess itemized deductions.

What kind of income merits averaging?

Again, if your income is $3,000 higher than 120% of your average income over the previous four years, you may average almost all of your income. This includes 40% of net long-term capital gain. But you may not average: throwback trust accumulation distributions; excessive or premature distributions from self-employment retirement plans; or other income subject to a separate tax imposition.

Suppose your average income over the last four years is $10,000 and this year you have earned $16,000. You may use the income averaging in this case since 120% × $10,000 = $12,000 and $12,000 + $3,000 equals $15,000, which is less than your current income. Note that your marital status, the property laws of the state in which you live, and the place where you earned the income may affect your computation of tax.

How to average your income and compute your tax

IRS Schedule G of Form 1040 details the procedure for averaging income and computing tax, but the general idea is as follows:

1. Find your income average over the last four years.

2. Determine "base income" by multiplying average income by 120%.

3. Subtract base income from this year's income to find your "averageable income."

4. Take averageable income and divide it by 5. Add this to your "base income."

5. Use Schedule G to compute the tax on your base income (from step 2) and then compute tax on base income + averageable income ÷ 5. Now subtract the one total from the other to get the tax difference.

6. Take this tax difference and multiply it by 4. Add this number to the tax on your base income plus ⅕ of the averageable income to get your final tax liability.

How much can you save?

Without averaging, a single individual with an average taxable income over four years of $10,000 pays $3,505 (based on 1979 rates) tax when he ends a year in which he makes $18,000. With averaging, this same individual pays only $3,383, a saving of $122.00

A single taxpayer with an average income of $17,000 over four years suddenly comes into a year in which he doubles his income. Without using income averaging he pays $9,722 tax. However, by using income averaging he pays only $9,106, a tax saving of $616.00.

The determining factor in income averaging isn't the amount of increase in income, but rather the proportion of increase over the previous four year income average.

When should you use income averaging?

You may use income averaging whenever you meet the requirements for it. You must elect to use it by filling out schedule G on the 1040 form. You may elect to use income averaging up to three years from the time the tax return was due or within two years from the time the tax was paid, whichever is later.

Disadvantages of income averaging

Usually, income averaging will yield a worthwhile tax saving, but bear in mind the following factors when you consider using it. If you elect income averaging, you may not in the same year take advantage of the maximum 50% tax on earned income or exclusion of income earned outside the United States.

Casualty Losses—Softening the Blow of Disaster

Casualty losses are property losses sustained as a result of a "sudden, unexpected, and unusual . . .identifiable event," according to the tax code. Furthermore, the tax code stipulates that the loss must stem from an event that is "an accident or sudden invasion by a hostile agency or force," like a forest fire that burns your house, a high velocity wind, or a tidal wave. But sunlight damage to curtains, termite damage to outdoor furniture, and breakage of family crystal due to your own clumsiness don't qualify. Common daily misfortunes of this sort are not deductible casualty losses.

Naturally, the issue isn't always black and white. Sometimes the individual suffering the loss will see the event as a natural disaster, but the IRS will disagree. If necessary, the court will settle the matter. If you're not sure if the deduction will be allowed, check with your accountant about deducting it anyway.

How to determine the deduction

For complete or partial loss of nonbusiness property you may deduct the difference between the before and after fair market value. The difference, however, is limited to the adjusted basis of the property. For a complete loss of business property you deduct the adjusted basis of the property. For partial loss of business property, you apply the rules used in regard to loss of nonbusiness property. Note, however, that the cost of the repairs necessary to restore property to its precasualty condition is an acceptable indicator of the property's loss in fair market value. If the value drops more than repair costs, the court has ruled that you may deduct the actual drop in value.

You may only deduct the amount of a nonbusiness loss that exceeds $100. In other words, if a flood hits your basement and destroys your $120 carpet down there, you may deduct $20 and no more. But what if that same flood also destroys your $1,000 furnace, a $200 antique bassinet, and does $150 damage to your pool table? In that case you subtract the $100 from the total loss suffered from the single casualty act and the remainder is deductible. In this case $120 + $1,000 + $200 + $150 = $1,470 and then you subtract the $100 and your total deductible loss is $1,370.

Other casualty loss considerations

• An uninsured casualty loss in inventory will show up in your inventory account. You may take a separate loss deduction only if you make a corresponding adjustment in your inventory account.

• You may not take a casualty loss on money or property that "just disappeared." You must document a theft either by reporting it in writing to the police or by obtaining a copy of their report of the theft.

• You may not deduct for sentimental or aesthetic value of nonbusiness property.

• You may not claim a casualty loss deduction on property that you do not own. If you damage your neighbor's boat, you may not deduct the amount it costs you to repair it, because it's his property, not yours.

• You may deduct costs incurred in attempting to recover stolen property and you may deduct costs for cleaning up after a deductible casualty loss.

Precautions

It helps in clearing up matters of casualty loss if you can prove condition and value of property before and after the accident. Save purchase checks, expert appraisals, newspaper clippings relating to the event, and anything else that will help document your casualty claim. Also, before and after photographs of property can help to expedite claims. Therefore, you might consider taking periodic photos of your property. All these things can, in the event of a deductible loss, bring about greater tax savings and quicker settlements.

Fear of insurance premium increases

Some people refuse to file for insurance reimbursement after a casualty loss because they fear an increase in insurance rates. However, the IRS usually tries to disallow the casualty loss deduction if you don't claim insurance reimbursement when you are clearly eligible for it. Note: recent court decisions have allowed casualty loss deduction, even if the taxpayer had insurance and did not file a claim.

Hobby Expenses and Losses May Be Deductible

The expenses and losses of your hobby are deductible if you can show that you engage in the hobby activity for a profit. When a hobby yields a profit it becomes a secondary business activity and as such is entitled to deductions usually permitted for a regular business. Also, a loss from the hobby may be deducted from other income if the hobby is deemed a business activity. Examples of profit-making hobbies might be: refinishing old automobiles for resale, painting salable works of art, or stamp collecting for profit.

Many people would like to deduct the costs of their hobbies. Consequently, the IRS had to find some way to define those hobbies that are entitled to business deductions. Section 183 of the IRS Code was designed to provide this definition, and to some extent it succeeds. Generally, an activity is deemed to be engaged in for profit if it produces a profit in any two of five consecutive years—unless the IRS can prove otherwise. Activities dealing with horses are an exception. You must make a profit on your horses in any two of seven consecutive years to qualify for hobby deductions. Section 183 applies only to individuals and Subchapter S corporations. It does not apply to regular corporations.

Proving profit motive

If you claim profit on your hobby for the required two out of five years, it's up to the IRS to disprove your claim if they want to disallow your deductions. Conversely, if you don't claim the needed two years of profit, you've got a long uphill fight ahead of you to prove that your activity is nevertheless a profit-motivated hobby. The following are nine important considerations used to determine the validity of profit motivation in a hobby:

• How much time is spent at the hobby? Is anyone else employed to continue work when the claimant isn't there?

• Will the assets used in the activity appreciate in value?

• Are accurate, businesslike records kept of expenses and profits?

• How is the track record of the hobby enthusiast? Has he made a profit at this kind of thing before?

• Are losses and expenses in accord with reasonable expectations for the start-up of a business?

• Are profits reasonable in relation to initial investment and claimed losses?

• To what extent is the hobby recreational or pleasurable? (The old idea that work cannot be fun.)

• Is there substantial income from other sources?

• Have experts been consulted to set up or run the activity?

It would hurt a taxpayer's claim if IRS decided that initial losses were too great, that there was too much income from other sources, and/or the hobby was too much fun. It would help the individual if he could answer the other questions affirmatively. In judging a claim, all the above factors must be taken into consideration. A disadvantageous answer to one or even a majority of the questions need not automatically mean the profit motivation will be disbelieved.

Tax strategy for hobbies

Keep your activity on a cash basis rather than an accrual basis so you can take advantage of opportunities to shift income and expenses into advantageous years to create a small profit for two of the five or seven years. You want those two years of profit, if you can get them, because then the burden of proof rests with the Internal Revenue Service.

What you may deduct even if it's not primarily a profitable hobby

You may not deduct loss on your hobby from your other income if yours is not a profitable hobby at all. However, you may take normal deductions for casualty losses, interest, and state taxes (and local taxes too). It doesn't matter if you turn a profit for these deductions. You may also deduct depreciation and other expenses up to the point where total expenses equal any profit, however small.

Uniform Gift to Minors Act

The UGMA is designed to facilitate the transfer of property to minors. Its simplicity is its most outstanding attribute. If you wish to make a gift of property to your child under the UGMA, you need only register the securities or the savings account in the following manner:

> John L. Smith, as custodian for John L. Smith, Jr.,
> under the Uniform Gifts to Minors Act.

Once this is done the property transferred belongs to the recipient (ownership cannot be revoked by the custodian) and interest or earnings are taxable to the minor. When the child reaches the age of majority, the custodianship is terminated and title is transferred to the child.

Custodianship

Any adult may be the custodian under the UGMA. The custodian may buy and sell securities or deposit the proceeds in a savings account subject to his judgment, but he must act with reasonable circumspection and honest intentions.

Under a short-term trust (earlier in this chapter) the donor can reclaim ownership after ten years and a day, but not so with a custodianship. When the child reaches the age of majority, he owns the property.

Additional considerations

• You may continue to claim your child as a dependent as long as you pay more than 50% of his support costs.

• A parent may not use the custodial account to pay for the child's support. If the parent is legally obligated to pay for such support and he uses the custodial funds, the payment will be taxed to the parent.

How to use the UGMA to save money

If you wanted to set up a savings account for your child's education, you could do it in your own account and never bother with custodianship. However, the tax you pay on the interest from a savings account in your own name would be determined on the basis of your personal tax rate. Usually, the tax you would pay on the interest or earnings from your own account would offset any real interest gains. On the other hand, if the account is set up in your child's name with you as custodian, the interest earned on the principal would be taxable to the child, which is to say in most cases it would be tax free. If you intend to save a few hundred dollars a year for your child's education, a custodianship under the UGMA could save you more than $1,000 in taxes over a ten to fifteen year period.

The best stock for a gift

If you wish to make a gift of stock to your children, be sure the stock's market value is as close as possible to your cost basis. If there is unrealized gain or loss when you give the stock, the recipient will either have to pay capital gains or give up some standard shelters for capital loss.

If there is unrealized gain on the gift stock, the child will pay capital gains tax when he sells it. The basis of the stock to your child will be your basis plus the amount of any gift tax paid.

If there is unrealized loss on the gift stock and the recipient sells it at a loss, his basis is your basis plus gift tax or the market value at the date of gift, whichever is less. Furthermore, you don't get to offset the loss against other gains, nor does your child.

Therefore, give your child stock with a market value that is closest to your cost basis. And when you make the gift, include with it a memo stating relevant tax information like purchase date of the stock, commissions paid, gift tax paid, and the market value at the time of the gift.

Important Aspects of Involuntary Conversion

When an owner is compelled by circumstances beyond his control to give up ownership of his property, an "involuntary conversion" occurs. If, for example, a thief relieves you of the burden of ownership of your car, this is an involuntary conversion. Similarly, if the government compels an owner to give up land so a freeway can go through, the property has undergone an involuntary conversion. Sometimes you are reimbursed by insurance for the conversion and other times you may receive money or other property from a party obligated to compensate you for your loss.

If you realize gain on an involuntary conversion (you have depreciated the value of the car to $1,000, but when it was stolen and destroyed insurance paid you $2,000), you may elect not to recognize the gain now and thus you will pay no tax on it now. However, when you buy replacement property, you must reduce its basis by the amount of the gain. This way, when you sell it later, the sales price and the basis will reflect the conversion gain and the gain will in effect be subject to tax at that time.

In general, you may elect not to recognize gain from involuntary conversion if the replacement property serves the same purpose as the converted property. If you buy a new tugboat with the insurance compensation to replace the old sunken tugboat, nonrecognition is not a problem, but if you replace the old tugboat with a yacht, you might run into problems. The more latitude you take in defining a like replacement for the old property, the more trouble you are likely to have convincing the IRS of your right to nonrecognition of gain.

Usually, it will be better for you to elect not to recognize gain from involuntary conversion and to thereby avoid the immediate tax on the gain. But always do your homework. Sometimes you can make a significant tax saving by recognizing the gain, paying capital gains tax, and depreciating the new property at its full value. Making the extra effort to put the numbers into columns and doing a little arithmetic can save you money.

How to Handle Bad Debts

There are two kinds of bad debts, business and personal, and each receives a different tax treatment. A bona fide business bad debt is fully deductible from ordinary income. A business bad debt may be deducted when it is completely worthless or partially worthless. But a personal bad debt may only be deducted when it is completely worthless, and even then it may only be deducted as a short-term capital loss that may be used to offset capital gains in full, with any remainder being applied to offset ordinary income up to $3,000 maximum per year. A personal bad debt may be carried over from year to year until it is used up.

Business debt vs. personal debt

Since the tax treatment of the two kinds of debt differs, there is often some confusion over what is in fact a business debt and what is a personal debt. Strictly speaking, a business debt is one that is acquired in the course of an individual's trade or business. A personal debt is one that is created outside of business. But to be more specific, here are some guidelines for distinguishing business debts from personal debts.

The following situations lead to bad business debts:

• Making loans to customers, suppliers, or lessees when such loans aid your business.

• Your primary business is loaning money.

• Merchandise was sold on credit and the recipient of the merchandise will not or cannot pay for it.

• Loans are necessary to protect your business reputation.

• Accounts receivable, retained after the liquidation of your business, become uncollectible.

• You make a loan to your employer in order to keep your job.

• You make a loan to a corporation, and that loan is instrumental in protecting your credit for a similar business activity you are engaged in.

• A loan to your partnership.

The following situations lead to bad personal debts:

• Debt from investment situations is not considered business debt.

• Money lent to someone else when he needs it for his business is, with some exceptions, considered a personal loan. It isn't your business, so to you it's a personal debt.

• You make a loan to a corporation that you own to keep it on its feet. This is not a business loan because the corporation is a separate entity and as such its business is not your business.

Naturally, if you have any question about the nature of a bad debt, consult a tax expert. The above situations are only designed to give you some idea about the differences between the two kinds of debt.

Making the Most of Business Interruption Insurance

Business interruption insurance is insurance that pays an owner for overhead expenses and loss of profits if the business is closed down for a while due to fire or some other casualty. Most businesses carry some form of business interruption insurance. There are two kinds of interruption insurance, "valued" and "nonvalued."

A nonvalued form of business interruption insurance pays for the estimated loss of profits due to casualty and the reimbursement money is taxed as ordinary income. The amount of payment depends on the amount of estimated profit lost.

A less common form of interruption insurance is the valued form, which pays a fixed amount to the business during the loss of operations due to casualty. The payments are not based on the estimated loss of profit. However, the income from valued form is taxed at the lower capital gains rate. If the money is used to replace damaged property, it may be treated as a nontaxable exchange and the capital gain tax can be deferred.

It could mean a substantial tax saving if you can take the time to look into the valued form of business interruption insurance. In some states this form is not allowed, but it can't hurt to find out.

Tax Exclusion on an Employee Death Benefit

The motivation behind a presentation of money to the family of a deceased employee will determine the tax treatment given that sum.

Compensation

In general, payment made by a company to the widow or other beneficiary of a deceased employee is tax-free income to the beneficiary up to $5,000 if the payment was made in compensation for the death. (This, of course, assumes that the deceased did not have a nonforfeitable right to such payment before his death. Note that the exclusion would still apply in the case of certain lump-sum distributions.) Not only can the beneficiary take the money tax free, but the amount is also fully deductible to the company as a reasonable business expense. It doesn't matter if the payment was made because of a written contract or because of the company's sense of duty.

Gift

Suppose, in addition to the $5,000 death benefit mentioned above, an additional $5,000 is paid as a gift out of charity, respect, or for some other reason besides legal and moral obligation. The result is that the additional $5,000 is completely tax free to the recipient but nondeductible to the company.

Additional compensation

If, however, the $10,000 payment is considered additional compensation—and the amount of additional compensation is reasonable—the company may deduct the full $10,000 as an ordinary business expense. The beneficiary would pay tax on only $5,000—the remainder is tax free. Usually, the IRS regards death benefit payment as additional compensation. It's often a struggle to prove it is a gift.

Personal Dividend Deduction

In 1982 the IRS will allow you to only a $100 exclusion ($200 if married and filing jointly) on income you receive from interest and dividends. Therefore, if a married couple has $600 in dividend income from stocks, they will pay tax on $400.

However, if you have a wife and a child and they have no income from dividends, you may transfer some stock to each of them and in this way get two extra $100 exclusions on the dividend income.

Therefore, in the above case, the family would have total exclusions of $400. If the couple is in a 40% tax bracket, this means a tax saving of $240 per year.

Energy Tax Act of 1978

The Energy Tax Act of 1978 encompasses several areas, all of which can save tax dollars for energy-conscious consumers. It breaks down like this:

Home energy conservation

A new tax credit for energy conservation expenditures (insulation, storm windows and doors, weatherstripping, caulking, etc.) is available. The improvements must have a useful life of at least three years.

The credit applies to qualified property installed after April 19, 1977 and before 1986 in principal residences substantially completed before April 20, 1977.

The credit is 15% of eligible expenditures up to $2,000, or a maximum credit of $300 (the total credit available for all years to which this provision applies). A carryover is allowed for unused credits through the tax year ending December 31, 1987.

Alternative energy equipment

Homeowners who install solar, geothermal, or wind energy equipment in their principal residences are allowed a maximum $4,000 nonrefundable cumulative tax credit. To be eligible, the equipment must be new, with at least a five year useful life. The cost basis of the property must be reduced by the amount of the credit claimed.

You may claim 40% of the first $10,000 expended (up to the maximum credit of $4,000). Like the home energy conservation credit, this credit may be carried over until the end of 1987.

Figure 6 illustrates how the tax credits would be calculated if you made the purchases for installations of energy-saving devices at your principal place of residence shown in the figure.

Note: If you spend up to $6,500 more on alternative energy equipment installations (before 1987), you will have up to $2,600 additional credit on future tax returns.

Deducting for Bad Debts Within the Family

You may not claim a bad debt deduction for an uncollectible loan to a member of your family unless you can prove to the IRS that it was a loan and not a gift. The way to prove it is a loan is to write it down in a businesslike form, stating maturity date and interest paid. It sounds rather cold for family business, but it could save you tax money if, for some reason, the family member decides not to pay you back.

Deducting Support of a Dependent Parent

If you pay more than 50% of the cost of supporting a parent, and meet other dependency tests, you may take the $1,000 deduction for a dependent. Here's how this can work to save you tax money.

Suppose you support a parent who gets $1,400 a year from Social Security and

249

other sources. The parent's medical expenses come to $200 a year (which you pay), and you also give the parent $100 per month to help with living costs. That adds up to only $1,400 in support per year. But if you gave the parent $100.50 per month, your yearly support total would be $1,406, which would put you safely over the halfway mark. Then you claim the parent as a dependent, take the $1,000 exemption, and add the parent's medical costs to your own for later tax deductions.

Figure 6

CALCULATION OF ENERGY CONSERVATION TAX CREDITS

Installations at Principal Residence

10/81	Reinsulating and caulking	$ 900
3/81	Storm windows	$1,400
2/81	Solar unit	$3,500

Home Energy Conservation Credit

Reinsulating and caulking	$ 900
Storm windows	1,400
Total 1981 expenditures	$2,300
Excess—credit not allowed	(300)
Maximum qualified expenditures	2,000
Allowable credit	15%
Credit claimed on 1981 return	$ 300

Home Alternative Energy Credit

1981 Solar unit	$3,500
Credit on $3,500 @ 40%	1,400
Credit claimed on 1981 return	$1,400

Professional Fees: When Are They Deductible?

When are your attorney and accountant fees deductible? And on which return? For tax purposes, professional fees fall into four categories:

• Business expenses—fees deductible as ordinary and necessary business expenses, taken on the business tax return.

• Nonbusiness expenses—fees incurred in connection with ownership or management of income-producing property and any expenses you incur concerning your own tax matters, deductible on your personal return.

• Nondeductible—fees that are not deductible on either business or personal tax returns.

• Capitalized—fees that relate to capital assets and thus must be added to the value of the asset.

Frequently, a professional fee will fall into more than one category. Your deduction could be disallowed unless you obtain from your attorney or accountant an itemized, detailed description of the services rendered with a portion of the fee allocated to each itemization.

If you are on a cash basis, you must deduct professional fees in the year paid. Conversely, if you are on an accrual basis, you can take the deduction in the year in which you receive the statement.

Thus, if you are on an accrual basis and did year-end tax planning work last December but did not receive a statement until January, you take a current year deduction. Alternatively, if you can ascertain the amount of expense incurred during December, you can take the deduction in December, even though you hadn't received a formal statement as of that time.

Figure 7 (which was taken from Revenue Rulings and Tax Court cases) lists examples of the tax treatment given to common legal and accounting fees. While you will find the chart a handy guideline, it is not comprehensive, and any fees you think might be deductible but are not included in the chart should be checked out in detail with your tax adviser.

Child's Income

A child is entitled to a $1,000 personal deduction and a zero bracket amount, $2,300, which combined allows him $3,300 of tax-free "earned" income. However, if the child has "unearned" income, he may not use the $2,300 zero bracket amount to offset it. A child's unearned income may be offset by his personal $1,000 deduction and by the $100 dividend exclusion if part of the unearned income is from dividends. Here's how it works. If a child has a total annual income of $3,600 with $2,600 of earned income and $1,000 of unearned income, he may partially offset the $2,600 with the zero bracket amount ($2,300) and use his personal ($1,000) deduction plus the $100 dividend exclusion to reduce his taxable ($1,000) income to $200. The child's total taxable income in this example is, therefore, only $200.

You can shift income from your own higher tax bracket to your child's lower bracket by, (a) employing your child in your business, or (b) transferring income-producing property to your child. However, keep in mind the following bits of information in regard to a child's tax situation:

• The parent may still claim the $1,000 dependency exemption if he provides

251

more than half of the child's support and the child is under 19 years of age or attends school five months or more per year.

• If the child is under 21 and is employed by a father-and-mother partnership or by a parent who is a sole proprietor, his wages are exempt from Social Security and federal unemployment taxes.

• If your child is employed by your corporation or by your sole proprietorship, his wages can be deducted as ordinary business expenses. Of course his wages must be reasonable in relation to his work and he must really work for you and make a contribution to the profit-making capabilities of the company.

• Children may claim exemption from income tax withholding by filing form W-4 with their employers—providing they did not pay tax in the previous year and do not expect to pay tax in the current year. This rule applies unless the child earns more

---

Figure 7

DEDUCTION OF PROFESSIONAL FEES

FEES DEDUCTIBLE ON BUSINESS RETURN

Business-related tax advice.

Credit and collection relating to business accounts.

Business advice on matters necessary for operation of business (Department of Labor regulations, advisability of change in business organization, etc.) Note: Fees relating to a recommendation for incorporation are deductible only if incorporation proceeding is not started.

Legal expenses for an auto accident claim where a business automobile is involved.

Antitrust litigation.

Legal expenses for any civil fraud suit involving the business.

Business accounting expenses.

Any legal or accounting expenses for winding up and/or liquidating the business.

The expense of a libel or slander suit (but only if you can prove that the libel or slander directly injured the business).

FEES DEDUCTIBLE ON PERSONAL RETURN

Legal fees paid by divorced spouse to collect spousal maintenance (alimony). Note that fees paid by opposite spouse to defend against the proceeding are not deductible.

Rent collection, tenant eviction, or services to get property taxes reduced.

Accounting fees for preparing books or auditing income property.

Tax advice relating to divorce.

Tax advice concerning personal income taxes, any property owned, gift taxes, estate taxes, etc.

Legal and appraisal expenses to collect insurance (fire, casualty, etc.) settlement on income property you own.

Expenses incurred to defend a tax audit of your personal return.

FEES NOT DEDUCTIBLE ON EITHER BUSINESS OR PERSONAL RETURN

Estate planning matters not relating to tax (e.g., preparation of will).

Defense of title to property.

Recovery of personal loan.

Any expense for pursuing an accident claim involving nonbusiness (personal) automobile.

Fees that must be capitalized (added to the value of the property).

Expenses to obtain or protect a patent.

Business lease arrangements. (Note: The cost to negotiate the lease must be capitalized. The tax advice portion is deductible.)

Organization of partnership or corporation. (Special rules apply here.)

Fees relating to purchase of real estate.

Fees relating to purchase of equipment and machinery.

Sale of stock of corporation.

Corporate reorganization, stock redemption, or merger.

Obtaining a zoning variance.

Enforcement of business "buy-sell" agreement.

---

than $3,300 or has a gross income over $1,000 that consists in part of unearned income.

DISC

The term DISC actually stands for Domestic International Sales Corporation. To stimulate exports and improve the balance of payments, Congress authorized in 1971 the creation of this new type of corporation. Specifically, a DISC is granted special status and tax benefits in return for acting as an export agent for its parent (if the DISC is a subsidiary) or for other unrelated manufacturers of export products. Here are some of the benefits a DISC can provide.

Taxation

The DISC itself is not subject to income tax. Instead, 50% of its profits are taxable to its shareholders in the year earned. So long as export sales grow, the IRS considers the balance taxable to the shareholders only when actually distributed to them. Hence, the tax on one-half of profits can potentially be deferred indefinitely.

Producer's loan

Under the proper conditions, the 50% of the DISC's income on which income tax is deferred may be loaned ("producer's loan") to the parent or shareholders without being considered as distributed and, hence, taxable.

Freedom from transfer-pricing problems

The DISC provides "safe havens" from the strict and complex intercompany pricing rules found elsewhere in the Internal Revenue Code. Rules governing DISCs effectively allow a liberal portion of the profit from an export transaction to be allocated to the DISC (where it receives the tax benefit) rather than to the manufacturer.

Requirements to set up a DISC

Because the DISC legislation had a definite purpose in mind—to increase exports—the law provides strict qualifying criteria:

• The DISC must be domestically incorporated, although it can operate in foreign countries.

• Not more than one class of stock may be outstanding, and capital must be maintained at $2,500 or more.

• At least 95% of assets and receipts must be related to the export function.

• The export corporation must make an election to be treated as a DISC.

To qualify for the 50% tax deferral granted to DISCs, the law says that the shareholders must make an election to have the corporation treated as a DISC 90 days prior to the beginning of the taxable year for which they want the deferment. Contact your local IRS office and the Commerce Department for helpful booklets concerning exporting and DISCs.

Rule of 78s—Accelerated Interest

The Rule of 78s allows the acceleration of interest payments on installment loans made at a discount and on discount loans. If the borrower needs greater interest deductions in the first year and/or the lender needs greater income from interest in the first year, each would be well advised to consider using the alternative Rule of 78s to compute interest payments.

How it works

Normally, interest is prorated evenly over the payment periods. You pay the same amount of interest on the first payment as you do on the last one.

But under the Rule of 78s, you determine interest payments by multiplying the total interest on a loan by a declining series of fractions.

The numerator (top part of the fraction) is determined by the number of months the loan has yet to run. The denominator (bottom of fraction) is computed by adding up the months of the loan (the denominator of a 12-month loan would be $1 + 2 + 3 + 4 + 5 + 6 + 7 + 8 + 9 + 10 + 11 + 12 = 78$—hence, the name, Rule of 78s. The denominator of an 18-month loan would be $1 + 2 + 3 + \ldots + 18 = 171$). A helpful formula to determine the denominator when using the Rule of 78s is $(n + 1)(n/2)$, where "n" is the length of the loan. For our 12-month example above, it would yield $(12 + 1)(12/2) = 78$.

So, if the total interest on a 12-month loan was $2,000, the interest due on the first payment under the Rule of 78s would be:

$$2{,}000 \times \frac{(\text{number of months yet to go} = 12)}{(\text{sum of months} = 78)} = \$307.69$$

The second month it would be $\$2{,}000 \times \dfrac{11}{78} = \$282.05$.

The third month it would be $\$1{,}000 \times \dfrac{10}{78} = \$256.41$.

The fourth month it would be $\$2{,}000 \times \dfrac{9}{78} = \$230.77$, etc.

If you are contemplating the use of the Rule of 78s, you should keep the following in mind.

• This accelerated computation of interest yields no tax benefit if the loan is for less than 12 months.

• If you want to switch from the standard pro rata method to the Rule of 78s, you must let the IRS know by filing Form 3115.

• The lender and the borrower may use different methods of accounting in regard to the interest. Each does as he pleases.

• A cash basis taxpayer may not deduct the interest expense until he has actually made the payment, and then only to the extent that it represents payment for the current tax year.

Deducting State Sales Tax

Since few, if any, taxpayers are likely to save all receipts as proof of state sales tax payments, the IRS does not require such proof for income tax deductions on the sales tax. Instead, the IRS provides a table in your Form 1040 by which you may estimate the amount of state sales tax paid and deduct accordingly. The following are a few suggestions for increasing the amount of your deduction for state sales tax.

Estimate according to your entire income. The IRS estimates of sales tax in the 1040 form are based on average sales tax paid by people in certain income levels. But the income you report on page one of the 1040 form isn't necessarily the income by which you may estimate your state sales tax. In determining your state sales tax deduction, you should include in your total income all nontaxable income for the year. This may be dividends deducted under the $100 exclusion, the 60% of your long-term gain that was not subject to tax, tax-exempt interest, and so on. By estimating by the higher income level, you get a greater sales tax deduction.

Out-of-state purchases. Not all state sales taxes are the same. If you have made significant purchases in a state with a higher sales tax rate, you may estimate the additional amount of sales tax paid and add that to your official estimate.

Rare purchases. The sales tax paid on an automobile should always be added to your official average amount of sales tax. This is an unusual purchase and its contribution to your sales tax total is important. Of course, any other major and unusual purchases like a boat or a motorcycle should be added.

Selling Your Home

Most people know that if you sell your house, you may use the proceeds to purchase a new house without paying tax on the proceeds of the sale of the old house. What most people don't know, however, is that the regulations governing this change of residence can be pretty strict. So if you want to take advantage of the tax benefit allowed you, pay close attention to the following:

The principal residence

If you want the house you sell to qualify for tax deferral, the house must be your principal residence. Sale of your skiing condominium at Vail, Colorado, doesn't qualify unless you can prove that it is your principal residence. The profits from the sale of your principal residence will be liable for tax unless they are spent on a new principal residence. If you rent a garret and buy a sailboat with the money acquired from the sale of your home, the sale will not be tax free.

Gain on the sale

If you make a gain on the sale of your house and that gain is not invested in your new home, it is taxable to the extent that it exceeds the cost of the new home. However, if you paid for cosmetic improvements ("fixing up" expenses) on the old house in order to sell it, those expenses may be deducted from the adjusted sales price for purposes of computing the current taxable gain. Building a new garage onto the old house or putting in a swimming pool don't qualify as expenses that affect the adjusted sales price of the home. But painting the living room or exterior or laying in new sod on the lawn do qualify and you may adjust the sales price to reflect this.

Price of old home $100,000
Price of new home 95,000
Taxable gain 5,000
Cost of presale cosmetic changes . 3,000
Current taxable gain 2,000

Note, however, that cosmetic costs to fix up the house before sale must be completed and paid within 90 days prior to the sale or within 30 days after the sale date in order to be used to adjust the sales price.

To maintain the tax deferred treatment of your home, you must occupy your new residence within 24 months of the sale of the old house. It may be 24 months before or after the sale, but you must eat and sleep in the new home to qualify as occupying it. Stuffing it with furniture is not occupying it.

If you build a new home you must begin construction within 24 months and actually occupy it within 24 months of the sale of the old home. If your contractor suddenly decides that he can't finish the new home in that time, you're out of luck. Therefore, it is wise to put a clause in the construction contract that grants you damages (to cover any tax loss due to delay moving in) if he doesn't finish your home on time.

If you are 55 years of age or over, the first $125,000 of gain on your home is tax free, whether you buy a new home or not. Note that this is a once in a lifetime election and the house must have been your principal residence for three of the last five years. See the example of how it's done:

Cost basis of home	$ 30,000
Adjusted sales price	180,000
Gain	150,000
Taxable gain	25,000

Loss on the sale

Not everyone makes a profit on the sale of his home. And unfortunately, a loss on the sale of your personal residence is not deductible. However, if you can convert your personal residence into a property held for trade or business, you can deduct the loss completely. You do this by renting your home for a substantial period before you sell. Rented property becomes business property, according to the tax court, which allows you to take the deduction.

If you inherit a house, and the house is not your personal residence, a loss on the sale of that house is deductible as a capital loss up to $3,000 per year until the loss is used up.

If, however, the house was up for rent before it was sold, you can take the entire loss in the year of sale.

If you are unable to sell your house, but the upkeep is getting expensive as it sits idle on the market, look for legal deductions that can cut some of these expenses. You can take quite a few deductions if you handle it correctly. First, the interest expense on a mortgage is deductible regardless. But what about all the upkeep expenses while the house is empty? The IRS says that if you are holding property for possible income production or profit, you can deduct any expenses for upkeep. You should either offer the house for rent with an option to buy (income production) or be able to demonstrate that by holding the house it may appreciate further in value (profit motive). This will allow you to deduct all reasonable expenses while the house is still on the market.

Transfer of a Lease

Rental income is taxable as ordinary income, but if you can sell your lease instead of subletting, your gain is taxed as capital gain. Here's how it can work:

Your firm has a 15-year lease on a building, but you want out after ten years. Happily, Mr. Smith's firm is willing to move into your old building. You were paying $5,000 per year and Smith is willing to pay $6,000 per year. If you sublet the property to Smith, you have $1,000 per year ordinary income for five years, $5,000 taxed at your ordinary income rate.

However, if you sell the lease outright to Smith for $5,000, the money comes to you as capital gain and is subject to the lower tax rate. If you give Smith a break on the price to entice him to go along, he is happy because he saves money (he can still amortize the cost) and you are happy because you save tax dollars.

Naturally, you don't want the IRS to suspect that the sale of the lease is actually only another form of sublet. Therefore, after you've arranged things with your landlord, write up a bill of sale for the lease and use terms like "buyer" and "seller," avoid any right on your part to repossess, and have the lease assigned to Smith. These little details help you to avoid trouble later.

Selling Investment or Business Real Estate

If you intend to sell investment property or business real estate that you have held for more than 12 months, you might consider the tactic of spending more money for repair of the property, jacking up the price to cover those repair costs, and then taking a tax profit on top of your sales profit. The key here is that profit on the sale of property is capital gain, but repair costs are deductible against ordinary income.

How it works to save tax dollars
Suppose you have a business property to sell, but the property could use some repairs. Your tax bracket is 25% and you have to pay $1,000 for the repairs. How can spending more money save you money?

1. Since repairs are deductible against ordinary income, these repairs have just created a $250 deduction in your ordinary income tax.

2. You raise the price of the property by $1,000 to recover the money spent on repairs. The profit on the property is taxed at your capital gain rate (40% × the ordinary income tax rate). Therefore, the capital gains tax on the repairs will be 40% × 25% × $1,000 = $100.00.

3. So you have increased your capital gain tax on the property by $100.00, but you have lowered your ordinary income tax by $250.00. Therefore you have a net saving of $150.00 that was brought about by spending more money! Of course, you must always be wary of cost recovery recapture on in this kind of arrangement. Check with your accountant if you have doubts.

Incorporating Before You Have a Business

Most people say that they would want to investigate very carefully before forming a new business, but sometimes you can actually save money when considering a new business by going into business first and worrying about the nature of the business later. Sounds odd? Here's how it can work.

The cost of obtaining information on a business

• When it relates to your present business. When you investigate new possiblities related to your present business, you may deduct the expenses of your investigation as necessary to your business. As long as the expenses are related to your present business, the IRS won't bother you.

• When it involves an unrelated business. If you are in the business of making cotton candy and you suddenly decide you want to look into making life rafts for submarines, you may not deduct as ordinary business expenses the costs incurred while investigating the general submarine life raft industry. Expenses for investigating a business not related to your present business are capital expenditures that may be deducted later through amortization, depreciation, sale, or abandonment—if you proceed with the new business. (Of course, if the investigation leads to a dead end, you're just out of luck in regard to the money expended for the investigation.) However, once you've decided whether to enter the business and, if you've decided to purchase a new company, which company you might want to buy, then any expenses related to the specific purchase would be deductible as incurred, whether or not you actually consummate the purchase.

A possible solution

Because of the restrictions on business deductions, you may find that you will save money by simply forming a new corporation before you investigate the new business area. Of course, this discussion is primarily aimed at investigations that require significant amounts of money. The idea here is to form a minimum-capitalized corporation and then write off the investigation expenses to the corporation to which they are directly related. Later, if the new business area doesn't seem feasible, you can deduct the expense of the investigation as an abandonment in a discontinued corporation. This can be done by claiming a deduction for the worthless corporate stock as either a capital or ordinary loss, dependent upon the nature of the stock that is involved.

Deducting Expenses for Education

You may deduct expenses for your education as long as the education is to maintain or to improve the skills needed for the business in which you are already established. You may not deduct expenses for education if that education will train you for a different business or even for a new job in the same field.

Related skills

If you make a living as a cowboy and want to go to school to learn electrical engineering, you may not deduct the expenses of your education. However, if you are an electrical engineer and you want to take an updated course on a new kind of circuitry that is now being introduced into your field, the deduction will probably be allowed.

Sometimes there is a very fine line between related and unrelated education. The tax court has held that an accountant who wanted to deduct the cost of his study for his CPA exam was not entitled to the deduction because the CPA qualification would have made him eligible for a new job. However, as suggested in the introduction to this chapter, when in doubt, consider an aggressive posture.

Travel expenses

If the education is job related, how much can be deducted for any travel expenses?

If you can show that the primary purpose for the travel expenditures was education, you may deduct transportation costs, meals, lodging, and other costs related to pursuing education away from home.

If you travel to a seminar or some other educational meeting, but the primary reason for the travel is pleasure, you may deduct for meals, lodging, and expenses while the educational function is underway, but you may not deduct transportation costs. You will notice that the restrictions here are similar to those governing business expenses as outlined early in this chapter.

Figure 8

COST OF EXTRA COVERAGE COMPUTED BY IRS

Age	Cost per Month per $1,000	Age	Cost per Month per $1,000
20-29	8 cents	45-49	$ .40
30-34	10 cents	50-54	.68
35-39	14 cents	55-59	1.10
40-44	23 cents	60-64	1.63

Saving Tax Money on Group Term Insurance

You might be able to save tax dollars by taking another look at your group term life insurance arrangements. Of course, many businessmen know that up to $50,000 of group term life insurance can be provided tax free to an employee—with costs deductible to the corporation. But often unknown is the fact that the corporation can provide more than $50,000 coverage to favored officers or employees and still receive a full tax deduction. The recipient, however, must include the cost of the coverage above $50,000 as taxable compensation to himself. But the "cost" is not the true cost of the extra coverage (as paid by the corporation). Rather, it is computed according to a schedule provided by the IRS (see Figure 8).

As you can see, because these rates don't include any loading charges, they can be substantially below the actual cost of the insurance.

Average Itemized Deductions

Although the statistics are generally not well publicized, the Internal Revenue Service does publish figures on the average dollar amount of deductions taxpayers claim in four major areas. (See Figure 9.) While it's probable that these "average" figures will not accurately represent your particular deductions, the statistics can be helpful:

1. Deductions that are significantly higher than the average. If your deductions are substantially higher than the average shown, you should be prepared to defend your claims, as your chances for audit will increase dramatically. It's a good idea to attach documentation to your return if you can see a potential problem area. This foresight could prevent an audit.

2. Deductions that are significantly lower than the average. On the other hand, if your deductions are quite a bit lower than the figures shown on the chart, reevaluate your financial records to make sure you haven't overlooked any legitimate deductions.

3. Evaluation of your record-keeping. The chart is also helpful for analysis of your record-keeping system. If, for instance, you find that your deductions are consistently on the low side, you should evaluate your personal bookkeeping system to ensure that deductible items are properly logged for tax preparation purposes.

This record-keeping system can be as simple as notations in a checkbook register or as complex as a complete double entry bookkeeping system. The important thing is

Figure 9

AVERAGE ITEMIZED DEDUCTIONS FOR 1979

Adjusted Gross Income Class	Average Deductions for Contributions	Average Deductions for Interest	Average Deductions for Taxes	Average Medical Dental Deductions
$ 4,000 – $ 6,000	$ 481	$1,775	$ 771	$1,539
6,000 – 8,000	535	1,909	834	1,623
8,000 – 10,000	517	2,188	970	1,215
10,000 – 12,000	582	2,047	1,020	1,264
12,000 – 14,000	573	2,169	1,140	1,071
14,000 – 16,000	584	2,190	1,260	882
16,000 – 18,000	554	2,334	1,334	814
18,000 – 20,000	593	2,499	1,511	635
20,000 – 25,000	583	2,589	1,699	590
25,000 – 30,000	654	2,792	2,053	549
30,000 – 40,000	795	3,110	2,526	518
40,000 – 50,000	1,115	3,609	3,327	514
50,000 – 100,000	1,793	5,131	5,017	696
100,000 or more	8,958	11,896	13,409	1,223

that it be an accurate and up-to-date reflection of those expenses that can be used to reduce your taxes come April 15.

Note that the figures in this chart are from 1979 returns—the most recent statistics available. Thus, you may want to increase the figures to compensate for inflation.

CHAPTER SIXTEEN

How to Survive an IRS Audit

Most IRS audits are actually quite routine—the IRS agent generally only wants substantiation of an item or two. As such, an audit should not cause you to be unduly concerned and generally should not require the services of your accountant or tax lawyer. However, even routine audits can get out of hand if not handled properly. Here are eight tips compiled by tax professionals to ensure that your audit goes smoothly.

1. Research the agent assigned to your case as soon as you are notified that your return has been pulled for audit. Notify your accountant and lawyer that you are being audited and that you will contact them if the audit is other than routine. Ask these advisers and other business associates for key facts about the agent's specialty or personality. This can give you valuable insight into handling of your audit.

2. Take the initiative and contact the agent to set up an appointment. Ask exactly what information he will need—this will help pinpoint contested areas. You will create a favorable first impression by accepting the audit as just another business matter.

3. Prepare worksheets and backup information substantiating the contested areas. This will not only cut audit time but will project an attitude of conscientiousness and detail.

4. Make the agent comfortable in a low-traffic area of your office when he arrives. Busy yourself with other work that will not be distracting to him. Do not let the agent browse through your records unattended, although you may offer to have your bookkeeper meet with him to explain your systems.

5. Don't feel rushed. If the auditor asks a question you have not anticipated, be honest and say you just don't know the answer—but will be happy to get more information. Never volunteer information not requested!

6. Consider the cost of protesting versus the cost of paying if the agent proposes a

deficiency. You may save more by accepting the agent's assessment than by tying up additional hours (and possibly later accountant's and lawyer's fees) in an appeal. Also, be selective in the issues you fight for. You'll stand a better chance of gaining ground on major issues if you'll gracefully surrender on the smaller ones.

7. "Prime issues" are those which the IRS will not compromise under any circumstances. Some of these are listed toward the end of this chapter. Before deciding on an appeal, make sure none of these issues is at stake.

8. Stay in control. Finally, if for any reason you feel uncomfortable with the direction the audit is taking, or that the agent is getting into areas you feel you are not prepared to defend, terminate the interview and call your accountant and/or tax lawyer immediately.

IRS Audit Survival Checklist

Almost inevitably either your business or personal tax returns will be audited by the Internal Revenue Service; yet few taxpayers are really prepared to handle an audit. Keep this checklist handy for eventual reference so you know what to expect and make no inadvertent blunders.

The first step you should take when you meet with any IRS agent is to examine his or her credentials. If the agent is a revenue agent, the audit is probably routine. If, however, you discover that you are dealing with a special agent, immediately terminate the interview, answer no questions, and phone your attorney. Revenue agents are concerned with ordinary civil tax questions whereas special agents investigate criminal tax fraud matters. While a special agent is supposed to read you a summary of your rights, they sometimes try to keep a low profile by quickly flashing their identification papers or working as a team with a revenue agent. Know which type of agent you are dealing with. Be firm but courteous in all your dealings with these agents.

The second step is to ask the agent to outline the scope of the audit and what records he would like. Generally, the agent is only looking for supporting evidence for certain claims you have made. By knowing exactly what the agent is looking for, you and your accountant can prepare the necessary documentation to support your case and quickly complete the audit. Answer all questions but do not volunteer information or give overdetailed answers. There is obviously a fine line between being evasive, which will only engender suspicion and prolong the audit, and being too helpful. Never allow an agent to go through your papers or records. It will only lead to more questions and may expand the scope of your audit.

Once the audit is complete, the revenue agent will prepare his report, called an RAR, stating his recommendations concerning the investigation. You will then be asked to sign a waiver Form 870 indicating that you agree with the agent's assessment of taxes due. If the amounts are small or the agent has discovered obvious mistakes, it is generally best to sign the form and conclude the audit. But if the agent touches on gray areas where you feel your position is defensible, you should tread carefully. If you agree to settle too quickly, the agent may feel that you have other things to hide that merit further investigation. Many agents shoot high, expecting to compromise eventually. In these situations and where the sums involved are substantial, it is preferable to let your accountant or tax attorney argue the technical points for you.

Tax experts generally agree that a case should be settled as early as possible—preferably at the audit stage. However, if you do not agree with the agent's findings and cannot come to a settlement, you will have to appeal the case either through the IRS administrative process or through the courts, which is a judicial process. In the administrative appeal, it is advisable to have a professional tax adviser or legal counsel accompany you. You should definitely have legal counsel for any judicial proceedings.

Administrative process

"30-day" and "90-day" letters. If you do not agree with the agent's assessment and refuse to sign Form 870, you will receive a copy of the RAR with a preliminary note advising you that you have 30 days to appeal your case. If you ignore the letter, you will then receive a 90-day letter advising you to pay or petition the tax court for a redetermination.

The Appellate Division. Formerly, the administrative process consisted of two levels: The District Conference or the Appellate Division. In October of 1978, the two divisions were combined into one Appellate Division.

After receiving the 30-day letter but before receiving the 90-day letter, you may request a hearing by notifying your Regional Appellate Office in accordance with the instructions in the IRS's transmittal letter. Unless your disputed amount is less than $2,500, your request should usually be accompanied by a written protest.

Representation. You may represent yourself at the appellate division hearing or in any of the tax court procedures, or you may be represented by an attorney, CPA, or an individual enrolled to practice before the Internal Revenue Service.

If your representative attends a conference without you, he or she may receive or inspect confidential information only in accordance with a properly filed power of attorney or a tax information authorization. Obtain Form 2848, Power of Attorney, or Form 2848-D, Authorization and Declaration, from any IRS office.

The written protest. To make an administrative appeal you may need to file a written protest with the District Director. You do not need to file a written protest if the disputed amount is less then $2,500 or the audit was conducted by correspondence or by interview in an IRS office. If required, the protest letter should be submitted in duplicate within the period allowed by the preliminary letter. Contact your tax adviser or the IRS for further specifics.

Judicial process

At any time after a tax deficiency has been determined, you may elect to bypass the IRS administrative process and proceed directly to the Tax Court, Court of Claims, or your U.S. District Court. These courts are independent judicial bodies and have no connection with the IRS. Your chances of success may be greater in court than with the IRS—about three-fourths of the cases brought to court are resolved out of court, and settlements average 30¢ for each dollar of original deficiency. These settlements, however, vary between IRS districts.

Tax Court. If your case involves a disagreement over whether you owe additional income tax, or estate or gift tax, you may go to the U.S. Tax Court. To do this, ask the IRS to issue a formal letter, called a "statutory notice of deficiency." You have 90 days from the date this notice is mailed to you (150 days if addressed to you outside the United States) to file a petition with the Tax Court.

Note that if your case involves a dispute of $5,000 or less for any one taxable year, a simplified alternative procedure is provided by the Tax Court. Upon your request and with the approval of the court, your case may be handled under the Small Tax

Case procedures. At little cost to you in time or money, you can present your own case to the Tax Court for a binding decision. If your case is handled under this procedure, the decision of the Tax Court is final and cannot be appealed. You can obtain more information regarding the Small Tax Case procedures and other Tax Court matters from the Clerk of the U.S. Tax Court, 400 Second St., NW, Washington, DC 20217.

District Court and Court of Claims. You may file a claim for refund if after you pay your tax you believe the tax is erroneous or excessive. If the IRS hasn't acted on your claim within six months from the date you filed it, you can then file suit for a refund. A suit for refund must be filed no later than two years after the IRS has disallowed your claim. You may file your refund suit in your U.S. District Court or in the U.S. Court of Claims. Generally, your District Court and the Court of Claims hear tax cases only after you have paid the tax and have filed a claim for refund. You can obtain information about procedure for filing suit in either court by contacting the clerk of the District Court in your area or the Clerk of the Court of Claims, 717 Madison Pl. NW, Washington, DC 20005.

An IRS audit is no reason for panic and it does not indicate that the IRS intends to delve into all of your personal or business affairs. As you can see, appeal to higher authorities generally results in a lower settlement, but, of course, costs more in legal fees.

What You Should Know About Tax Rulings

A "Revenue Ruling" is the IRS's specific answer to a taxpayer's specific question. As such, it gives the IRS's interpretation of all applicable laws and regulations to a given set of circumstances. Generally, "Rev Rulings" relate to a prospective transaction—that is, most rulings are obtained in advance.

Why get a ruling?
Generally, the IRS will not contest a transaction on which a ruling was obtained beforehand, assuming that the taxpayer acted in accordance with the ruling. And, generally, you are safe in relying on rulings written for others, if the substantial facts and circumstances are the same. However, bear in mind that revenue agents are allowed discretion in interpreting individual cases, so any transaction entered into based upon a ruling issued for another case may not hold up on audit in your case.

An additional benefit of obtaining a revenue ruling is that the revenue agents who research and write rulings are highly knowledgeable tax law specialists. Requesting a ruling is essentially getting expert consultation for free.

When not to get a ruling
There are several situations when a taxpayer is wiser not to request a ruling.

If you suspect the IRS would not rule in your favor, you would be alerting them to a possible flaw in your tax preparation. The transaction in question may be routine, but research and investigation may point out another area of your business or personal finances that may produce unexpected complications.

Also, there are areas where the IRS will not issue rulings. Some of these include:

- "Reasonable" compensation (§162).

- Whether a corporation is acquired for the purpose of avoiding income tax (§269).

• Determination of the amount of earnings and profits of a corporation (§312).

• Whether transactions lack a "business purpose" or the purpose is to evade taxes (Rev. Rul. 74-17, 1974-2 CB 491).

• Matters involving hypothetical situations.

Other areas where the IRS generally will not issue rulings include:

• Depreciation issues, such as salvage value, useful life, and depreciation rates (§167) for pre-1981 Tax Act property.

• Whether Section 306 stock redemption in a closely held corporation is principally designed to avoid taxes.

How to apply for a ruling

Unnecessary delays can be avoided if thorough and accurate details are provided the IRS at the time a ruling is requested. The request should be submitted in duplicate and should be addressed to the Commissioner of Internal Revenue, Attention: T:PS:T, Washington, DC. Your request should include:

1. Complete information on all taxpayers involved or affected (including corporate taxpayers). Include names, addresses, Social Security or employer identification numbers, where returns are filed, and, in the case of a corporation, the state of incorporation.

2. A summary of the proposed transaction and the reasons for it. Attach true copies of any supporting documents, but relevant facts contained in the documents should also be included in the statement of facts. It is not sufficient to incorporate such facts by reference.

3. A statement as to whether the same issue is currently under investigation by the IRS, to the best of the taxpayer's knowledge. (If so, the Service will deny your request for a ruling.)

4. A request for a specific ruling and a statement of citations of relevant rulings or regulations.

5. The request must be signed by the taxpayer or his representative. If signed on your behalf by your CPA or attorney, a Power of Attorney (Form 2848) must be attached.

6. Include your telephone number and request an oral conference.

7. If you wish to apply for an "expedited" ruling (normally, rulings take three to four months), that request should be made separately. Your "expedite" request must show good cause.

In 1976, the IRS adopted an informal conference procedure to help expedite rulings. Approximately two weeks after a request for ruling is received, an agent will contact you for an informal discussion on whether additional information is required, and a tentative opinion on how the IRS will rule. However, the agent's comments are not binding on the Service.

Withdrawal of request

You may withdraw your request for a ruling at any time. You need not state a reason. All that is necessary is a letter to the Commissioner asking that the request be abandoned.

Naturally, you would want to withdraw your request if you were advised that the ruling will not be favorable. While there is some danger that your regional office will be alerted to the fact that a ruling was applied for, generally speaking, the Service does not pursue issues which have been abandoned.

How to Do Your Own Tax Research

Every tax law change—like the Tax Reform Act of 1976 or the 1978 Revenue Act—is an amendment or codification to the 1954 Code. A proposed tax change follows the same legislative procedure as any other law: it is submitted to Congress in the form of a bill that, after debate and amendment, is passed by both the House and the Senate and submitted to the President for signature.

The various stages of a tax law's development may be tracked through the *Congressional Record* or committee reports. It is important to remember that tax laws are merely guidelines that Congress has formulated but which must be interpreted by other agencies—in this case, the Internal Revenue Service. Therefore, it becomes critical to know what the attitudes of the legislators were at the time the law was formulated. The *Congressional Record* and committee reports often indicate the intent of Congress and can be very helpful in substantiating a position, although the research is time-consuming and tedious. Keep in mind that the IRS relies on committee reports for documentation of its position, too. Thus, availing yourself of this research tool just might disarm the IRS's "secret weapon" on an audit or in a tax court hearing.

Two tax services (Prentice-Hall, Commerce Clearing House) send committee reports periodically to subscribers. Large public libraries and law libraries will also have files on both the committee reports and the *Congressional Record*.

Figure 1

SOURCES OF TAX RESEARCH INFORMATION

Source	What it contains	Where it is found	Ease of research
Congressional Record and committee reports	"Journal" of legislative debate throughout all stages of enactment into law. Shows congressional intent.	Commerce Clearing House, Prentice-Hall, other major tax services, public library, law library.	Fairly difficult to research; much "wading through" required.
IRS regulations	Interpretation of IRS Code by Commissioner of Internal Revenue.	*Federal Register; Internal Revenue Bulletin;* Internal Revenue Service offices. Also available through Government Printing Office.	Paperback copies issued by major tax services easiest to work with. Check your library or gain access to law library.
Revenue Rulings and procedures	Individualized interpretations of specific taxpayer questions.	Weekly *Internal Revenue Bulletin;* semiannual *Cumulative Bulletin,* both available by subscription or individually through the Government Printing Office. Major tax services provide weekly updates.	Tax services provide indexes for ease in finding specific rulings. IRS bulletins organized by subject.
Court decisions	Precedents set by judicial decisions on individual points of law.	Bound volumes of *Tax Court Reports* and *Tax Court Memos* available through Government Printing Office; tax services publish weekly reports.	Law libraries will give best access to decisions. To save time, enlist the help of an experienced law librarian.

IRS regulations

A regulation (or "Reg") is an interpretation of the IRS Code made by the Commissioner of Internal Revenue. As such, it is nearly as good as law to revenue agents, and the agents themselves are bound by it. A court case is the only way you can win if a regulation is against you. And even after you get to court, you may face an uphill battle. Tax courts regard regulations—particularly those that have been on the books for years—as law for all practical purposes.

Of course, the process of interpreting the regulations may bring out points in a taxpayer's favor. However, if your research turns up a Reg clearly in opposition to your line of defense, it would be wise for you to consider compromising or dropping the point entirely.

The *Federal Register* publishes proposed regulations, to which taxpayers may comment or object. Final regulations, or Treasury decisions, are printed first in the *Federal Register,* then in the *Internal Revenue Bulletin.* Regulations are also available through the Government Printing Office or your local IRS office and through the various commercial tax services.

Revenue rulings

"Rev Rulings" are interpretations, based on the Code, regulations, and court decisions, on specific taxpayer questions and are issued in response to written requests. A revenue ruling is published in the *Internal Revenue Bulletin;* unpublished rulings are referred to as letter or private rulings.

Rulings do not carry the same weight as regulations, although they are considered an official interpretation of the tax law. They can be a critical research aid when your facts and circumstances are basically the same as those already decided.

Weekly bulletins and a six-month *Cumulative Bulletin* are available through the Government Printing Office. Commercial tax services also provide regular updates of rulings.

The *Internal Revenue Bulletin* periodically announces "acquiescences" and "nonacquiescences" with regard to court cases it has lost. An acquiescence means that the IRS basically agrees with the interpretation of the law (in favor of the taxpayer) and would probably rule in the taxpayer's favor again, given similar circumstances. A nonacquiescence indicates that the precedent set will not necessarily have any bearing on a similar case. Thus use acquiesced cases whenever possible in preparing your defense.

Tax courts

Perhaps the greatest source of precedent for tax questions comes from the various tax courts.

Two types of decisions are handed down from the U.S. Tax Court: regular decisions (which generally carry more weight as precedent), and memorandum decisions (which generally uphold previously decided issues).

If you intend to do significant research into tax court case law, it would be helpful to have access to a law library. Check with your public library, colleges and universities, downtown office buildings, or your attorney to arrange entry. The tax services cover major cases, regulations, and rulings in a reasonably simple format. (See Figure 1 for a summary of sources.)

Doing your own tax research obviously requires considerable time and energy. However, it can save hundreds or thousands of dollars in professional fees. An added bonus—by doing your own research you will gain valuable insight into the details of your particular tax question.

What Is the Auditor Looking For?

When an IRS revenue agent scrutinizes your return, what is he really looking for? Here is a portion of the actual standards and techniques used by agents in auditing income tax returns, taken from the official IRS guidelines.

Individuals—Nonbusiness
Wages and salaries:

• Review compensation arrangement with an eye toward special privileges (paid vacations, use of company car, etc.).

• Particular consideration should be given to the source of taxpayer's income, as certain occupations and trades are more susceptible than others to omitted income.

• Be alert to outside employment, prizes, tips, etc.

Travel and entertainment:

• The amounts spent for travel and entertainment items are deductible if they are ordinary and necessary business expenses. The records should be in sufficient detail to establish the following: the relationship of the expenditure to the business; the payee and place of expenditure; the amount of the expenditure; the identity of the persons involved, including parties entertained, if any.

• Ascertain if the questions on the return pertaining to expense account information have been completed. If unanswered, inquiry should be made.

• Discuss with the taxpayer his employer's reimbursement policy to determine the correctness of the answers to the questions and to establish whether the taxpayer may have received additional compensation through the use of company-owned facilities, paid vacations, etc.

• If the taxpayer has claimed a travel or entertainment deduction, procure an analysis of all expenses, both reimbursed and unreimbursed. Such expenses should be broken down into the broad categories of transportation, meals, and lodging.

• Consider whether the facts of the case warrant fraud referral, or the application of the civil fraud or negligence penalty.

Contributions:

• Verify amounts claimed and determine that the deduction has been taken in the proper year.

• Determine whether the payments were made to qualified organizations.

• Ascertain that percentage limitations have not been exceeded.

• Determine if contributions claimed are nondeductible personal expenses and ascertain if donor received benefits or consideration in return.

Corporations
Sales and consignments:

• Review the cutoff. Determine if year-end sales have been included in the proper accounting period. Determine if the accounting method is acceptable and consistent with prior years.

• Review and inquire into entries in the account that appear to be unusual in source, nature, or amount.

• Determine whether merchandise is being withdrawn for personal use by corporate officers or others and make appropriate adjustment.

• Test the recording procedures regarding returned merchandise, discounts, claims, and rebates, looking for pocketing of funds, offset of personal items.

• Where records appear unreliable or inadequate, consider the possibility of approaching the audit from another standpoint (bank deposit method, net worth method, etc.).

Officers' salaries:

• Determine total compensation paid or accrued to principal officers, taking into consideration any compensation claimed under headings other than officers' salaries, such as manufacturing salaries, supervisory salaries, etc.; contributions to pension plans for the officers; payments of personal expenses; year-end or other bonuses, etc.

• Determine if and to what extent each principal officer's compensation is unreasonable, taking into account such factors as nature of duties, background and experience, knowledge of the business, etc.

• Be alert to closely held multiple corporation situations in which compensation may be split between two or more related corporations, and which in the aggregate may be considered excessive to the officer-stockholder.

Travel and entertainment:

• Determine the corporation's policy with respect to reimbursing or giving allowances to officers and employees for T&E expenses.

• Prepare a summary of the totals posted to the accounts containing T&E items, and identify same with the deductions for T&E expenses claimed on the tax return.

• Select a representative test period (or periods). All T&E items within said period (or periods) must be broken down and classified in the suggested broad categories shown in the sample workpapers.

Settling Your Case: What Are Your Options?

At some point in the audit procedure, the revenue agent will present his adjustments in your return and, most likely, will advise you of the additional tax you owe. At this point, you have several options: you can accept the assessment, pay the tax, and have the audit settled; you can request a conference with the Appellate Division; or you can pay the tax and file for a refund. The first (and best) line of defense is to settle at this level. Here's how to proceed.

Dealings with the agent

Never settle or concede any issue until the agent has completed his examination. By making sure the agent's cards are all on the table, you allow yourself more leeway in planning your negotiation strategy.

You are within your rights to request some time to consider the agent's proposed settlement. Use this time to determine:

• Has the agent properly construed the facts of your situation? If you can prove that your version of the facts is correct (through your books, records, or the supporting affidavits of persons familiar with the situation), the revenue agent will usually concede without argument. If, however, the issues are still open to interpretation, probably the best you can hope for is a compromise.

• Are the agent's proposed adjustments correct under the IRS Code and Regulations? Remember that interpretations of the tax statutes are not always clear-cut; if you can raise a reasonable argument as to the agent's interpretation, do so.

• Are there adjustments in your favor that can be used to offset some of the deficiency? Or, alternatively, if there are many issues, can some be conceded in exchange for favorable adjustment on others?

• Is the agent assigned to your case completely unreasonable? A frequent question asked by taxpayers undergoing audit is when—if ever—it is advisable to ask that an agent be removed from a case. Usually, it is poor strategy to run the risk of alienating the auditor. If you find it impossible, or nearly so, to work with the auditor assigned to your case, a telephone call or meeting with his group chief may resolve matters.

Advantages of settling with the agent

There are several advantages to settling your audit at the revenue agent level. The most obvious is that the deficiency involved may not justify the cost in time and dollars of pursuing it to a higher level. In addition, the agent is more likely to interpret technicalities liberally if it appears that a settlement can be reached.

If you find that you would be willing to settle on all but one or two points, you have the option of paying the entire deficiency. Then you can apply for a refund of part or all of it any time within two years. This procedure stops the interest clock; it is also possible to concede only the minor issues and appeal the more important ones.

What if you can't settle with the agent?

On October 2, 1978, the IRS combined the appeals structure into one level. The elimination of district conferences is designed to simplify record keeping and reduce taxpayer inconvenience, while maintaining taxpayer rights.

Thus, your level of appeal from the findings of the revenue agent is now only one step—the Regional Appellate Office. An "Appellate Conferee" from the staff will meet with you and discuss the disputed issues fully.

The conferee's orientation at this point is the revenue agent's report (RAR), and the burden of proof is on the taxpayer to provide clear and convincing evidence that the agent's report should be amended. Documentary evidence (books, records, worksheets) are the most effective proof. Supporting evidence that may have bearing includes affidavits and oral statements by disinterested persons, copies of relevant correspondence, etc.

When the hearings are concluded, the conferee will review the facts and testimony and will submit a report reflecting his decision. If you agree with his findings, you may sign the waiver (Form 870) attached and pay the tax. If you still disagree, your case must be pursued at the judicial level.

Note that the appeal procedure within the IRS remains informal, held at the taxpayer's convenience, with no transcript. Furthermore, if the original audit was held at an IRS office—called an "office examination"—the taxpayer does not even have to file a written protest to begin the appeals process. In "field examinations" of income tax returns—normally held at the taxpayer's place of business—no written protest is required unless the disputed amount is over $2,500.

270

How to prepare a written protest

If your field audit resulted in a disputed amount of over $2,500, a written protest will be necessary. Your protest should contain:

1. A statement that you want to appeal the findings of the revenue agent to the Appellate Division.

2. Your name and address (for a corporation, the address of the principal place of business).

3. The date and case reference on the letter from the IRS transmitting the findings you are protesting.

4. The taxable years, periods, or returns involved.

5. An itemized schedule of adjustments or findings with which you do not agree.

6. A statement of facts supporting your position in contested factual issues. This statement and all major evidence submitted with the protest should be sworn to as true, under penalties of perjury.

7. A statement outlining the law or other authority upon which you are relying.

8. The protest should be filed in duplicate.

Advantages of appeal

The idea of going beyond the revenue agent stage with your audit may seem frightening, especially since the appellate conferee is evaluating your case based on the RAR. However, the advantages of taking your case further up the ladder include:

• The issues will be debated before a more experienced tax technician. Conferees have generally had years of experience as field or office agents, and are more knowledgeable than revenue agents, as a rule.

• Any personality clashes between you and the agent are no longer present. You have a chance for a fresh start with a new agent, who has the responsibility of looking at the issues objectively.

• Issues may be interpreted more favorably to you by the higher authority. Again, you have the advantage of dealing with a more experienced agent, who may well interpret the same evidence in a different way.

• The informality of the conference hearings is designed to save taxpayer time and trouble. The IRS wants to resolve the issues with as little difficulty as possible, and the appeal process is designed to accomplish this purpose.

Over 75% of all cases are settled using the procedures described above. Therefore, we have not discussed in detail the judicial procedures that the taxpayer can utilize. Appeals to the courts generally require the expert assistance of your CPA or tax lawyer. (See Figure 2.)

Prime Issues

On certain issues, the IRS will not compromise. These "prime issues" have recently been made available to the public through the Freedom of Information Act. A partial list follows.

• Convertible debt: whether attribution of part of the issue price of convertible debt to the conversion privilege gives rise to amortizable discount.

Figure 2

APPEALS PROCEDURE

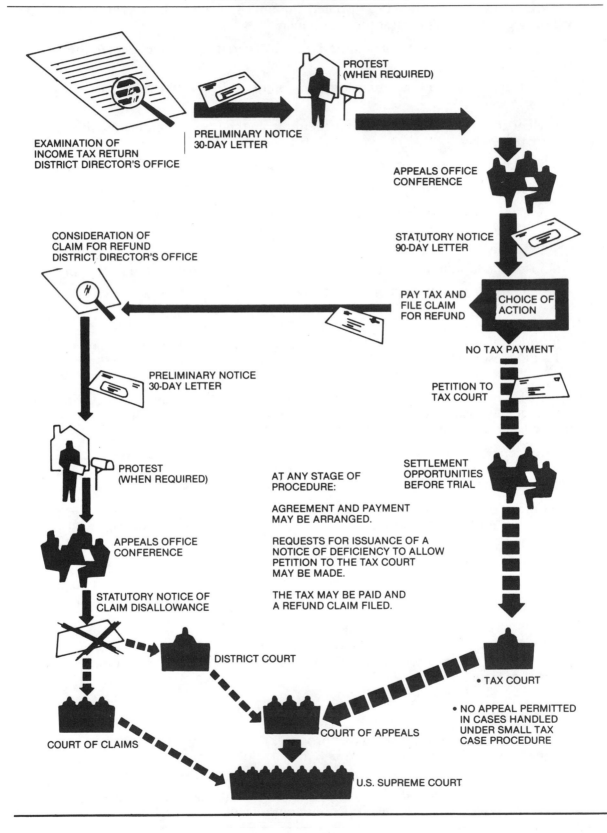

EXAMINATION OF
INCOME TAX RETURN
DISTRICT DIRECTOR'S OFFICE

PRELIMINARY NOTICE
30-DAY LETTER

PROTEST
(WHEN REQUIRED)

APPEALS OFFICE
CONFERENCE

CONSIDERATION OF
CLAIM FOR REFUND
DISTRICT DIRECTOR'S OFFICE

STATUTORY NOTICE
90-DAY LETTER

PAY TAX AND
FILE CLAIM
FOR REFUND

CHOICE OF
ACTION

NO TAX PAYMENT

PRELIMINARY NOTICE
30-DAY LETTER

PETITION TO
TAX COURT

PROTEST
(WHEN REQUIRED)

AT ANY STAGE OF
PROCEDURE:

AGREEMENT AND PAYMENT
MAY BE ARRANGED.

SETTLEMENT
OPPORTUNITIES
BEFORE TRIAL

APPEALS OFFICE
CONFERENCE

REQUESTS FOR ISSUANCE OF A
NOTICE OF DEFICIENCY TO ALLOW
PETITION TO THE TAX COURT
MAY BE MADE.

STATUTORY NOTICE OF
CLAIM DISALLOWANCE

THE TAX MAY BE PAID AND
A REFUND CLAIM FILED.

DISTRICT COURT

• TAX COURT

COURT OF CLAIMS

COURT OF APPEALS

• NO APPEAL PERMITTED
IN CASES HANDLED
UNDER SMALL TAX
CASE PROCEDURE

U.S. SUPREME COURT

- Loss by shareholder on guaranty of corporate loan: claim of ordinary loss rather than capital loss.

- Deductions in connection with residence listed for sale: whether a taxpayer who ceases to live in residence and lists it for sale can take deductions applicable to investment property, e.g., maintenance and depreciation.

- Stock options: readily ascertainable fair market value.

- Pension and profit sharing plans: whether a plan covering only a single class of employees is discriminatory and whether a plan that fails to meet requirements for qualification in its operation loses its qualification.

- Family leasebacks: rent deductions where property is transferred to a trust and promptly leased back.

- Mandatory contributions to deferred compensation plan: whether mandatory contributions withheld from an employee's pay and contributed to a qualified deferred compensation plan are includible in the employee's income in the year they are withheld.

Special Handling of Fraud Investigations

You may never encounter a fraud investigation. But if you do, be prepared for the worst: the dogged determination of the IRS in pursuing fraud cases results in guilty pleas for 71% of those indicted, and of the 17% who go to trial, 65% are convicted.

Special agents investigate tax fraud, so if you find yourself dealing with one, it can mean nothing but serious trouble. Therefore, your safest route is to run—not walk—to your attorney and let him represent you throughout the investigation.

If you are investigated for fraud

A special agent is supposed to give you a Miranda warning (advising you that you do not have to answer any questions you feel may incriminate you and that anything you say can and will be used against you). He is further supposed to identify himself as a special agent, show his credentials, and tell you that he is making a criminal investigation. However, most court cases have upheld the decision that the only time an agent absolutely must read a taxpayer his rights is when the taxpayer is actually in custody. The distinction, then, is that although Internal Revenue Service administrative guidelines require that an agent provide you with these warnings, information obtained and statements made can be admitted into evidence even without the warnings, if the data are disclosed in a noncustodial interview.

It can't be repeated enough. Take the initiative, ask to see the agent's credentials, and confirm that he is not a special agent.

Assuming that you are dealing with a revenue agent (whose role is to investigate routine tax matters), there are still certain procedures that may tip you off to the possibility that a special agent will be brought in. If the revenue agent requests extensive photocopies of seemingly unimportant records. . .if the revenue agent subpoenas records from your stockbroker or bank. . .if the revenue agent asks you for a net worth statement or cost of living statements. . .be alerted to the possibility that the civil investigation may be turning in the direction of a criminal one. At that point, your best course of action is to turn the matter over to your tax attorney.

Your Constitutional rights

Under the Fourth and Fifth Amendments to the Constitution, you are protected against unreasonable search and seizure and self-incrimination. (Constitutional rights do not apply to corporations.) The most vital of these rights are the rights to counsel and silence. Although the special agent will advise you that you "may wish" to seek the advice of counsel, he may leave you with the impression that counsel can be obtained at any time. This is not the case. Once you divulge any information at all to the special agent, you have waived your right to these protections.

If you say anything at all, tell the truth. Intentional misrepresentation can open new doors to additional criminal proceedings under the "false statements" section of the U.S. Criminal Code, regardless of what happens to your criminal audit.

Probably the worst thing you can do in the early stages of a fraud investigation is to pay what tax the agent says you owe. By doing so, you may be providing the government with the very evidence it needs to make its case.

Few people realize...

If an attorney is representing you, he is bound by the attorney-client privilege, and no court can force your lawyer to disclose "privileged information." However, accountants are not provided such privileges, and records or discussions you have shared with your accountant may be subpoenaed as evidence against you. Keep this in mind whenever you give records to your accountant.

CHAPTER SEVENTEEN

How Much Is Your Business Worth?

Would you know how to set a fair price if someone wanted to acquire your company?

How will the government value your business for estate tax purposes?

Basically, valuation methods for closely held corporations fall into two categories: (1) those considering the value of physical assets, and (2) those based on the value as a going concern.

Value of physical assets

The most common approaches to asset valuation are:

• Liquidation value, or the value of the assets if the business were liquidated. Generally, this value is computed because it represents a minimum price and tends to put a floor under the valuation reached by other methods.

• Reproduction value, or the cost to reproduce the assets of the business at current prices. This method tends to yield a ceiling price on valuations reached by other methods.

• Book value, or the excess value of assets over liabilities. While there are refinements to this approach, the true value of the assets may be difficult to determine because of accelerated cost recovery LIFO/FIFO conventions. Additionally, the net worth of a company may be high because it has accumulated earnings over a considerable time period. Yet recent earnings may be down, and its future prospects depressed.

Because of these shortcomings, the book value is most useful for appraising companies with mostly liquid assets subject to accurate accounting valuation, for example, banks, insurance companies, and investment trusts. Even in these cases, book value is seldom used alone as a criterion of value. Nevertheless, it provides a useful benchmark when used in conjunction with other methods.

Going concern value

While businesses are often bought and sold solely on the basis of asset value, most investors are more concerned with the profits these assets can generate. The most common technique used to measure going concern value is the "capitalized earnings" method. In this method the company's true annual earning capacity is first estimated, based on past performance and future prospects. These earnings are then multiplied by a "capitalization factor" to arrive at a final value as follows:

• Estimate of true earnings. Past earnings are usually a good indication of what can be expected in the future. To arrive at an annual earnings figure, most analysts take the average earnings for the past five years. However, several adjustments must be made: (1) Any extraordinary profit or loss must be eliminated, such as gain from the sale of part of the business or a loss from inventory write-offs, (2) salaries and special perquisites to shareholder-employees must be deducted from earnings, and (3) any nonstandard accounting practices must be adjusted, e.g., certain expenses may have been capitalized when they should have been written off.

• Determining the capitalization factor. Suppose that an investor wants a guaranteed 10% return on his money. If you have an investment that yields a guaranteed $8,000 per year, he should be willing to pay you $80,000 for it. This is the amount he can afford to invest and still receive a 10% return. The investor capitalized the investment at ten times that return by taking the reciprocal of the yield he wanted and determining how much he could afford to pay ($1/.10 \times \$8,000 = \$80,000$). Figure 1 is a rough guide to capitalization factors. This chart, showing typical capitalization rates, was compiled many years ago. While the factors may vary depending on the economic climate, it is a useful guide to relative values of various types of businesses. Keep in mind, however, that in today's circumstances, many solid companies are selling below book value and at earnings multiples well under these.

Figure 1

TYPICAL CAPITALIZATION RATES

Business	Capitalization Factor (number of times earnings paid for the business)
Established business with considerable growth potential.	10+
Established business with solid position in market and good management. Limited growth potential.	10
Established business requiring managerial attention but otherwise sound.	8
Business relatively vulnerable to general industry or economic fluctuations.	6-7
Small, highly competitive industrial, retail, or service business where capital investment is relatively small.	4-5
Industrial, retail, or service business dependent on the special skills of one or a few managers. Capital investment is small and business is highly competitive.	2-3
Personal service business requiring little capital. Highly dependent on present owner.	1

Guidelines for determining the capitalization factor

Depending on the growth potential of the business and the risk that projected earnings may not be realized, capitalization factors vary. The higher the growth potential and the less the risk, the smaller the return that the investor will accept and the more the business is worth. Several other considerations that affect the value of a business are:

• State of the economy. How vulnerable is the company to economic change and what is the projected state of the economy?

• Position in the industry. Is the company a leader in its field or is it highly dependent on the actions of others? Is the company's business seasonal or affected by scarcity of certain key resources?

• Financial. How dependent is the company on debt? Will heavy interest expenses or possible acceleration of debt repayments cause problems?

• Management. Will present key management stay with the company or must new (and unproven) executives be recruited? (Note: This is an especially critical point for a small business heavily dependent on one or two individuals.)

An actual example

Now that we have seen some of the factors that need to be evaluated in placing a price on a business, let's use some real numbers to see how these systems can work to give you a clearer picture of a company's net worth (see Figure 2).

When you attempt a reasonable evaluation of a business, keep in mind that, generally, a business owner's estimate of the value of the stock held for his close corporation has been shown through cases in tax court to be about one-third the estimate given by the IRS. Usually, the court settled the value about halfway between the two estimates.

Figure 2

VALUE OF COMPANY XYZ

Physical assets:	
Liquidation value	$50,000
Reproduction value	150,000
Book value	75,000
Going concern value:	
5 year annual average earnings (after tax)	10,000
Amount of extraordinary earnings (after tax)	10,000
Capitalization factor	10
Going concern value ($10,000 × 10)	100,000
Influence of fluctuation in economy	none
Position in industry	good
Management	good/stable
Financial	no substantial debt
Estimate of price	$100,000

CHAPTER EIGHTEEN

Buying or Selling a Proprietorship

When a sole proprietorship is bought or sold, it is no longer a single entity, but rather a group of separate assets, according to tax laws. The assets are divided into three categories: capital assets, noncapital assets, and other property used in trade or business (Sections 1231, 1245, 1250 type property). Each receives different tax treatment. (Explanation and tax treatment of each of these types of assets was discussed in Chapter 15.) These assets may all be sold or purchased at the same time, but they must remain separate when it comes time to determine tax. The key to a successful sale or purchase, once the overall price is agreed upon, is the most advantageous allocation of price to the three kinds of assets. Generally, what is good for the buyer is bad for the seller and vice versa. But if these things aren't clearly settled in the sale, the IRS will allocate value for you and it will probably not be to your liking.

Advantage to the seller

If the seller could have it all his way, he would have most of the sales price allocated to his capital assets and Section 1231 assets because gain on these is taxed as capital gain rather than as ordinary income. Sale of noncapital assets produces ordinary income that is taxed at a higher rate, so the seller does not want much price allocated to things like inventory and accounts receivable.

Goodwill, which is the premium over the book value of the business that is paid for brand name and prestige, should have high value in the sale from the seller's point of view because it is considered capital gain and is taxed at the lower capital gain rate. Unfortunately, it is not deductible to the buyer so he won't be anxious to agree to a high value on goodwill.

Advantage to the buyer

For the most part, the opposite of what the seller wants is the arrangement the buyer wants. He want low price allocation to capital assets, high allocation to prepaid expenses, and medium or low allocation to Section 1231 property.

Figure 1 provides a general summary of the price allocation desired by seller and buyer. In this case the assets are assumed to have been held for more than 12 months and to have been sold at a gain. Selling an asset at a loss reverses the party's position on that asset (i.e., if the buyer wanted it high, he now wants it low, and if the seller wanted it low, he now wants it high).

Other considerations

When you weigh the possibilities of the sale or purchase of a sole proprietorship, here are a few other items to keep in mind.

Investment credit: The seller should note that the sale may trigger recapture of investment credit, which can have adverse tax consequences.

Installment sale: Under the restrictions of an installment sale, inventory is not included in the installment method of reporting income. This means that you can sell

Figure 1

PRICE ALLOCATION DESIRED BY SELLER VS. BUYER

Seller	Class of Asset	Buyer
I. Non capital		
Low. It is treated as ordinary income.	Inventory or stock in trade.	High since cost of goods sold allows recovery.
Low. It is treated as ordinary income.	Accounts receivable.	High. The cost will be recovered as they are collected.
Low. Ordinary income.	Covenant not to compete.	Medium price since it may be recovered through amortization.
II. Capital		
Low treated as ordinary income.	Prepaid expenses.	High. They are deductible against future income.
High. It is treated as capital gain.	Goodwill.	Low. It is not depreciable.
III. Section 1231, 1245, 1250		
High—capital gain.	Lease.	High. It is recoverable through amortization.
High—capital gain.	Land.	Low. It is not depreciable.
Low—capital gain, except for recapture, which is ordinary income.	Buildings, machinery, equipment.	High. Can be recovered by cost recovery and eligible for investment tax credit.

the inventory in a sale of a proprietorship separately to increase the total first-year payment without affecting the gain reportable under installment sale rules.

Accounts receivable: The seller's allocation to accounts receivable should equal the value of the accounts after reducing them by the bad debt reserve. If not, the reserve will be deemed taxable income.

Section 1245 property: When you sell a section 1245 property (which is personal property subject to cost recovery), capital gain is produced only if the gain exceeds previous cost recovery deductions. Usually, a buyer wants a medium allocation to this type of asset, but he may gain by a higher allocation if he stands to get a large investment credit upon buying it. If there is going to be a large cost recovery recapture on that asset, the seller wants a low allocation because the recapture will be taxed as ordinary income.

If you agree to an allocation that is favorable to the other party, you should receive in return some kind of concession on the price. And remember, if the allocation chosen is not thought reasonable by the IRS, they may reallocate in a more unpleasant manner. However, including the allocation in written agreements will help substantiate your position.

CHAPTER NINETEEN

Sale or Acquisition of a Corporation

At one time or another, almost every business manager will become involved in the purchase or sale of a business. There are many ways such transactions can be structured, and the tax consequences to the buyer and seller can be very important. Some transactions, for example, result in immediate taxable gain to the seller. In others, the transactions can be qualified as "tax free," meaning that taxes are deferred. Your knowledge of the basic methods of structuring an acquisition can save on legal expenses and negotiating time and can result in an arrangement that is highly favorable to your interests.

Taxable transactions

The most straightforward and frequently used method of purchasing a business is to offer cash and/or notes for the stock or assets. While any gain from such a transaction is immediately taxable to the seller, he presumably has enough liquidity from the sale to meet the tax bill. Following are two ways that a purchase of this nature can work.

Purchase of stock: If the business is a corporation and if it is desirable to transfer the business as a going concern, the buyer will normally purchase the stock of the corporation from the seller. Three potential problems must be watched: (1) The buyer must take steps to be sure he doesn't assume any hidden liabilities of the corporation and that accounts receivable are collectible; (2) the excess of the purchase price over the book value of the corporation is classified as goodwill and cannot be deducted for tax purposes; and (3) there may be a problem if minority shareholders of the acquired corporation do not wish to sell out.

Purchase of assets: To overcome some of the problems of stock transactions, often only the assets of a business are sold. Such a sale avoids unforeseen liabilities, but it may be difficult to transfer certain leases or contracts if they are not specifically assignable. A great advantage to the buyer in this type of transaction is that the

Figure 1

TYPE A REORGANIZATION: MERGER

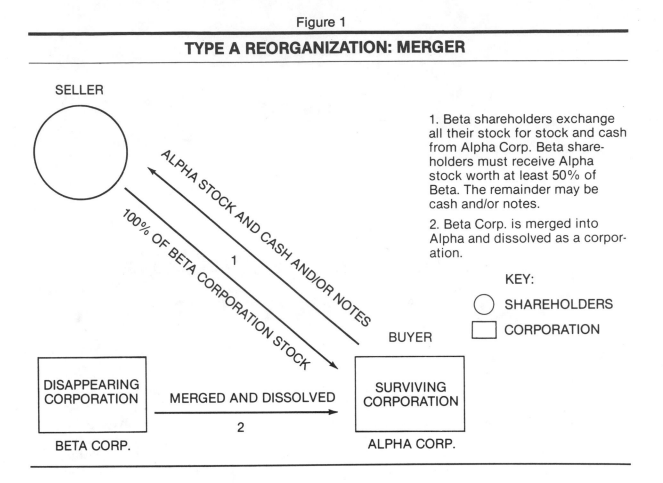

SELLER

1. Beta shareholders exchange all their stock for stock and cash from Alpha Corp. Beta shareholders must receive Alpha stock worth at least 50% of Beta. The remainder may be cash and/or notes.

2. Beta Corp. is merged into Alpha and dissolved as a corporation.

KEY:

◯ SHAREHOLDERS

▢ CORPORATION

ALPHA STOCK AND CASH AND/OR NOTES
1

100% OF BETA CORPORATION STOCK

BUYER

DISAPPEARING CORPORATION — MERGED AND DISSOLVED → SURVIVING CORPORATION
2

BETA CORP.

ALPHA CORP.

depreciable assets take on a stepped-up basis that yields increased depreciation deductions.

Tax-free transactions

The IRS recognizes three common types of acquisitions as tax free: Type A, Type B, and Type C "reorganizations."

Type A: Merger or consolidation. This transaction is sometimes called a "statutory merger" because it must be done in strict compliance with the merger provisions of the corporate statutes of a given state. It consists of combining two corporations into one as follows: (1) The shareholders of both corporations must approve the merger, and (2) the shareholders of the disappearing corporation must retain a significant interest in the survivor. Generally, the IRS will accept a figure equal to 50% of the value of the shareholders' interest in the disappearing corporation as significant. (See Figure 1.)

Note that a Type A reorganization is the only one where the stock issued by the acquiring corporation does not have to be voting stock to obtain tax-free treatment. In fact, cash or debt may also be used as long as the seller pays taxes on it.

Type B: Stock-for-stock acquisition. This is the most common tax-free acquisition method. It occurs when the buyer exchanges only voting common or preferred stock for at least 80% of each class of the voting and nonvoting stock of the seller.

This type of acquisition is popular with small companies that sell out to larger public concerns. Since the stock received is not taxed until it is sold, the seller enjoys

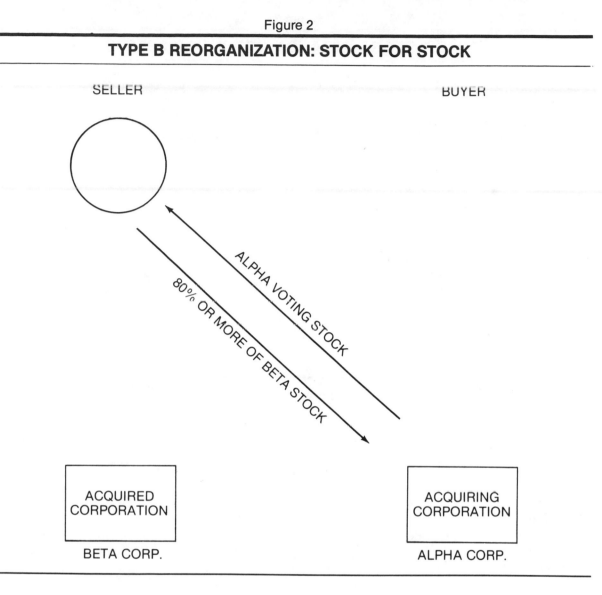

Figure 2

TYPE B REORGANIZATION: STOCK FOR STOCK

SELLER

BUYER

ALPHA VOTING STOCK

80% OR MORE OF BETA STOCK

ACQUIRED CORPORATION

BETA CORP.

ACQUIRING CORPORATION

ALPHA CORP.

considerable flexibility as well as liquidity. Note that in this type of reorganization, the acquired corporation stays alive. As a result, there is generally less paperwork and expense than with other types of acquisitions. (See Figure 2.)

Type C: Stock-for-assets acquisition. In this type of transaction, voting stock of the buyer is exchanged for substantially all the assets of the seller. In practice, the IRS usually interprets this to mean that at least 90% of the seller's assets must be acquired and more than 80% of the consideration given to the buyer must consist of voting stock. The remaining 20% can be cash or debt. This type of acquisition is generally used when the buyer does not wish to acquire certain assets or assume certain known or any unknown liabilities of the seller.

Note that in this type of transaction, the sellers (Beta) retain the old corporate shell including any assets that were not sold. To obtain the Alpha shares, the Beta shareholders will normally exchange their Beta stock for the Alpha stock and then liquidate Beta corporation. This exchange is noted in Figure 3. If the exchange is ac-

Figure 3

TYPE C REORGANIZATION: STOCK FOR ASSETS

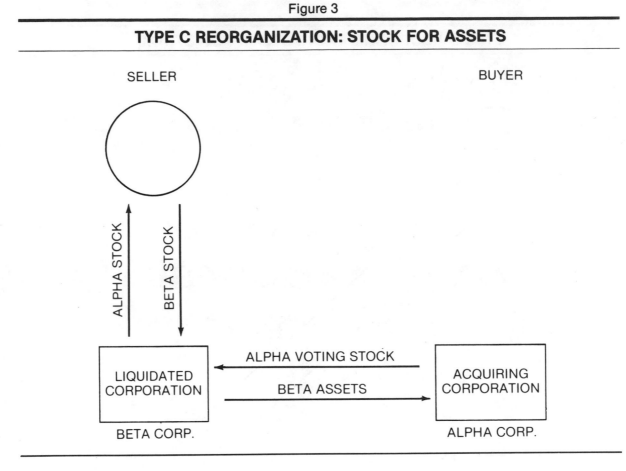

complished properly, the sellers will not be taxed on their Alpha stock until they actually sell it.

While a basic knowledge of acquisition methods is valuable, it is a specialized area requiring expert assistance. Always retain competent legal and tax counsel to advise you.

CHAPTER TWENTY

How to Sell to Yourself—
Disproportionate Stock Redemptions

You've worked hard to build your business, which probably represents most of your personal assets. Naturally, you would like to cash in on some of the rewards. You could raise your salary, but the IRS might disallow any undue increase and treat it as a dividend. This would result in a double tax—once at the corporate level and once as ordinary income at the personal level.

Or you could sell a portion of your stock, but the other stockholders probably wouldn't have the money to buy your shares, and you wouldn't want to sell to outsiders. Looks hopeless. But there is a solution that few businesspeople are aware of: a "disproportionate stock redemption."

What is a 302 redemption?

According to the law, whenever a corporation buys back shares from a stockholder during his lifetime, the proceeds are normally treated as a dividend for tax purposes. But if the redemption qualifies as disproportionate according to Section 302 of the Internal Revenue Code, the transaction is considered a "sale or exchange" and is afforded capital gains treatment.

There are two basic requirements for a disproportionate stock redemption. The first deals with the ratio of the redeeming shareholder's stock to the total outstanding stock before and after the redemption. The redeeming shareholder's percentage of ownership after the redemption must be less than 80% of his percentage of ownership before the redemption. Second, the redeeming shareholder must own less than 50% of the outstanding voting stock after the redemption. (If more than one class of voting stock is outstanding, this requirement applies to all classes.)

Here's a simple example. Suppose your corporation has 1,000 voting shares outstanding, of which you own 600. To qualify for capital gains treatment via a disproportionate redemption, you would have to sell at least 231 shares back to the company, computed as follows:

Your percentage of ownership prior to the redemption was 60% (600/1,000). After the redemption, your percentage of ownership would be 47.98% (369/769). As the percentage owned after redemption (47.98%) is less than 80% of the percentage owned prior to the redemption (60%) [i.e., 80% × 60% = 48%, which is greater than 47.98%], the redemption meets the 80% test under Code Section 302(b)(2)(C). Also, the requirement that the shareholder own less than 50% of the total combined voting power of the corporation immediately after the redemption would be met pursuant to the 47.98% ownership. Thus, the redemption would qualify as a sale as opposed to a dividend.

The trap of "stock attribution"

When determining a stockholder's interest for purposes of the 80% and 50% tests mentioned above, the rule of stock attribution must be applied. This means that a stockholder is deemed to have a "constructive interest" in any shares owned by certain related parties. Here are five situations where stock attribution applies:

Family. Spouse (unless legally separated), children, grandchildren, and parents (but not brothers and sisters).

Partnerships and estates. Any stock owned by a partnership or an estate is considered owned proportionately according to the interest of the partner or beneficiaries. (If you are equal partners with three others and the partnership owns 100 shares of XYZ stock, you will have 25 shares of XYZ attributed to you if you redeem any personal XYZ shares you own.)

Trusts. Proportional attribution applies (similar to partnerships and estates).

Corporations. If an individual owns 50% or more of a corporation, any stock held by the corporation is attributed to the individual's ownership interest in the corporation.

Options. Stock will be considered constructively owned and fully attributable if the individual has an option to buy it.

Complete redemption and termination of interest

You can also qualify for capital gains treatment by selling all your shares to the corporation, terminating your interest in the company. You will not have to worry about attribution as long as: (1) the retired shareholder retains no interest in the corporation other than as a creditor (an interest includes being an officer, director, or having a consulting retainer); and (2) the retired shareholder does not acquire an interest (except by inheritance or bequest) for ten years.

How your spouse can help you convert dividends into capital gains

The great advantage of a complete redemption is that you can sell a substantial part of a family-owned company at capital gains rates—and still retain undiluted control of the corporation. However, it does involve a step-by-step ten-year game plan:

1. Give your spouse a substantial amount of stock when you set up the corporation or as soon thereafter as possible.

2. Make sure the stock is held for at least ten years.

3. Have the corporation redeem all your spouse's stock.

4. Make sure your spouse does not acquire any more stock or any other interest in the corporation for the next ten years.

As a result, all the gain is capital gain, and you retain control of the corporation. For example, suppose you form a corporation and issue 100,000 shares at $1.00

per share. You give 50,000 to your spouse and retain the other 50,000. After ten years the shares are worth $5.00 per share. You would like to get some money out of the company, but almost anything you do will be treated as a dividend—nondeductible to the corporation and fully taxable as ordinary income to the individual. The solution?

Redeem all of your spouse's stock for $250,000. The first $50,000 is tax-free—it's a return of capital. The remaining $200,000 will be taxed as a capital gain rather than ordinary income. Finally, you will still have control of the company because you own the remaining shares. Here are several points to consider:

Gift tax. There would be no gift tax implications since the 1981 Tax Act allows unlimited marital deductions (i.e., unlimited gifts between spouses).

Filings with the IRS. After redeeming the stock, your spouse must file with the IRS an agreement to notify them if any additional stock is acquired within ten years of the distribution. Furthermore, a timely return must be filed in the year of redemption or the capital gains treatment may be lost.

Appreciated property. Your spouse's stock can be redeemed with appreciated property held by the corporation, such as land or securities. The corporation would escape tax on the asset's appreciation and preserve its working capital. The spouse still gets capital gains. Note: This type of redemption escapes the normally very restrictive new tax rules that apply to using appreciated property to redeem stock, but only if the spouse owns at least 10% in value of the distributing company's stock for the 12-month period ending on the date of distribution (IRC Section 311(d)(2)(A)) and the redemption qualifies as a complete termination of interest under IRC Section 302(b)(3).

In this area, as with all complex tax areas, you should consult your tax adviser.

CHAPTER TWENTY-ONE

Special Considerations

Installment Sale of Real Estate

How you can save

A businessman can realize substantial tax savings on the sale of property by making it an installment sale. The drawback of an outright sale (one which does not qualify for the installment method) is that you must pay tax on the full amount of the gain in the year of the sale, regardless of whether or not you have really received the full payment on the sale.

So if you sell a property for $100,000 and the property is on your books at $10,000, you would pay tax on the full $90,000 profit if the sale is not treated as an installment sale. However, you may be able to report taxable gain as installments are received if you meet any one of these tests:

- You are a dealer in merchandise and regularly sell on the installment basis.

- The property sold is real estate; or

- The transaction is a "casual" sale of personal property.

It used to be that in order for a real estate sale or a casual sale to qualify for installment sale tax treatment, the seller could receive no more than 30% of the total price in the first year. But the Installment Sales Revision Act of 1980 repealed that requirement, and now any sale described above will qualify for favorable tax treatment. Now, you pay tax only on the amount of gain you receive, even if the payment in the year of sale is more than 30%.

The installment method of reporting gain is now automatic, unless an election to the contrary is made by the taxpayer. Note the following additional points concerning installment sale treatment:

What are "payments"?

Payments in the year of sale include any cash, property, or tradable securities given the seller by the buyer. They do not normally include notes given by a buyer that are merely promises to pay, not actual payment. However, notes payable on demand are treated as payment for this purpose.

The interest trap.

The interest incurred on the installment payments must be 6% or more. If less, the IRS feels that the seller is trying to dodge his taxes and the IRS will compute the interest at 7%. As of press time, proposed regulations would raise the minimum interest to 9%, or the IRS would compute interest at 10%. If these regulations pass, they may be retroactive. Therefore, discuss with your tax adviser the possibility of inserting a "contingency clause" in your installment sales contracts. This contingency clause would allow the retroactive change of interest rate to the degree necessary to comply with any retroactive law change.

Be sure to work closely with your accountant or tax adviser when setting up an installment sale. The rules are relatively simple, but there are several pitfalls to watch for.

Goodwill and the Noncompetition Covenant

"Goodwill" is a term applied to the amount paid for a business over and above the value of the tangible assets. For example, if you purchase a business for $150,000 and the value of all the assets is $100,000, you have paid $50,000 for "goodwill," which covers such things as the firm's reputation, high morale of employees, future earning power, and good management.

In financial terms, goodwill is treated as a capital asset. The seller treats the payment for it as capital gain. However, the buyer can't deduct the cost of goodwill. He only gets his money back for the goodwill if and when he sells the business. There are ways to recapture some tax breaks, however.

Customer lists

In the buying and selling of firms like publishing houses, insurance agencies, and many service industries, the purchase of the customer list can be an important part of the deal, especially when buying out a competitor. Too often, however, the price of the customer list is included under goodwill and the buyer misses an opportunity to deduct the cost of this list.

Usually, the IRS will say that a customer list is a single asset and may not be broken down into individual accounts for the purpose of deducting losses. However, if the buyer can determine the dollar value of each account on the customer list by means of reasonable calculation, he may later deduct the cost of these accounts if he loses them. Or, he may take annual amortization deductions over the determined useful life of the list.

For example, if you were buying a dry cleaning business and you wanted to find the dollar value of the accounts on the customer list, you could find the average sales per customer account and then multiply it by the frequency of a given customer's patronage. You could then discount the amount by an attrition rate of, say, 15% per year. Once a dollar value is established for a customer's account, it becomes a separate asset and may be deducted later if lost.

Note: This area of customer lists is one the IRS frequently challenges.

Noncompetition covenant

The buyer of a business would usually like some assurance that the seller won't turn right around after the sale and start a new, competitive company. Therefore, the buyer would like to have a "covenant not to compete" and he is willing to pay extra for such an agreement. Usually, this noncompetition agreement states that the seller will not compete with the buyer for a set period of time or within a given geographical or market area.

However, whereas the goodwill portion of a sale price is taxed as capital gain to the seller and is nondeductible to the buyer, a noncompetition covenant is taxed as ordinary income to the seller and is deductible to the buyer over the agreed-upon time period.

It is usually best for the buyer to establish the noncompetition covenant as being distinct and separate from the agreement for the purchase of the business. This separation is important because if the covenant not to compete is deemed by the IRS to be a necessary condition for the enjoyment of the purchased goodwill, the covenant will be considered part of the goodwill and as such will no longer be deductible to the buyer.

CHAPTER TWENTY-TWO

Retirement Planning

High on any hierarchy of human needs is security. During the past few years, security at retirement has become a prime political, economic, and social problem.

Social Security alone does not provide a comfortable retirement income, and the corrosive effects of inflation make it all but impossible to accumulate sufficient personal savings to provide for longer life expectancies.

Hence, the question of a properly designed retirement program must eventually be addressed in almost any business.

Corporate Employees—Qualified vs. Nonqualified Plans

Retirement plans fall into two broad categories—"qualified" and "nonqualified." A qualified plan is simply one that meets the stringent requirements of Section 401 of the Internal Revenue Code and qualifies for highly favorable tax benefits. Nonqualified plans do not receive such benefits but are significantly easier to set up and administer. A typical nonqualified plan would be a deferred compensation arrangement in which a company agrees to pay an employee at some future date (usually after retirement) for services he is currently performing.

A typical nonqualified plan: deferred compensation
Suppose you are a corporate officer, 60 years old, and in a 38% personal tax bracket. Your firm wants to give you a raise of $4,000 per year until you retire at age 65. The firm now pays taxes at a 20% average rate.

If you accept the raise now, you pay personal tax on it at your present rate (38% × $4,000) and take home just $2,480 per year [($4,000) – (38% × $4,000) = $2,480]. This raise has an after-tax cost to the company of $3,200 [$4,000 – (20% × $4,000) = $3,200]. Over the five years until you retire, you take home only $12,400. The after-tax cost of your raise to the company is $16,000 over those five years (5 × $3,200).

But if you take the raise as deferred compensation, payable after retirement when you will probably be in a lower tax bracket—say 20%—you receive the $4,000 per year at the lower tax rate (20% × $4,000 = $800 tax), which is $3,200 take-home. The corporation, which we will assume has expanded over the five years so that it now pays at a 46% tax rate, has an after-tax cost of [$4,000 − (46% × $4,000)] = only $2,160 per year for your raise. Over five retirement years, you take home $720 more per year, a five-year tax saving of $3,600. Similarly, the company pays (5 × $2,160) = $10,800 after-tax over the five years, a tax saving for the company of $5,200.

A nonqualified deferred compensation plan is subject to the following guidelines established by the IRS. The tax court reasons that, if these rules are followed, the tax on the income may be deferred because the employee doesn't actually get his hands on the extra money until he is in fact retired.

Rules for deferred compensation plans

- The deferred compensation arrangement must be established before the employee actually earns the income.

- The employee must be on a cash basis.

- The agreement may not be unconditionally funded by placing the deferred payment in an escrow or a similar type of account. The employee can have the company's promise of payment, but the compensation may not be secured in any way.

- The employee may not demand the compensation before the date agreed upon.

- The amount of compensation must be reasonable. If either current or deferred compensation is deemed unreasonable, it will not be deductible to the employer.

Usually, the employee agrees to the following in a deferred compensation agreement:

- The employee may not receive any part of the deferred pay until he reaches the established retirement age or becomes disabled. His heirs may receive the compensation if he dies.

- The employee may not join the competition or engage in competitive activity.

- The employee must remain in the employer's service for an established period of time in order to receive the deferred pay.

- The employee will, as an outside contractor, be available for consultation if needed after retirement. (Note: It must be clear that the employee is acting as an independent contractor when he does consulting work for the company. There should not be confusion about the retiree's relationship to the company.)

Advantages of deferred compensation

- No legal restrictions exist on who or how many employees

can take advantage of deferred compensation plans. The plan may cover any number of employees.

• The employee makes a substantial tax saving by deferring part of his salary into lower tax years.

• The employer may realize a substantial tax saving if he anticipates a higher tax rate in later years.

• The employer may have access to the deferred funds during the time of deferment.

• The arrangement is easy to set up.

Disadvantages of deferred compensation

• There is no guarantee that the company will be able to pay the deferred compensation when the employee is ready to retire.

• Since IRS regulations forbid unconditional funding via an escrow account, it may be a good idea to have the company purchase a high cash value life insurance policy on the employee with the employer as beneficiary. When it comes time for the employee to retire, the policy is cashed in and the monies are available for the deferred payment.

• The employee doesn't get the use of the deferred monies until the agreed-upon date.

Figure 1

COMPARISON OF QUALIFIED PROFIT SHARING VS. PENSION PLANS

	Profit Sharing	Pension
Orientation	Favors younger employees.	Favors older employees.
Benefits	Retirement benefits need not be provided.	Retirement benefits must be provided.
	Other benefits, such as accident and health, may be provided.	Other benefits limited to disability coverage.
Contribution	At discretion of management and based only on profits. Cannot exceed 15% of total payroll.	Fixed obligation which must be made in both profit and loss years.
Forfeiture	May be allocated to remaining participants of plan.	Used to decrease employer's cost.
Distribution	After as few as two years.	Only on retirement, death, disability, or termination of employment.

- Deferred compensation may not benefit a retiree with high income already in a 50% maximum tax bracket.

Qualified plans

As we have seen, in a nonqualified compensation deferment plan the employee, and often the corporation as well, winds up paying a reduced tax on the compensation. Furthermore, the nonqualified plan is free from the more stringent IRS requirements for qualified plans.

Qualified plans, on the other hand, have these advantages:

- Current tax deduction. Pretax corporate money goes into the plan as a deductible contribution.

- Tax-free accumulations. Income from investments in the plan may accumulate and be reinvested tax free.

- Deferred tax on benefits. Benefits are not taxed until actually received. Even if the entire amount due an individual is paid out in a lump sum, the distribution usually receives preferential tax treatment under a special ten-year averaging method.

- Distribution of employer securities. Under certain circumstances, employer securities credited to an individual's account may be distributed, but tax is not due on any appreciation until the securities are actually sold.

- Stockholders. In no way are stockholders prohibited from participating in a qualified plan as long as they are also employees of the company.

Pension vs. profit sharing

Many businesspeople are confused by the differences between the two major types of qualified plans—pension and profit sharing.

Under a pension plan, the company has a fixed obligation to continue to contribute a certain amount of money each year toward the plan, rain or shine. With profit sharing, there is no such fixed commitment—contributions are contingent on profits and can be skipped or reduced in a bad year. Usually, a formula is established that defines the way in which the employer's profit sharing contributions will be made. For example, it might be 15% of pretax profit over the first $10,000 in profit. But the retirement benefit under profit sharing will vary according to the amount of contributions and the fund's accumulated earnings.

Generally, profit sharing plans tend to be more attractive to smaller or recently formed businesses with unstable year-to-year profits. On the other hand, pension plans are generally more attractive to older management and employees who want the security of a fixed contribution by the company to the plan each year. A little-known fact about profit sharing plans: Retirement benefits do not necessarily have to be provided for the plan to qualify for the tax break. Other benefits, such as house mortgage financing, tuition assistance, and emergency loans, can sometimes be offered. Hence, profit sharing tends to be more attractive to younger individuals. Figure 1 summarizes the major differences between the two types of qualified plans.

Requirements to qualify

To obtain IRS approval and the tax benefits, the main requirement is that a qualified

298

plan be permanent and not discriminate in favor of a particular employee group, such as top management.

It is generally possible, however, to design the plan so that long-term employees (including management) indirectly receive preferential treatment. For example, some plans stipulate rigorous "vesting" provisions. Any employee who leaves in the first four years of employment forfeits all contributions to the plan. (These funds then accrue to the remaining members in the plan.) After four years there is 40% vesting, with additional increments each year, resulting in full vesting only after ten years of continuous employment.

Furthermore, there is no requirement with qualified plans that all employees receive the same amount of benefits. Allocation of contributions among participants can vary according to (1) years of service, (2) age, and/or (3) compensation. A payout formula based on a combination of compensation and years of service generally works out best for long-term employees and management.

Other requirements for qualified plans

- Who must be included. Qualified profit sharing plans and pension plans must cover 70% of all eligible employees who work more than 1,000 hours in 12 months. Also, an owner of two separate businesses may not establish a plan for one business that discriminates against his employees in the other.

- Voluntary contributions. In a profit sharing plan, a participant may pay extra money voluntarily into his retirement account. This is in addition to the amount paid in by the employer. There is, however, a limit to the amount of voluntary contributions, and such contributions may be deductible to the participant. Once in the account, they escape tax on their compounded earnings.

- Benefit limitation. The limit on the amount a retired employee may receive each year under a pension plan is the average compensation received over his three consecutive highest paid years or $124,500 in 1981, whichever is less. (This figure is adjusted annually for inflation.) The benefit limitation on the profit sharing plan is limited by the restrictions on the amount that may be paid into or credited to his account.

- Benefit taxation. Retirement benefits are taxed as ordinary income if they are disbursed as annuity payments. Of course, the ordinary income tax rate is usually significantly less as a retiree. A lump-sum payment of the benefit—be it at retirement time or when the plan is terminated—is taxable as long-term capital gain if attributable to contributions and earnings made before 1974. Payments attributable to earnings after 1973 are usually treated as ordinary income subject to a special ten-year averaging stipulation.

- What if a participant dies before retirement age? Then the beneficiary of the employee may exclude $5,000 from income tax as an employee death benefit.

- Allowable investments. In most cases, funds contributed to a retirement plan may be invested in bonds, savings accounts, real estate, life insurance contracts, stock, or mutual funds. However, there is a diversification requirement in regard to such investments.

• Rollover. Rollover or "portability" is the term applied to the tax-free transfer of accumulated retirement benefits from one company to another or to an Individual Retirement Plan. Usually, an employee who terminates his employment is taxed on the vested interest he withdraws when he leaves. But if he transfers the amount taken out into his new employer's retirement program within 60 days, he is not taxed on his accumulated retirement benefits.

Two more qualified plans

Before moving out of this area of retirement planning, it should be noted that there are two other common forms of retirement plans, a stock bonus plan and a "money purchase" plan.

Under a stock bonus plan, a company contributes its own stock to the retirement plan instead of cash. In virtually all other respects it is the same as a profit sharing plan.

A money purchase plan resembles a pension plan in that the employer must contribute a fixed amount annually to the retirement fund. However, the employee is not promised a specific amount of retirement compensation. Rather, when he retires, a pension annuity will be purchased with the money that has been allocated to his retirement account.

Employers are finding employees increasingly restive for catch-up wage increases. Rather than paying out higher salaries with attendant higher Social Security taxes, worker's compensation, and other taxes, it might make sense to investigate a retirement plan instead. With the double benefits of a current corporate tax deduction for contributions to the plan plus tax-free accumulation of all proceeds, employees can be provided the security of a retirement program—at a net cost to the company of perhaps no more than current wage demands.

And, do not overlook the morale and loyalty factor involved here. Security can mean a great deal to an employee and it is likely to make him stay on.

Of course, pensions and profit sharing are no jobs for a novice to tackle. See if your trade association has any qualified plans already approved by the IRS for your industry. Then get the advice of your attorney and a good insurance agent.

Self-Employed—The Keogh or HR-10 Plan

Few business managers will be content to retire on Social Security benefits alone. Consequently, almost everyone needs a personal savings and investment program. However, investments are usually made with after-tax dollars—that is, after all federal, state, and Social Security taxes have been paid. Any interest, dividends, or gains earned by your investments are also taxed. But now you can use pretax funds to invest for your later years, and all gains can accumulate tax-free. You only pay tax after you retire and start to withdraw funds. Then, your tax rate would probably be considerably lower than it is now.

What is a Keogh Plan?

Prior to 1963, only those who conducted their business in the corporate form and employees of corporations received a tax break in their retirement planning. The estimated 9 million self-employed businesspeople were left out in the cold. However, in

1962 Congress passed the Keogh Act. Based on this law, any self-employed individual or partner could set aside a maximum of $2,500 per year as a tax-deductible contribution to a retirement plan. However, because of the relatively low amount that could be contributed, only an estimated 10% of those eligible had formed Keogh Plans after 12 years.

Under the 1981 Tax Act, the maximum deductible amount has now been raised to $15,000. Here are the specifics, for a person who owns 10% or more of his business.

Contributions

General rule. You may set aside 15% of your earnings, up to a maximum of $15,000 per year. And no matter how little you earn, you may contribute and deduct $750 or 100% of earned income, whichever is less, so long as adjusted gross income does not exceed $15,000. However, if you have employees, you must make equal percentage contributions for those who have been with you for three years or more (i.e., if you contribute 15% of your income, you must contribute 15% of their wages).

Figure 2

THE EFFECT OF KEOGH CONTRIBUTIONS

Note: This graph shows the dramatic difference between an investment of $7,500 (before tax) in a Keogh Plan and the $3,750 you would have available to invest each year after paying income taxes at a 50% rate. A constant 8% return is assumed and all income is invested. Needless to say, these are quite conservative assumptions.

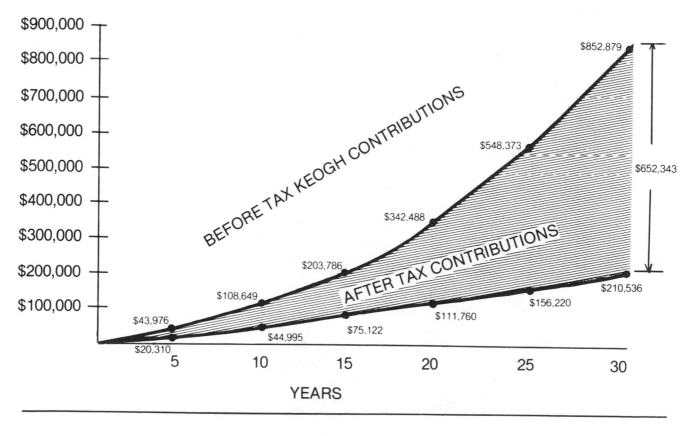

• Voluntary contributions. The 1981 Tax Act will now allow additional voluntary deductible contributions to a Keogh plan up to a maximum of $2,000 ($17,000 total).

• Defined benefit. The system described above is called a "defined contribution" plan. It is also possible to set up a "defined benefit" plan. According to this scheme, you may contribute an amount each year sufficient to give you a certain income upon retirement. In this case, actuarial tables are used along with current income to compute the allowable contribution. For some self-employed people with few years until retirement, this can result in tax-deductible contributions in excess of $15,000 per year.

Accumulations

Earnings on any money salted away accumulate tax-free, and taxes are not paid until the funds are withdrawn. For most people, this will be in their retirement years when their tax bracket is lower because of reduced total income and old-age dependency exemptions. The effect of pretax contributions and tax-free accumulation is shown in Figure 2.

Rollover

Under certain conditions, an account in a Keogh Plan may be rolled over tax-free into a qualified retirement plan of a corporation or into an Individual Retirement Account.

Vesting

Full vesting begins immediately with Keogh Plans. Unlike some corporate procedures that call for forfeiture of any accumulated retirement funds if the employee leaves before five years, a Keogh Plan demands that every dime you put in on behalf of your employee belongs to him, starting with the first day.

Withdrawals

The whole idea of a tax-sheltered retirement program is to encourage savings for later years, and the law discourages with stiff tax penalties any "premature distributions." However, funds may be withdrawn without difficulty under the following circumstances:

• Normal retirement. Fund withdrawal cannot begin before age 59½ and must start by age 70½. But employees may start drawing when they reach the age agreed upon in their retirement plan, as long as the limits are observed.

• Disability. Benefits may begin any time an individual becomes disabled, i.e., unable to engage in substantial gainful activity because of physical or mental impairment which is expected to be of indefinite duration.

• Death. In the event of death, proceeds due an individual may be distributed to beneficiaries within five years. Alternatively, the funds may be used to buy an annuity payable over the beneficiaries' lives.

Individuals—The Individual Retirement Account

The Individual Retirement Account (IRA) is a plan that allows an individual who is not covered by any other retirement plan to set up his own tax-exempt retirement account. Almost any wage earner can now set aside $2,000 per year, or 1% of income (whichever is less) for retirement investment. In the case where the spouse is working, up to $4,000 can be set aside.

Like the Keogh Plan, the two most outstanding advantages of the IRA are: (1) contributions to the retirement fund are deductible from current taxable income; and (2) investment earnings are tax-free until they are withdrawn at retirement age.

However, unlike the Keogh Plan: (1) the IRA allows a maximum contribution of $2,000 ($4,000 if working spouse is included); (2) it need not cover employees; and (3) it is open to anyone who is self-employed or a corporate officer even if otherwise covered for retirement.

Contribution restrictions

● General rule. The annual contribution must be made in money (i.e., no notes) and it is deductible from gross income.

● Excess contribution. Contributions in excess of the deductible may be subject to a penalty tax of 6%.

● Spouse's IRA. A working spouse may set up his/her own IRA and may contribute to it out of his/her income up to the limit. A joint return may include each spouse's deduction. The maximum total IRA deduction on a joint return is $4,000.

Investing IRA funds

Investment of IRA funds may follow any one of three basic structures. In all cases the earnings compound tax-free.

● The funds may go into an individual retirement annuity or endowment purchased from a life insurance company. However, the cost of the life insurance premium may not be deducted.

● Investments may go into an individual retirement account where contributions may be invested in savings accounts, mutual funds, trust accounts, or stock and bonds under the trusteeship of a bank or some other fiduciary. This must be done in accord with a written agreement with the IRS.

Withdrawals

Like the other retirement plans, the idea behind the IRA is to put money aside for later. Therefore, if you try to withdraw the money before retirement, you will have to pay tax penalties. Here are the withdrawal regulations:

● Premature distribution (withdrawal of funds) is subject to income tax plus a 10% penalty tax, except in the case of rollover, disability, or death.

● Funds may not be withdrawn until age 59½ but if you don't begin to withdraw by age 70½ there is a 50% penalty tax.

● Withdrawals are taxed as ordinary income and may be eligible for regular income averaging.

> • They are not excluded from estate tax (except for certain annuities) and they may be subject to state income tax.

How an employer is affected by IRA

In addition to setting up his own IRA, an employer may also set up IRAs for his employees. Of course, there is no restriction on the number of employees who may be covered. Here are the guidelines for an employer-sponsored IRA.

The employer may deduct the cost of the contribution made on behalf of his employee and the cost of administration of the account. He must withhold Social Security and unemployment tax, but he does not withhold income tax. The employer may contribute all or part of the maximum contribution. Funds in an employer-sponsored account may go into a common investment account, but a separate accounting is required to establish the interest of each participating employee.

The employee must declare the employer's contribution as income, but he may take a corresponding deduction. He may contribute additional funds voluntarily to supplement the fund up to the limit allowed if the employer doesn't contribute the maximum.

Rollover

Retirement funds from an IRA may be transferred tax-free to a qualified retirement plan in a new company if the monies are put into the new retirement plan within 60 days of withdrawal. Usually, such a withdrawal would be subject to the premature distribution penalty tax, but the penalty is avoided as long as the funds are rolled over into the new plan.

Social Security: It's Worth More Than You Think

In the foreseeable future, probably no single piece of legislation will affect you, your employees, or your company more than the Social Security Act. Yet many businessmen are unaware of the basic provisions of this law and how it can influence their personal and business planning.

Scope of the law

The Social Security law actually covers 12 major programs, but the benefits of most concern to the executive are these four:

> • Retirement benefits.
>
> • Survivor benefits.
>
> • Disability benefits.
>
> • Lump-sum payment at death.

Retirement and survivor benefits

Figure 3 summarizes the retirement and survivor benefits available to the executive and his family.

Survivors' benefits are an especially valuable life insurance benefit for young families. If the head of the family dies or becomes disabled before age 65, the spouse

Figure 3

SOCIAL SECURITY BENEFITS SUMMARY

	Status	Percent of Basic Benefits
Executive	Age 65 or over	100 %
	Age 62	80 %
Spouse	Age 65 or over or age 62 with child under 18, student under 22, or disabled child	50 % *
	Age 62, no children at home	37½ %
Widow(er)	Age 65 or over	100 % **
	Age 60	71½ %
	Age 50 and disabled	50 %
Child	Under age 18 (22 if full-time student, unmarried, and dependent) or disabled child at any age if disability began before age 22	50% if wage earner alive 75% if wage earner deceased

*Subject to family maximum
**of spouse's benefit

and children under 18 will each receive a monthly benefit. The amount of current life insurance you now have under Social Security depends on your age. If you and your wife are both 35, for example, with two young children, it can be worth about half-a-million dollars.

For an executive who retires at age 65 in 1990, the "basic benefits" are estimated to be $1,071.66 per month. In other words, you and your wife could expect to receive $1,071.66 per month plus her 50% if she is age 65, totalling $1,607.49 per month. And the 1972 revision to the basic act stipulates that all benefits are to be corrected for inflation using the Consumer Price Index.

Disability benefits and lump-sum payment at death

There are two other Social Security benefits which should interest an executive. First, if you become blind or expect to be disabled for 12 months or more, you will receive your basic benefits at any age. Second, your survivors will receive in a lump sum up to $225 toward your burial expenses at death.

Eligibility

The rules that must be met to be considered "fully insured" under Social Security are complex, but almost every executive, whether self-employed or working for an employer, should be fully qualified.

Watch these gaps

While Social Security provides a base for you and your family's personal security, there are important gaps that you should consider. One concerns widows' benefits. If you should die, your spouse will get benefits only if she is over 60 or caring for a child under 18. Hence, you should consider an insurance program to meet this shortcoming. Also, if you become a widower with dependent children, it could cause a substantial financial burden. More and more executives are considering life insurance on their spouse to meet this unfortunate need. Another problem area is disability benefits; the government's definition of disability is exceedingly strict and it is often difficult to collect. Consider a private program to at least supplement Social Security benefits.

CHAPTER TWENTY-THREE

Insurance Planning

With the stock market in disarray and stock options in disfavor, many employees and employers alike are seeking refuge in new "tax-attractive" incentives and perquisites. However, recent tax acts put an end to many attractive fringe benefits. Here's a little-known one that came through unscathed—it's called "split-dollar."

Lawful discrimination

Adequate life insurance is a concern of every executive. But during heavy spending years when an executive most needs insurance, he has the least money available to buy it. Furthermore, insurance premiums are not deductible to the individual and, hence, have to be paid with after-tax dollars. This is where "split-dollar" comes to the rescue. It provides a way for a corporation to assist executives with their personal insurance programs by "splitting" the premiums with them. Additionally, it is one of the few compensation benefits that can be awarded on a discriminating basis to selected individuals.

Split-dollar in practice

Every permanent life insurance policy (as opposed to the term variety) has two aspects: the cash value and the death benefit. With split-dollar, the corporation pays that portion of each annual premium which represents the increase in cash value of the policy. The favored executive pays the remainder of the premium. With respect to the death benefit, two beneficiaries are designated—the corporation for an amount equal to the cash value of the policy at the time of death and the executive's beneficiary for the remainder.

A look at the numbers

Let's look at the numbers for a typical plan (summarized at Figure 1). Consider the case of a $100,000 split-dollar policy on a 36-year-old executive. The first year, the policy has a cash value of $225, which the employer pays, and the executive pays the remaining premium of $1,940. (To make it easier, many companies advance executives the amount of their portion of the first year's premium which is then repaid out of future salary.) The second year, the executive's payment drops to $275, and the company pays $1,825. By the fifth year, the cash value increases as much as the premium, so the company pays the entire premium thereafter for the life of the policy.

Death benefit

At all times, the death benefit stands at $100,000 and eventually goes to the two beneficiaries—the company for an amount equal to the cash value (ranging from $225 in the first year to $37,000 by the twentieth) and the executive's widow or family for the remainder. In other words, with split-dollar, the executive receives far more insurance than he could normally afford if he bought it himself, and the employer is absolutely sure of getting back whatever was spent on the policy, whether the executive lives, dies, quits, or retires.

Minimum Deposit Insurance

Adequate life insurance can be expensive, and the premiums are not tax deductible. Many businesspeople, especially those in their early years, feel that they can afford only term insurance, although they know its protection is temporary. It's surprising how few businesspeople realize that they can purchase whole life insurance at less cost than term insurance.

Financing life insurance

Interest on house or car payments is tax deductible. If policyholders borrow to pay life insurance premiums, that interest is also deductible, leading to the innovative practice of borrowing against the cash value of whole life insurance to pay the premiums. After the third or fourth year, the cash value normally grows by more than the premium each year, so the policy can effectively become self-financing. When certain rules are followed, the result is a triple benefit.

- The expense of carrying the policy can effectively become tax deductible.

- All proceeds still pass to beneficiaries free of income tax.

Figure 1

SPLIT-DOLLAR PLAN
$100,000 ORDINARY LIFE POLICY—ANNUAL PREMIUM $2,350

Year	Dividend	Net Premium (Annual Premium Less Dividend)	Cash Value	Increase in Cash Value (Employer Pays)	Net Premium Less Employer's Contribution (Employee Pays)	Employee's Death Benefit
1	$ 185	$ 2,165	$ 225	$ 225	$1,940	$99,775
2	250	2,100	2,050	1,825	275	99,950
3	315	2,035	3,900	1,850	185	96,100
4	385	1,965	5,775	1,875	90	94,225
5	445	1,905	7,680	1,905	0	93,230
1-20	$12,600	$36,200	$37,000	$33,300	$2,490	$63,000 (end of 20th year)

- Whole life protection can usually be obtained at a cash outlay below that of an equivalent amount of term insurance.

Minimum deposit practice

The chart at Figure 2 illustrates how a $100,000 minimum deposit policy could work out for a person 35 years old.

The tax laws (Section 264 of the Internal Revenue Code) state that a deduction for interest payments to finance life insurance is allowable as long as at least four full premiums are paid in the first seven years of the policy's life ("minimum deposit"). All other premiums may be borrowed from the insurance company.

Therefore, for the first four years, the full premium is paid (Column 5). In the fifth and subsequent years, the amount of the net annual premium is borrowed from the cash value of the policy (Column 6), and a tax deduction is taken for interest payments (Columns 8-9). Over a 20-year period the net cash outlay would total $19,690 (Column 10).

However, to obtain the true net cost so that it may be compared with an equivalent amount of term insurance, the residual cash value must be deducted because term insurance normally has no cash value.

As shown, the net cost is $409 per year, which works out to $4.60 per $1,000 of in-force coverage. The result is permanent protection at a price less than that of an equivalent amount of term insurance.

As funds are borrowed against the cash value of the policy to pay the annual

Figure 2

MINIMUM DEPOSIT PLAN
$100,000 ORDINARY LIFE POLICY—ANNUAL PREMIUM $2,300

(1)	(2)	(3)	(4)	(5)	(6)	(7)	(8)	(9)	(10)	(11)
	Premiums			How Paid		Cash Value	Interest		Outlay	In-Force Insurance
Year	Annual Premium	Annual Dividend	Net Annual Premium	Premium Paid	Premium Borrowed (total loans)	Cash Value (after loans)	Annual Interest (8%)	Value of Interest Deduction (40% tax rate)	Net Cash Outlay (Cols. 5 + 8 − 9)	Death Benefit ($100,000 − Col. 6)
1	$2,300	$ —	$ 2,300	$2,300	$ —	$ 500	–	–	$ 2,300	$100,000
2	2,300	115	2,185	2,185	—	2,900	–	–	2,185	100,000
3	2,300	165	2,135	2,135	—	4,900	–	–	2,125	100,000
4	2,300	240	2,060	2,060	—	6,900	–	–	2,060	100,000
5	2,300	315	1,985	—	1,985	5,900	–	–	–	98,015
6	2,300	385	1,915	—	3,900	5,625	$ 153	$ 61	92	96,100
7	2,300	450	1,850	—	5,750	5,730	312	125	187	94,250
8	2,300	520	1,780	—	7,530	5,740	460	184	276	92,470
•										
•										
•										
20	2,300	1,050	1,250	—	25,100	11,500	1,915	766	1,149	74,900
Total			$33,780	$8,680	$25,100	$11,500	$18,350	$7,340	$19,690	$ 74,900

Calculation of Net Cost of Insurance

$19,690 (Total net cash outlay from Column 10)
− 11,500 (Residual cash value from Column 7)
$ 8,190

= $ 409/year = $4.60/$1,000 of in-force insurance

premium, the death benefit (Column 11) is reduced by an equal amount. To retain full coverage, many minimum deposit plans allow for application of part of the annual dividends to pay for one-year term insurance equal to the amount borrowed. This is referred to as the "fifth dividend option." Each year as the policy loan increases and death benefits decline, the term insurance guarantees that the death benefits to beneficiaries (after deducting the amount of the loan) will equal the full face value of the policy.

How to "raid" the cash value

As noted above, IRS regulations state that at any time during the first seven years of a policy, no more than the amount of three net annual premiums may be borrowed. Since the cash value grows faster than the annual premium after the first year, a residual cash value builds up (Column 7), which cannot be borrowed without jeopardizing the tax status of the previous loans. However, beginning in the eighth year, the full cash value not yet taken out ($5,740 for the above example) may be borrowed without upsetting the interest deduction. Since most people feel that they can obtain a greater return on funds than the 5% to 8% it costs to "raid" the policy, they normally withdraw all available cash value and make up the reduction in death benefits with additional one-year renewable term insurance.

Integration of minimum deposit with an existing estate plan

The minimum deposit concept can be applied to any existing whole life policy. Check with a competent insurance adviser for assistance. Also note that on a new policy the sequence of premium payments does not have to be the same as above. In summary, minimum deposit offers the following significant advantages:

> • Whole life protection can be obtained at a net cost (after taxes) below that of term insurance.

> • The loan plan may be discontinued at any time, and the original premium rate will still be guaranteed for life, even though the individual may no longer be insurable.

Selling Your Life Insurance Policy to Your Corporation

If you currently own your own life insurance policy, you may be able to realize substantial gain by selling that policy to your corporation, a transaction that is perfectly acceptable to the IRS as long as you are an important member of the corporation. Here are four ways in which you can gain by giving up ownership of your life insurance policy:

1. By getting tax-free money out of a corporation you own.

2. By increasing your annual spendable income.

3. By eliminating estate liquidity problems.

4. By removing surplus funds from the corporation at the lower capital gains rate.

Getting accumulated funds out of your own corporation tax free

One of the principal problems with incorporation is that the income is taxed twice, once at the corporation level and once again when it is distributed to the stockholders. However, if you could sell your life insurance policy to your own corporation, the cash value of the policy comes to you as a tax-free exchange and in this way you avoid the second level of taxation on income. The results of this transaction are:

> • Corporate earnings come directly to you without the second tax.

> • The corporation's surplus funds are virtually unaffected since it can cash in the policy anytime.

> • The corporation becomes the beneficiary of the policy.

> • Upon your death your heirs receive your stock which has increased in value as a result of payment of the policy benefit to the corporation.

Of course, if the corporation pays you more than the actual value of the policy, the excess over the face value of the policy will be taxable to you as ordinary income.

One other advantage to this type of transaction is that selling to your corporation increases your income. This logic is very straightforward. If you are paying $1,000 per year for the life insurance policy that you own personally, and you sell that policy to your corporation at its fair market value, you no longer have to pay for the annual premium and you now have an extra $1,000 in spendable income.

Eliminating estate liquidity problems

Suppose your main reason for carrying life insurance is to cover possible estate liquidity problems. But, by the time you're 55, you realize that the insurance you are carrying won't be adequate to cover estate liquidity needs. At this age you can't afford the higher premiums necessary for the additional coverage, so you sell the policy to your corporation for its fair market value, and the corporation buys the needed additional insurance coverage. Upon your death, the corporation receives the benefit of the policy and your heirs may redeem an amount of stock sufficient to cover estate liquidity needs. Redemption proceeds will be taxed at capital gain rates, but there should be no income tax because the funds will be withdrawn as a Section 303 Stock Redemption. (See Chapter 24.)

Who owns the life insurance policy?

If you are planning to carry a life insurance policy through your business, be sure to establish who is in fact the owner of the policy. Confusion over true legal ownership can lead to substantial tax cost.

If you wish your corporation to own your life insurance policy, you must be certain that you do not retain any "incidents of ownership," according to the tax court. These would include:

> • The right to change the beneficiary.

> • The right to use the policy as security in obtaining a loan.

> • Your right or the right of the estate to any of the economic benefits of the insurance policy.

> • Any power to benefit from the disposal of the policy during your lifetime.

> • Your right to cash in the policy.

If you retain just one of these rights or incidents of ownership, you are considered the owner of the policy and the proceeds of the policy will be taxed accordingly. (See Figure 3.)

311

Figure 3

TAX TREATMENT OF INSURANCE COSTS AND BENEFITS

Type of Insurance	Description of Benefits	Tax Considerations	
		Insured or Beneficiary	Company
1. Split-Dollar (Life)	Company pays the portion of premiums on whole life policy representing increase in cash value of policy. Beneficiary pays balance.	Insured not taxed on cash advances by company to pay portion of premium represented by increase in cash value. No income tax on proceeds at death.	Recovers cash value portion of policy tax free at death of insured.
2. Section "101" Death Benefit (Life)	Up to $5,000 can be paid by company to beneficiary.	Tax free to beneficiary.	If funded by insurance, premiums not deductible. Payments to beneficiary are deductible.
3. Group Term (Life)	Life insurance tax free to individual up to $50,000 coverage.	At death, beneficiary receives proceeds income tax free.	Premiums deductible to company.
4. Disability	Salary continuation.	Premiums paid by company not taxable to employee. Proceeds tax free to beneficiary with certain restrictions.	Premiums for insurance coverage deductible to company.
5. Health, Accident, Medical Reimbursement	Expenses for accident and health insurance can be paid by company. (Check new 1980 rules for medical reimbursement expenses.)	Premiums paid by company not taxable to employee. Medical bills paid not taxable to employee with certain restrictions.	Premiums deductible to company. Medical bills paid by company deductible with certain restrictions.
Minimum Deposit (Life)	Individual borrows from insurance company against cash value of policy to pay premiums. Can effectively obtain whole life coverage at near term rates.	Interest on borrowing tax deductible so long as four full premiums are paid in the first seven years of the policy.	N/A
1. Cross Purchase Buy/Sell (Life)	Used by remaining owners to purchase ownership interest of deceased.	Proceeds income tax free to remaining beneficiary owners.	Premiums not deductible.
2. Key Man (Life)	Insurance taken by company on key executive(s) with company as beneficiary.	Company receives proceeds tax free upon key executive's death.	No deduction allowed company for premiums paid.
3. Section "303" Redemption (Life)	Used by company to redeem an owner's stock at death. Provides estate liquidity.	Proceeds income tax free to company. Allows partial redemption of stock at capital gains.	No deductions for premiums if funded by insurance.

CHAPTER TWENTY-FOUR

Estate Planning

People write scornful wills, vindictive wills, and generous wills. They can be as short as Rabelais' one sentence will, "I have nothing, I owe a great deal; the rest I leave to the poor," or as long as a small publication. But even though most people would like a voice in the disposition of their affairs after they die, nearly three out of four people die "intestate"—without a will.

If you die without a will

Outside of tax law, there is no federal law regarding wills. Each state has its own intestacy statutes, and your estate will be distributed according to the laws of the state of your legal residence. These laws fractionally divide an estate according to rigid formulas. And, of course, they cannot provide for the desired disposition of family treasures, which are often sold to pay taxes and provide for the survivors.

It may surprise you to learn that if you die intestate, the bulk of your estate may not go to your spouse. The laws of many states award from one-third to two-thirds of the estate to the children. If there are no children or grandchildren, the state intestacy laws may give your parents, siblings, or other blood relatives a portion of your funds—even if they are less needy than your spouse! If you think your view of your affairs would differ from that of the state, you will probably decide to make a formal will—and soon.

Will willing make it so?

Even if you have made a written will, it may not be accepted as a valid one by the court if it is:

> Handwritten. The statutes of many states hold that handwritten (sometimes called "holographic") wills are invalid, unless they conform to specific requirements.

Do-it-yourself. Many standard will forms obtainable from stationery stores or books do not conform to the letter of the law, and are easily contested and often declared invalid on a technicality.

Out-of-state. Your will is administered according to the laws of your domicile, not where you had the will drafted. If you have moved, be sure your will conforms to the laws of your new state of domicile.

Witnesses. Strict requirements are stipulated for witnesses in many states.

Marriage, divorce, and children. In most states, marriage, divorce, and the birth of children cause automatic revocation or alteration of part or all of a will.

Modification of a will

After it has been properly prepared and executed, it is not necessary to redraft the basic will to make changes or updates. Instead, the changes are incorporated in a separate document known as a "codicil" that is appended to the will. However, the codicil must be executed with the same formality as the basic will. Under no circumstances should you simply cross out certain clauses in the will and insert changes.

Probate and priority of claim

No will is legal until the proper court or official declares that it meets all statutory requirements. This act is known as the decree of probate.

Once the will has been admitted to probate, several claims have priority before any distribution can be made under the terms of the will. While the exact order varies by state, they follow this general pattern:

1. Funeral expenses.

2. Administration. Fees due the court, attorneys, and others for administering the estate.

3. Family allowance. An amount, often set by the court, to provide for the immediate needs of the decedent's family while the will is being administered.

4. U.S. Government. Any taxes and other claims due.

5. Last illness. Expenses pertaining to the decedent's final illness.

6. State, county, and local governments.

7. Wages due others.

8. Claims secured by liens.

9. All other debts.

Settlements outside the will

Not all of your property and personal matters can be settled within the will. Here are some other arrangements you should consider:

1. Contract benefits. Ample life insurance is a good way to tide

the family over until your estate is settled. The payments are made to the beneficiary named in the contract, apart from any will. However, the total value of the benefits may be treated as part of the taxable estate. Remember that the security of a paid-up life insurance policy does not obviate the real necessity for a well-drawn will.

2. Joint tenancy. Securities, real estate, and bank accounts that are jointly owned can bypass probate and go directly to the survivor. But you cannot avoid federal and state estate taxes by the use of joint tenancy—and at the death of the survivor, this property can be taxed again. Moreover, while you can easily change a will, some joint tenancy holdings create a legal title which cannot be changed without the consent of the other party.

3. Last instructions. If you have specific wishes regarding your funeral and interment, it is wise to leave a memo (a letter of last instructions) with a trusted friend or relative describing the funeral arrangements you desire. It should also give the location of the will, other important papers, ready cash, and valuables.

Watch these items

If you have a will, here is a checklist of sometimes omitted items you should review with your attorney:

Does the will take advantage of the unlimited marital deduction? Also, has your adviser considered whether it would be better to use a *partial* marital deduction and pass the remainder directly to other heirs, trusts, etc.?

Has your adviser considered the new QTIP (Qualified Terminable Interest Property) Trust, which allows the decedent to direct the disposition of a marital trust upon death of the spouse?

How are death taxes to be allocated among beneficiaries?

Have all insurance arrangements been considered in the will?

Have safeguards been provided to ensure minimum double taxation of the estate—once at the death of each spouse?

Have proper provisions been made to establish who legally died first in the event of apparent simultaneous death of both spouses?

Should the executor of the estate have the power to run or dispose of your business?

Also, have you considered disposing of part of your estate via gifts during your lifetime? The 1981 tax law allows you to give away tax free $10,000 ($20,000 if married and spouse joins in gift) per year per donee.

Section 303 Redemption

In the event of the death of an owner of a closely held corporation, stock owned by the decedent may be redeemed tax free or as capital gain up to an amount that equals funeral, administrative expenses, and death taxes. This provision is found in Revenue Code Section 303 and it is designed to avoid tax squabbles over the tax treatment of stock redeemed to cover estate liquidity of the owner of a closely held corporation.

The problem was that the IRS sometimes viewed such redemption gains as ordinary dividend income and, by the time enough money was taken out of the company for the estate income to pay taxes on the dividend income, the estate's tax bracket was higher and thus more tax was due.

Requirements for Section 303 stock redemption

All the following requirements must be met before a Section 303 redemption can be made:

- The decedent's gross estate (as determined for estate tax purposes) must include the stock that is redeemed under Section 303.

- The stock owned by the decedent at time of death must have a greater value than 35% of the adjusted gross estate. This applies to the stock held in his own corporation.

- If the decedent held stock in more than one corporation and 20% of the value of all such stock is included in his estate, all the stock is treated as if it were stock in a single corporation.

- The Section 303 redemption must usually be made within 39 months of the filing of the federal estate tax return, unless you elect to pay in installments.

Of course, if stock is redeemed in excess of the established costs of estate liquidity, the excess may be taxed as ordinary income.

How to Set Up a Sprinkling Trust

A sprinkling trust is a trust established for the grantor's children or grandchildren that is flexible enough to "sprinkle" funds out to the children in proportion to the varying needs. Flexibility of distribution of funds is the primary motivation behind a sprinkling trust, whereas primary motivation for other types of trusts may be avoidance of litigation; tax minimization; efficient management of funds; or reduction of administrative costs and court costs.

There are two common methods for structuring a sprinkling trust, fixed share and single fund. Although each has advantages and disadvantages, keep in mind the system you might use to provide for your children's needs if you were paying for them right out of your wallet.

Fixed share

Under this method each child covered by the sprinkling trust is allotted a fixed share of the principal. The child's needs are then paid for by sprinklings from his share of the income and principal of the trust. When the trust is terminated, the child receives whatever is left of his allotment.

Single fund

The single fund approach provides that all the principal and income from the trust be kept in a single fund and that sprinklings be taken from the fund as needed to meet the different needs of the children. Therefore, if one child falls ill and another decides to go to graduate school, the extra expenses for each child are met by the whole of the trust fund instead of just by the children's individual shares. When the single trust fund is terminated, the remaining assets are distributed (usually) evenly among the children. Generally, the single fund method for a sprinkling trust is considered to be most flexible in meeting the needs of the children. Therefore, the bulk of this discussion will center on single fund sprinkling trusts.

At some point you may want to terminate the single fund and distribute the principal to the children. When is the right time to do it? No matter when you choose to terminate the trust, the needs of one child will differ from the needs of the others at the time of distribution of the funds. You must gauge your optimal termination time upon your estimate of the needs of your family. Here are four common situations upon which terminations hinge:

> 1. After a specified period of time. You may choose to terminate the trust after 15 years have elapsed. The advantage here is simplicity and apparent equality. But this is not always the case. What if the oldest child needs the principal to buy a house before the termination date or the youngest child—at age 17—will use his share to buy the motorcycle you never wanted him to have?

> 2. When the oldest child reaches a specified age. You might design the trust to terminate when the oldest child reaches a specified age, say age 30. Again, a simple system, but what if the youngest child is only halfway through college and would be better served by a trust that is set up to cover his remaining costs of education?

> 3. When the youngest child reaches a specified age. Obviously, this one too has its problems. By the time the youngest no longer needs the trust, the oldest may be up to his ears in debt or may already have gone through bankruptcy as a result of not having access to the principal in his trust.

> 4. A set age for each child. If you establish the trust so each child's share is distributed to him upon reaching age 25, you systematically reduce the principal of the youngest child. If there are four children, the first reaches 25 and withdraws his 25% of the principal. The second soon turns 25 and does the same thing. Finally, the third child withdraws his 25% and now the youngest is left with sprinklings from one-quarter of the original principal. The youngest enjoys only 25% of the financial security given the oldest child.

Another alternative is to switch from single fund to separate shares when the first child comes due for his distribution. Of course, this brings on the disadvantages of separate share method for the other children and the youngest gets the worst of it since he has only the separate share to rely on for the longest period of time.

Getting around the disadvantages

Although the disadvantages of these variations seem discouraging, they are by no means prohibiting because a sprinkling trust can often be designed with sufficient flexibility to get around most of them. Here are a few ways some of the drawbacks can be dealt with:

> 1. Special funds within the trust. One of the drawbacks of ter-

minating the trust when the youngest child comes of age is that the older children have to wait too long. This can be dealt with by having a separate fund within the overall trust to meet the specific needs in one area, like education or medical costs. Once this separate fund is set aside to meet special needs, the rest of the funds can be distributed.

2. Special distributions. The trustee may be given the power to make special distributions as needed before the termination of the trust. So, if an older child needs to buy a house, the trustee can give him a special distribution of part of his share of the principal without bringing about a complete dissolution of the trust. Of course, these premature distributions would be deducted from the recipient's share of the trust upon final termination.

3. The younger they are, the larger their share. If it is clear that the needs of the younger children will for some reason be greater than those of the older children, it is sometimes best to give the younger children a larger share of the trust when you are using the separate share method. This is not more equal, but it may be more equitable.

Usually, a sprinkling trust can be as flexible as you need it to be to cover the needs of your children, but you should certainly be aware of the above variables when you approach your attorney to have him set it up.

"Flower" Bonds—How to Get the Government To Help Pay Your Estate Tax

A flower bond is a certain issue of U.S. Treasury bond that can be used at par value to pay estate tax. If you've come to that time when you must consider ways to pay your estate tax, consult your bond broker about these.

What is the advantage?

U.S. Treasury bonds pay taxable interest, but if you can buy flower bonds at a discount there may be a tidy tax-free profit to be made when your estate tax is paid. If, for example, you know that your estate tax will be about $20,000, you could buy 20 flower bonds at a discount cost of $900 each. These bonds pay 4% interest on a par value of $1,000 so that you have income from the interest to start. But later, the bonds may be used to pay your estate tax. The cost of the bonds was $18,000 but the par value makes them worth $20,000 when used to pay the estate tax. Although the bonds must be included in your estate at full value ($20,000), your estate will realize a profit of $2,000 less any estate taxes applicable to the profit.

Index